# THE MIDDLE EAST IN THE NEW MILLENNIUM: ECONOMIC DEVELOPMENT & BUSINESS LAW

*To Nitzi and Shushi, with my love and pride*

Note to the Reader:

**Dr. Gil Feiler**
Info-Prod Research (Middle East) Ltd.
Diamond Tower, Floor 30
Jabotinski 3a, Ramat Gan 52520, Israel
Tel: 972-3-751-2780
Fax: 972-3-751-2781
E-mail: ipr@netvision.net.il
www.infoprod.co.il

Dr. Gil Feiler is the executive director and co-owner of Info-Prod Research (Middle East) Ltd. and a senior lecturer at the Interdisciplinary Center in Herzeliya Dr. Feiler has published extensively on labor migration, regional economic cooperation prospects, business opportunities and other related issues. His most recent books include: *Rethinking Business Strategy for the Middle East and North Africa* (London: The Economist, 1997); and *From Boycott to Economic Cooperation: The Political Economy of the Arab Boycott of Israel* (London: Frank Cass, 1998).

<u>Info-Prod Research (Middle East) Ltd.</u>

Info-Prod Research (Middle East)—IPR is a consultancy specializing in research and economic analysis at the country, sector and product levels in the Middle East and North Africa.

Additional services are based on IPR unique databases of Middle East business information, which are constantly updated for on-line vendors, including Reuters, Lexis-Nexis, Gale Group, The Dialog Corporation, Genios and the Financial Times.

# The Middle East in the New Millennium: Economic Development & Business Law

*by*

*Dr. Gil Feiler*

KLUWER LAW INTERNATIONAL

The Hague • London • Boston

Published by Kluwer Law International,
P.O. Box 85889, 2508 CN The Hague, The Netherlands.

Sold and distributed in the U.S.A. and Canada
by Kluwer Law International,
675 Massachusetts Avenue, Cambridge, MA 02139, U.S.A.
tel: (617) 354-0140; fax: (617) 354-8595

In all other countries, sold and distributed
by Kluwer Law International,
P.O. Box 85889, 2508 CN The Hague, The Netherlands
tel: 31 70 308 1562; fax: 31 70 308 1555

Library of Congress Cataloging-in-Publication Data

Feiler, Gil.
    The Middle East in the new millennium : economic development & business law /
by Gil Feiler.
        p. cm.
    Includes bibliographical references.
    ISBN 9041188444 (hardcover)
        1. Commercial law--Middle East.  2. Commercial law--North Africa.
    3. Middle East--Economic conditions--1979-  4. North Africa--Economic conditions.
    I. Title.
KMC242.F45 2000
338.956--dc21                                              00-039086
                                                          CIP

ISBN 9041188444

# Acknowledgments

I would like to express my gratitude for the assistance provided by the following lawyers: Mr. Wagdi Bishara, an attorney in the law offices of Nadoury & Nahas who worked on the legal review section in the chapter on Egypt; Mr. Michael T. Dabit, senior counsel in Michael T. Dabit & Associates who worked on the legal review section in the chapter on the Hashemite Kingdom of Jordan; Mr. Seddik Zaari, a senior partner in the law firm of Seddik Zaari Law Offices who worked on the legal review section in the chapter on Morocco; Mr. Sharhabeel Al Za'eem, a senior partner in the law offices of Sharhabeel Al Za'eem & Associates who worked on the legal review section in the chapter on the Palestinian Authority; Mr. Adly Bellagha, a senior partner in the law offices of Adly Bellagha & Associates, who worked on the legal review section in the chapter on Tunisia.

The exchange of information forms the basis of understanding, and the cooperation of these colleagues is an affirmation of the possibilities of peace and development in this region.

I extend my sincere appreciation to the staff of Info-Prod Research (Middle East) Ltd. In particular, I wish to highlight the tremendous assistance provided by Mr. Doron Peskin, head of research at IPR, and senior consultants Mr. Andrew Wohlberg, Mr. Randal Slavens and Mr. Shawn Cramer.

Finally, I would like to extend a special acknowledgment to Mr. Yaacov Yisraeli from the law firm Shiboleth, Yisraeli, Roberts, & Zisman. Mr. Yisraeli, in addition to several attorneys and articled clerks at his firm provided tremendous research and guidance in the preparation of the Legal Review sections of the chapters of this book.

**Gil Feiler**
February 2000

# Table of Contents

# Introduction

The closing of the 1990s has provided the vantage point of seeing what the Middle East used to be, not yet what it will become. The events of the last decade have torn down the old edifices of regional relationships and economies. But unresolved issues still prevent the building of new ones. So, as the millenium comes to an end, the region remains in a transitional flux, with questions about how peace will factor into the crystallization of the reshaped region and how, and if, economic liberalization will proceed, at what pace and at what benefit to the people. What is certain, however, is that the last decade of the first millenium has offered images and hopes of a more peaceful and prosperous future for all of the region's inhabitants.

Perhaps the greatest of these images was Israeli Prime Minister Yitzhak Rabin and Palestinian leader Yasir Arafat shaking hands at the White House – a handshake that set the region on a new course. On the political level, the quest for peace has been the region's top story of the decade. Comprehensive peace between the Arabs and Israelis has been elusive, but in the century's closing days, it seems more within reach than ever. If and when this peace does materialize it will not guarantee that the Middle East will meld into a single market with countries coordinating economic strategy, but it can at least open that possibility. It will almost certainly, though, inject the kind of stability that lures foreign investors needed to propel the region into the 21st century.

Another aspect adding to the decade's uniqueness is the changing guard of leadership. An entire generation of leaders who were schooled on Cold-War politics and had rarely breathed the air outside their countries is passing on and being replaced by a younger, dynamic western-oriented-and-educated generation whose gaze travels far beyond the Arab-Israeli conflict. New leaders in Jordan, Morocco and Bahrain do not only know how to turn on a computer, but also how to roam the Internet and teach their fellow countrymen how to do so.

These leaders, and many of the remaining older ones, are steering their traditionally socialistic countries toward open-market economies, seeking help from the very bastions of global capitalism such as the IMF and the World Bank in restructuring their macro-economic foundations. For many countries there is really no choice, unless allowing their citizens' standard of living to fall further and further behind the rest of the world constitutes a choice.

The challenges meeting these new leaders in a new era are daunting. Population, for example, is becoming an increasingly important issue. The Middle East has one of the world's fastest population growth rates, with some countries averaging 3.5 percent to as high as 4.8 percent. The population growth rate in some countries is outpacing the economic growth rate. This growth rate is either pushing many infrastructures to their limits or beyond, or aggravating other areas such as water usage.

The region's population is also young, with an estimated 60 percent below the age of 20. In 1998, the region's labor force grew 3.5 percent to 85 million, with an estimated 12.5 million unemployed. Without liberalizing the economies, jobs will not be created fast enough to meet the growing demand, foreign investment will not flow in and living standards will not rise.

Another challenge will be economic diversification. Many countries of the region must do more to further diversify their economies and wean themselves from over-reliance on natural factors. The Gulf states, excluding the UAE, are much too dependent on their hydrocarbon resources. These countries' economies were battered in 1998 when oil prices collapsed and tens of billions of dollars were lost. And what oil is to these countries rainfall is to the agriculture-based economies, such as Morocco. In recent years a drought has dragged down GDP in these countries by about four percent.

A further challenge will be managing natural resources, especially water and hydrocarbons. At Syria's current rate of oil production, the country is expected to extinguish its petroleum resources in the next 5-6 years unless more wells are discovered.

The decisions that these new leaders must make to address difficult issues will always be arduous and sometimes painful. They will include relaxing price controls, reducing subsidies, lowering public expenditure, reducing import quotas and tariffs, adjusting foreign exchange controls, diversifying and passing new investment legislation. They will also need to quicken the privatization of lumbering state-owned enterprises and continue to pour billions of dollars into developing roads, electricity, water and telecommunications.

Perhaps making these tough decisions will be made easier for the leaders as they are able to see that their investments and growing pains are already paying off. During the first half of the 1990s, the Middle East and North Africa (16 Arab counties, the Palestinians Authority, Iran and Israel) had the second fastest growth rate in the world, with Qatar experiencing the world's highest growth rate during a several year stretch. Between 1991 and 1995, the average annual GDP growth rate in the Middle East and North Africa reached 3 percent. In 1996 alone, real GDP growth peaked at 4.8 percent. The main drivers of this growth were increased oil prices, an improved political atmosphere and internal political stability.

Of all Arab countries, however, Egypt stands above all others in growth terms. In the last two years, the country had annual growth rates of between 5 and 5.8 percent. Its GDP grew from $37.4 billion in 1992 to $66 billion in 1999. GDP per-capita grew over the same period from $610 to $1,000. Israel, however, remains a regional anomaly with the strongest, healthiest, petroleum-free economy. Its GDP in the same 7-year period grew from $61 billion to $93 billion and GDP per capita grew from $11,200 to nearly $16,000.

The future for the region appears brighter. The peace process is progressing forward while the potential for greater regional integration and cooperation increases. Macro-economic conditions at the end of the 1990s are much stronger than at the beginning. There are important economic sectors that are not yet fully developed but which stand to propel the region's economy during the coming decades. The region is rich with mineral resources. It has tremendous tourism potential and its strategic global position creates an environment ripe for free trade zones and ports. And in the coming decades, there is a real chance that this potential will be met.

The Middle East for many can be a daunting place to do business. There are many differences in language, culture and business practices. Furthermore, although there are many areas attractive for investment, myriad foreigners are not even aware of them. This book seeks to remedy that. The following chapters will paint a picture of the region's business and economic environment. The beginning of each chapter examines recent economic, political and business issues, followed by an overview of business legislation. In general, the chapters focus on trends and new developments as well as growth sectors. Moreover, detailed information is provided to give the reader a complete view of economic and business events and understanding of opportunities.

Furthermore, the book provides an overview of business legal issues in the region. It is important to note that many countries of the Middle East are slowly beginning to adopt more liberal legislation that increasingly conforms to policies promoted by international organizations. The countries hope that such steps will help to attract the foreign investment needed to propel them into the next millenium.

It is the author's sincere wish that this book will contribute, in some small way, to the process of normalization in the region and to the bringing together of peoples through economic growth and prosperity. The author hopes that the information contained in this book will help to dispel the uncertainties and misgivings that may exist at the onset of any new business union.

# ALGERIA

## Recent Political Developments

In April 1999, Abdelaziz Bouteflika was elected unopposed as Algeria's new President. Since taking office, Bouteflika has offered amnesty and released thousands of Islamist insurgents from prison. Bouteflika succeeded in securing a truce with the Islamic Salvation Army and received the backing of the front's "Historic Chief," (as Algerians like to refer to their leaders) Abassi Madani.

| Population | 31 million (1999) |
|---|---|
| GDP ($bn) | 47.1 |
| Religions | 99% Sunni Muslim |
| Government | Republic |
| Languages | Arabic (official), French, Berber |
| Work Week | Saturday–Wednesday Banks and Insurance Companies: Saturday–Thursday |
| Monetary Unit | Algerian Dinars (AD) |
| Exchange Rate | AD 67=$US 1 |

The militants freed in early July 1999 consist of men and women who had sheltered or financed armed extremists, not those guilty of violent crimes or rape. These recent developments offer a ray of hope that the savage war may end. Some analysts, however, remain skeptical regarding the future of Algeria's internal politics. This skepticism was fueled in August 1999 and January 2000 when terror attacks occurred in different parts of the country (although not in the capital, Algiers). The renewed violence waves came following new reconciliation measures adopted by the President.

In late 1999, Algeria's new Prime Minister, Ahmed Benbitour, 53, chose a group of technocrats to head the important oil, finance, and trade portfolios in his new government. The makeup of the new cabinet, which is headed by a former Finance Minister and consists of various senior ministers with business backgrounds, is President Bouteflika's technique of signaling to the local and international business communities that Algeria is serious about implementing promised economic reforms.

Meanwhile, on the international scene, Bouteflika has been trying to improve ties with Morocco and France—two strategic partners with whom Algeria has had rocky relations in recent years. Algeria hopes that warming ties with these regional neighbors will send a positive signal to the international business community that its environment has become more investment-friendly.

Nevertheless, a hyper-militant Armed Islamic Group in Algeria, composed primarily of original Afghan war veterans and those schooled by them, refuses to surrender arms or cease activities. The group is believed to be responsible for the worst massacres and other outrages both prior to and since the Islamic Salvation Army ceased active operations in 1997.

These armed groups in Algeria issue death threats against civilians through notices sent to the media and posted in public places, or telephone calls and letters delivered to individuals. Targets of these death threats include civil servants, relatives of members of the security forces, journalists and artists.

The internal disorder started when in January 1992, the Algerian military abolished parliamentary elections after it became clear that Islamic groups were the clear victors. This cancellation sparked a nearly decade-long violent confrontation between the military and Islamists.

In the last eight years, the conflict is estimated to have claimed the lives of over 70,000 people. Islamists have targeted not only security services but also civilians (elderly men, women, and children), journalists and intellectuals as well as foreigners. Roughly 130 foreigners have been murdered since the end of 1993. For foreigners, it is dangerous to be outdoors at all in Algiers unless they are accompanied by someone who knows the city well. The last foreigner to be killed in Algiers was a Bulgarian entrepreneur who had lived there for many years. He had his throat cut while walking in a public park in the northern section of the city.

## Recent Economic Developments

Amidst the carnage and bloodshed that have ensconced this North-African nation since the early 1990s, Algeria, with IMF and World Bank support, has taken impressive steps in implementing a structural economic adjustment program. Thus far, the country has successfully met and surpassed all macro economic performance criteria. The government has stabilized its currency, lowered inflation and recorded a positive balance of payments. Furthermore, despite the terror and chronic high unemployment (about 30 percent), Algeria has continued to achieve positive economic performance, much of it coming from its enormous hydrocarbon resources.

The microeconomic story, however, is significantly bleaker. Industrial output is declining and restructuring is proceeding slowly. And although the country's privatization law offers numerous advantages to private investors, such as tax incentives, deferred payments, and an employee ownership option, just few enterprises have been privatized which is necessary to lure the investors.

Strong opportunities for foreign investment in Algeria have come from the country's investment code. As part of this code, the country established in April 1997 a free trade zone in Bellara. This has positioned the hydrocarbon, agribusiness and construction sectors for substantial expansion.

The continuing, albeit abating, violence remains one of the most significant deterrents to attracting investors. Simply visiting the country requires businesspeople to ensure that an Algerian national accompanies them from the time of arrival to departure. The extent of security necessary to provide company workers and the cost of such security must be factored into any decision regarding investment in Algeria.

Algeria's economy overwhelmingly relies on its hydrocarbons resources. In recent years, the oil and gas sector accounted for an average of 30 percent of the country's GDP and about 95 percent of its export earnings. This dependence places the economy at the mercy of crude petroleum prices, which in the past few years have been unusually volatile.

Besides this exposure to oil price swings, the national stabilization scheme has thus far failed to improve the living standards of most Algerians. Pressure is mounting on the government to increase wages and social project expenditures and to eliminate the 2 million job and housing shortage.

To reduce its reliance on oil, the Algerian Government continues to pursue industrial reforms. Progress has, however, been slow, because employee dismissals have provoked much social dissent.

Algeria's GDP presently amounts to $47.1 billion, while its per capita GDP hovers around $1,500. But in purchasing power terms (which adjusts for exchange rates and costs of living), per capita GNP is approximately $4,000. The agricultural sector contributes 12 percent to the GDP, while the industrial and services sectors contribute 49 percent and 39 percent, respectively.

In 1996, Algeria achieved real growth of 4 percent, but in the following two years this rate dropped to between 1-1.5 percent. In the past two years, Algeria's hard currency reserves depleted rapidly. By the end of 1999 they amounted to $4.66 billion. In comparison, by the end of 1998, the Algerian foreign currency reserves had contracted 15 percent to $6.846 billion versus $8.047 billion in 1997. This collapse was primarily due to declining international oil prices. Consequently, the government decided to limit spending and slashed the 1999 budget by roughly 30 percent. State administrators and public sector enterprises have been advised to dramatically lower their expenditures, except in the areas of wages, debt reimbursements and imports.

Higher imports and a steep drop in the value of its oil and gas exports caused the country's trade surplus to shrink from $5.79 billion in 1997 to $803 million in 1998. Imports totaled $9.3 billion in 1998, up 7.4 percent from the previous year. Oil and gas exports—which accounted for more than 96 percent of total exports—amounted to $9.7 billion in 1998, compared to $13.6 billion in 1997.

Algeria's leading trade partner was the European Union, which absorbed 63.5 percent of its exports and provided 57 percent of its imports. Meanwhile, the trade surplus dropped to $460 million in the first half of 1999, down almost 50 percent from the same period in 1998. Exports totaled $4.86 billion, compared to $5.66 billion in the first six months of 1998, while imports reached $4.4 billion, compared to $4.7 billion in the corresponding period last year.

In general, the government is continuing to liberalize foreign trade and payments. But the pace of reform has slowed since its mid-1990s peak. Some imports, particularly luxury goods, continue to be restricted to a limited number of importers as state-owned banks refuse to provide all importers with the necessary customs clearance documents. The Algerian Customs Authority is also attempting to stop the rotten food imports through more stringent controls, including a regulation that contains a minimum validity period for imported food products.

## Economic Indicators

| | 2000p | 1999e | 1998 | 1997 |
|---|---|---|---|---|
| GDP ($ billions) | 53.84 | 49.7 | 47.1 | 45.9 |
| GDP Growth (percent) | 5.0 | 6.2 | 2.0 | 3.0 |
| GDP Per Capita ($) | | 1,637 | 1,608 | 1,608 |
| CPI Inflation (percent) | 4.5 | 4.5 | 5.0 | 5.7 |
| Unemployment (percent) | 30.0 | 30.0 | 27.0 | 28.0 |
| Foreign Exchange Reserves ($ billion) | | — | 3.0 | 4.5 |
| Exports ($ billion) | | 9.72 | 10.12 | 13.89 |
| Imports ($ billion) | | 8.8 | 9.3 | 8.6 |
| Trade Surplus ($ billion) | | 0.92 | 0.82 | 5.29 |
| Foreign Currency Reserves ($ billion)* | | 4.6 | 6.8 | 8.0 |
| Foreign Debt ($ billions) | | 32.0 | 33.4 | 32.7 |
| Budget Deficit ($ billions) | 3.38 | | | |

* As of the end of December
p—projections based on an average price of $15 per oil barrel

To expand the country's economic base, the Algerian government is offering significant export incentives to increase non-hydrocarbon exports. The authorities have established the Algerian Foreign Trade Promotion Company as well as the Foreign Trade Promotion Fund, which is financed by a luxury-imported goods tax. The Algerian Export Management Company manages an export credit insurance agency, while an Export Promotion Fund was created in June 1997 to give logistic and financial assistance to export enterprises.

A black market for hard currency exists for small-scale importing and personal travel abroad. The gap between the official and black market rates is approximately 10-15 percent.

Algeria's industrial sector continues to be characterized by large and inefficient state-owned enterprises (SOEs). These firms have survived primarily on credit extended by Algeria's state-owned banks. In the mid-1990s, the SOEs were adversely affected by successive dinar devaluations, which raised the cost of servicing their foreign currency loans.

Because of this and other causes of their insolvency, the government continues to aggressively restructure public enterprises, including the rescheduling of SOE foreign debt. In the fall of 1998, 11 specialized holding companies were established according to different sectors to manage the public sector companies, which they are commissioned to privatize.

In recent years, the Algerian government has liberalized the country's import regime. Supplier financing is no longer required to import capital equipment. Furthermore, the rescheduling of Algeria's foreign debt released substantial foreign currency for imports. Algerian importers can access this foreign exchange provided they have enough Algerian dinars to cover the hard currency cost of imports.

## Hydrocarbon Sector

Algeria's vital hydrocarbon sector has remained immune to terrorist acts. Sonatrach, the state-owned hydrocarbons company, plans to raise annual export earnings to over $16 billion next year. A key element to this plan is the doubling of natural gas exports to 60 billion cubic meters per annum. Toward the end of 1996, the Trans-Maghreb pipeline linking Algeria's Hassi R'Mel gas field to Spain and Portugal via Morocco commenced operations. By the end of this year, Sonatrach hopes to expand the Trans-Med gas pipeline's capacity to Italy to 24 billion cubic meters per year.

Sonatrach strongly encourages foreign oil exploration. During the past ten years it has signed roughly 40 oil/gas exploration and production sharing agreements with foreign firms. Several American energy companies, such as Anadarko, Arco, and Louisiana Land & Exploration, are pursuing projects in Algeria.

Plans include much more extensive hydrocarbon exploration, a larger liquefaction capacity to boost LNG exports, additional pipelines, and more contracts with foreign companies skilled in enhanced oil recovery methods for use at existing oil fields. American, French, German, and Japanese firms dominate this sector. The most lucrative markets are for wellhead and down-hole equipment and supplies, and drilling machinery.

## Agriculture

Agriculture production depends on weather conditions and thus is volatile. In 1996, for example, agricultural output rose 19.5 percent, but subsequently dropped 76.1 percent the following year due to drought.

The potential for agricultural exports will rise after the government institutionalizes procedures making it easier for farmers to own and sell land and to access medium-long-term credit. The government hopes that a merger between one of the country's insurance companies and the state-owned Agricultural Bank for Rural Development will result in more funding being channeled to the agricultural sector. The inauguration of a leasing company would enable Algeria's farmers and fishermen to obtain capital equipment through lease-purchase agreements, which would provide them with an opportunity to raise productivity.

Improving the water resource supply and enhancing agricultural productivity are among the Government's top priorities. Its irrigation program offers lucrative opportunities for direct sales and licensing arrangements. Several Algerian companies seek to manufacture irrigation and waste water treatment equipment locally, and all have expressed interest in collaborating with foreign firms. The most promising markets therefore, are for drilling, irrigation, and waste water treatment equipment.

Algeria's agricultural sector has the potential for substantial development in the next few years. There are particularly strong opportunities for foreign manufacturers of farm equipment and supplies because Algerian farmers need such things to increase productivity.

## Construction
Historically, the state has played a predominant role in providing housing. Yet, Algeria's government has been unable to satisfy the housing market's demand. In recent years, the government's control of this sector on the one hand, and its inefficient management on the other, have led to construction delays and a mounting housing deficiency. At times, this housing gap has been covered by illegal construction. Despite these difficulties, Algerian authorities boast of their achievement in doubling the annual supply of housing units from about 80,000 in 1993 to over 160,000 in 1997 and 1998. Nevertheless, this remarkable augmentation has fallen short of the sector's rising demand.

## Privatization
In mid-July 1999, the head of Algeria's National Privatization Board, established in September 1998, said the country's privatization program had resulted in both positive and negative consequences. He said that profit-oriented transactions, rather than privatization-oriented operations, had thus far been executed. Eighty-nine of Algeria's 384 large public sector enter-

prises had been privatized. Of the new companies' owners, 20 percent are foreigners, 25 percent internal employees, and 55 percent national private firms.

The Algerian government in recent years has taken steps to implement and push forward its privatization program. Algeria's Parliament has amended the privatization law to facilitate the privatization process. The law now includes flexibility in pricing and payment terms. It authorizes the sale of non-autonomous public firms and abolishes the buyers' obligation to maintain a firm's activity and its labor force intact for at least five years. The law also allows for the sale of some enterprises to the general public, in particular to workers. Furthermore, the law provides for an employee stock ownership option, whereby up to 30 percent of the capital of a company being privatized may be offered to its workforce.

## Business Environment

### Distribution and Sales Channels
Algeria's well-developed distribution system includes an extensive network of wholesale and retail outlets, most of which are controlled by private entrepreneurs. Although state-owned wholesale marketing firms continue to sell importer foodstuffs, pharmaceuticals, and industrial supplies and equipment, private wholesalers are becoming increasingly active in these sectors. The government is in the midst of privatizing state-owned distribution outlets, and Algeria's retail trade is almost exclusively controlled by private businesspeople.

### Use of Agents/Distributors
Within the framework of Algeria's 1993 Investment Code, foreign suppliers no longer need to invest in Algeria to establish distributorships. They may use local agents or distributors, or alternatively, may establish their own distribution companies. Algerian law prohibits foreign firms from using commercial agents to bid on government tenders.

### Franchising
Although franchising is not widespread in Algeria, private firms are becoming increasingly interested. Coca-Cola and a private Algerian food process-

ing company, for example, established a successful local bottling operation in 1993.

## Leasing

In January 1996, the Government declared a law allowing Algerian companies to lease foreign-produced equipment. Private firms recently have expressed growing interest in leasing, particularly construction equipment. The Agricultural Mutual Bank, in partnership with a large insurance company and the privately-owned Union Bank, established an agricultural equipment leasing company in July 1997.

## Joint Ventures/Licensing

Recognizing that the country lacks the resources to upgrade state-owned manufacturing plants, the Algerian government is actively encouraging foreign investors to assist them. Algerian companies—desperate for technical expertise from foreign partners necessary to compete at the national, regional and global levels—are offering equity incentives in joint ventures.

## Selling to the Government

Algerian government agencies (including ministries and local government units) purchase foreign-made goods through tender processes that are open to all potential suppliers. The Law on Public Tenders administers Algerian government procurement. It mandates a 2 percent bid bond and a 5 percent performance bond. Foreign bidders must deal directly with the client agency, but tender documents, which list tender procedures and requirements, can also be obtained through local representatives or embassies.

Government agencies and public companies may choose to work directly with foreign companies within the framework of what are termed "limited consultations" with at least 3 suppliers. It is common practice for government entities and state-owned enterprises to request financing in their tenders.

## Advertising and Trade Promotion

Direct advertising of equipment and machinery has only a marginal impact on the local end user. Advertising does not influence state-owned companies, since they import on the basis of international open tenders. On the other hand, with the liberalization of Algeria's import regime, advertising is becoming increasingly effective for consumer products. Algeria's Radio and Television Service does accept advertisements.

The annual Algiers International Fair in June is the hub of Algerian trade promotion events. In recent years, the Algerian Fair Authority (SAFEX), and a private firm, Group ABH, have organized several fairs centered around industrial sectors. Ongoing economic reforms may increase international interest in such events.

## Customer Support

Suppliers of capital goods to the Algerian market are expected to provide sales service and customer support. Fee sales service is normally provided for a one-year period. After this period expires, suppliers may enter into agreements to provide customers remunerated sales service, referred to in Algeria as "technical assistance."

Foreign suppliers provide customer support services through local liaison offices. Since these offices are prohibited from engaging in commercial activities, they cannot import or distribute equipment and spare parts. The Algerian end-users must import these items either directly or through distributors.

Recent legislation makes it mandatory for distributors of foreign products to provide a warranty of 6-18 months, depending on the type of good, to stock parts in Algeria, and to provide customers with after-sales service.

## Leading Business Opportunities

| Rank | Sector | Rank | Sector |
|------|--------|------|--------|
| 1 | Oil and Gas Field Machinery | 5 | Food Processing and Packaging Equipment |
| 2 | Water Resources Equipment | 6 | Drugs and Pharmaceuticals |
| 3 | Computers and Peripherals | 7 | Building Products |
| 4 | Telecommunications Equipment | 8 | Mining Industry Equipment |

# Legal Review

## Currency and Banking

### Banking System

The country's banking system includes the Central Bank (Banque d'Algerie), six state-owned banks, one public development bank, and one private bank. An Islamic Bank is jointly owned by a state-bank the Saudi Al-Baraka Group. Algeria's sole private bank, Union Bank, operating since 1994, concentrates on merchant banking. For an extended period, Algerian banks were merely depository institutions, which helps account for their inefficiency. These banks lent mainly to the public sector, which left the banks with a legacy of non-performing debt and managerial difficulties. The country's implementation of World Bank and IMF reform programs has led to their recapitalization and to the banking system's liberalization. The Government encourages leading international banks to establish branches in Algeria.

### Foreign Exchange Controls

Except for a few anomalies, Algerians are prohibited from holding real and financial assets abroad. Algerian importers are permitted access to foreign currency as long as they possess the dinar equivalent of the hard currency cost of the imports.

## Intellectual Property

Algeria's intellectual property practices do not have any adverse effects on its foreign trade. Foreign firms have not reported losses on export or investment opportunities due to imported or locally produced counterfeit or pirated goods.

Patents are protected by a law introduced on December 7, 1993, which is administered by the Institut Algerien de Normalisation et de Propriete Industrielle (INAPI). INAPI grants patents for 20 years from the date a patent request is filed and for all types of technology. For further information, foreign firms may contact the Directeur de la Protection Industrielle.

The Laws of March 19, 1966 and July 16, 1976 accord trademark protection in Algeria. In 1986, the authority for granting and enforcing trademark protection was transferred from INAPI to the Centre National du Registre du Commerce (CNRC). A law that would transfer trademark authority back to INAPI is presently being discussed.

In 1973, Algeria ratified its 1952 Convention on Copyrights. In April 1973, the Government passed a law providing copyright protection for books, plays, musical compositions, firms, paintings, sculptures, and photographs. This law accords authors the right to control the commercial exploitation and marketing of these products. A proposed revision of this law is now in the process of being drafted to provide protection for video, radio, and Internet programs. The Office National Du Droit D'Auteur (ONDA) manages copyright protection.

### Investment and Trade Issues

The Government of Algeria welcomes foreign investment to help drive, diversify and modernize the national economy.
In 1993, the Government announced an Investment Code that does not distinguish between investments made by foreigners and Algerians. The Government developed a composite regime that provides similar or more attractive incentives than the regimes offered by neighboring states. Algeria's investment code grants new investors:

- a three-year exemption from the value-added tax on goods and services acquired locally or imported;
- a two-to-five year exemption from corporate income taxes;
- an exemption on property taxes;
- the right to pay 3 percent customs duties on 30 products (for which duties are normally between 25-45 percent);
- the right to pay no more than 7 percent of gross wages as the employer contribution to social security (the standard rate is 24.5 percent).

### *Encouragement of Foreign Investment*
Investment incentives are stronger for companies whose production is export-oriented. For example, enterprises exporting 100 percent of pro-

duction are entirely tax exempt; they must pay only the 7 percent employer contribution to social security. Firms exporting 50 percent of production receive a 50 percent tax exemption.

In March 1995, the Government established an investment promotion agency (Agence de Promotion, de Soutien, et de Suivi des Investissements, APSI). APSI registers investment applications and determines what advantages investors should be accorded under the law. The Government has also established regional investment promotion agencies to assist investors in obtaining land and to facilitate their business with local authorities.

## Investment Tax Incentives

In October 1993 the Government lowered the income tax for foreign technical and supervisory personnel. Prior to the decree, most foreign workers faced marginal tax rates that could be up to 70 percent of income earned. Now, foreign company personnel whose monthly salaries exceed AD 80,000 (roughly $1,333) pay a flat 20 percent rate.

### Hydrocarbons Investments
The 1986 Law Governing the Exploration, Exploitation, and Pipeline Transportation of Hydrocarbons, and subsequent amendments to it regulate investments in Algeria's hydrocarbons sector. This law grants foreign companies the right to establish joint ventures with the state Hydrocarbons Company, Sonatrach. In December 1991, this law was amended to allow foreign firms to control up to 49 percent in the production of existing oil fields. It also permits foreign investment in natural gas projects and provides for tax incentives to stimulate hydrocarbon exploration.

### Capital Markets for Portfolio Investment
In Algeria, no capital market exists outside the banking system. In order to finance part of its deficit, the Government commenced selling bonds in late 1994. In 1996, the central bank began initiating open market operations.

### Conversion and Transfer Policies
Algeria's Investment Code authorizes foreign investors to repatriate all revenue earned by hard currency investments within 60 days of such a request.

### Dispute Settlement
The Algerian Government is a signatory of the convention establishing the International Center for Settlement of Foreign Disputes. It is also a member

of the Multilateral Investment Guarantee Agency (MIGA). International arbitration is permitted under Algeria's Code of Civil Procedure.

## Trade Regulations

In recent years, Algeria has taken significant measures to liberalize its trade regime. Its association agreement with the European Union, along with its desire for membership in the World Trade Organization should promote further trade reforms. The import categories that remain subject to restrictions include firearms, explosives, narcotics and pork products.

### Trade Barriers
Algeria's procurement practices make minimal use of countertrade, laws to encourage local production, or non-competitive bidding practices.

Although Algeria's customs operations are being modernized, in many instances administrative procedures remain arduous. Algerian imports are subject to payment of ad valorem customs duties ranging between 3 percent and 40 percent. A value-added tax of 7, 14, or 21 percent is levied on imports, which are also subject to another import tax, the Taxe Specifique Additionnelle (TSA). This tax ranges from 20 percent to 110 percent. While the VAT is based on the import's purchase price plus customs duties, the TSA excludes the latter in its calculation, and applies primarily to luxury goods.

### Services Barriers
Algeria's Post, Telephone, and Telecommunications Ministry maintains a monopoly on all telecommunications services. The production, importation, and distribution of equipment are open to the private sector. In the second half of 1999, the Algerian Stock Exchange opened for trading activities. The Exchange, which has a weekly trading session, only lists several companies.

### Import Licenses
Import licenses are not required, but the importation of certain luxury goods remains restricted because of the state-owned bank's unwillingness to provide all importers with the necessary documents to clear such items through customs.

## Export Controls

Algeria's authorities have succeeded to remove virtually all export restrictions. The main exceptions include palm seedlings, sheep, and historical and archaeological artifacts. The Government is encouraging non-hydrocarbon exports, and has established the Algerian Export Insurance and Guarantee Company.

## Temporary Entry

Equipment and machinery brought into Algeria temporarily for the purpose of a specific project or exhibition are exempt from payment of customs duties and taxes. In order to obtain such a waiver, importers must complete a customs form, which they must subsequently present to the customs authorities when the goods are re-exported.

## Labeling Requirements

All imported products must be labeled in Arabic. Imported drugs must receive authorization from the Ministry of Health and Population prior to being distributed locally. Such drugs must have been marketed in their country of origin prior to being sold in Algeria. Algeria's Customs Service has imposed more stringent controls over food imports, and regulates the minimum validity period of imported foodstuffs.

## Free Trade Zones/Warehouses

In April 1997, the Government designated the site of Bellara (in the Jijel district, near the port of Djendjen) as a free trade zone. Foreign investors in this zone are exempt from taxes and customs duties.

## Membership in Free Trade Arrangements

In 1989, Algeria, Tunisia, Morocco, Mauritania, and Libya formed the Arab Maghreb Union (UMA). The countries agreed on a free trade agreement, but no timetable has been established. Moreover, international sanctions imposed on Libya have rendered the UMA impotent. In 1998, Algeria finalized an association agreement with the European Union.

# BAHRAIN

## Recent Political Developments

After 28 years of leading his country, including declaring Bahrain's independence from Britain, Emir Sheikh Isa bin Salman al-Khalifah died of a heart attack in March 1999 at age 66. His eldest son, Sheikh Hamad, 49, immediately replaced him.

The new leader faces many difficult situations. A majority of the roughly 600,000 Bahrainis are Shi'ites and reject the legitimacy of the Sunni regime. Criticism is also directed toward the family-style rule of the country. Many family members hold key cabinet positions.

| Profile | |
| --- | --- |
| Population | 0.63 million (1999) |
| Religions | 85% Muslim; 15% Christians, Jews, Bahais, Hindus and Zoroastrians |
| Government | Emirate, limited monarchy |
| Languages | Arabic (English is widely spoken) |
| Work Week | Saturday - Wednesday (some offices are open half days on Thursdays) |
| Monetary Unit | Bahraini Dinar (BD) |
| Exchange Rate | BD 1 = US$ 2.65 |

Another source of strife is the ban on political parties. In 1975, internal political agitation and discontent toward the Assembly's operation led to its dissolution. In December 1994, anti-government protests erupted following the arrest of a Shi'ite clerk who was arrested for distributing leaflets signed by 20,000 people demanding the restoration of Parliament.

In 1996, Bahrain announced it had foiled a pro-Iranian plot to topple the government and subsequently downgraded its ties with the Islamic Republic. Sheikh Hamad must also deal with the country's border dispute with Qatar regarding a small but potentially oil-and-gas rich groups of islands, including Hawar Island.

Sheikh Isa, however, did leave his son with a modernized country. The late Sheikh said he believed his greatest accomplishment was the construction of the causeway that opened in 1986 linking Bahrain and Saudi Arabia.

As mentioned, the country's demographics are a serious cause of internal political turmoil. Shi'ite Muslims constitute a slight majority. They accuse the Sunni minority of employment opportunity discrimination. The rising unemployment rate is becoming an important social and political factor. The official government figure of less than 2 percent is unreliable, with various estimates placing the actual figure as high as 15 percent. A higher unemployment rate, of course, is more likely to affect the young - those more inclined to turn to desperate political acts regarding the government's policies. Shi'ite arsonists were suspected in a wave of attacks in Bahrain's capital city of Manama in early May 1996, just 40 days after the execution of a Shi'ite demonstrator found guilty of killing a police officer.

## Recent Economic Developments

Bahrain is the smallest oil producer in the Gulf and the least wealthy in terms of hydrocarbon resources. It produces roughly 40,000 barrels per day from its own fields and receives 120,000 bpd from an offshore field it shares with Saudi Arabia. Still, its economy is oil-based and, thus, its economic health fluctuates with oil prices. Like its neighbors, the state is taking steps to reduce its dependency on oil through economic diversification.

To achieve this goal, this tiny nation is investing in industries like aluminum smelting, petrochemicals and ship repair. With government encouragement, Bahrain has long been established as the principal banking and financial center of the Gulf region. To protect its reputation in this field, the country is set to promulgate a new law that will combat money laundering. The government has also established the Bahrain Promotions and Marketing Board, a special office set up with inter-ministerial, joint public and private sector membership, which is responsible for coordination efforts to attract businesses and investments. It is also creating a regulatory framework to develop Bahrain as a regional financial and commercial hub.

Bahrain offers a prime location from which to do business within the much larger regional market. It is working to develop a tourism industry and trying to position itself for international economic conferences and fairs. But

Dubai and other Gulf regional centers are seriously challenging its historical position as a regional trading center. In 1998, Bahrain attracted $3 billion worth of foreign investment.

Currently, wholly or partially government-owned enterprises dominate the economy, yet laws and regulations have been overhauled in recent years, particularly since 1990, in a bid to make the business climate as welcoming as possible for free enterprise and in order to lure foreign companies. Foreign investors are welcome to set up licensed export industries, with 100 percent foreign ownership. Commercial firms are likewise encouraged to set up 100 percent foreign-owned regional offices and distribution centers.

Toward the end of 1999, there were indications that Bahraini exports, along with oil prices, were bouncing back from the lows of 1998. The trade surplus in the third quarter of 1999 was at BD 79.9 million. Total exports in that period were BD 420.2 million, up 17.5 percent from BD 357.6 million in the previous quarter. The value of oil exports rose 38 percent to BD 284.3 million from BD 205.5 million in the second quarter. Imports also rose 11 percent from BD 306.5 million to BD 340.3 million. (BD1=$2.65).

The effects of the deflated oil prices in 1998 and the beginning of 1999 are noticeable on virtually all of the country's economic indicators. The 1999-2000 budget deficit is expected to be BD 300 million, twice that of the previous year when the deficit was BD 150 million. The Government's total revenues are estimated at BD 1.138 billion, 9 percent lower than in 1998-1999. Government spending is predicted to shrink by 4.5 percent.

1998's low oil prices brought the country's oil export earnings to a 10-year low, reducing BD 260.8 million worth of export earnings between January and September 1998 as compared with the same period in 1997. The country's oil exports reached BD 498.9 million during the first 9 months of 1998 a 34 percent decline over the same period the year before. According to provisional figures, oil exports totaled BD 637 million for the year.

Oil exports represented nearly 76 percent of total export earning in 1988 and 78 percent in 1990. That trend, however, has been downward during the 1990s, dropping to 59.7 percent in 1995, rising to 67.2 percent in 1996 but declining again to 62 percent in 1997. During the first 9 months of 1998, the percent of oil exports reached its lowest level since 1988, declining to 52.9 percent. Non-oil exports remained at almost the same level of BD 431.2

million between January and September 1998, compared with BD 432.3 million in those months of 1997.

The country recorded a trade deficit in the first three quarters of 1998 because of the low oil prices. Exports fell to BD 943.8 million and imports were BD 950.1 million, whereas during the same period in 1997 a trade surplus was recorded.

The government is trying to bring increased private participation into areas that have been traditionally under the government's sole domain. Besides the petroleum industry, the country's growth sectors, are aluminum, financial services, telecommunications and information technology, education, tourism and food processing.

New infrastructure will involve private financing. Public unrest at rising unemployment rates force the government to take further measures to encourage job-creation for Bahrainis. A policy of "Bahrainization" is likely to be expanded, and the Ministry of Labor will take a tougher stance on targets for the employment of nationals, while introducing new legislation to make it easier and cheaper for firms to take on Bahraini workers. To help maintain investment in infrastructure, Bahrain at the end of May 1999 signed a $25 million agreement with the Arab Fund for Economic and Social Development to finance an electricity network project.

## Business Environment

Bahrain is seeking to privatize its Hidd power and water complex. Two Bahraini banks bid for the facility and the winner will enter into partnership with an international developer to run the complex and raise its capacity to 930 MW by 2005. The facility now has two 140 MW gas turbines and four 7.5 million-gallon-a-day desalination units.

The government's strategy for promoting private enterprise and expanding joint industrial projects included the preparation of a 80-hectare piece of land in the South "Alba" region at a cost of BD 1.5 million. The government also built a BD 7 million electricity generating station in that area.

Furthermore, in August 1999, when Texaco signed an agreement to evaluate oil and gas exploration potential, it became only the second foreign company to be involved in an energy-related project. Earlier that year, the

## Economic Indicators (In BD millions, unless otherwise indicated)

| | 1998* | 1997 |
|---|---|---|
| GDP (Current Prices BD millions) | 2,369.7 | 2,261.5 |
| Real GDP Growth (%) | 4.8 | 3.1 |
| Inflation (%) | 0.6 | -5.4 |
| Total Exports | 1,229.6 | 1,648.2 |
| Oil Exports | 637.0 | 1,020.7 |
| Non-Oil Exports** | 592.6 | 627.5 |
| Total Imports | 1,336.4 | 1,513.6 |
| Oil Imports | 274.0 | 529.2 |
| Non-Oil Imports | 1,062.4 | 984.4 |
| Bahrain Crude Oil Production (thousand U.S. barrels) | 13,751 | 14,159 |
| Total Government Revenue | 554.0 | 705.8 |
| Gov't Revenue from Oil & Gas | 259.4 | 422.7 |
| Total Expenditure | 704.5 | 703.6 |
| Private Sector Deposits at Commercial Banks (excluding interbank deposits) | 1,747.0 | 1,481.3 |
| Government Deposits at Commercial Banks (excluding interbank deposits) | 408.7 | 443.1 |
| Interest rates on time deposits | 4.39 (Q4) | 5.40 |
| Interest rates on savings deposits | 2.29 (Q4) | 2.40 |
| Interest rates on business loans | 8.60 (Q4) | 8.70 |
| Interest rates on personal loans | 12.72 (Q4) | 12.10 |

*Provisional
**Includes re-exports

Supreme Council decided to merge BAPCO with Bahrain national oil company, the state's producer and distributor. A year earlier, Chevron was invited to drill for oil in the northern and western offshore areas near Saudi Arabia. Drilling will begin in 2000.

*Major Projects*
In the late 1990s, the government approved a variety of infrastructure projects, including housing projects to accommodate at least 50,000 people, expanding the sewerage system and a sewerage treatment system to recycle

water for irrigation purposes. Other projects include aluminum joint ventures and a coke calcining plant.

But the biggest project is the $458 million Hidd Power and Desalination Project headed by Zurich-based Asea Brown Boveri. The plant will have a capacity of 280Mw and 30 million gallons of water a day. It is being built on a 420,000 sq. m plot of land.

## Franchising

Fast food franchises are highly sought after by local contacts. Many of the major food franchise companies are operating presently in Bahrain. There is also an increasing interest in non-food, service-sector franchises with proven international attractiveness. A local sponsor is required to set up a franchise in Bahrain.

## Leading Business Opportunities

| Rank | Sector |
|------|--------|
| 1 | Financial Services |
| 2 | Educational Services |
| 3 | Insurance Services |
| 4 | Telecommunications Services & Equipment |
| 5 | Electricity |
| 6 | Water Treatment & Conservation |
| 7 | Information Technology Services |
| 8 | Port/Shipbuilding Equipment |
| 9 | Apparel |
| 10 | Air Conditioning |
| 11 | Automobiles |

# Legal Review

## General

A large part of the laws of Bahrain are based on published statutes, which derive from the *Shar'ia* (religious law). The Contract Law and Civil Wrongs Ordinance are based on principles of English common law, which were originally adopted during the British protectorate period. Much recent legislation is based upon and follows a civil-law format, much in the style of Egypt and France.

## Judiciary

Bahrain's Civil and Commercial Procedures Law of 1971 provides the framework for the jurisdiction of the civil and commercial courts. Generally, the civil courts are composed of: (1) the Junior Court; (2) the High Court; (3) the High Court of Appeal; (4) the Court of Execution; and (5) the Summary Actions Court.

### *The Junior Court*

The Junior Court has jurisdiction to hear both civil and commercial cases of claims involving small sums, and cases involving certain real property rights. Junior Court cases may be appealed to the High Court.

### *The High Court*

The High Court has jurisdiction to hear all civil and commercial cases not falling within the jurisdiction of the Junior Court. The High Court is also authorized to hear cases concerning the personal status of non-Moslems and cases which are placed under its jurisdiction by law. The High Court also maintains jurisdiction over non-Bahraini citizens, including companies, that are resident or domiciled in Bahrain except in cases involving real property situated outside Bahrain. The High Court has jurisdiction to hear appeals from the Junior Court and the Court of Execution. The High Court has exclusive jurisdiction over appeals of judgments from the Summary Actions Court. Judicial precedent followed by the High Court is set by decisions of the High Court of Appeal and the High Court of Justice sitting as a court of appeal.

### *The High Court of Appeal*

The High Court of Appeal sits as a court of appeal regarding all appeals made from the High Court.

## The Execution Court

The Execution Court has jurisdiction to execute all final judgments made by the Junior Court, the High Court and the High Court of Appeal.

## The Summary Action Court

The Summary Action Court hears claims that may be adversely affected by the lapse of time. Hearings are usually set to take place not less than twenty-four hours after the filing of an application for a summary trial, although, in cases of extreme urgency, this period can be reduced.

## Business Forms and Structures

## General

The Law of Commercial Companies, Decree 28 of 1975, as periodically amended, governs most of the principal types of business entities in Bahrain. This decree contains the law relating to companies, partnerships and branches. In addition to the aforementioned entities, Ministerial Order 25 of 1977 created a specific entity known as the exempt company, an off-shore company introduced in order to encourage foreign companies to locate their regional headquarters in Bahrain. To further promote Bahrain's goal of being the regional financial center, many of the offshore entities are banking units and investment banks.

In order to establish a joint-stock company, limited liability company, or partnership in Bahrain, at least 51 percent of the capital must be owned by Bahraini nationals. The laws and regulations governing the establishment of offshore exempt companies and offshore banking companies significantly relax the usual restrictions against foreign ownership.

The terms used in the legislation are difficult to translate precisely. For example, the term "company" is often used to mean both company and partnership and the term "partner" to mean both partner and shareholder. A company or partnership is defined by the Law of Commercial Companies as a contract under which persons undertake to participate in a financial enterprise with a view to profits, each contributing money or services and dividing the profits or losses resulting from the enterprise.

Bahraini law allows for the establishment of the following types of companies and partnerships: (1) general partnership (a partnership under a collective name); (2) limited partnership; (3) partnership limited by shares; (4) joint stock company; (5) limited liability company; and (6) joint venture.

Any association which does not assume one of the prescribed forms will not be recognized by law and any persons who enter into a contract in the name of such an unrecognized entity are liable jointly and severally to third parties for resultant obligations.

## Companies Law

### Joint Stock Companies
A joint stock company is a pure shareholding company in which all of the members are liable for company debts to the extent of the nominal value of their shares. This type of company can take the form of an exempt joint stock company, a closed joint stock company or a public joint stock company. While the latter type requires a minimum of 51 percent Bahraini ownership, the exempt and closed joint stock companies may be 100 percent foreign owned. All forms of the joint stock company must maintain permanent offices in Bahrain.

Public stock companies may only be established with permission from the Ministry of Commerce and supported by an Emir decree. Seven founding shareholders are required in order to establish a public stock company. Together they must subscribe for between 7 and 20 percent of the shares of the company.

An application to register a public stock company must be filed with the Directorate of Commerce and Industry in the Ministry of Commerce and Agriculture along with the company's Memorandum and Articles of Association. Public stock companies are authorized either for a fixed period of time or for the period of time necessary to achieve a specified objective. The Minister of Commerce and Agriculture makes a determination whether to register the company within thirty days of receipt of the application and recommendation of the Directorate of Commerce and Industry. Registration is completed after the approval of the Minister is published in the Official Gazette. Public subscription for shares must begin after the publication in the Official Gazette of the decree incorporating the company. A prospectus must be published prior to the opening of the subscription. The subscription is made through a bank where the proceeds are to be deposited in the name of the company. If the company cannot be established after the subscription period due to being under-subscribed, the founding shareholders are responsible for returning all subscriptions received.

The public stock company may have a board of directors composed of between three and twelve directors, each nominated for a three-year term. A majority of the directors must be resident Bahrainis. Shares of a public stock company may be transferred freely. Bahraini shareholders, however, can sell their shares only to other Bahraini nationals.

Closed stock companies are formed in the same manner as public stock companies and may be formed without an Emir decree provided that the founders submit an affidavit affirming that they undertake to have the company Memorandum and Articles of Association comply with the law; that all the shares of the company have been subscribed for by the founders and the value of the shares has been deposited in an authorized bank; that shares paid in kind have been evaluated in accordance with the law and are fully paid up; and that the founders have established the necessary management for the company. Five founding shareholders are required to establish a closed stock company.

## Limited Liability Companies

The limited liability company, a shareholding company whose shares are not open to public subscription, is one of the most common forms of doing business by foreign investors. The company must have at least two and no more than fifty shareholders who are liable for the debts of the company only to the extent of their respective interest in the capital. At least one shareholder must be a Bahraini national, and the total shareholdings by Bahrainis may not be less than fifty-one percent. The words "With Limited Liability" must follow the name of the company. The limited liability company must have a limited life span not exceeding twenty-five years, which may be extended by a unanimous approval of the shareholders. The company must be managed by one or more managers who need not be partners. There is no legal requirement for a board of directors unless the number of partners exceeds two. A percentage of the company's profits must be allocated on an annual basis for depreciation and a certain rate of the net profits thereafter must be allocated to a legal reserve until such reserve equals 25 percent of the company's capital. Limited liability companies may not engage in banking, insurance or brokerage activities.

## Partnerships

### General Partnerships
A general partnership must be comprised of two or more Bahraini nationals; foreign investors can participate in partnerships, but Bahraini national participation must be at least 51 percent. In a partnership, the liability of the partners is unlimited, and they are jointly and severally liable with respect to the partnership's obligations to the entire extent of their assets. The name of the partnership must consist of the name of one or more of the partners adding thereto the words "Bahraini Partnership" or an indication that a partnership exists.

### Limited Partnerships
A limited partnership is comprised of at least one general partner and one limited partner. The extent of a limited partner's liability for the partnership's commitments is restricted to the amount of capital invested by the limited partner in the partnership. A limited partner may not participate in the management of the business and if this is done, the limited partner will be jointly and severally liable for the partnership's liabilities in the same way as the general partners. All general partners must be Bahraini nationals and at least 51 percent of the capital must be owned by Bahraini partners.

### Partnerships Limited by Shares
A partnership limited by shares consists of at least one general partner and at least ten shareholders. Management is the responsibility of the general partners and they are liable, to the extent of their entire assets, for the debts and commitments of the partnership. The shareholding partners are not responsible for the debts of the partnership, except to the extent of the value of their shares in the partnership. Shareholding partners may not interfere in the management of the partnership, and if they do so, they are personally liable for losses caused as a result thereof.

### Joint Ventures
A joint venture, also known as an association in participation, is a company that does not enjoy a separate legal personality. Joint ventures are formed by the conclusion of a Memorandum of Association specifying the rights and

obligations of the partners and the division of profits and losses. Joint ventures are not subject to any prescribed formalities.

A joint venture affects only the legal relations between the partners, however, it does not acquire legal status recognizable *vis-à-vis* its relationship with third parties. Third parties have a right of legal recourse against the partners with which they deal and the partners may thereafter proceed against each other for contribution.

## Legal Structures for Non-Bahrainis

### General

Commercial life in Bahrain can be broadly divided into the offshore and onshore sectors. In the offshore sector, which consists of exempt companies and offshore banking units, the rules regarding foreign participation are quite liberal. In the onshore sector, the rules governing each type of business entity impose certain limitations on foreign participation; all the partners of a general partnership must be Bahraini and foreign participation in other forms is limited to 49 percent. There are, however, certain exceptions to this rule.

The Commercial Companies Law allows for the establishment of 100 percent foreign owned companies under the following terms: (1) the purpose of the company is to establish an industrial enterprise in the country; (2) a majority of the company's capital is to be invested in an industrial development project; or (3) the company's objective is to use this establishment as a primary center for the investment of funds related to the distribution of its goods and/or services. If the wholly foreign owned company takes the form of a joint stock company, it must be a closed joint stock company.

Certain exceptions to the partnership rules allow some service sector partnerships, such as accounting, architectural and engineering firms to engage in partnership relations between Bahrainis and foreigners. In the event that there is only one foreign partner, the Bahraini partners must be entitled to at least 51 percent of the capital and operational earnings, and, if there are several foreign partners, to at least 30 percent thereof.

### Exempt Companies

Exempt companies are joint stock companies that have been exempted from some or all of the requirements of the Law of Commercial Companies by the Minster of Commerce and Agriculture. An exempt company must register and situate its main office in Bahrain, but is set up to conduct its activities outside of Bahrain. This type of company may operate for a maximum twenty-five year period. The exempt company's activities must be conducted outside Bahrain. No more than 20 percent of the capital of an exempt company may be owned by Bahraini nationals without the permission of the Minister. An exempt company takes the form of a joint stock company. The phrase "Bahraini Exempt Joint Stock Company" and an indication of the entity's capital must follow the company's name. The company's activities may not include insurance, banking or brokerage. It is exempt from the requirements of local Bahraini participation in ownership applicable to most Bahraini companies. Without the consent of the Ministry of Commerce and Agriculture, an exempt company is not allowed to conduct any business or to undertake any commercial activities within Bahrain.

Exempt companies must have at least two members, and the maximum number of members is unlimited. Exempt companies are managed by a board of directors of no less than two and not more than ten directors. A percentage of profits of the exempt company must be allocated each year for depreciation and 10 percent of the net profits thereafter must be allocated to form a compulsory reserve until the amount of such reserve equals 25 percent of the capital.

The Directorate of Commerce and Companies' Affairs of the Ministry of Commerce and Agriculture has complete discretion to accept or to reject an application for the registration of an exempt company. It may exercise this discretion in accordance with its views as to the contribution that the proposed company will make to the economy of Bahrain and to Bahrain's reputation as an offshore center for business activity. Upon its incorporation, the exempt company is required to deposit a portion of its capital with the Bahrain Monetary Agency in order to guarantee any liabilities which might be outstanding upon the company's dissolution and may be paid only to the liquidator of the company.

## Foreign Company Branch

The Law of Commercial Companies provides that companies established outside Bahrain may open branches or offices in Bahrain provided that the approval of the Minister of Commerce and Agriculture is obtained and a local sponsor is appointed. The Minister will not grant approval unless he is satisfied that the parent company is financially sound and will assume full responsibility for liabilities of the branch. The sponsor must be a Bahraini merchant, either a company or an individual. The Companies Law exempts branch offices of foreign companies from having a Bahraini sponsor if these offices use Bahrain as a regional center or as a representative office for their business activities.

### Commercial Agency

The Commercial Agency Law of 1992 regulates the establishment of commercial agencies in Bahrain. In accordance with this law, overseas companies can distribute or sell their products and commodities in Bahrain through agents who may be either Bahraini nationals or majority-owned Bahraini companies. The Bahraini Commerce Ministry has been attempting since 1995 to implement the 1992 law in a more transparent manner and is preparing further reform legislation.

There are two types of commercial agency: commission agency and commercial representation. A commission agency is a contract under which an agent acts in his own name for the account of the principal in return for a certain consideration. The agent carries out the commercial activities independently and, consequently, customers have no right of recourse against the principal.

A commercial representation corresponds to the ordinary agency relationship according to which the acts of the representative bind the principal with respect to third parties. The agency relationship is usually governed by a contract of service or employment.

An agency contract should, *inter alia*, contain the names and nationalities of the principal and agent, the rights and obligations of both parties, the amount of profit or commission to be paid, the agent's area of business activity, the term of the agency, etc. According to the Agency Law, agents are required to renew agreements with their principals once every two years. The law requires that agents assume responsibility for providing all customers the spare parts and tools necessary to maintain and to repair any machinery and equipment sold by the agency.

All commercial agency agreements must be registered with the Commercial Registry of the Directorate of Commerce and Companies' Affairs in the Ministry of Commerce and Agriculture. Under the Agency Law, the Council of Ministers may limit the number and type of agency agreements which an agent may register. Any unregistered commercial agency shall not be recognized.

A principal may appoint only one agent within the area of activity for which he is appointed. The agent is entitled to commissions for all transactions concluded in his area of activity irrespective of whether they are the result of the agent's endeavors, unless otherwise agreed upon by the parties. The Agency Law permits persons other than the authorized agent to import goods by paying the local agent a 5 percent commission.

Either party cannot terminate agency agreements which are concluded for an indefinite period unless the other party commits a breach of contract without justifiable cause. If the agency is terminated by the principal prematurely or for any reason beyond the agent's control, the agent shall be entitled to compensation from the principal equivalent to any losses incurred and for loss of profits. If the agent terminates the agency agreement prematurely or without justifiable cause, the principal is entitled to compensation for any losses incurred as a result thereof.

## *Bankruptcy and Liquidation*

As of 1996, Bahrain had passed no laws relating to insolvency, the bankruptcy of individuals, and the rights of creditors in cases of insolvency or provisions for the compulsory winding-up of companies.

Bahraini Courts have been persuaded to turn to the legislation of other countries in cases where a judgment debtor was unable to pay the judgment debt. In other situations, under court supervision, creditors have been persuaded to appoint a receiver or a liquidator to collect the assets of a debtor (whether an individual or a company).

Provisions regarding the distribution of proceeds of sale of a debtor's movable or immovable property are contained in the Civil and Commercial Procedures Law of 1971. The only type of secured creditors are employees in respect to salary accrued, due and unpaid. Remaining assets are distributed on a *pro rata* basis to all unsecured creditors. It is provided that if the proceeds of sale are insufficient to satisfy a creditor who has seized and sold property of the debtor and no agreement to the contrary has been made between the seizer of the property and the other creditors, the proceeds of the sale will be divided amongst them *pro rata* to their respective debts. Bahraini law's recognition of the prior rights of mortgages is an example of an agreement to the contrary.

Furthermore, Bahraini law has occasionally appointed an official receiver to take custody of sequestered property or property in dispute. A receiver must keep, manage and return the property to the person who establishes a right to it and must submit an account of the proceeds of his management of the property. The disputing parties must agree to the appointment of the receiver.

The Commercial Companies Law of 1975 contains provisions relating to the liquidations and winding-up of companies and the dissolution of partnerships and other entities.

In general this law relates to the winding-up and dissolution of solvent entities although there are provisions relating to the winding-up of companies which are unable to proceed with conducting business as a result of all or a substantial part of their assets having been lost or destroyed, or as a result of incurring substantial losses. A partnership may be dissolved when one of the partners is declared bankrupt or insolvent.

Detailed rules regulate the appointment of liquidators and the liquidation process. Liquidators are obliged to notify creditors of the commencement of the liquidation and to invite them to submit their claims. Liquidators may also advertise for creditors if the identity and domicile of the creditors are not known.

The law provides that the costs and expenses of the liquidation will take priority over the debts owed to the company's creditors. Following the payment in full of all debts owed to creditors, the remaining assets of the company are divided among the company's shareholders *pro rata* to their respective holdings.

The Commercial Companies Law does not provide for fraudulent preference and voidable transfers of assets made prior to liquidation by a company.

## Currency and Banking

### *Currency Control*

The Bahrain Monetary Agency (BMA) is the regulatory body that oversees the commercial banks and other financial institutions operating in Bahrain and is the rough equivalent of a central bank. The BMA controls the issuing of currency and is the authority in charge of exchange matters. In addition, the BMA sets maximum interest rates for all loans made in Bahraini Dinar and recommends maximum rates of interest payable on deposits of Bahraini Dinar.

### *Banking*

#### *General*

Over the past twenty years, Bahrain has developed as a regional financial center for the Gulf region and for much of the Arab world. Bahrain's financial institutions attract funds from the Gulf region since, unlike most other countries in the region, Bahrain does not prohibit the use of interest in banking operations. Law of Commerce No. 7 of 1987, expressly permits interest in transactions; rates agreed to by parties to a contract will be enforced if not exorbitant in opinion of Bahrain courts. No hard and fast rule exists, but based on past cases interest in excess of 15 percent could be viewed as exorbitant.

While other GCC countries like the UAE permit the use of interest, legislative initiatives like offshore banking units continue to attract foreign funds.

In the past few years, however, there has been a rise in the number of Islamic banks operating in Bahrain that do prohibit the use of interest. In 1996 Citibank opened an Islamic bank.

Bahrain has a well-developed commercial banking sector which includes many of the large international banks. A number of offshore banking institutions offer specialized commercial services. There is a housing bank, which provides long term finance for housing and commercial real estate developments. Additionally, there are several Islamic banks and financial institutions that constitute a significant factor in the financial community. The distinctive feature of Islamic banking is that no interest is paid; instead the bank charges fees and shares its profits or losses. In addition, the Bahraini Stock Exchange, established in 1989, has been open to foreign as well as Bahraini investors since 1990.

## Offshore Banking Units

Bahrain has been encouraging the establishment of "offshore" banking units (OBUs) since the mid 1970s. An OBU is not allowed to provide local banking services but is allowed to accept deposits from governments and from large, regional financial organizations and to make medium-term loans for local and regional capital projects. The OBUs serve to channel money from the petroleum-producing region back into world markets.

A license from the BMA is necessary in order to establish an OBU. The OBUs operate under the following conditions: (1) OBUs may be branches or joint ventures; (2) OBUs must be fully staffed and operational at all times; (3) OBUs may transact business with the Government of Bahrain, its agencies, or any licensed bank operating in Bahrain (conducting business with any other entity or individual resident in Bahrain requires the prior permission of the BMA which is normally given only if the transaction is related to a development project); (4) OBUs may provide non-residents of Bahrain with all banking services except checking accounts; (5) OBUs which are branches are not required to maintain any reserves with the BMA; (6) OBUs are required to supply to the BMA such information as may be prescribed by it from time to time; (7) OBUs are required annually to submit to the BMA a balance sheet and profit and loss account audited by auditors; (8) OBUs which are partly or wholly owned by banks or other entities are required annually to file with the BMA a copy of the consolidated accounts of the owners; and (9) OBUs are required to pay to the BMA an annual license fee of an amount as may from time to time be prescribed by the BMA.

## Representative Offices

Foreign banks may open a representative office in Bahrain. This is often done by international banks wishing to establish a presence in Bahrain until such time as they are able to justify the additional cost of setting up an offshore banking unit. Representative offices are prohibited from conducting trade or business in Bahrain and are limited to collecting general financial, economic and commercial information, offering general representation and rendering assistance to customers of the bank. These offices have to be approved by the BMA and pay an annual license fee.

## Investment Banks

Investment banks, characterized as non-bank financial institutions, operate under a licensing system by the BMA. They may not offer current account services, although deposits can be accepted from non-bank institutions in a minimum value of US$ 50,000 or the equivalent. Deposits may also be accepted from banks inside and outside Bahrain. Investment banks are allowed to grant loans to both residents and non-residents provided they are not in the form of an overdraft. In addition, they may also undertake all forms of business in securities including underwriting, placing and trading in securities, consultancy on issues of investment and the raising of capital. Investment banks may be formed as exempt companies.

## Intellectual Property

## General

While Bahrain does have laws pertaining to the protection of patents, trademarks and copyrights, they are often considered inadequate by Western standards despite the fact that Bahrain has recently ratified the Berne Convention for the Protection of Literary and Artistic Works and the Paris Convention for the Protection of Industrial Property, and is contemplating joining the Madrid Agreement regarding the International Registration of Marks. Bahrain's intellectual property legislation includes the Copyright Law of 1993 and the Patent, Design and Trademark Law of 1995. Notwithstanding the Copyright Law of 1993, works may be separately registered through a cumbersome and expensive process with the Ministry of Information which grants greater protection to the creator of the copyrighted material than the Copyright Law. The country is a signatory to the Trade Related Aspects of Intellectual Property Rights agreement (TRIPS) and must become compliant by January 1, 2000.

## Patents and Designs

### Patents
Patents, trademarks and designs are protected in Bahrain by virtue of the Patent, Design and Trademark Law of 1995, as periodically amended. Pro-

tection is based on registration at the Patents and Trademarks Registration Office.

If a registered patent or design is not used within two years of the filing date of the application to register, third parties may apply to the court for the registration to be revoked.

The validity of a patent registration is for fifteen years only. It can be renewed for five years provided that the patent is of special significance and the income realized from it during the original term is not reasonable relative to the expenses incurred. The other procedures and protection regarding patents are similar to those of trademarks. One exception is that registration of patents in Bahrain requires either a home registration or any other foreign registration of the patent.

## Designs
The validity of a design registration in Bahrain is for five years, renewable for two further terms of five years each. The other procedures of registration are similar to those of trademarks. One exception is that a design registration of designs in Bahrain requires either a home registration or any other foreign registration of the design.

## Trademarks

According to the Patent, Design and Trademark Law, a trademark registration is valid for ten years from the date of filing the application. Thereafter, a trademark registration is renewable for periods of ten years each. Trademarks are defined as everything that takes a distinctive form such as names, words, signatures, characters, number, drawings, etc., if used in distinguishing products, goods or services.

Trademark rights are acquired by registration, however, a trademark application can be opposed successfully upon producing sufficient proof of the prior use of the mark in Bahrain and elsewhere around the world. Marks which are not renewed will be canceled by the Commercial Registry. Unlawfully registered marks may be canceled by a court.

Once a trademark application is filed, the trademark is examined as to its registerability. Trademark applications accepted by the Registrar are in the Official Gazette. There is a sixty-day period open for filing an opposition by any interested party. An authorized agent or the proprietors themselves as from the date of publication should present an opposition to the registration of a trademark before the Registrar within the prescribed period. Such an opposition case is settled by the Registrar. In the absence of opposition, a published trademark is registered, and the certificate of registration is issued.

Use of trademarks in Bahrain is not compulsory for filing applications for registration nor for maintaining trademark registrations in force. But a trademark is subject to cancellation and may be canceled by any party who can establish that the trademark was not actually used during the five years immediately preceding the application for cancellation or that there was no *bona fide* intention of using the trademark on the goods in respect of which the trademark was registered.

Unauthorized use of a trademark registered under the law or an imitation of such trademark applied on goods of the same class, or sale, storing for the purpose of sale, or exhibiting for sale of goods bearing a counterfeit mark, or using a mark duly registered under the law by another person to serve the purpose of unauthorized promotion of goods of the same class are offenses punishable by law in Bahrain.

## Copyright

The Copyright Law was introduced to Bahrain's legislative system in 1993. The Copyright Law protects authors of intellectual property such as books, paintings, photographs, cinematographic, radio and television works and personally created computer software and databases and was enacted in order to combat pirating of videotapes, audiotapes, artistic work and computer software.

Ministerial Order 4 of 1993 established a Copyright Protection Office in the Ministry of Information. The Copyright Protection Office examines applications for copyright protection, accepts the deposit of works after payment of fees, and registers the transfer of copyrights. The Office is also responsible for examining international copyright agreements and implementing those which Bahrain has executed.

The Copyright Law applies to: (1) the works of Bahraini authors which are published for the first time, whether in or outside of Bahrain; (2) works of foreign authors that are published for the first time in Bahrain; and (3) works of Arab authors who are nationals of a Member State that has ratified the Arab Copyright Protection Agreement of 1958 and whose work is published for the first time in a Member State.

Copyright protection lapses, in general, fifty years after the death of the author or, in the event of jointly owned intellectual property, fifty years after the death of the last surviving author.

With respect to the following works, the protection lapses fifty calendar years after the date of publication: (1) films, photographs and applied art; (2) works published under a pseudonym; (3) works which belong to a corporate entity; and (4) works first published after the author's death.

In the case of computer software, the copyright protection will lapse either fifty years after the completion of the work or forty years from the date of publication, whichever is earlier.

## Taxation

### Taxation of Companies

The single corporate income tax in Bahrain is levied on oil, gas and petroleum companies at a rate of 46 percent. This tax is applicable to any oil company conducting business activity in Bahrain of any kind, including oil exploration, production, or refining, regardless of the company's place of incorporation.

Deductions are allowed for taxes and customs and duties, which are paid by the taxpayer. The costs of raw materials, production and management, may also be deducted from taxable income. Capital assets may be depreciated over the useful life of assets.

### Taxation of Individuals

There is no individual income tax in Bahrain.

### Municipal Tax

A municipal tax is payable by individuals or companies renting property in Bahrain. The rate of the tax varies according to the nature of the property, namely: unfurnished residential property, furnished residential property and commercial property.

## Social Security Taxes

Employers who employ more than ten employees, irrespective of their nationality, must pay 10 percent of the employee's gross income to social welfare taxes. The employer's contribution is 7 percent of gross wages for pension insurance, disability and death (applicable only to Bahraini employees) and 3 percent of gross wages for insurance against employment injuries (applicable to all employees). The employee's contribution is five percent of gross wages for pension insurance, disability and death (applicable to Bahraini employees only).

## Withholding Taxes; Sales Tax

No withholding of taxes exist. The only tax on sales or turnover is a tax on gasoline which is levied at a low rate of 12 percent. Bahrain has no value-added tax, property tax or production tax.

## Treaties for Prevention of Double Taxation

While there is no existing provision in the law expressly preventing double taxation, the foreign tax paid on income subject to a foreign country's tax system will generally be deductible from the tax imposed on taxable income in Bahrain.

## Investment and Trade

### Investment Incentives

The Bahraini government actively promotes foreign investment and, in recent years, has promulgated regulations permitting 100 percent foreign ownership of new industrial establishments and for the establishment of representative offices or branches of foreign companies without local sponsors. Most other commercial investments, however, are subject to government approval and generally must be made in partnership with a Bahraini national controlling 51 percent of the equity. Foreign nationals are not permitted to purchase land in Bahrain with certain exceptions made for GCC nationals. The government encourages the employment of local nationals by setting local-national employment targets in each sector and by restricting the issuance of expatriate labor permits.

*Investment Incentives Applying to Both Foreign and Bahraini Firms*
The Government of Bahrain, in recent years, introduced an industrial incentive program for private companies to employ locals and special measures to support new and existing small and medium-sized industries. These incentives include:

- *Labor:* A subsidy of US$ 11,925 per year for the first three years, for each Bahraini employed by companies setting up factories in pioneering industries; US$ 7,950 per year for downstream industries, and US$ 2,650 per year for companies setting up factories in existing industries.
- *Electricity Charges:* A 50 percent rebate for the first five years in all industries.
- *Land Rental:* A 100 percent rebate of rental fees in Government industrial areas for the first five years, for all industries.
- *Customs Duties:* A 100 percent rebate of customs duties for the first five years, for all industries.
- *Export Credit Facility:* Available to all industries.
- *Tariff Protection:* Subject to the approval of the National Committee on Tariff Protection, 10 to 20 percent protection may be given to pioneering downstream industries.

## Trade Agreements

The Basic Statute of the Gulf Cooperation Council (GCC) was signed in 1981 and the signatories thereto are Saudi Arabia, Oman, Kuwait, the United Arab Emirates, Qatar and Bahrain. The GCC aims to attain cooperation in all fields, to draw up comparable legislation in finance, trade, education, health, tourism and administration, to establish research centers and to encourage scientific development in industry. The ministers from the GCC countries are cooperating with a view towards unifying customs tariffs, establishing a regional stock market and allowing Gulf companies to open representative offices in other Member States.

The Uniform Economic Agreement was executed on 11 November 1981. It sets out various objectives which are to be realized by domestic legislation in the Member States. The Agreement deals with the free movement of goods within the Member States and exemption of goods from customs and other duties imposed by on imports. It contemplates uniform customs tariffs for goods entering the area of the GCC from outside. It also deals in general terms with the issue of free movement of workers between Member States, leaving the practical realization of these goals to separate legislation to be agreed upon by Member States. The Agreements also cover development programs, oil policy, scientific policy and cooperation on technology transfer agreements with third parties.

The Member States have formed a customs union and have adopted a unified customs schedule based on the Brussels Tariff Nomenclature, the international standard for the classification of goods for customs.

## Customs

Bahrain is, in some respects, a free port. There is no regulation restricting foreign trade with the exception that all goods imported into or exported from Bahrain must comply with certain requirements. Anyone wishing to import goods into Bahrain for sale or consumption must obtain a general license from the Customs and Ports Directorate of the Ministry of Finance and National Economy.

Customs duties are levied only on goods imported for sale in Bahrain. The rates of duty include the following: 5 percent on foodstuffs from non-GCC countries; 5 percent on non-luxuries; 10 percent on general luxuries; 20 percent on cars and boats; 70 percent on cigarettes and tobacco; and 125 percent on alcoholic drinks.

The Government of Bahrain permits the duty-free importation of raw material inputs for incorporation into products for export and the duty-free importation of equipment and machinery for newly established export industries. Except under special license, the private importation of weapons is generally prohibited, and only one private company is authorized to import explosives. The Government of Bahrain provides indirect export subsidies in the form of preferential rates for electricity, water and natural gas to select industrial establishments.

Imported and exported goods are classified according to the Standard International Trade Classification (SITC), Revision 1.

## *Public Sector Procurement*

The Government makes major public purchasing decisions through public tender processes. For major projects, the Ministry of Works, Power and Water extends invitations to selected, pre-qualified firms. Construction companies bidding on Government construction projects must therefore be registered with the Ministry of Works, Power and Water. Smaller contracts are handled by individual ministries and departments and are not subject to pre-qualification procedures.

### Environmental Law

Bahrain is party to several international conventions pertaining to environmental issues. The Kuwait Regional Convention for Cooperation on the Protection of the Marine Environment from Pollution was enacted to help prevent, abate and combat pollution of the marine environment, to deal with pollution emergencies and to establish appropriate rules and procedures for the determination of civil liability and compensation for damage related to pollution of the marine environment. The Convention was adopted on April 24, 1978 and its date of entry into force was July 1, 1979.

Bahrain is also a party to the Agreement for the Establishment of a Commission For Controlling the Desert Locust in the Near East, adopted on July 2, 1965, and entered into force in Bahrain on February 24, 1969. The Agreement's objective is to promote national and international research and action to control the desert locust in the region.

# EGYPT

## Recent Political Developments

Since the early 1990s, Egypt has made a dramatic economic turnaround making its economy an envy of the region. GDP during the last few years has increased by between 5.3 percent and 6 percent and is expected to jump to 8 percent in the coming years.

The turnaround began in 1991 when the country, faced with large external debt service arrears, declining growth, 20 percent inflation and a worsening balance of payments, initiated a comprehensive economic reform program supported by the IMF. The program included freeing interest and exchange rates, dramatically reducing the budget deficit and disciplined monetary growth.

| Profile | |
| --- | --- |
| Population | 68 million (1999) |
| Religions | 92% Muslim; 8% Other |
| Government | Presidential/ Parliamentarian Republic |
| Languages | Arabic (English and French are widely spoken) |
| Work Week | Commercial Saturday–Thursday 9:00–15:00; 18:00–21:00 Government Saturday–Thursday 8:00–15:00 Banking Sunday–Thursday 8:30–15:30 |
| Monetary Unit | Egyptian Pounds(£E) |
| Exchange Rate | £E 3.4=US$ 1 |

Egypt also received assistance from the World Bank in developing a framework for reforming the public sector, privatizing state-owned enterprises and liberalizing trade and investment policies. These reforms have led to exchange rate stabilization, lower inflation, a balance of payments surplus and a liberalized banking regime.

The government is continuing with its reform program, particularly in privatization. Egypt has implemented one of the region's most aggressive programs, earning it an IMF ranking as one of the top four of emerging markets. As of March 31, 1999, Egypt had privatized 33 percent of its public-sector enterprises, generating $2.7 billion in government revenue.

It is likely that these reforms will remain on track as President Mubarak, who has overseen the economic turnaround, was elected in September 1999 to a fourth six-year term. Soon after, he reshuffled his cabinet to prove his commitment to economic reform, appointing former Minister of Public Enterprises Atef Ubeid as Prime Minister.

Mubarak has also taken measures, albeit often drastic, to control one of the biggest threats to the country's economic recovery: Islamic fundamentalism. Since the November 1997 Luxor massacre, which targeted the lucrative tourism sector in an attempt to shake the pillars of the regime, Egypt unleashed a harsh and successful campaign to combat extremists. The massacre, which virtually crippled tourism, one of the country's leading economic sectors, revealed how one sensational event could nearly erase years of progress and delay further economic growth.

Mubarak will face increasing pressure during this term to appoint a successor. This need has been highlighted with a July 1999 assassination attempt (the fourth such occurrence during Mubarak's tenure). Egypt's Constitution has no effective mechanism in place to nominate heads of state.

Maintaining internal stability will be vital for attracting the foreign investment necessary to continue the economic expansion. And this expansion is crucial if the country wants to be able to provide better living standards for its exploding population, now at nearly sixty-eight million. In the last century, the population has increased almost six times and three times since 1950. Even under a moderate growth scenario, Egypt will have more than ninety million citizens by the year 2035. Under more rapid growth, as has been the case in recent years, Egypt may reach 103 million in the next forty years.

## Recent Economic Developments

During the fiscal year 1998-99, Egypt met its goal of maintaining a deficit of around 1 percent of GDP. The current deficit, for the year ending June 30, 2000, was budgeted at 1 percent of GDP, but ministers say they managed to trim it to 1.1 percent in the first six months of the fiscal year. Government spending in 1999-2000 is budgeted at $29.5 billion. While the government is practicing tight fiscal policy, it is also increasing some social programs, such as doubling since 1998 the number of bakeries providing subsidized bread to 20,000.

As part of the Camp David accords, Egypt receives more than US$ 2 billion per year in US-based economic and military aid. Foreign reserves are estimated at approximately US$ 18 billion, exceptionally high for an economy engaged in many of the liberal economic reforms that Egypt has undertaken. Egypt's budget deficit is now roughly 1 percent of GDP. Inflation is also down to under 4 percent of GDP. Because Egypt served as a linchpin in the 1990-91 Gulf War, it has benefited from a US$ 10 billion write-off in debt relief.

For fiscal 1999-2000, the government is aiming at a 6 percent growth rate, followed in the coming year by an 8 percent growth rate, 18 percent savings rate and 23 percent investment rate. The drivers of growth will be the construction, transportation and industrial sectors. While these figures represent the positive picture of the economy there are some trouble spots, such as an unemployment rate hovering in between 7 percent and 8 percent and a trade deficit that grew from $10.22 billion in 1997 to $11.77 billion 1998.

In other fiscal matters, the government did not raise taxes in 1999-2000 for the fourth consecutive year. External loans, according to the 1999-2000 budget, are £E 700 million, less than one percent of the budget. External debt accumulated during seven years is $28.2 billion. Internal debt rose from £E 125 billion in June 1997 to £E 136.8 billion pounds, with the money earmarked for transportation, communications, drinking water and sanitary drainage projects.

During the last decade, Egypt's economy has strengthened and become increasingly popular with foreign investors. The factors enticing investors are numerous. Egypt has the largest population in the Arab world, including a market of between 5 million to 10 million people who follow western consumption patters, and its labor force is relatively well-educated and English speaking.

Furthermore, the country continues to privatize major industries, attracting foreign investment. Major infrastructure projects are underway from airports to telecommunications and port projects. The tourism industry has also drawn large foreign investment.

In fact, during FY 1998-99, Egypt had a successful year in terms of attracting foreign investors. The volume of foreign and Arab investments in Egypt increased to £E 24,960 billion, 18 percent of which was generated in the free zone. Saudi Arabian firms were the top Arab and foreign contributors with £E 4.5 billion.

Although the investing climate is generally positive, there are detractions. Some loud complaints, for example, have been directed at the government for its lack of transparency and high price setting in its public offering of government-owned companies. There are also the age-old problems of doing business in Egypt such as relatively high transaction costs, bureaucratic processes and red tape.

**Economic Indicators**

| | 1998/99[1] | 1997/8 | 1996/7 |
|---|---|---|---|
| GDP Growth (percent) | 5.8 | 5.7 | 5.3 |
| Inflation (percent) | 3.8 | 6.2 | 7.0 |
| Unemployment (percent) | 7.5 | 8.3 | 8.5 |
| Debt Service Ratio | 10.80 | 10.90 | 12.66 |
| Govt. Budget Deficit (£E mln) | −3,990 | 2,699 | 2,328 |
| Balance of Payments (US$ mln) | −2,117 | −135 | +1,912 |
| Trade Balance | −12,524 | −11,771 | −10,219 |
| Exports | 4,445 | 5,128 | 5,345 |
| Oil | 1,000 | 1,728 | 2,578 |
| Non-Oil | | 3,400 | 2,767 |
| Imports | 16,969 | 16,899 | 15,565 |
| Services Balance | +5,946 | +4,595 | +6,194 |
| Transfers Balance | +4,869 | +4,404 | +4,145 |
| C/A Balance | −1,709 | −2,772 | 119 |
| Capital Account | 880 | 3,766 | 2,041 |

[1]Projection, according to Egypt's Ministry of Economy

## Main Economic Domains

In terms of foreign currency revenues, the Egyptian economy is dependent on four main sources: remittances from expatriates working abroad, gas exports, Suez Canal dues, and tourism. In recent years, revenues from these sectors dropped, due to several factors. These include an international oil price slump (in 1998 and early 1999), the November 1997 Luxor massacre, which deterred tourists, and a gradual decline in Suez Canal dues (spurred by the Asian economic crisis).

## Industry

The most important products of Egyptian industry include cotton yarn, jute yarn and fabrics, wool yarn, refined sugar, sulfuric acid nitrogenous fertilizers, paper, cement, motor-vehicle tires and television receivers. Other industrial activities include the manufacturing of iron and steel, assembling of motor vehicles and oil refining (at several locations). Smaller-scale industrial enterprises of significance to the economy include tanning, brewing, and the manufacture of pottery, perfumes, handicrafts, cottonseed oil, flour and other processed foodstuffs, and asphalt. Most industrial activity is centered around Cairo and Alexandria.

## Agriculture

Agriculture has fallen from 20 percent of GDP to 17.3 percent and from 36 percent of total employment to 29.5 percent as of July 1999. This is a sector in which the government has placed a top priority, pushing economic reform the farthest. The result has been a steady increase in productivity and production. Impressive growth has been achieved both in terms of increases in cultivated areas and in production levels. Despite this, Egypt is the world's largest food importer.

Cultivation is concentrated in the Nile and Delta regions, and less than 3 percent of total land area is cultivated. Some steps were taken during 1998-1999 to change this ratio, as the government added 1.8 million feddans of farmable land. But Egypt is looking to the estimated $85.5 billion Toshka Canal Project next to Lake Nasser to dramatically alter the landscape. The project, which began in October 1996, is expected to double the country's arable land. It is scheduled to be completed in 15 years.

Currently, Egyptian farmlands are capable of some of the highest yields in the world. In 1998-1999, for example, grain production increased from 8 million to 18 million tons. Egypt is the world's most important producer of long-staple cotton. Other leading crops include rice, tomatoes and wheat.

Also produced are sugarcane, watermelons, millet, barley, onions, vegetables, citrus fruits, mangoes, dates, figs and grapes.

## Tourism

As of 1999/2000, tourism became Egypt's top foreign exchange earner, and its success depends greatly on foreign perception of internal stability. This susceptibility was highlighted in 1997 following two terrorist attacks on tourists, including the massacre of 58 foreigners at Luxor. The result was a 19 percent drop in tourism revenues in FY 1997/98 to $2.9 billion. This, combined with a drop in oil prices, also led to a dollar shortage, which impacted the stock exchange as foreign investors were unable to redeem their shares for dollars.

Egyptian tourism offers tremendous attractions in terms of cultural heritage and of natural beauty. Tourism is a major growth industry, especially along the Mediterranean and Red Sea coasts, and is attracting foreign project management expertise and quality building systems and equipment. Tourism is also important for the government, since it is an important source of easy employment.

Egypt's goal is to draw six million tourists annually by the year 2000. Meanwhile, accommodation capacity will expand to 75,000 hotel rooms. Related construction by German, French and Italian investors will create about 17,500 new jobs. Foreign marketing campaigns are expected to draw a large number of foreign tourists.

## Energy

The country's oil and gas industries comprised 6.7 percent of the GDP and 33.7 percent of merchandise exports in 1997/98. Egypt's oil revenues suffered with other oil-producing countries when prices dropped, decreasing the value of the country's petroleum and related products exports from $2.4 billion in 1996/97 to $1.2 billion the next year.

Oil prices in 1998/99, however, have again begun to rise, along with Egypt's oil production, increasing from 34 million tons to 55 million tons. Not only did the country's consumption of oil increase, its reserves also increased by one-and-a-half times.

Egypt produces approximately 800,000 to 900,000 barrels of oil per day (approximately forty-five million tons per year). Natural gas accounts for approximately 28 percent of total energy consumption in the country. Production of natural gas and its derivatives is anticipated to augment by at least 4 percent annually.

There have been important developments in the gas sector, with important finds located in the offshore region of the Nile Delta.

Egypt's electrical capacity has grown substantially over the last decade. In 1999 it increased its capacity from 18 billion kWh to 102 billion kWh, with that number expected to rise to 601 billion kWh after the Sidi Krir power station's scheduled opening in December 1999.

Hydroelectric power represents over 8 percent of the total annual energy production in the country.

## Trade

Egypt offers an import market nearing US$ 17 billion annually. The United States is the largest foreign supplier, capturing approximately 20 percent of Egypt's imports in 1998, hovering between $3 billion and $4 billion for several years.

The principal imports of Egypt are agricultural products, foodstuffs, transportation equipment, chemicals, mining and quarrying machinery and metal products. The country has become increasingly dependent on imports and food grants, especially for wheat, flour and meat, due to rapid population growth.

The major exports of Egypt are crude petroleum, raw cotton, cotton yarn, fabrics and rice. The chief customers for these and other exports are Italy, the US, Germany, France, the former USSR, Japan and Great Britain.

## Business Environment

### Privatization

The Egyptian government made a formal commitment to privatization in the early 1990s and announced a plan for the divestiture of 125 public enterprises over the following five years. The government has also decided to sell off its shares in more than 250 public joint venture companies. However, some observers claim that the privatization process has proceeded slowly due to a lack of serious government commitment. These sources feel that privatization is being implemented primarily to appease international financial institutions and send positive signals to the world.

The privatization program in Egypt is two-fold. The first and most extensive part involves divestment of public sector holdings in production and manufacturing companies. To that end, two approaches are being undertaken: sales of shares through the stock exchange and sales of a strategic stake to anchor investors through public auction.

The second stage of the program is the encouragement of private sector investment in sectors historically controlled and operated by the public sector including electricity, roads, airports, ports, oil and gas transmissions. For that purpose, new laws were passed by the Egyptian government authorizing private sector investment in public services.

Law 203 of 1991 established the legal basis for privatization by removing the 314 public sector enterprises from the control of government ministers and restructuring them as affiliates under sixteen independent holding companies. In principle, the holding companies operate as private sector companies with full financial and managerial accountability.

The government plans to privatize 99 companies in 2000 and aspires to complete privatization of all public-sector companies by 2001. Analysts believe this goal will be difficult to attain because of the time needed to restructure financially strained companies before they can be sold.

For the most part, privatization has occurred in the construction, finance, tourism and transportation industries. Egypt is coming under increasing American and European pressure to open more of its service sectors, especially telecommunications. Investors are particularly interested in the country liberalizing this industry and ending the state's fixed-line monopoly, which will enable cheaper Internet access. The government has announced that it would sell a 10 percent stake in Telecom Egypt in 2000 and another 30 percent soon after.

Other sales expected during late 1999 and 2000 include seven regional power companies. The government also approved in September 1999 the sale of the largest parts of the Suez Company for Loading and Unloading. It also agreed to sell equity in the Misr-Aswan Company for Fishing and Fish-procession and the Asyut company, which repairs vehicles.

Other scheduled sales are for the Isma'ilia Tourism Company, the Helnan Dahab Hotel, the Cosmopolitan Hotel in Cairo, Delta Spinning & Weaving and Wadi Cotton Ginning. During 1999, Egypt sold two cement companies—Asyut Cement and Beni Suef Cement, for a total of about $500 million.

As of the beginning of September 1999, there were still no plans to privatize the state-owned media, military production, the oil sector, Egypt Air or the Suez Canal Authority. While Egypt has been interested in privatizing its four leading banks since 1997, continuing disagreements concerning a sales method and the allowance of foreign shareholders continues to delay the sales.

## Other Reform Efforts

In 1996, the Egyptian cabinet abolished a long-standing ban on foreign ownership of real estate in the country, which dated back to the socialist and nationalist policies of the 1960s. In 1998/99, the government passed further laws that would open the way for foreign and private sector involvement in the banking and insurance industries.

Additionally, the Ministry of Interior has increased the number of raids on suspected technology pirates to stamp out Egypt's reputation of offering poor intellectual property rights. As a result, foreign computer software companies have committed to investing there.

The government food subsidies, however, are likely to remain in place for some time, as Egypt learns from the Jordanian experience when it lifted bread subsidies in August 1996 that sparked riots. The government is doubling for 1999/2000 the number of bakeries supplying subsidized bread to 20,000.

## Major Development Projects

President Mubarak continues to pursue ambitious development projects, including a free industrial zone in the Gulf of Suez. This venture aims to employ more than 250,000 workers and attract large-scale investment. The East Port Said container terminal, adjacent to the industrial zone, represents

Egypt's first harbor to be built and operated by foreign partnership. The port's strategic location off the Mediterranean could be Egypt's gateway to international trade. It will also provide the private sector with an opportunity to manufacture export-oriented products.

In another step to encourage non-oil exports, the government in mid-1999 cancelled taxes on exporters' income. Exporters had already received rebates of sales taxes and customs duties on inputs used to produce export commodities, but these allowances are still overdue. The latest decision will encourage companies currently producing for the domestic market to consider export opportunities, and should therefore increase non-oil exports in the long term.

The vehicle assembly sector is showing impressive results. Most major international models are now produced at twelve assembly plants employing 75,000 workers. General Motors, Peugeot, Suzuki, Citroen, Daimler-Benz, and Hyundai all produce in Egypt. During 1999, Egypt signed its first comprehensive vehicle manufacturing venture between Daewoo Motors and Nasr Automobile Company. Operations will be located in Wadi Houf, a southern Cairo suburb.

Telecommunications is another area where major changes are underway. In 1999, the government granted two licenses to foreign companies for the right to operate 20,000 nationwide public payphones, each for a 10-year period. Egypt, like other countries in the region, is seeing a significant rise in mobile phone usage. By January 1999, six months after assuming control of the mobile network established by Telecom Egypt, Mobinil (France Telecom, Motorola and Orascom Technologies) nearly doubled the number of subscribers from 83,000 to 159,850. Mobinil's competition is Misr-Fone, which has 180,000 users.

Multinational companies are particularly active in the petroleum sector in Egypt. Among these are the Gulf of Suez Petroleum Company (GUPCO) which is a joint venture between the Egyptian General Petroleum Corporation (EGPC) and Amoco of the US, with more than $5 billion in investments. Amoco is also active in the development of compressed natural gas for automotive use and is developing an integrated business in Egypt involving a public station for vehicle and other fueling facilities.

Other multinationals operating in Egypt in both oil and gas include Shell; Italy's Agip; Repsol of Spain; Mobil and Norsk Hydro of Norway. Technology has been bought from ABB Lummus Crest (USA) for the implementation of an ethylene/polyethylene plant at Ameriya-Alexandria; and EGPC has also signed a licensing agreement with British Petroleum for the production of polyethylene.

Food processing is another industry that has attracted multinationals in Egypt. Production units have been set up to serve both the local market and neighboring countries. Thus, recent newcomers include Nestle, Heinz, Kellogg's, Cadbury, Pioneer Hi-bred and Unilever. Both Heinz and Cadbury are also working in association with the Kuwait Food Company in Egypt.

## Build Operate Transfer

A government policy established in 1999 states that all power generation projects would be constructed on a build-own-operate-transfer basis. Thus far, three contracts have been awarded.

In general, foreign and local investors are intensifying their involvement in both build-operate-transfer (BOT) and build-own-operate-transfer (BOOT) schemes in Egypt. Projects which have already been initiated include the construction of a thermal power station on a BOOT basis with two 325-megawatt generators, to be located at Sidi Krier on the Mediterranean coast, at an expected cost of about US$ 450 million (Siemens KWU has already won the contract to supply the generators), and a water-driven pumped storage plant at Ataqa near Suez, which will also have two 325-MW generators and is expected to cost some US$ 600 million. The pumped storage system would pump seawater into a basin in the mountains when the grid has plenty of slack and lower the water level to generate extra power during peak periods. Plans are also being drawn for a wind farm at Za'afarana on the Gulf of Suez, which will include a 300-MW turbine and cost about US$ 350 million.

An additional project involves the construction of a private airport at Mersa Alam on the Red Sea Coast, 300 kilometers south of Hurgada and 800 kilometers south of Cairo, also to be built on a BOOT basis. Plans for a second international airport project, to be located on the Mediterranean coast near El Alamein, have been announced, and an offer for tenders has been issued.

Other projects expected to go ahead on a BOT or BOOT basis include the construction of roads, hotels, restaurants, rest-stops and service stations along roadways, as well as the setting up of agricultural production and marketing schemes along urban and rural arteries.

The four toll roads to be constructed are between Alexandria-El-Fayyoum, El-Fayyoum-Aswan, Dairout-Farafra and El-Kharga-El-Dweinat highways, and have a total length of 1,850 kilometers (1,150 miles).

In the medium-term, the General Authority for Investment (GAFI) foresees BOT and BOOT being applied to other transport projects, such as the construction of new railroads and metropolitan lines to serve the huge new industrial and residential cities which have been built in desert areas. The Ministry of Transport and Communications is considering private sector involvement in the development of a new telecommunications infrastructure.

## Franchising

Franchising has become a popular business practice for both foreigners and Egyptians, particularly in fast-food restaurants and clothing stores. Franchises in do-it-yourself systems, languages and computer training centers, pest control and gold plating have also sprouted. This market has experienced remarkable expansion since it began in 1970, and market sources expect continued growth at an annual rate of 10 to 20 percent.

Brand conscious Egyptians, approximately 3 percent of the population or over two million consumers, are drawn to the increasingly popular and convenient service. Fare prices are high because of franchiser quality assurance standards and imported ingredients.

The fastest growing area is primarily US fast-food restaurants. As of 1999, there were 33 American franchisers including, Kentucky Fried Chicken, McDonalds, Pizza Hut, Subway, Taco Bell and Hard Rock Cafe. To address common problems such as customs delay, an International Franchise Committee was established as part of the American Chamber of Commerce in Egypt to meet with Egyptian government officials.

Garment franchising is a relatively new and growing industry in Egypt. Using Egyptian workers and materials, garment franchises have met with great success in Egypt's increasingly freer market economy. Currently, approximately fifteen garment franchises exist in the Egyptian market. Egyptian businessmen themselves have begun their own homegrown franchises, particularly in the clothing industry, franchising their businesses to others.

**Leading Business Opportunities**

| Rank | Sector |
|------|--------|
| 1 | Medical Equipment |
| 2 | Packaging Equipment |
| 3 | Oil & Gas Field Machinery |
| 4 | Automotive Parts & Maintenance Equipment |
| 5 | Construction Equipment & Building Materials |
| 6 | Computers & Peripherals |
| 7 | Paper & Paper-board |
| 8 | Agricultural Equipment |
| 9 | Telecommunications Equipment & Services |
| 10 | Environmental Equipment & Services |
| 11 | Franchising |
| 12 | Electrical Power Systems |
| 13 | Plastic Materials & Resins |
| 14 | Food Processing Equipment |
| 15 | Architectural, Construction and Engineering Services |

# Legal Review

## Judiciary

A basic understanding of Egyptian law requires some knowledge of the origin and basis of Egyptian jurisprudence. Egyptian legislation can be traced to three major sources: Napoleonic Code, Roman law and Islamic law (Shar'ia).

Egypt is a constitutional democracy based on the principle of separation of powers between the legislative, the executive and the judicial branches. The 1971 Constitution of Egypt, amended by the referendum of May 22, 1980, is premised upon respect for individual freedoms and for the rule of law. The Constitution is the supreme law of the land and provides for an independent judicial branch. Judges are subject to no other authority but that of the law; they serve until the age of sixty-four, until which time their jobs are secured.

Egyptian legislation is instituted according to the following hierarchy: the Constitution, Parliament legislation, Presidential decree, Prime Minister's decree, ministerial decision and acts of governors and governmental body heads and public corporations.

Laws, Presidential decrees and Decrees of the Prime Minister are published in Egypt's Official Gazette, usually within two weeks of their issuance, and, unless they provide otherwise, they become effective one month from the date of publication. Ministerial decisions as well as other decisions and acts approved for publication are published in the Egyptian Proceedings, a supplement of the Official Gazette.

Until the first half of the 19th century, Egypt, under the leadership of Khedive Ismail and his successors, underwent a rapid process of westernization, which included, inter alia, the adoption of modern codes of law modeled after the French Napoleonic Code. Since that time, Egypt has adopted a more Roman (Civil Law) system, in which matters involving personal status such as marriage, inheritance and divorce were made subject to Islamic substantive law. Currently, the procedural and substantive laws of Egypt are applied throughout the Republic, except in cases of personal status which are decided in accordance with Islamic substantive law in cases involving Muslims whether Egyptians or aliens, Church substantive law in cases involving non-Muslim Egyptians, or, according to the substantive law of the nation of the litigant parties in cases involving non-Muslim foreigners.

The Egyptian judicial system consists of two separate court structures: the ordinary courts of law and the administrative courts.

## The Common Court System

The Common Court System is composed of four tiers: the Summary Courts, Courts of the First Degree, Courts of Appeal and the Supreme Court (Cour de Cassation).

## Summary Courts

The Summary Courts have jurisdiction to decide cases involving misdemeanor and minor offenses; civil and commercial cases in which the value does not exceed £E 5,000 as well as minor personal status issues and labor disputes arising between employers and employees.

## Court of First Degree

The Courts of the First Degree have jurisdiction to decide all cases involving matters in which the value exceeds £E 5,000 and all major personal status matters, subject to a right of appeal to the Court of Appeal. They also have jurisdiction to hear appeals against decisions of the Summary Courts in civil and commercial cases and misdemeanor criminal offenses.

## Courts of Appeal

Courts of Appeal are located in the major cities of Egypt. They have jurisdiction to hear appeals from civil, commercial and personal status cases decided in the first instance by the Courts of First Degree. Furthermore, they have jurisdiction to decide cases involving major crimes the penalty for which is death or imprisonment with hard labor of between three and twenty-five years.

## Supreme Court

The Supreme Court (Cour de Cassation) only hears appeals on final judgments of the Courts of Appeal and is only available if a breach of law is claimed as the basis for the appeal.

## The Administrative Court System

The judiciary in Egypt, similar to those of France and Italy, does not have jurisdiction to interfere with, repeal or nullify an administrative decree. Nonetheless, a court may award compensatory damages caused to a party by such administrative decree.

The only possible recourse regarding administrative decrees is to bring suit before the Council of State. The Council of State is composed of university trained judges. It alone is vested with the power to declare invalid and to revoke illegal, arbitrary, or abusive administrative decrees issued by government officials and ministries.

The Superior Constitutional Court was established in 1969 and is given exclusive jurisdiction to decide questions regarding the constitutionality of laws, rules and regulations.

## Business Forms and Structures

### *Companies Law*

Investors interested in establishing businesses in Egypt are subject to four laws: Corporate Law No. 159 of 1981; Investment Law No. 8 of 1997; New Communities Law No. 59 of 1979; and the Desert Land Law No. 143 of 1981. All companies established in Egypt are governed by the Corporate Law No. 159 of 1981 and the Commercial Law of 1883. Foreign companies may receive incentives and guarantees granted by other laws provided that they will be working in one of the fields prescribed therein.

Investment Law No. 8 of 1997 specifies those fields in which a company may receive the incentives and guarantees. These fields include: reclamation and cultivation of barren and desert lands; animal, poultry and fish production; industry and mining; hotels, motels, boarding houses, tourist villages, tourist travel and transport; transport of goods in cooling vans, cold stores for preservation of agricultural products, industrial products, food stuffs, containers stations and grain silos; aviation transportation and the services directly connected therewith; overseas maritime transport; all service for digging and exploration operations, transport and delivery of gas; housing projects, the units of which are leased wholly empty for non-administrative housing purposes; the infrastructure comprising drinking water, drainage water, electricity, roads and communications; hospitals and medical treatment centers which offer 10 percent of their capacity free of charge; financial leasing; guaranteeing subscription to securities; risk capital; production of computer software systems; and projects funded by the social funds for development.

The principal forms of companies under the Corporate Law No. 159 of 1981 are: the joint stock company and the limited liability company. These two forms of companies are the preferred form of incorporation for foreign investors.

Joint stock companies working under the umbrella of the Investment Law No. 8 of 1997, may be wholly controlled by a foreigner. Also, limited liability companies may be 100 percent foreign owned provided that at least one of the general managers is an Egyptian national.

## Joint Stock Companies

The joint stock company (JSC) is a company the capital of which is divided into shares of equal value; the liability of the shareholder is confined to the value of the shares to which he subscribes, and he is not liable for the debts of the company except within the limit of those shares. The JSC must have at least three founders. The founders are jointly responsible for the obligations they undertake. When the company is established in accordance with the Investment Law, founders may be foreigners. Each share may not be less than £E 5 and may not exceed £E 1,000.

The capital of the JSC is divided into nominal shares of equal values. At least 49 percent of the shares of JSCs should be put to public subscription at the time of their foundation or at the time of increase of their capital. Such subscription should be restricted to Egyptians for a period of one month, unless the Egyptians already own the 49 percent of shares. If this percentage has not been satisfied after being put to public subscription, the company may be founded without the total or partial completion of this percentage.

In companies that put their shares to public subscription, the issued capital shall not be less than £E 500,000. The founders cannot subscribe less than £E 250,000 in the issued capital or, 10 percent from the authorized capital, whichever is the highest amount.

In companies that do not put shares to public subscription, the issued capital may not be less than £E 250,000. A quarter of this amount must be paid at the company's foundation, and the remaining amount should be paid within ten years.

The shares in the JSC are characterized as follows: (1) negotiable shares and in kind shares; (2) capital shares and enjoyment shares; (3) common shares and preference shares.

## Limited Liability Companies

The limited liability company (LLC) is a company in which the number of shareholders does not exceed fifty. Each shareholder is only responsible within the limit of his portion of the shares. The foundation of the company, the increase of its capital or borrowing to its account is not permissible through public subscription. The LLC is not allowed to issue negotiable shares or bonds. The transfer of the shareholders' portions shall be subject to recovery from the other shareholders, in compliance with special conditions laid down by law. The company may adopt a particular name, which may be derived from its purpose and may include the name of one or more of its partners.

Features of the LLC are: the limited liability of each shareholder; a minimum of two shareholders; prohibition on public subscription; issuance of negotiable shares or bonds; restrictions for the assignment of shareholders' portions; transfer of the portions due to the death of a shareholder.

The capital of the company may not be less than £E 50,000, divided into equal shares of not less than £E 100 each, to be paid in full. There is no maximum for the portion's value, although there is for the shares' value. The shares of an LLC are indivisible; representations of the shares by negotiable bonds are not allowed, and every share will have a vote even if it is otherwise prescribed in the statutes.

## Mergers and Acquisitions

Mergers and acquisitions are governed by the Corporate Law No. 159 of 1981. A merger may take place by combining one or more companies into an existing company or by the consolidation of two or more companies.

The offering of assets from one company to another company, specially established for such purpose is not considered a merger. Following a merger, the merged company's shareholders should be accepted into the merging company. If the shareholders obtained bonds, foundation shares or cash money in lieu of company shares, a merger has not taken place.

A merger requires the dissolution of two existing companies or at least one of them. The purchase of one company by another is not considered a merger. The purchaser may only enjoy the right to representation in the general assembly within the limits of its shares. In this case, each company will keep its legal personality.

A merger requires the unification of the companies' purposes in order to achieve certain goals, including the focusing of projects, the termination of competition, the reduction of general costs, the unification of management or the strengthen the merging company's credibility.

A merger requires that the following conditions be met: (1) the merger is effected by a resolution of the executive general assembly of both the merged and merging companies; (2) the merger is effected by a resolution of the competent minister after obtaining the approval of the Committee for Examination of the Applications for Foundation of Companies (CEAFC); (3) shareholders who object to the merger during the meeting or who, for a plausible reason, demand to exit from the company and recover the value of their shares, may do so by a written demand which should reach the company within thirty days from the date of publishing the resolution to merge.

The value of the shares or portions will be decided according to agreement or by the court, taking into consideration the current value of all the assets of the new company. The uncontested value of these shares, or portions, must be settled with their owners before finalizing the merging procedures. The court will decide the amount the company must pay to compensate concerned parties who have sustained damage as a result of the merger. The compensation amounts decided upon will have priority over all the assets of the merging company.

As a result of the merger the manager of the dissolved company will no longer have any authority to represent the company. The merging company will inherit all the merged company's obligations and rights within the limits agreed upon in the merger agreement, without prejudice to the creditors' rights. The projects within the purposes of the merged companies, which were already in operation, will not be dissoluted. These projects will be transferred to the merging company. The founder of the merged companies will be considered founder in the merging company. The merging companies and their shareholders, as well as the merged company or the new company, will be exempted from all taxes and fees that become due as a result of the merger. The creditors of the merged company and its bondholders will be considered creditors to the merging company. They may protest the merger before a competent court.

Finally, it is permissible by a decision of the competent minister, after approval of the CEAFC, to authorize JSCs, the two types of partnership companies, limited liability companies and the collective companies, whether Egyptian or foreign-owned companies exercising their main activities in Egypt, to be merged into Egyptian JSCs or to merge with such companies into a new Egyptian company. Branches, agencies or establishments of these companies are considered merging companies.

## Companies Liquidation

The liquidation of companies is regulated by the Companies Law (Law No. 159). In case of loss of half the capital of the company, the directors are required to submit to the General Assembly an order for dissolution of the Company. The issuance of such an order requires the majority of the shareholders' votes necessary to modify the company's articles of incorporation.

In addition, a court order for dissolution of the company may be demanded by shareholders in possession of a quarter of the capital if the loss attains three-quarters of the capital, and by any interested party if the loss entails the decrease of the capital below the minimum share capital.

After its dissolution, a company is considered to be in a state of liquidation. The General Assembly will nominate one or more liquidators and fix their remuneration. In case a court order is issued ordering the dissolution, the court shall indicate the mode of liquidation and will nominate the liquidator and fix his remuneration.

The company organs will remain standing during the period of liquidation, but their powers will be confined to the affairs that are not in the competence of the liquidator.

The liquidator shall fulfill all the duties requisite for the liquidation, including: paying the company's debts, selling the company's assets and representing the company in court. The liquidator shall execute all that is needed for the conservation of the funds and rights of the company. He should also take all actions necessary to obtain all the company's rights from others. The liquidator is not allowed to establish new business unless such business is requisite for previous affairs.

The company is bound by every disposal that is necessary for liquidation and that the liquidator fulfills under its name even if it surpasses the restrictions included in the authority of the liquidator and unless those who contracted with the liquidator are ill intentioned.

The liquidator must terminate the liquidation within the time period fixed in the document of his nomination. If this period is not fixed, every shareholder or partner may bring the matter to court, for fixation of the period in which the liquidation should be ended. The liquidator shall present to the General Assembly or to the group of partners a provisional account on the business of the liquidation followed by a final account. The liquidation is to be concluded by ratification of the final account. After termination of the liquidation, the liquidator shall demand the removal of the company from the commercial registrar. The liquidator will be responsible toward the company for damages caused to the company by his mishandling of its affairs.

## Partnerships

### General Partnership
Two or more persons (individuals or legal entities) may form a general partnership. Such a business association is governed by the terms of the partnership contract as well as by civil and commercial laws. The partnership contract must be notarized and registered with the Ministry of Finance. Unless otherwise specified in the contract, all partners have equal rights, liabilities and powers, and they are jointly and severally liable for the debts of the partnership to the extent of their entire wealth.

### Limited Partnership
In a simple limited partnership, there are two types of partners. General partners are liable for partnership debts to the extent of their entire personal wealth, and limited partners are liable to the extent of their investment in the partnership. Establishment requirements are similar to those governing general partnerships.

### Partnership Limited by Shares
In a partnership limited by shares at least one partner must assume unlimited liability for the debts of the partnership. The liability of the other partners is restricted to their respective capital contributions represented by negotiable shares. Partnerships limited by shares are subject to most provisions that apply to joint stock companies, apart from capital participation requirements and certain matters concerning the board of directors.

### Converting a Partnership into a Joint Stock Company
A decree from January 1995 enables the conversion of a partnership into a JSC, subject to the procedures of preliminary foundation, providing the company's assets and liabilities shall be valued by means of a committee to be formed for that purpose.

## Joint Ventures

A contractual or unincorporated joint venture is formed when two parties, one of whom is Egyptian, join with one another in a venture for their mutual benefit. If the parties choose not to set up a company for the venture's purposes, the legal aspects of their cooperation will be dictated by the contractual relationship between them. This form of business association is particularly popular in natural resources development projects. It is notable that contractual joint ventures are often treated as partnerships for taxation purposes.

The parties to the joint venture may include all the terms and conditions contained in the joint venture agreement in their articles and statutes. The parties may add to these forms any additional clauses provided that such additions shall not violate the public order.

## Branches and Representative Offices

Branches are subject to the system of dividend distribution to workers as mentioned in Law No. 159 of 1981. They are subject to exemption from taxation for a period of ten years if they exercise their activities in new urban communities and employ a certain percentage of Egyptian nationals as specified in the Companies Law.

Representative offices are prohibited from the exercise of any trading activity. Approval of the foundation of such offices may take as long as eight weeks. Foreign companies or establishments may not establish scientific, technical, consultative or other service offices, unless these companies or establishments have an appointed commercial agent in Egypt, according to the provisions of the Commercial Agents Law No. 120 of 1982.

Such companies, establishments or offices may not exercise any trade representation (agency) activities or middleman works, except through a commercial agent and middleman register provided for the purpose at the Ministry of Economy and Foreign Trade.

## Commercial Agency and Representation

Egypt's foreign trade system (importation and exportation) is based upon commercial agency and representation. Special registries for commercial agents, importers and exporters are arranged by laws and decrees, including

Law 120 of August 5, 1982 and its executive regulations, concerning agents and distributors, and Law 121 of 1982, and its executive regulations, concerning importers.

According to Law 120, only Egyptian legal entities, individuals born to Egyptian fathers and long-standing naturalized Egyptians may represent foreign principals in importing goods into Egypt. Commercial agents and mediators must be approved by and registered with the Ministry of Foreign Trade. Corporate and partnership representatives must be 100 percent Egyptian owned and managed. If the partner is a juridical person, it must be an Egyptian entity, the majority of whose capital is owned by Egyptians. In case of naturalized Egyptians, ten years must have passed since acquiring Egyptian nationality.

Yet, in compliance with the Egyptian government's efforts to attract foreign investment, an important exemption has been provided for investment projects, enabling them to import their requirements and export their products directly.

## Currency and Banking

### Foreign Currency Control

In February 1991, Egypt removed most foreign exchange controls, allowing rates to reflect market forces. Soon thereafter, Egypt fully unified its two-tier exchange system and opened the exchange market to non-bank dealers.

Law No. 38 of 1994 enables the free transfer of foreign currency into or out of Egypt and from one person to another within the country. The only foreign exchange restriction provides that the proceeds from sale of real estate in Egypt that is owned by foreigners residing outside of Egypt may not be transferred abroad for a five year period following the sale. The Egyptian pound remains non-convertible and may not be taken outside the country.

### Banking

The Central Bank of Egypt sets policy for almost all of the country's bank with the exception of three: Misr African International Bank, the Arab International Bank and the Egypt Export Development Bank.

Banks can set their own interest and exchange rates within guidelines set by CBE, such as T-Bill auctions and discount rates. Also, a large increase of foreign and domestic banks operating in Egypt has caused the Central Bank of Egypt (CBE) to set restrictive guidelines for new comers.

From 1957-1974, only fully owned Egyptian banks were permitted to operate. The Investment Law 43 of 1974 allowed foreigners to obtain a less than 50 percent stake in a joint-venture commercial and investment bank. Further laws continued to open the banking system, including permitting foreign bank branches to operate in Egyptian currency. Finally, on June 16, 1995, the government approved majority foreign ownership joint-venture banks.

In 1999, there are numerous American banks operating in Egypt including Citibank, American Express Bank, Bankers Trust, Bank of New York, Chase Manhattan and one Egyptian-American Bank.

At the end of June 1998, total bank assets were $73 billion, deposit base $54 billion and loan portfolio of $48 billion.

Egyptian banks are generally considered overly conservative. They often demand a counter guarantee equal to the amount borrowed as a condition for granting a loan. Short-term lending makes up about 80 percent of the major banks' portfolios.

There are over 100 banks in Egypt including thirty-eight commercial banks that are controlled by four government-owned banks (Banque Misr, National Bank of Egypt, Bank of Alexandria, and Banque du Cairo) and numerous joint ventures and specialized banks. These four government-owned banks hold two-thirds of the banking community's assets.

Presently, some major international investment banking institutions are entering the Egyptian market, including HSBC Investment Banking, ING Barings, Credit Suisse and Morgan Stanley.

The Egyptian Government has revised many of the banking laws and practices. Egypt's banks have benefited from the government's reforms of the exchange rate and interest rate systems, and many have made substantial gains by investing in government bills and bonds. Nonetheless, banks still suffer from low capitalization and heavy debt burden from the former socialist period.

## Intellectual Property

The legal regime regarding patents and trademarks is similar to that of England, and registered owners of intellectual property are provided with adequate protection. Egypt is a signatory to the Paris Convention of the Protection of Intellectual Property and the Madrid Agreement regarding international registration of trademarks. Furthermore, Egypt is a member of the World Intellectual Property Organization.

### Patents

The law on Patents and Industrial Designs, Law No. 132 of 1949, as amended, grants inventors fifteen years of patent protection from the date of application. In some cases, it may be extended for an additional five-year term. The patent holder has exclusive rights to the invention and may license, assign, pledge or in any other way act with regard to the patent. At the end of the patent protection period, the invention enters the public domain.

A new patent law has been drafted recently. The new law, if approved, would extend the patent protection period to twenty years and widen the definition of an "invention" as protected by the law. Unlike the current patent law, the draft law provides for a substantive examination of the patent application before granting the patent. The draft law also provides that not only the patentee but also any other party who introduced adjustments, improvements or additions to a patent invention shall have the right to apply and obtain an independent patent.

Egypt has adopted the Paris Convention, and, accordingly, a patent application filed in a member country entitles the applicants to apply for a patent in Egypt within one year.

### Trademarks

The Trademarks Law No. 47 of 1939, as amended, grants a ten year protection period to trademark holders from the date of application. The trademark is renewable for similar periods without restriction; an application must be filed for each renewal period.

## Copyright

The Copyright Law No. 354 of 1954, provides copyright protection for, *inter alia*, written works, paintings, sculpture and architecture, theater and musical pieces, photographs and cinematographic films, television and radio works for publication, maps, and speeches. A 1992 amendment to the Copyright Law stiffened the penalties available under the Copyright Law and also provides for protection of videotapes.

A 1994 amendment to the Copyright Law treats computer software as literary work and guarantees it a fifty-year term of protection. Protection under the Copyright Law terminates fifty years following the demise of the author. Should the copyrighted material be owned by a legal entity rather than a natural person, then the fifty year protection period begins on the date the material was first published. The author may assign the rights granted to him by the law to other persons, subject to certain limitations set by the law.

## Industrial Designs and Models

Some industrial designs and models (such as design features of products and designs new in many items) can be registered with the Office for Registration of Industrial Designs. Registration provides protection for a period of six years and is renewable for two additional five-year terms.

## Unified Intellectual Property Act Draft

A committee was formed at the Ministry of Commerce and Supply to draft a unified act to govern all elements of intellectual property. The new act is to include the existing laws concerning copyrights, models, industrial designs, and patents of invention and trademarks. In addition, the act will extend the protection period for industrial designs and models to renewable periods of ten years. It will also provide for substantive examination of the model, design or patent to ensure that it is novel and innovative. The proposed act sets severe penalties for intellectual rights infringement.

## Taxation

Taxes in Egypt may be divided into two categories. The first one concerns direct taxation of individuals and legal entities on their income or profit.

The second involves indirect taxation of goods, services and events. The Egyptian taxation framework is statutory based. Tax administrators are given, under the relevant legislation, few discretionary powers. Courts are primarily responsible for the interpretation of statutes. The nature of the Civil Law system operating in Egypt allows precedent to have an influential but not necessarily a binding effect.

Over the last several years, Egypt has made many changes in its tax system. Some of these changes are merely cosmetic while others are rather substantial. Given this trend, it is advisable to seek up-to-date advice on recent and future changes to the tax law before pursuing commercial plans in Egypt.

## Taxation of Companies

The Egyptian corporate tax regime applies to joint stock companies, limited liability companies, partnerships limited by shares, foreign companies and branches of foreign companies whose head office is situated abroad. This tax is also applicable to banks and public sector companies.

As of January 1, 1994, companies are subject to corporate profit tax at a standard rate of 40 percent. Special rates, however, apply to companies engaging in the following activities: (1) Petroleum companies—40.55 percent; (2) Companies with export activities—32 percent; and (3) Industrial (manufacturing) companies—32 percent.

Corporate income tax is based upon taxable profits computed according to generally accepted accounting principles and certain modifications as provided by statute, the most important of which involve depreciation, inventory valuation and inter-company transactions. Capital gains arising from the sale of fixed assets are treated as ordinary profits. Dividends received by resident companies from foreign sources are subject to tax on income from moveable capital at a rate of 32 percent, but foreign taxes paid on such dividends are deductible. Interest derived from securities listed on the Egyptian Stock Exchange is exempt from income tax.

Virtually all legitimate business expenses are deductible including depreciation, other taxes and duties, interest and royalties, bad and doubtful debts, rent, director's remuneration, profit sharing payments to employees, legal expenses, pension and Egyptian state social insurance contributions. Losses may be carried forward and applied against future profits for up to five years.

All operations owned by the same company must be aggregated for reporting purposes. If operations are carried out by separate companies which are owned or controlled by one parent company, however, consolidation is not permitted.

It should be noted that general partnerships and simple limited partnerships are not taxable entities under Egyptian law. The partners in such partnerships, are personally liable for the tax due on their respective shares in the partnership's profit. Partners, therefore, are taxed in the same manner as individuals.

## Taxation of Individuals

### Income Tax

Law No. 187 of 1993, also known as the Unified Tax Law, abolished the general income tax previously levied on individuals pursuant to Tax Law No. 157 of 1981. Under the new Unified Tax Law, individuals, including partners in partnerships, are subject to tax at various rates on income from five sources:

- Income from Movable Capital: This tax is levied at a rate of 32 percent of gross income usually collected through withholding. This category refers to interest (other than interest on deposits), foreign-source dividends (less foreign taxes paid), executive director's fees and attendance fees.
- Income from Immovable Capital: This tax is levied at rates ranging from 20 percent to 48 percent. This category applies to net income derived from land and buildings.
- Commercial and Industrial Profits: This tax is charged on a sliding scale at rates ranging from 20 percent to 48 percent. This category applies to net commercial and industrial profits of enterprises which are not subject to corporate tax.
- Professional Fees: This tax includes rates that range from 20 percent to 48 percent. This category covers the net income of professionals such as engineers, accountants and lawyers.
- Salaries: This is a tax imposed on salaries paid in Egypt or abroad for services performed in Egypt. Taxable salary includes the value of all benefits, apart from housing allowances given to foreign experts. The salary tax is levied at 20 percent on the first £E 50,000 of net

taxable salary, after deductions and allowances, and 32 percent on the excess.

## General Tax on Income

In addition to the specific taxes that are levied on specific types of income as mentioned above, the Egyptian legislature has imposed a general tax on income which is applicable to individuals. This tax is an additional tax, and the tax base is regarded as the total net income that the individual receives during the year. Only income that is subject to a specific tax is included in the tax base for the general tax on income.

The general tax on income is progressive and reaches 65 percent for income in excess of £E 200,000 per annum. It should be noted that foreign employees in Egypt are subject to this tax unless there is a particular statutory or regulatory provision exempting them from the tax.

## Other Taxes

### Real Property Tax
Real Estate taxes are levied on the assessed annual rental value of improved and agricultural property at rates ranging between 10 percent to 40 percent.

### Stamp Duty
Most classes of documents, contracts, checks, receipts, bills, letters of guaranty, various banking transactions, transfer of unlisted securities, leases and many other instruments require payment of stamp duties. For example, between £E 150-£E 300 of stamp duty is charged upon the formation of companies, £E 50 is charged for the registration of companies in the Commercial Registrar and £E 0.01 is levied on bank checks.

### Withholding Taxes
There are no withholding taxes as such in Egypt, apart from scheduled income taxes which are withheld at source in many cases. Dividends distributed by an Egyptian company are not subject to withholding tax. The main instances where taxes are withheld are summarized below.

Tax on income derived from moveable capital is withheld in many cases, including payments to a foreign company that has no branch in Egypt and payments to non-resident individuals. Royalties and technical assistance fees paid to a foreign company with no branch in Egypt are normally subject to the 40 percent corporate income tax rate. The tax is imposed on the net amount after an arbitrary deduction for expenses. Amounts are also withheld on account of taxes due at 10 to 15 percent on the amount payable for professional services, at 3 percent on commercial services and at 10 percent on commissions paid to commercial agents. Lastly, employers must withhold the scheduled tax on salaries and wages from their employee's pay.

## Inheritance and Gift Taxes
Succession tax is imposed on gifts and inheritances at rates between 3 to 15 percent. No tax is charged on an inheritance of less than £E 10,000. Resident foreigners are subject to inheritance and gift taxes on real estate and moveable assets. Non-residents are subject to these taxes only on real estate assets located within Egypt.

## Development Duty
A 2 percent development duty is levied on the annual taxable income of individuals and companies that exceeds £E 18,000.

## Social Insurance Contributions
Employers and employees must pay social insurance contributions to the Ministry of Social Insurance and Social Affairs. The social insurance laws do not apply to expatriates. The rate paid is based on the employee's monthly salary and is contributed to at a rate of 26 percent by the employer and 14 percent by the employee.

## Sales Tax
Law No. 11 of 1991 provides for a general tax on sales. The tax applies to most goods and certain types of services (mainly tourism, telecommunications and entertainment services). Goods imported from abroad for commercial purposes are also subject to the tax. The tax rate for goods ranges from 10 percent (the general rate) up to 50 percent for certain specified goods. The tax rate for services ranges from 5 to 10 percent. The tax is added to the price of the goods or services in question and is payable by the consumer at the point of sale and remitted by the billing entity to the tax authorities.

## Treaties for the Prevention of Double Taxation
Egypt has concluded treaties for the prevention of double taxation with a number of countries, including: Austria, Canada, Cyprus, Denmark, Finland, France, Germany, India, Iraq, Italy, Japan, Libya, Norway, Oman, Pak-

istan, Romania, Singapore, Sudan, Sweden, Switzerland, Syria, Tunisia, the United Kingdom and the United States. Draft treaties which have not yet been ratified were concluded with Indonesia, Korea, Malaysia and Morocco. It is notable that since Egypt does not levy withholding tax on dividends, its tax treaties provide reduced withholding tax rates only for interest and royalties.

In the absence of a tax treaty, unilateral tax relief is available by way of deduction rather than by a tax credit. A taxpayer who derives foreign-source income which is subject to foreign as well as to Egyptian taxes will be allowed to deduct the amount of foreign tax paid in order to compute the taxpayer's taxable income for Egyptian tax purposes.

## Investment and Trade

### Investment Law

On May 11, 1997, Egypt's new Investment Incentives and Guarantees Law (Law No. 8 of 1997), which repeals and replaces Investment Law No. 230 of 1989, was legislated. The new law aims to boost production and foreign and domestic investment and offers potentially good incentives for investors, including:

- The prohibition of nationalization, confiscation, and freezing of assets;
- The right to own buildings and land for project purposes regardless of investors' nationality and place of residence;
- The right to maintain foreign currency bank accounts;
- The exemption of manufacturing projects from price controls or profit limitations;
- The right to repatriate capital and profits;
- The right of 100 percent foreign ownership of ventures.

In addition, the new law provides extended tax holidays for projects in target areas. It allows companies, once established, to gain their tax incentives automatically without receiving the prior approval of any administrative authority. It also provides incentives for exporters. Whereas the previous law extended tax incentives for any capital increase or any project expansions, however, the new law provides no such tax concessions.

The law specifies a list of priority sectors that automatically benefit from its guarantees and incentives. These sectors include land reclamation, manufacturing and mining, transport, software and computer systems development and production, medical services, certain financial services, oil field services, agriculture and tourism. For these and for most other projects, investments are automatically approved.

The new law expressly preserves the benefits and incentives, as well as investment guarantees granted under law No. 230 for companies established under that law or existing prior to the promulgation of the new law under Law No. 230, all foreign investment projects are exempted from taxes and duties applied in Egypt for a period of five years which may be extended by another five years, regardless of the location of the project.

The new law has also abolished the highly bureaucratic General Authority for Investment (GAFI). The entity that will replace GAFI and its functions are to be determined by a presidential decree. Pending issuance of the decree, GAFI will remain the authorized administrative agency.

## Tax Incentives

Law No. 8 of 1997 grants the projects working under its rubric a tax holiday that includes provisions of interest to investors.

Profits on projects and shareholder shares are exempted from the tax on industrial and commercial profits and from the corporate tax for a period of five years starting from the first fiscal year following the beginning of production or activity. The exemption may be extended to ten years for projects established in new industrial zones, new urban communities, remote areas and those projects financed by the Social Fund for Development.

Profits on projects operating outside the Old Valley and profits of shareholder shares shall be exempted from tax on industrial and commercial profits and from the corporate tax for a period of twenty years starting from the first fiscal year following the beginning of production or activity.

An amount equivalent to a percentage of the capital paid in, to be determined by the Egyptian Central Bank for Lending, and discount rates, for the year of fiscal treatment, shall be exempted from the corporate tax, provided that the company is a JSC and its stocks are registered at one of the stock exchanges.

Yields of bonds, finance share warrants and incomes of the other similar securities portfolios as issued by the JSCs shall be exempted from the tax on revenues of movable capitals, providing they are placed for public subscription and registered at one of the stock exchanges.

A customs tax at a unified rate of 5 percent of the value is levied on the value of all imports (machines, equipment and instruments) imported by such projects.

The profits resulting from the merger, division or the change of the legal entity of a project are exempted from the taxes and duties payable on the merger, division or change of legal entity. Such projects shall enjoy the exemptions prescribed before the merger, division or change of legal entity, until the relevant exemption periods expire. The merger, division or change of the project's legal entity shall not result in any new fiscal exemptions.

The result of assessing the in-kind portions forming the foundation of JSCs, Partnership Limited by Shares and LLCs shall be exempted from the tax on revenues of commercial and industrial activities or the tax on corporate companies' profits according to each case.

## Free Trade Zones

Projects set up in one of the active free zones enjoy certain benefits that may be of interest to foreign investors. Such projects are not subject to exchange-control regulations nor are they subject to any customs duties on imported goods or equipment. In addition, they are exempt from taxes for an unlimited period. These projects, however, are subject to annual duty of 1 percent of the value of products entering or leaving the free zone or on the annual value added to the project, as the case may be. Licenses to operate in free zones may be granted for the following activities: storage of goods in transit from one port to another; storage of Egyptian goods intended for export (provided taxes have been paid); storing, mixing, blending and repackaging operations; manufacturing, assembly and processing; and ancillary activities or services required by companies operating in the free zones.

The existing free zones are located in Nasr City, Alexandria, Port Said, Suez, and Ismailia. In addition, new free zones are being established in Damietta, Cairo Airport, Safaga, Al Arissh and in Sinai east of Port Said.

## Trade Agreements

Egypt is not a signatory to any free trade agreement. Egypt, however, has been negotiating with the European Union (EU) to realize a free trade agreement which will replace the earlier agreement concluded in 1977 that gave Egyptian industrial products free access to the European market. Negotiations have focused on the abolition of quotas on oil, textiles and other manufactured products and a relaxation of restrictions on agricultural produce.

While Egypt is a member of the Arab Common Market, along with Syria, Jordan, Iraq and Libya, this endeavor has not produced notable trade relations.

Egypt has entered into extra-regional trade relations with the EU and the US, among other countries, relating to the preferential treatment of certain specified goods. Egypt has pursued similar kinds of preferential treatment trade agreements with the Czech Republic, Greece, Jordan, Kuwait, Malta, Poland, Saudi Arabia and Syria. In March of 1995, Egypt and China entered into a trade accord. Egypt has also signed an Economic Treaty with Russia.

Egypt and Israel signed the Agreement on Trade and Commerce in May of 1980. The peace between the two countries, until recently, may best be described as "cold". In the wake of the peace process with the Palestinian Authority, the Joint Committee on Trade of Egypt and Israel met in November 1994 and issued the Taba Declaration in February 1995; it is hoped this step will lead to a new chapter in the trade relations between the two countries.

## Customs

Egypt has complex tariff and non-tariff barriers. The latter include: a banned import list, quality control inspection standards, a prior approval list, quotas, Egyptian selling prices imposed on imported goods for customs valuation purposes and government procurement practices. Tariffs range from 5 to 55 percent, with certain rare exceptions such as automobiles (up to 135 percent).

The current tariffs are a result of a presidential decree issued in 1996 which lowers Egypt's highest customs tariffs by 10 to 15 percent across the board. In early 1996, the government also announced the reduction of tariffs on a wide variety of capital goods needed for industrial investment to 10 percent from previous rates that ran as high as 70 percent.

The government, however, has levied a 3 percent to 4 percent surcharge on the value of imported shipments as a fee paid for the inspection, listing, classification and re-examination of the shipment.

Overall, high tariffs have not crimped trade by foreign countries because the tariffs apply to all imports equally, and clever importers have been successful in discovering where exceptions and loopholes exist in the system. Exemptions to the banned import list are available for many sectors including the petroleum, tourism and military industries.

The list of banned import items was created to protect domestic industry and to reduce foreign exchange expenditures on luxury goods (called provocative items under customs terminology). Goods on the list include passenger cars, textiles, apparel, leather, steel pipes, PVC and batteries. Exemptions to the ban may be granted by the Ministry of Economy and Foreign Trade if no equivalent product exists in the local market or if the banned item is required for the survival of an industry. As the Egyptian Government has been rapidly reducing the items contained on the banned list, it has become less of a barrier to trade. A number of years ago the list covered 37 percent of all imports. Today, this percentage is lower and eventually is expected to be reduced to 5 percent of imports.

Egypt's quality control inspection standards adversely affect certain products, particularly food items. The Government has expanded the list of products subject to inspection to include many manufactured products, in addition to the previously monitored foodstuffs. Policy makers who point to the need to protect consumers from fraud and counterfeits see quality control as a moral issue. The major hurdle for foreign suppliers is that these quality standards often are ill defined or not written at all. The restrictive features of this system are in the process of revision.

Egypt's 1996 agreement with the IMF provides for the reduction of the maximum tariff rate to 40 percent, a reduction of certain rates to 30 percent, and the limitation of the number of tariff bans to seven by 1998. This is also, according to the agreement, the deadline for the reduction of the current 4 percent and 3 percent import surcharge rates to a uniform 1 percent and for the government to eliminate all remaining non-tariff barriers.

## Public Sector Procurement

Tendering in Egypt is regulated by Law No. 9 of 1983. According to this law, tendering should be subjected to the principles of publicity, equality and freedom of competition. Law No. 9 grants the government with three methods to select the party to an administrative contract: tendering, selective tendering and direct agreement.

Contracting for the purposes of purchase of movables, rendering services and concluding works and transport contracts are through a general tender.

Contracting through selective tendering may be employed in the following cases: (1) products or services subject to monopoly; (2) products or services that are available only through one particular person; (3) projects or services that cannot be defined with precise specifications; (4) consultative or technical works, which according to their nature, are required to be carried out by means of technicians, specialists or specific experts; (5) animals, poultry and fowls of all kinds required for purposes other than nourishment; (6) supplies, works, transportation and services that are urgent or that must be carried out in secrecy.

In case of urgency, the administrative authority may conclude its contracts through direct agreement (negotiation) within the limits of £E 2,000 regarding regular purchases, services and transport contracts. The limits are £E 4,000 regarding works-projects and £E 8,000 regarding the purchase of products monopolized by foreign companies that have no agent in Egypt. A tenderer must reside in Egypt or conduct the tender through a local agent.

### Environmental Law

Environmental issues in Egypt are governed by Law No. 4 of 1994. This law provides for the creation of an agency for the protection and promotion of the environment, the Environment Affairs Agency (EEAA). The EEAA is destined to formulate the general policy and to prepare the necessary plans for the protection and promotion of the environment. It should also follow up the implementation of such plans.

The law provides for a mandatory environmental review, to be undertaken by the competent administrative authority according to EEAA's instructions, as part of the approval process for all proposed projects.

The law forbids the handling of hazardous substances and wastes or the construction of any establishment for treating such substances without a license from the competent administrative authority. It is also forbidden to import hazardous waste or to allow its entrance into or passage through Egyptian territories. It is mandatory for all those who produce or handle dangerous materials to take precautions to ensure that no environmental damage shall occur.

All establishments (industrial and others) are required to ensure that while practicing their activities no leaked or emitted air pollutants (caused by the burning of fuel, etc.) shall exceed the maximum permissible levels. It is also prohibited to incinerate, to dispose of or to treat garbage and solid wastes as well as to spray pesticides or any other chemical compound unless it is done according to the conditions and safety measures specified in the Executive Regulations of the law.

Ships of any nationality, offshore platforms and any other companies or agencies authorized to explore or exploit natural marine resources are forbidden to discharge into the territorial sea of Egypt any polluting substances resulting in harm to the water environment.

The law further provides for a system of incentives to be offered to those who implement environmental protection activities or projects and sets penalties for those who are in violation of its provisions.

The Egyptian government has developed a five-year environmental action plan (1997/98-2001/02) for attacking the country's solid waste, air and water pollution problems.

The plan's priorities include: preparing feasibility studies for planned development projects, urging companies to work toward ISO 14000 environmental standards certification and urging the use of scientific management techniques and waste recycling to preserve natural resources.

Egypt is a signatory to various conventions concerning environment protection, among which are: the Environmental Modification Convention;

the African Convention on the Conservation of Nature and Natural Resources; the Vienna Convention for the Protection of the Ozone Layer; the Convention for the Prevention of Pollution from Ships; the Barcelona Convention for the Protection of the Mediterranean Sea against Pollution; the Brussels Convention on Civil Liability for Oil Pollution Damage and the Moscow Treaty for Nuclear Weapon Tests in the Atmosphere.

# ISRAEL

## Recent Political Developments

Following 50 days of exhausting and erratic political negotiations, Ehud Barak was sworn in on July 6 1999 as Israel's Prime Minister. He immediately promised that his foremost concern would be the pursuit of a "true, lasting peace." Some local analysts feel that the composition of his coalition, which combines secular liberal elements with conservative religious parties, is problematic and will eventually lead to the bloc's early dissolution. Other experts, however, contend that the massive Knesset faction Barak heads (75–85 seats out of 120) will enable him to gain majority support on any given issue.

Barak's preliminary negotiations with the Palestinians have proceeded relatively smoothly. The July 1999 Sharm El-Sheikh Agreement marks the resumption of final status talks. Within its framework, more land was transferred to Palestinian control, scores of Palestinian prisoners have been released, and a "safe passage" route linking the West Bank and Gaza was opened.

Still, a tough road remains ahead for the Israeli administration. Within the framework of final status negotiations with the Palestinian Authority, a compromise solution must be reached regarding sensitive issues such as the

| Profile | |
| --- | --- |
| Population | 6.1 million (1999) |
| Religions | 82% Jewish; 14% Muslim; 3% Christian; 1% Druze and other |
| Government | Parliamentary Democracy |
| Languages | Hebrew, Arabic (English is widely spoken) |
| Work Week | Public Sector: Sunday–Thursday 8:30–16:30 Banking: Sunday–Friday 8:30–12:30 Sunday, Tuesday, and Thursday 16:00–18:00 Embassies: Sunday–Thursday 8:00–16:30 |
| Monetary Unit | New Israeli Shekel (NIS) |
| Exchange Rate | NIS 4.10=US$ 1 |

return of refugees and Jerusalem. Barak also promised his constituency a complete withdrawal from Southern Lebanon within 12 months. This issue, however, is connected to peace on the Syrian front. As of mid-December 1999, direct Israeli-Syrian negotiations are resuming.

## Recent Economic Developments

Israel is an economic anomaly in the Middle East. It has perhaps the least amount of hydrocarbon resources and is still the highest per capita GDP. But what the country lacks in oil and petroleum, it makes up in brain power. National literacy is higher than 90 percent. The country has more scientists and technicians per capita than any other country in the world. About 30 percent of the population possess at least 13 years of education.

This people power combined with the government's support of high-tech endeavors and a highly skilled immigration pool have helped drive the country's high-tech capabilities that have been used in fields as diverse as weaponry to agriculture.

This world-class high-tech sector has helped drive the country's diversified economic base, which is further supported by a sophisticated service sector, including banking, accounting, legal and technological services.

While the country is the region's economically strongest, growth has slowed in the late 1990s after several years of strong expansion. This has been in part due to tight monetary policy seeking to curb inflation.

But growth may be again spurred in the coming years, in part by improving prospects for peace. Israel continues to seek peace with Syria, Lebanon and to determine its relationship with the Palestinians. But already, since the Oslo agreements and the peace treaty with Jordan, there have been some tangible sings of economic benefits. There has been increased trade, albeit minimal, with Jordan. Israelis are taking advantage of Jordan's Aqaba port. Many countries are establishing diplomatic relations with Israel and many companies who once shied from doing business with Israeli companies because of the Arab Economic Boycott, are now doing business as the boycott has been eased.

Since 1996, the Israeli economy has been stuck in a deep slowdown. The recession worsened in 1998— GDP grew by only 1.9 percent, compared with

2.4 percent in 1997 and 4.7 percent in 1996. This low growth rate creates a strong possibility that Israel's per capita GDP will decline in 1999. After rising by 1 percentage point to 7.7 percent in 1997, Israel's unemployment rate continued to climb in 1998 and 1999 as a result of the downturn, and reached a level of 8.8 percent and over 9.0 percent, respectively. The government failed to keep inflation at 4 percent in 1998, which was one of its main targets. Following a rapid devaluation of the Israeli shekel in October, inflation for 1998 reached 8.6 percent.

The government of Ehud Barak, elected in May 1999, must exert considerable efforts to fulfill its election commitments. These include alleviating the state from its 3-year recession and creating 300,000 new jobs during its term. Avraham Shochat, the new Finance Minister, has stated that his top priority is to rekindle economic growth. Economists stress that he must first tackle the mounting budget deficit, which reached 7.9 billion shekels ($1.9 billion) in the first half of 1999. Future plans include a NIS 6 billion (roughly $1.4 billion) cut in the year 2000 budget.

Financial analysts do expect the Israeli economy to overcome its current woes, as soon as the new leadership resumes the peace process and tourists arrive for millennium celebrations. Thus, optimistic estimates predict year 2000 growth at 3.5 percent. Infrastructure investment, primarily land transportation infrastructure, is expected to continue to grow in the upcoming year and beyond. This investment will be financed by an increase in the budget deficit and at the expense of other budget items. When implemented, such a change in economic policy focus is likely to lead to an accelerated pace of growth.

The Oslo agreements and the peace with Jordan were both expected to boost Israel's economy, help further integrate the country's marketplace into the world economy and increase its attractiveness to foreign investors. The peace process has also led to the opening or renewal of diplomatic relations with numerous countries, including the nations from the former Soviet bloc, China and India.

The agreements have also positively impacted the capital market as well as financial policies of large corporations. But they have not yet had the anticipated far-reaching long-term benefits, particularly in terms of returns on foreign investment.

In the medium- to long-term future, the increased economic growth Israel expects from the peace process will not be dependent on increased commercial contacts with its Arab neighbors. Rather, it will come from improved economic ties with the West, which will be seen in increased foreign investments, particularly, as the Arab boycott of Israel loses its impact.

Still, there will be some growth from trade with Arabs. Jordan and Israel traded goods worth US$ 18 million in the second half of 1996 after opening the border to cargo in June 1996 for the first time in nearly fifty years. Israel exported US$ 9 million in goods and imported US$ 5 million from Jordan. In the following year, these totals increased 130 percent, to $20 million and $12.5 million respectively. In 1998, Israel exported $25 million in goods to Jordan, while importing $17 million in Jordanian products.

Israeli merchants have made increasing use of the Aqaba port in their trade with third countries, as evident in the container traffic at the Arava terminal, mostly en route to the port of Aqaba. In 1998, container traffic at the Arava terminal increased 218 percent from the previous year. During the first nine months of 1999, there was a 156 percent increase in traffic versus the corresponding period last year.

## Inflation Rate

Inflation during the first half of 1999 was affected by the Bank of Israel's contractionary monetary policy, the recession and the Shekel's large depreciation during the third quarter of 1998, which was followed by a large appreciation. The 18.5 percent depreciation during August-November 1998 was the main reason for the 5.8 percent increase in the CPI between September-November. In the second quarter of 1999, the index rose by a cumulative rate of 1.1 percent, and 1999's inflation amounted to 1.3 percent.

## Exchange Rate

During the last quarter of 1998, the Shekel depreciated by nearly 20 percent against the dollar. A large cut in the Bank of Israel's interest rate is expected, which would reduce interest rate differentials between Israel and abroad, subsequently leading to a substantial one-off depreciation within the diagonal band. In such a case, a new equilibrium exchange rate will develop at a higher level.

**Economic Indicators**

| | 1991 | 1992 | 1993 | 1994 | 1995 | 1996 | 1997 | 1998 | 1998 ($ million) | 1999 (projected) |
|---|---|---|---|---|---|---|---|---|---|---|
| Gross Domestic Product | 6.3% | 6.6% | 3.5% | 6.8% | 7.1% | 4.5% | 2.7% | 2.0% | 97,900 | 2.0% |
| Gross Domestic Product per capita | 0.1% | 3.2% | 0.7% | 4.2% | 4.0% | 2.1% | 0.2% | -0.4% | 16,400 | -0.4% |
| GDP—Business Sector | 7.6% | 8.3% | 3.5% | 8.0% | 8.7% | 5.6% | 2.6% | 1.8% | 65,300 | 1.7% |
| Private Consumption | 7.2% | 8.0% | 7.3% | 9.5% | 7.2% | 5.0% | 4.1% | 3.3% | 59,800 | 2.4% |
| Government Consumption (excl. defense imports) | 2.5% | 1.4% | 4.2% | -0.2% | 0.3% | 5.7% | 1.9% | 2.3% | 28,700 | 2.7% |
| Exports of goods and services | -2.0% | 14.1% | 9.9% | 12.8% | 10.71% | 6.8% | 7.6% | 6.0% | 32,100 | 4.3% |
| Imports of goods and services | 15.5% | 8.8% | 14.1% | 10.9% | 8.5% | 8.1% | 2.8% | 2.1% | 42,000 | 5.0% |
| Investment in fixed assets | 38.8% | 6.8% | 1.7% | 13.3% | 9.0% | 9.30% | -2.3% | -3.3% | 20,100 | 0.5% |

Source: Bank Hapoalim Economic Report, July 1999.

## The Budget

During the first six months of 1999, as in the previous two years, budgetary developments were affected by the slowdown in tax receipts. This slowdown results from the recession, the decrease in real estate activity and the Shekel's depreciation, which increased companies' financing expenses in 1998 and reduced their reported profitability.

The domestic budget deficit reached NIS 5.4 billion through the first half of 1999 compared with NIS 2.8 billion in the corresponding period last year. The 1999 budget deficit for the whole of 1999 is expected to total NIS 12 billion, or 3 percent of GDP versus the targeted deficit of 2 percent of GDP.

The Law for the Reduction of the Budget Deficit was formed in 1992 and created the basis for determining the 1999 target deficit. Calls to amend the law have been voiced since the economy slipped into recession, and have recently won support from academic circles, the business sector and government. The objective of the change is to facilitate "built-in stabilizers," i.e., a larger deficit during periods of recession and a smaller one during times of prosperity.

## Labor Force

Israel's unemployment rate rose from 8.6 percent in the first quarter of 1999 to 8.8 percent in April and May. Since October 1998, the number of job seekers has risen by an average monthly rate of 1.2 percent. During the first half of 1999, the number of job seekers amounted to 158,000.

A large proportion of Israel's labor force is highly skilled and well-trained. The national literacy rate is higher than 90 percent; many Israelis speak several languages, and, are often fluent in English. Israel has more scientists and technicians per capita than any other country in the world. About 30 percent of the population possess at least 13 years of education and about 20 percent of the population holds academic degrees. Almost one-quarter of the work force is involved in scientific, academic or technical professions. Another quarter is employed in industry. Israel publishes more scientific articles per capita than any other country in the world.

Israel's labor force is not cheap, although average wages are lower than those prevailing in Europe or in the United States. Israel, however, has an especially professional labor force. Productivity in the high-tech fields increased from US\$ 45,000 in sales per worker in 1985 to over US\$ 90,000 presently.

## Immigration

Immigration has been crucial to the Israeli economy, particularly the large number who have arrived since 1989. Many came from the former Soviet Union and were highly skilled, providing deep professional and technological resources that spurred economic growth in terms of know-how and supply and demand.

According to figures provided by the Israel Central Bureau of Statistics (CBS), since 1990 more than 850,000 immigrants arrived in Israel, comprising roughly 16 percent of Israel's population today. A large number of these immigrants have already been absorbed into the Israeli economy, although not all have succeeded to find employment in their trained fields.

## Principal Economic Domains

Roughly 40 percent of the business sector product is comprised of services. Industry accounts for 30 percent, transport and communications, 13 percent, construction 9 percent and water and electricity 4 percent. Agriculture contributes the remainder.

## Industry

Israel has been cursed with a lack of most basic raw materials but blessed with a highly skilled labor force. It has thus focused its economic energies on manufacturing products with high added value. During the past few decades, Israel has made important international contributions in the fields of medical, electronics, biotechnology, telecommunications, fine chemicals, computer hardware and software, diamond cutting and polishing.

The country's highest growth rates are in the high-tech sectors, which require large R&D investments, sophisticated production techniques but are not capital intensive. Traditional industrial branches include food processing, textiles and fashion, furniture, fertilizers, pesticides, pharmaceuticals, chemicals, rubber, plastic and metal products.

## Transportation and Communications

Transportation accounts from roughly 9 percent of GDP and 11 percent of exports of goods of services. This sector also employs 6 percent of the country's work force. Of this, 48 percent works in land transportation, 23 percent in shipping and aviation, 19 percent in communications and the rest in various services, including storage and parking.

## Construction

Between the early years of statehood and 1991, residential building comprised between 70 to 75 percent of total construction output. After 1991, the rate leaped to 86 percent as tens of thousands of immigrants needed housing.

The percentage of private investment in all construction has gradually overtaken government increasing form 33 percent in 1958 to 83 percent in 1989. This percentage did temporarily decline as large wave of immigrants created enormous demand for government-sponsored or subsidized housing.

## Agriculture

A combination of domestic production and imports meets most of the country's food needs. Imports consist primarily of grain, oilseeds, meat, coffee, cocoa and sugar, which are financed by agricultural exports.

Israeli farms produce mostly dairy, poultry, flowers, fruits and vegetables. Lucrative winter produce include long-stemmed roses, spray carnations, melons, tomatoes, cucumbers, peppers, strawberries, kiwis and avocados are especially successful exports.

Israel's high-tech capabilities have also spurred the country's agricultural success. Farmers and researchers work cooperate to develop and apply sophisticated agricultural methods as well as technological advancement, new irrigation techniques and innovative agro-mechanical equipment.

## Tourism

More than 2 million people visit the country each year, attracted by its geographical diversity, archaeological and religious sites, almost unlimited sunshine and modern resort facilities. Most tourists to Israel come from Europe and the Americas.

Tourism, with its enormous potential, is a major factor in Israel's economic plans to eliminate its balance of payments deficit. Tourism is a major source of foreign currency earnings. Some 70,000 employees are directly involved in the tourism infrastructure throughout the country.

In 1997, total sales of hotel accommodations amounted to over $1.1 billion. The country's tourism infrastructure consists of over 48,000 rooms in hotels, kibbutz guesthouses and holiday villages. According to Israel's Ministry of Tourism, over the next ten years facilities providing over 50,000 rooms must be built. The Israeli government also aspires to promote regional tourism with Egypt, Jordan and the Palestinian Authority.

## External Trade

The country's small domestic market limits the country's economic growth potential and forces it to rely on external trade for sustainable economic growth.

Exports of goods and services will be an important factor in helping the Israeli economy disengage itself from the recession in the year 2000. At the same time, the resumption of growth will lead to a more rapid increase in imports. In 1999, exports of goods and services are expected to grow by 4.3 percent in real terms, while imports of goods and services are expected to expand by 5 percent.

Israel imports 40 percent of its oil from Egypt, valued at approximately US$ 500 million per year. Total oil imports amount to 9 to 11 million tons per year.

## Business Environment

### Privatization

Two significant problems with the Israeli economy are the amount of funds earmarked for defense (20 cents of every dollar are spent on weaponry and preparedness) and government ownership of Israel's largest companies; e.g., Israel Electric Corporation, Israel Aircraft Industries, Oil Refineries

Ltd., El Al (the national airline), and Bezeq (the telephone and communications company).

Furthermore, the country's largest, the Labor Federation (Histadrut) controls other major industries and services such as Tnuvah (an agricultural marketing cooperative), and Kupat Holim (a huge system of health care clinics and hospitals).

In 1998, privatization raised approximately $1.2 billion through public offerings on the Tel-Aviv Stock Exchange (TASE). Highlights included sale of the Government's remaining 30 percent interest in Israel Chemicals (ICL) and its disposition of interest in United Mizrahi Bank, Bank Leumi, Bank Hapoalim and Bezeq. In addition to privatization through the TASE, the government sold some of its bank holdings to Lehman Brothers and Goldman Sachs, which purchased 2 percent of Bank Leumi and 1.8 percent of Bank Hapoalim, respectively. These investment banks subsequently resold the shares to international institutional investors.

During the first half of 1999, privatization activity via the TASE slowed noticeably—to less than $400 million. The Government raised $145 million from Lehman Brothers and Goldman Sachs, which purchased 4 percent of Bank Leumi and 2 percent of Bank Hapoalim, respectively and which again resold the shares to their investors. In July 1999, Bank Hapoalim sold a further 6 percent of its shares on the London Stock Exchange, marking the first offering of an Israeli bank on an international stock exchange.

Prospective privatization activities in the near future include the reduction of government holdings in Israel Discount Bank, Bank Leumi, Bank Otzar Hashilton, El Al Airlines and Bezeq.

## Major Projects

The country's electrical capacity has struggled to keep pace with the economic growth, forcing state-owned monopoly power utility, Israel Electric Corporation (IEC), to accept competition from private producers.

Since 1996, Israeli law has permitted private generators to generate 20 percent of total capacity: 10 percent from within Israel and 10 percent from cross-border projects. All the independent power projects must to sell electricity to the IEC.

The Israeli Ministry of National Infrastructure plans to issue two international tenders for 350-400 MW combined cycle power plants. An interministerial committee is working on determining the exact parameters of the projects, in particular the quantity of electricity the plant will be allowed to sell to the IEC and to the private sector. There have been numerous delays to the privatization of Israel's electricity sector. These obstacles were mainly due to the fact that the IEC itself was involved in the process by issuing the Independent Power Production tenders. The Ministry of National Infrastructure will issue the upcoming tenders, thus creating market expectation that the IPP program will receive new impetus, creating substantial opportunities.

Opportunities in natural gas projects are also expected to increase due to their environmental advantages. Interest has been high in a planned 320 MW plant, to be fueled by Egyptian natural gas. Enron and Gaz de France have shown interest in developing the US$ 1 billion pipeline from Egypt, while ABB, British Gas and Amoco are among interested bidders for the plant.

However, official negotiations on the supply of natural gas between the Egyptian and Israeli governments were suspended in 1998. Sources in both Egypt and Israel indicated that the suspension was due to political, not commercial considerations. Nevertheless, in late-1999, Egypt announced officially its willing to provide Israel (as well as the Palestinian Authority and Jordan) with natural gas.

In the construction sector, the Shalom Project is the largest project ever undertaken in the Middle East. With an aggregate cost of US$ 400 million, it includes the construction of three business skyscrapers, the tallest of which reaches a height of 180 meters, and has become one of the leading shopping malls in Israel.

A Canadian firm, Magil, and its local Israeli partner, Cementcal Ltd., built more than 300,000 square meters of the project, including a parking lot. A single management company belonging to Canit Hashalom Investments Ltd. manages the project.

## Build Operate Transfer

There are three major transportation projects scheduled for the next 5 years and valued at a combined US$ 4 billion. The projects are the Cross-Israel

Highway, the Tel Aviv Metro and the Carmel Tunnel. All may be conducted on a BOT basis.

BZW and Poalim Capital Markets and Investments, the investment banking arm of Bank Hapoalim, are advising the government on the Cross-Israel Highway, the country's first toll-road. The first phase of the project, to be constructed on a BOT basis, consists of a ninety kilometer central section of the road stretching from the Yad Benjamin region, near Gedera, to Hadera, in the north of the country.

The winning consortium will build and operate the highway for up to thirty years. The US$ 750 million estimated cost of the project will be met by toll levies.

The proposed Carmel Tunnel, which would alleviate the traffic bottleneck into Haifa, has progressed further than both the Cross-Israel Highway and the Tel Aviv Metro projects. In other sectors, the scope for project finance is more limited. Water and sewerage is a municipal sphere, but some BOTs are being discussed.

Airport and port expansions and are also areas where private money is being considered. At the end of 1997 the Israeli Airports Authority issued the first tenders for construction of the new Ben Gurion international airport terminal. A new terminal was built at Haifa airport, which has been opened to short distance international flights. Privatization of Haifa airport is under consideration. Expansion of ground facilities and upgrading the main runway will be delayed until a decision regarding the airport's future is made. Furthermore, agreement has been reached between the governments of Israel and Jordan regarding joint use of Aqaba airport. Israel will close the Avdat military airfield to civilian wide-body aircraft and build a new terminal at Ein Evrona, north of the current Eilat terminal.

The Israeli Ports and Railways Authority plans to issue a preliminary international tender for the expansion of Ashdod Port. The project will involve marine excavation, extensions of breakwater and construction of new quays to increase the Port's container handling facility by 50 percent to 1.7 million containers annually. The cost of the project will exceed $500 million. The deepening of the Port will provide anchorage for vessels capable of handling up to 6,000 containers. In addition, some of the new quays will have facilities for anchorage of bulk vessels with a capacity of 100,000 tons.

## Franchising

Between 1992 and 1995, franchising nearly doubled from US$ 90 million to an estimated US$ 160 million. More than 50 percent of franchises come from America and include Domino's Pizza, Pizza Hut, McDonald's, Kentucky Fried Chicken, Kenny Rogers Roasters, Burger King, Dunkin Donuts, Ben and Jerry's and Haagen Dazs. Additionally, Ace Hardware and Office Depot opened franchises in the early 1990s. Toys-R-Us opened in 1995.

Most franchises in Israel are owned by a main franchisee, who owns and operates branches throughout the country. Subway is an exception, operating a network of individually owned outlets. Mailboxes Etc. is entering the market with individually owned franchises. The key to success in Israel lies in strong management and ongoing, in-country training programs.

## Shopping Malls

Consumer malls have sprouted up across the country. Trendy, specialized national chain stores and franchises have become increasingly popular, replacing traditional food and consumer goods monopolies. Success lies offering a variety of new products, customer service and changing consumer consumption habits.

### Leading Business Opportunities

| Sector | Sector |
|---|---|
| Telecommunications Equipment | Toys and Games |
| Computers and Peripherals | Franchising (especially in the fast food sector) |
| Computer Software | Machine Tools/Metalworking Equipment |
| Processed Food (including beverages and cigarettes) | Food Processing/Packaging Equipment |
| Airport/Ground Support Equipment | Information Services |
| Chemical Product Machinery | Leasing Services |
| Industrial Chemicals | Electronic Components |

## Legal Review

Israel inherited much of its legal system from the two powers that ruled the country prior to its independence: the Ottoman Empire and the British Mandate. Since its foundation on May 14, 1948, however, Israel has adopted new legislation that replaced most of the laws borrowed from those powers. Today, Israel can boast its own modern and independent legal system.

Israel has no written constitution, but several Basic Laws that enjoy judicial supremacy have been enacted, and together with Israel's Declaration of Independence, they form the basis for Israeli constitutional law.

## Judiciary

The judiciary enjoys independence from the executive and legislative branches of government. Judges are nominated by the Judicial Appointments Committee and are confirmed by the President.

The court system consists of three tiers: Magistrates Courts, which are located in most sizable communities throughout the country; five District Courts, located in Jerusalem, Tel-Aviv, Beer Sheva, Haifa and Nazareth; and the Supreme Court, which resides in Jerusalem. In addition to the aforementioned courts, there are several specialized courts, including the traffic courts, juvenile courts, labor tribunals, family courts and the religious courts. The latter mostly deal with personal status issues (i.e., marriage and divorce). If, however, both litigants consent, any civil claim may be brought before the religious courts.

### *Magistrates Court*

The Magistrates Courts have jurisdiction over both criminal and civil cases. This jurisdiction is restricted, however, with certain statutory exceptions, to criminal cases for which the maximum punishment is a fine or imprisonment for less than seven years, and to civil claims unrelated to real property (except for issues of possession or use) or that do not exceed the amount of approximately US$ 285,000. Cross-claims in civil cases, which arise from the same circumstances as a claim that is being tried before the Magistrates Courts, may be heard in the Magistrates Courts regardless of value.

Any judgment of the Magistrates Courts may be appealed before the District Courts. Interim decisions of the Magistrates Courts on civil matters, however, may only be appealed to the District Courts subject to a leave by the Magistrates Court or by a District Court judge.

## District Court

The District Court has residual jurisdiction, hence it may hear any civil or criminal case that is not under the jurisdiction of the Magistrates Courts or under the exclusive jurisdiction of another tribunal. The District Court also serves as a court of appeal on judgments of the Magistrates Courts.

Similar to the Magistrates Courts, one judge ordinarily hears matters brought before the District Courts. Criminal cases in which the penalty is death or imprisonment of ten years or more and civil appeals from lower instances and other tribunals, however, are heard by a tribunal, except for interim decisions and orders or temporary injunctions.

Judgments of the District Court as a court of first instance may be appealed to the Supreme Court. Other decisions of the District Courts in civil cases, and judgments of the District Courts in appeals, may be appealed to the Supreme Court by leave of the District Court or the Supreme Court.

## Supreme Court

The Supreme Court sits in two capacities. First, it sits as the highest court of appeal in both civil and criminal cases. Second, it sits as the High Court of Justice deciding on matters concerning administrative law and conflicts with the government, as well as petitions for equitable writs such as habeas corpus, mandamus and certiorari.

The Supreme Court ordinarily sits as a panel of three judges; however, in certain circumstances the President of the Supreme Court may decide that a greater odd number of judges is necessary and may increase the number to as many as 13 judges. In other situations, a single residing judge may grant motions for temporary injunctions and other interim relief or hear appeals on judgments of the District Court that were decided by a single judge.

## Business Forms and Structures

### *Companies Law*

A foreign person or enterprise can operate in Israel through several types of business entities. Of primary importance are corporations and partnerships.

Furthermore, except in unique circumstances, no limitation is placed on the nationality of the shareholders or officers of an Israeli corporation. In fact, all the shareholders, officers and directors may be foreign residents or citizens.

### *Corporations*

Corporations are governed by the Companies Ordinance (New Version) of 1983, which was modeled on British legislation and are the most common form of business entity in Israel. They may be private or public, limited by shares or guarantees, unlimited or foreign.

The procedure for incorporation includes the filing of a memorandum of association and articles, in accordance with the provisions of the Companies Ordinance, with the Registrar of Companies. Those documents may be submitted in English.

It should be noted that a new Companies Law has been proposed and is now being debated in the Knesset, the Israeli parliament. If enacted, as is anticipated by many legal scholars, it will bring Israeli legislation even more closely in line with modern, western corporate law, especially that prevailing American law.

### *Private Companies*

Israeli private companies are either limited by shares or by guarantee and may have between two to fifty shareholders. They may not offer their shares or debentures to the public, and any transfer of their shares is subject to a board approval. In addition, a private company is not obliged to publish a prospectus in order to issue securities, nor is it required to submit audited financial statements to the Registrar of Companies.

## Public Companies

Israeli public companies must have a minimum of seven shareholders. Unlike private companies, they may offer shares and debentures to the public on the stock exchange by issuing a prospectus approved by the Securities Authority or through private placements if the offer is to 35 investors or less. They must file financial statements with the Companies Registrar, and if their shares are listed on the stock exchange, they must also abide by the rules of the exchange and the laws relating to securities and the regulations promulgated by the Securities Authority. In addition, a public company must hold a general meeting of its shareholders at least once a year, at which its management report and audited financial statements must be presented. In those meetings, the shareholders can, inter alia, approve dividends, elect directors and appoint auditors. A publicly traded company must include two independent, non-executive directors on the board, who serve as representatives of the public.

## Companies Limited by Shares

Among corporations, this is the most common corporate form. The Companies Ordinance provides the general protections afforded to shareholders in limited liability companies throughout western countries, including the shareholders' limited liability towards the liabilities of the company, which is regarded as a separate legal entity. This protection is not absolute, and may be withdrawn by the courts, by "lifting the corporate veil". This may occur in circumstances where shareholders abuse the corporate form in order to commit criminal acts or to wrongfully depreciate the corporation's assets.

## Foreign Companies

A foreign company may operate in Israel through a branch or through a subsidiary formed under Israeli law.

A foreign company wishing to set up a branch in Israel must register as a foreign company with the Registrar of Companies. According to the requirements of the Israeli Companies Ordinance, a list of its directors and a power of attorney authorizing an individual residing in Israel to receive legal process served on the company must be filed with the Registrar of Companies.

## Directors' Duties and Liabilities

Recent legislation has confirmed the case-law based duty of care and fiduciary duty owed by company directors to their company and imposed greater responsibility upon directors. Directors must act competently, in good faith and in the interest of the company. They must not put themselves in a position that may create a conflict of interest between themselves and the company or that may place them in competition with the company. Furthermore, company directors may not take advantage of any business opportunity arising as a result of their position in the company and must disclose any personal interest they may have in a transaction to which the company is a party. Provided full disclosure is made, a company director may enter into a transaction with the company. Transactions with interested parties require board approval, approval of the audit committee, and transactions not in the ordinary course of business require shareholder approval. The interested party may not participate in the board meeting review of the transaction, and at least one-third of the non-interested shareholders participating in the shareholder meeting must vote for the resolution approving the transaction.

## Securities Regulations

The issuance of securities to the public is governed by the Securities Law of 1968 and the rules and regulations of the Tel-Aviv Stock Exchange and of the Ministry of Finance. The main subjects covered by the Securities Law include, *inter alia,* the establishment, composition and powers of the Securities Authority; the rules relating to prospectuses and the permit for their publication; the manner and form in which the subscription to securities issued by prospectus takes place; the possible liability for a misleading prospectus; and rules concerning insider trading and class actions.

The basic requirement of the Securities Law of 1968 is that securities will be offered to the public only under a prospectus whose publication was authorized by the Securities Authority. The prospectus is then scrutinized by the Securities Authority and is made public within a few days. The prospectus requirement reflects the principle of disclosure as a primary instrument for investor protection. The liability of the signatories to the prospectus for misrepresentation or inaccuracy is strictly enforced.

# Partnerships

Partnerships are governed by the Partnerships Ordinance (New Version) of 1975. A partnership may not have less than two nor more than twenty members. The relationship between the partners is usually determined in accordance with the partnership agreement. In the absence of such an agreement, partners are entitled to their share of profits in proportion to their share in the partnership's capital. Unless stated otherwise in the partnership agreement, a partner may withdraw at any time from the partnership. Withdrawal of a partner will liquidate the partnership unless otherwise provided in the partnership agreement.

Partnerships must register with the Registrar of Partnerships, although the Partnerships Ordinance states that failure to register shall not be taken into account when considering whether or not the partnership exists. A limited partnership may not commence business until it has been registered.

## Limited Partnerships

A limited partnership must have at least one general partner and one limited partner. The general partner, as in a general partnership, has unlimited liability for the obligations of the partnership. The liability of a limited partner is limited to the sum invested in the partnership. The limited partner may not participate in the management of the partnership and does not have the power to bind the partnership. In addition, a limited partner may not, while the limited partnership is in existence, draw on or receive in return, either directly or indirectly, any part of his investment in the partnership. Violation of this principle may make him liable for the obligations of the limited partnership up to the amount so withdrawn.

## General Partnerships

In a general partnership, all partners jointly and severally share unlimited liability for the partnership's obligations; such liability may extend to the partners' personal assets. Each partner is permitted to participate in the management of the business and is held to be an agent of the partnership.

## Foreign Partnership

A foreign partnership may conduct business in Israel, but it may not establish a place of business in Israel unless it has first registered with the Registrar of Partnerships and received a permit from the Ministry of Justice.

## Other Corporate Forms

### Joint Ventures

Joint ventures are an effective method for conducting business between entities from different countries. A joint venture can be formed by a contract or be structured as a partnership or a company.

### Commercial Agency

Agency arrangements may also be of interest to foreign investors. It should be noted that there is no specific legislation dealing with commercial agents and distributors in Israel (except with respect to limitation of commission payable for supplying goods or services to the government). Therefore, there are no statutory requirements regarding the form and content of an agency agreement. In addition, there is no limitation on the nationality or domicile of such agents.

### Cooperative

This form of organization is found mainly in agriculture, transportation and in certain types of marketing operations associated with agricultural products. The liability of a member in a cooperative society is generally limited to the amount of shares owned by the member or to an amount specified in the society's articles.

### Non-Profit Organization

A special law enables non-profit activities to be conducted through an organization. This is a simplified form of an incorporated body and is generally used by charitable organizations.

## Anti-Trust Law

Israel's anti-trust law is governed by the Trade Restrictions Law of 1988 and is enforced by the Trade Restrictions Authority headed by a Commissioner. The Law and the Authority deal primarily with three issues: restrictive contractual arrangements, mergers and prohibition of monopolies. According to the Law, a contractual arrangement would be considered restrictive if at least one party to an agreement restricts itself in a manner that may prohibit competition in the business between the parties to the agreement or between one of the parties and a third party. An arrangement is deemed restrictive if the restriction concerns the price offered or paid, the profit which may be derived, the division of the market according to the location of the business or the people or type of people engaged with it, or the quantity, type or quality of the assets or services rendered.

The Authority also certifies ventures involving the consolidation of companies. A merger is defined as including the purchase of the majority of the assets of one company by another company, or the purchase of shares of one company by another company that provides the purchasing company with either more than 25 percent of the issued share capital, the voting power, the power to appoint more than 25 percent of the directors, or the power to participate in more than 25 percent of the purchased company's profits. The Law applies only if the joint annual turnover of the consolidated companies exceeds US$ 14.5 million or if the merger would either create a monopoly or lead to the vesting of a significant purchasing power in a particular industry in the hands of a single entity. The Authority has the power to prohibit such a merger and also to separate already merged companies if, as a result of their merger, competition was restricted.

The Law also prohibits monopolies. A monopoly is defined as the concentration of more than half of the total supply of assets or purchase of assets, or more than half of the total services rendered or purchased, in the hands of one individual. The Authority's role is to define business entities as a monopoly and to restrict them from abusing their position.

The Authority's involvement in Israel's business environment has increased significantly in the past several years. The Law is enforced rigorously, as its violation would constitute a criminal offense.

## Currency and Banking

### Foreign Currency Control

Israel abolished most of its remaining foreign exchange control in 1998, except for restrictions placed upon Israeli institutional investors' holdings of foreign securities and foreigners' access to certain hedging instruments.

Despite the virtual elimination of exchange controls, foreign exchange transactions must still be reported to the Bank of Israel. Foreign residents and new immigrants can maintain an unrestricted, freely transferable account (entitled "Patakh" nonresident accounts) with Israeli commercial banks. Once the "Patakh" account is established, foreign investors can open a shekel account, which allows them to freely invest in Israeli companies and securities. These shekel accounts are completely convertible into foreign exchange.

Most foreign currency transactions are conditioned upon being carried out through an authorized dealer. Specifically, an authorized dealer is a banking institution licensed to arrange, *inter alia,* foreign currency transactions for its clients. The authorized dealer operates in accordance with the procedural instructions of the Comptroller of Foreign Exchange.

## Banking

Israel has a highly developed and modern banking system. There are commercial banks, mortgage banks, financial institutions, merchant banks, representative offices of foreign banks, and an investment finance bank. A full range of commercial services and support is provided by those banks, many of which maintain branches and offices in the major international financial centers. Approximately 75 percent of the total assets of the commercial banks is held by three major banking groups (Bank Hapoalim, Bank Leumi and Israel Discount Bank).

In 1983, the Israeli banking industry went through what became known as the "bank share crisis." As a result, the Israeli government intervened and became a major non-voting shareholder of the leading banks. The government has sold controlling interests in several banks and is continuing the privatization process with respect to the remaining shares held by the government in more banks as well as with respect to the other banks.

The Bank of Israel is the official central bank. Among its numerous responsibilities, the Bank of Israel is also responsible for the issuance of currency, monetary policy, and regulations.

## Intellectual Property

Israel adheres to the major multilateral IPR agreements. While Israel has a legislative framework to ensure protection of intellectual property rights, enforcement is lacking in all areas. The government's lack of sufficient resources for IPR enforcement is the primary cause for inadequate arrests, prosecutions and convictions. Furthermore, most of Israel's current laws regarding IPR protection are outdated and require revision. The country has been drafting and reviewing new legislation for over four years in the areas of patents, copyrights, trademarks, industrial designs, integrated circuits, and cable broadcasting.

## Patents

Israel, a member of the Paris Convention for the Protection of Industrial Property, protects patents under the Patent Law of 1967 for a period of twenty years from the date of filing the application. Any novel invention, whether a process or a product that involves an inventive step and is used in industrial or agricultural applications may be patented.

In order to register a patent, the Israeli Patent Law also requires the patent to be new and novel worldwide. Any publications or exploitation of a patentable invention anywhere in the world, prior to the date of registration in Israel will prevent the patent from being registered.

A patent application must be filed with the Patent Office and include the specifications of the patent. The Patent Office conducts an examination, which may take up to three years from the date of filing the applications, to determine whether the patent conforms to the Patent Law and regulations. At the end of the examination, if the application is approved, a notice of acceptance is published in the Patent Journal. From the date of publication and for a period of three consecutive months thereafter, any person may oppose the registration of the patent. If no objection is filed or if such objection is dismissed, the patent may be granted and registered.

## Trademarks

Under the Trademark Ordinance of 1972, registered trademarks are protected for periods of 14 years each, renewable indefinitely upon the payment of renewal fees.

The Trademark Ordinance provides that a trademark shall not be registered unless it distinguishes between the goods of the owner of the trademark and the goods of others. An application for the registration of a trademark must be filed with the Registrar of Trademarks and must include a description of the trademark and goods.

The Trademark Office conducts an examination of trademarks, which usually lasts for a period of about two years. After such examination, if a trademark conforms to the requirements of the Trademark Ordinance, a notice of acceptance is published. Within three months of this publication, any person may object to the registration on the grounds of ineligibility. Unless such an objection is filed, or if such an objection is filed but is dismissed, the trademark will be granted and registered.

Recent Israeli legislation regarding pharmaceutical patents has raised foreign concern about adequate protection for patented foreign pharmaceutical products registered in Israel. In 1998, Israel passed an amendment to its patent law, permitting Israeli firms to begin pre-expiry activity regarding international patented drugs for purposes of registration in countries other than Israel. In 1999, Israel passed an amendment allowing parallel imports of foreign patented drugs.

## Copyright

Under the United Kingdom Copyright Law of 1911, protection is given to rights of the creators of works that are original and are literary, artistic, dramatic or musical works. Such protection is automatic and no formal application is required in order to obtain such right. The Copyright Law extends the protection for the lifetime of the creator or author; an additional 50 years of protection are granted for musical and artistic work, and 7 years for literary and dramatic work. Computer programs are within the framework of this Law.

### Taxation

Israel's primary laws on income taxes are the Income Tax Ordinance (New Version) (ITO) and the Income Tax Law—Inflationary Adjustments of 1985 (the Inflation Law). According to the ITO, companies and individuals are subject to tax on "all income derived from, accrued in, or received in Israel." Taxable income includes business and trade profits, wages and salaries, as well as passive income such as dividends, interest, royalties, rent, real estate profits and capital gains.

## Taxation of Companies

Resident and non-resident companies are liable to pay corporate tax at a rate of 36 percent on income derived from, accrued or received in Israel. Companies that are residents of Israel are also liable to pay a capital gains tax on capital gains, regardless of where such gains are derived. A non-resident company is also liable to pay a capital gains tax on capital gains derived from the disposition of an asset located in Israel or an asset that, although not located in Israel, represents a direct or indirect right to an asset in Israel. An Israeli resident company is defined as a company registered in Israel and whose main activity is in Israel. A foreign registered company, however, will be deemed an Israeli resident company only if it so requests or if it is controlled and managed in Israel.

## Taxation of Branch Operations

An Israeli branch of a non-resident company is taxed as though it were a regular resident company with respect to all of its profits derived from, accrued or received in Israel. The branch may deduct from its taxable income all expenses incurred in the production of its Israeli source income, regardless of where such expenses were made. Branch profits after tax, which are remitted abroad, are not subject to either the branch profits tax or withholding tax (except in the case of an "approved enterprise," as discussed in the Encouragement of Capital Investments Law section below, in which case a branch profits tax of 15 percent is imposed).

## Taxation of Partnerships

A partnership is not subject to income tax. Rather, the partnership's income is apportioned to its partners according to their respective shares in the partnership's income. A partner's share of losses incurred by the partnership in a particular tax year may be offset against the partner's income from other sources in the same tax year.

## Taxation of Individuals

Individual Israeli residents are subject to taxation on their income derived from, accrued or received in Israel. The tax rates applied to individuals are graduated and include various tax credits depending upon the taxpayer's personal status. The maximum marginal tax rate for individuals is currently 50 percent. Non-residents who have Israeli source income or derive capital gains from the disposition of assets located in Israel or assets located outside Israel that represent, directly or indirectly, a right to an asset in Israel, are subject to income tax and capital gains tax accordingly.

## Capital Gains Tax

Capital gains tax is imposed on the gain derived upon the disposition of fixed and intangible assets. In computing the amount subject to capital gains tax, a distinction is made between real and inflationary profit (inflationary profit is equal to present value minus the actual cost adjusted by the rise in the consumer price index). Inflationary profit for the period during which an asset was owned and until December 31, 1993 is taxed at 10 percent, and inflationary profit derived after that date is exempt from tax. Real profit, if derived from the disposition of such assets, is subject to the particular taxpayer's ordinary income tax rate (36 percent for companies and up to 50 percent for individuals).

Capital gains derived from the sale of stock of Israeli companies traded on the Tel Aviv Stock Exchange (and certain foreign stock exchanges) by foreign investors who do not conduct business in Israel and by Israeli individuals and other entities that are not subject to Part B of the Inflation Law are exempt from taxation. It should be noted that gains derived from such transactions in stock are not exempt from taxation if earned by a securities "dealer".

Also exempt from capital gains tax are gains from the sale of personal effects, sale of state-issued bonds and the sale of assets held outside Israel by a new immigrant, provided such sale took place within seven years from the date of establishing Israeli residency.

## Interest

Interest received or accrued is generally taxed at the same rate as the particular taxpayer's ordinary tax rate. According to the ITO, however, a company given a loan that bears interest at a rate less than the rate of the increase in the consumer price index, shall be liable to pay corporate tax on the deemed interest income amounting to the difference between the interest rate charged and the consumer price index increase plus 2 percent per annum.

Loans granted by financial institutions in the ordinary course of business are exempt from this rule.

## Dividends

A corporate entity that receives dividends distributed by an Israeli company that is subject to Israeli corporate tax is not liable to pay tax on such dividends. Dividends paid by an Israeli company to an individual Israeli resident are generally subject to withholding tax at a rate of 25 percent. Dividends paid by an Israeli company to a non-resident shareholder are also subject to withholding tax at a rate of 25 percent unless a lower rate is applicable under a tax treaty. Dividends distributed from an approved enterprise, under the provisions of the Encouragement of Capital Investments Law, are subject to a reduced withholding tax rate of 15 percent, which is applicable to both corporate and individual shareholders.

## Deductions

Under the provisions of the ITO and related regulations, a company may deduct expenses incurred in the process of producing income.

## Depreciation

Depreciation of fixed assets is allowed to be deducted from companies' taxable income, at rates determined under the various tax laws and regulations relating to such fixed assets. Industrial "approved enterprises" under the provisions of the Encouragement of Capital Investments Law are usually entitled to use accelerated rates of depreciation, which may result in allowable depreciation.

## Indirect Taxes

### Value Added Tax

The Value Added Tax (VAT) is an indirect tax based on the consumption of goods and services in Israel. VAT applies to every taxpayer conducting business or engaged in trade in Israel that sells assets or provides services during the course of business.

VAT is ordinarily charged at a rate of 17 percent of the sale price of a transaction. The VAT law exempts certain transactions, however, such as residential rentals for a period not exceeding ten years and sales of buildings approved after 1979 under the Encouragement of Capital Investment Law of 1959.

In addition, certain transactions are "zero rated." The primary transactions to which a zero rate applies are certain export sales, and services rendered to tourists in hotels. Applicability of the zero rate is pre-conditioned upon payment for the transaction in foreign currency that is deposited in Israel with an authorized dealer (i.e., an Israeli bank), along with a written receipt evidencing such transaction.

### Real Property Tax
Property tax on vacant real estate is levied at a rate of 2.5 percent of the value of the land. Real estate that is considered inventory is taxed at a rate of 1.2 percent. Agricultural land is not subject to this tax.

### Land Betterment
Gains arising from the sale or disposition of real estate property in Israel are subject to tax under the provisions of the Land Betterment Tax Law of 1963. The rates of land betterment tax are levied and computed in a manner similar to the taxes levied on capital gains. Thus, the inflationary profit is taxed at a rate of 10 percent (inflationary profit after January 1, 1995 is not subject to tax), and the real gain is taxed at a rate of 36 percent for corporations, and at graduated rates up to a maximum of 50 percent in the case of individuals. Transactions that are considered a sale, the profits of which are subject to this tax, include most types of real estate transfers and leases of real estate for a period exceeding ten years.

### Acquisition Tax
Acquisition tax is levied on transactions in real estate at a rate of 3.5 percent of the value of developed real estate, and 5 percent in the case of vacant land. Transactions for the sale of a residence are stated at progressive tax rates ranging between 0.5 percent to 4.5 percent of the value of a residence.

### Stamp Duty
Most legal documents are subject to a stamp duty, which varies between 0.4 percent to 1 percent depending on the nature of the document. Failure to pay the assessable stamp duty does not impinge on the validity of the legal document, unless payment of the duty is an expressed pre-condition intrinsically contained in the document. A document for which stamp duty has not been paid may not be accepted as evidence in a court of law or ac-

cepted by official government offices. Stamp duty not paid within 30 days will incur penalties of between 25 percent to 50 percent.

### Gifts and Inheritance Taxes
There are no gift or inheritance and estate taxes in Israel.

### Taxation under Inflationary Conditions
The Inflation Law, which applies to companies that have business or commercial income, is intended to protect the net equity invested in a business from erosion by inflation. It is also intended to remove distortions derived from the effects of inflation when assessing companies' taxable income. Under Section 6 of the Inflation Law, the appreciation in value of traded securities held by companies to which the Inflation Law applies is added to such companies' taxable income, even if such appreciation has not been realized by the sale of such shares.

### Treaties for the Prevention of Double Taxation
Israel is a party to several treaties for the avoidance of double taxation. These treaties generally provide for the reduction or elimination of withholding taxes levied on dividends, interest and royalties paid by a resident of one of the treaty countries to a resident of another treaty country, and some of the treaties provide for the reduction or exemption of capital gains tax imposed on a resident of one of the treaty countries on gains derived from the sale of assets in another treaty country. Furthermore, the treaties avoid double taxation by allowing a taxpayer to take a credit against such taxpayer's domestic tax liability for taxes withheld in the income source country.

Tax treaties have been signed, inter alia, with the following countries: Austria, Argentina, Belgium, China, Canada, the Czech Republic, Denmark, Finland, France, Germany, Greece, Hungary, India, Ireland, Italy, Jamaica, Japan, the Netherlands, Norway, Uruguay, the Philippines, Poland, Romania, Singapore, South Africa, Sweden, Switzerland, Thailand, Turkey, the United Kingdom and the United States.

## Investment and Trade

Israel offers a variety of well-developed investment incentive programs, including the Approved Enterprise Scheme under the Encouragement of

Capital Investments Law, free trade zones and research and development grants from governmental and quasi-governmental sources.

## Encouragement of Capital Investment Law

The government's primary statutory measure for encouraging both domestic and foreign capital investments is embodied in the Encouragement of Capital Investment Law of 1959. Under this law, the government grants substantial benefits in a variety of forms to "approved enterprises." The status of an "approved enterprise" may be granted to companies incorporated in Israel and to partnerships registered in Israel. Such enterprises generally engage in industry, shipping, export or tourism.

Applications for approval of enterprises are filed with the Investment Center of the Ministry of Industry and Trade and must be approved before any investment is made. The Investment Center may approve or reject proposals in full or in part. One of the conditions to receiving such a grant is that 30 percent of the total investment in the project must have been financed by the owners' investment in paid up share capital.

Approved enterprises may be entitled to receive grants, which vary in amount according to the geographic location of the enterprise in Israel and the nature of the enterprise. In the case of industrial enterprises, the grants may reach up to 24 percent of the total investment in fixed assets of the project.

Approved enterprises may also receive tax benefits, including reduced rates of corporate tax, the ability to use accelerated depreciation on fixed assets and a reduced withholding rate on dividends distributed to shareholders. For example, reduced corporate tax rates may be between 10 percent and 25 percent, depending on the proportion of foreign investment made in the project, in contrast to 36 percent, which is the usual corporate tax rate.

An approved enterprise may alternatively choose to waive its right to receive government grants and to receive, instead, tax exemptions, which may, if approved, include a full tax exemption of up to ten years. Furthermore, an approved industrial or tourist related enterprise might elect to apply for state guaranties of loans instead of grants. Dividends distributed by an approved enterprise will be subject to the equivalent of branch profits tax of between 10 percent to 25 percent depending upon the percentage of foreign shareholding of the enterprise, in addition to withholding tax of 15 percent.

## Research and Development

Research and development grants and assistance programs are available through the Ministry of Industry and Trade. To attain such grants or assistance, which can provide as much as 66 percent of research and development costs, a proposal must be submitted by the entity conducting the research and development activity to the office of the Chief Scientist in the Ministry of Industry and Trade. If a research and development project results in a saleable product, the funding will generally be repaid as royalties at 3 percent of the product's sales revenues. The product developed as a result of such a grant must be produced in Israel, except if otherwise approved by the Research Committee of the Office of the Chief Scientist.

Similarly, up to 50 percent of industrial research and development costs of joint ventures between Israeli and US companies may be underwritten by the Binational Industrial Research and Development Foundation (BIRD), and funds for agricultural projects are available from the Binational Agricultural Research and Development Foundation (BARD), both of which are sponsored by the Israeli and United States governments.

Furthermore, the Canada-Israel Industrial Research and Development Foundation (CIIRDF) was established by the governments of Canada and Israel to promote collaborative research and development between companies in those two countries. CIIRDF will contribute up to 50 percent of the research and developments costs of joint feasibility studies, pilot projects or full-scale projects.

The United States, Israel and Jordan have recently initiated the TRIDE program, now in its pilot stages. Each TRIDE project is a joint venture involving private companies from all three countries, which will draw on complimentary strength in research and development, manufacturing, and marketing to develop new products and technologies for domestic and international markets. The three governments will support up to 50 percent of the direct costs needed to bring new product to market. The three governments have equally contributed a total of $2 million.

Israel is a member of the European Community's Fourth RTD Framework Program. The program funds research and technological developments and has a total budget of more than US$ 10 billion.

The Chief Scientist is also responsible for the Incubator Technology Centers which offer infrastructure support at reduced or no cost and finance 85 percent of the approved budget for technology based startup businesses. The Incubator Centers have been very successful in starting out several new ventures that have gone on to become highly successful businesses.

## Free Trade Zones

In an attempt to maximize the advantages of investing in Israel, the government enacted legislation to allow the development of the free trade area in Eilat, which provides for a 20 year income tax reprieve and a 15 percent flat tax on distributed profits of an investing company. It affords full exemption from import and export duties and taxes, allows full repatriation of profits with the foreign investor corporation and lifts otherwise applicable currency controls.

## Qualifying Industrial Zone

Pursuant to the United States - Israel Free Trade Area Implementation Act of 1995, the governments of Israel and Jordan agreed to the creation of the Irbid Qualifying Industrial Zone (QIZ). This zone is located in the Irbid duty-free zone in Jordan in conjunction with the Israeli side of the border-crossing at the Sheikh Hussein—Nahar Hayarden Bridge. On March 13, 1998, the Office of the United States' Trade Representative designated the first Jordan-Israel "qualified industrial zone" at the Al-Hassan Industrial Park in Irbid, Jordan. According to this special status, goods from the zone that are produced through Jordanian-Israeli commercial cooperation, and which meet certain minimal criteria, are eligible for duty-free entry into the United States. This initiative has already significantly increased Jordanian-Israeli dialogue on commercial issues and has generated notable private sector interest from both countries. More than $140 million worth of new projects have been set up at the Irbid QIZ in 1999. These new investments will bring to $350 million the aggregate value of projects in the zone, whereby most of these factories produce textiles and apparel. In 1998, the United States imported from the QIZ goods valued at approximately $17 million (see Chapter on Jordan).

## Trade Agreements

Israel has had free trade agreements with the European Union (EU) since 1975, the United States since 1985 the European Free Trade Association

(EFTA) since 1992, followed by agreements with Canada, Turkey, Hungary, Slovakia and the Czech Republic. Those agreements allow Israeli enterprises and Israeli-based enterprises to access freely foreign markets, which cover more than two-thirds of Israel's external trade.

Since the signing of the Declaration of Principles with the Palestinian Liberation Organization in 1993, Israel has signed a free trade agreement with the Palestinian Authority and began negotiations with a number of other Middle Eastern and other countries. So far, Israel has concluded agreements with Jordan, India, CIS, Russia, South Korea and Poland. Israel has had a most favored nation trade agreement with Egypt since 1981. Indonesia, Bangladesh and Pakistan have all indicated an interest in establishing closer economic ties with Israel. Morocco, which has established diplomatic relations with Israel, has increased its importation of Israeli-made agricultural related products such as agro-chemicals and irrigation equipment.

## Customs

Since January 1998, Israel has implemented the Customs Valuation principles of the WTO code. Under the new regulations, the basis for valuation is the Transaction Value, in most cases the CIF price. Under the 1975 EU-Israel Free Trade Agreement, industrial products not produced in Israel may be imported into Israel free of any customs charge. Such products usually include raw materials and semi-processed goods.

In the case of raw materials imported for the purpose of producing products intended for export, it is usually possible to defer payment of import duties, provided that guaranties are made that such duties will be paid if the products are not exported within a given period of time.

## Environmental Law

Environmental legislation enacted in recent years, together with greater public awareness, has resulted in increased environmental enforcement in Israel. The law can be divided into two groups: general laws whose provisions reflect environmental considerations, and specific environmental regulations. General laws predated the modern environmental era but their broad and stringent language has been used by environmental agencies to promote environmental regulation and planning.

The Ministry of Environment encourages local authorities to search for solutions to all types of environmental concerns. Opportunities exist for foreign exports of environmental technologies in areas related to Israel's particular concerns. The leading environmental matters include: the decrease in levels of water available for irrigation purposes; the increasing amount of municipal solid waste; the growing demand for re-useable wastewater; and the increasing quantities of hazardous waste.

Israel is also interested in new environmental technologies. The first international tender for a waste-to-energy plant was issued in January 1998, and construction of a model desalination "chimney" is underway. Israel's development of regional sanitary landfills, a national air pollution monitoring system and state-of-the-art municipal wastewater treatment plants, even in remote regions, are characteristic of a growing awareness for environmental issues.

## General Statutes Concerning Environmental Issues

The Planning and Building Law of 1965 regulates all building and land use management in Israel and establishes both institutional and substantive framework for environmental planning.

The Licensing of Business Law of 1968 creates a bureaucratic framework for licensing businesses by including the concept of "environment quality." This refers to the license qualifications that require, *inter alia*, the existence of appropriate sanitary conditions, the effective prevention of hazards and nuisances and compliance with planning and building laws.

The Public Health Ordinance of 1940 regulates a variety of aspects of public health, including environmental issues such as sanitation and water quality. The Ordinance also includes provisions on environmental hazards and a list of nuisances. Private and public nuisances are treated also by the Penal Law of 1977 and the Civil Wrongs Ordinance (New Version) of 1968.

## Environment Protection Legislation

There are various specific pollution laws: The Prevention of Nuisances Law of 1961, which primarily deals with air and noise pollution; The Water Law of 1959, which regulates water usage in general and water quality specifically; The Hazardous Substances Law of 1993, which regulates the disposal of solid and hazardous waste; the Prevention of Sea Water Pollution by Oil Ordinance (New Version) of 1980 and the Prevention of Sea Pollution (Dumping of Waste) Law of 1993, which deal with the prohibition on the discharge of oily substances and pollutants into the sea.

# JORDAN

## Recent Political Developments

| | |
|---|---|
| Population | 5.4 million (1999) |
| Religions | 99% Sunni Muslim; 100,000 Christians (Greek Orthodox, Armenian and Catholic) |
| Government | Constitutional Monarchy |
| Languages | Arabic (English is widely spoken) |
| Work Week | Public Sector: Saturday–Thursday 8:00–14:00 Commercial: Saturday–Thursday 8:30–13:00; 15:30–19:30 Banking: Saturday–Thursday 8:30–12:30 |
| Monetary Unit | Jordanian Dinars (JD) |
| Exchange Rate | JD 0.71=US$ 1 |

Shortly before King Hussein's death in early 1999, the late Monarch selected his son Abdullah as the new heir and abruptly ousted his brother, Hassan, from the position he had occupied since 1965. Close sources indicated that Hussein was unhappy with the behavior of his brother during his absence. According to these sources, while the King was undergoing cancer treatments in the United States, Hassan conducted himself as "more king and less heir."

In Abdullah's first year as Jordan's ruler, he has won accolades both at home and abroad with his policies. He has managed to repair Jordan's relations with Arab states such as Syria, Kuwait and Saudi Arabia. Although Gulf assistance to Jordan and remittances from Jordanian workers in the Gulf may never again regain their importance of the 1980s, there is now scope for closer commercial cooperation, which would favour Jordanian exports.

Abdullah has also forged a role for himself in the regional peace process as intermediary between Syria and Israel. He has endeared himself to his people by rooting at soccer matches and by mingling with citizens, often undercover, to discover what is occurring among his populace and to experience the bureaucratic annoyances afflicting the Kingdom's fragile economy and quality of life.

Additionally, the monarch has taken bold initiatives to combat potentially threatening internal opposition elements. In mid-September 1999, indigenous authorities arrested 3 senior Hamas officials as they attempted to return from Iran. This followed the August 30 raid of Hamas offices in Amman and arrest of several of the radical movement's officials. Hamas constitutes the main opposition to Palestinian Chairman Yasser Arafat.

Jordanians are increasingly frustrated with the lack of progress in the peace process, claiming that Israel hinders Jordan's trade with the Palestinians (presently this trade volume does not exceed $23 million annually.) Another source of anxiety between Jordan and Israel is over water. According to the peace treaty, Israel is obliged to supply Jordan with certain annual quantities of water. Last winter's drought has caused Israel to announce that it could no longer completely fulfill its commitments. This delicate issue will be a serious test-case for the two countries.

The government is committed to improving the nation's infrastructure in order to support new investment and continued economic growth. Jordan is in the process of liberalizing its investment and customs laws in an effort to attract foreign investment. Foreign investors are now allowed to invest in Amman's stock market and in its financial markets.

On January 15, 2000, Jordan's Prime Minister Abdul Rauf al-Rawabdeh reshuffled his 24-member cabinet appointing seven new ministers and dismissing six others. The key portfolios of foreign affairs, interior, finance and planning all remained unchanged. Officials have indicated that the new ministers are mostly technocrats who will boost the government's drive for economic reforms in accordance with IMF recommendations. The new Trade Minister, Mohammed Halayqah, is a former official who was credited with securing Jordan's entry to the World Trade Organization last month. Mr. Halayqah has already announced that one of his key priorities is to promote Jordanian exports.

An even more significant political alteration took place two days earlier when King Abdullah appointed Fayez Tarawneh as new royal court chief, replacing Abdul Kareem Kabariti. The royal court chief, one of the most influential posts in the Kingdom, is responsible for managing daily affairs of the royal family and serves as *de facto* liaison officer between the Monarch and the government. Unlike Kabariti, who supported accelerated free market reforms, Tarawneh believes that the government should garner as much solid support as possible for controversial reforms.

The government reshuffle is aimed at assembling widespread support for the Rawabdeh-led cabinet, which has recently launched a series of contentious social, economic and administrative reforms. The Prime Minister has been the subject of attacks from the public and opposition parties for his attempts to privatize major state-owned enterprises, his crackdown on Muslim dissidents, and his decision to levy a 10 percent consumption tax, which triggered a subsequent price hike.

Moreover, Rawabdeh is encountering fresh charges that he knew of bribes solicited by his son, Issam. Mahmoud Kharabsheh, head of the House Legal Affairs Committee, has alleged that Issam demanded a $21 million bribe from two Gulf nationals who sought to invest $100 million to construct a tourist village near Queen Alia Airport. Rawabdeh has denied that he was aware of any such occurrence, but has vowed to resign if the house of deputies proves such allegations to be true.

Kharabsheh first brought up this charge during the latest 2000 budget debate, whereby other deputies urged the government to combat high-level corruption, abuse of public funds and nepotism among senior government officials. The government has promised to enhance transparency as part of its IMF-guided reform agenda. But parliament has yet to pass a controversial law that obliges senior government officials to declare their sources of income.

## Recent Economic Developments

Jordan's feeble economy has traditionally been reliant on foreign aid, mainly from Gulf states and worker's remittances. In recent years, the Jordanian government has been seeking cooperation from foreign governments and international organizations to forgive its massive debt to unburden the nation. The country's debt ratio – about 100 percent of GDP – is one of the world's highest.

Leaders from the Group of Eight in June 1999 called on the world community to help alleviate Jordan's $7 billion debt encumbrance.

Such forgiveness would go a long way to helping the country's new king, Abdullah. On February 7, 1999, King Hussein died after over 45 years of leading the country. Hussein, one of the region's more popular figures—led his country through turbulent eras, including external wars with the Israelis and an internal war with the Palestinians. He bequeathed to his son a peace with the Israelis but a rickety economy as well.

The new king is looking to both external help and internal reform to meet his chief goal of creating an improved economic climate for Jordanians.

One beginning area to meet this goal is by improving the nation's infrastructure to support new investment and continued economic growth. Jordan is continuing to liberalize its investment and customs laws in a way that will attract foreign investment. And while the government controls roughly 60 percent of the economy and is the country's largest employer, it is pushing ahead with a privatization program that seeks to place the private sector as the engine of economic growth.

On the sectoral level, construction, agricultural and manufacturing sectors have played the leading roles in driving economic growth in recent years. While the country has limited natural resources, it is one of the world's largest exporters or phosphates.

The death of King Hussein raised a serious concern regarding the Kingdom's economic stability. These fears were concentrated on a scenario whereby the dinar would rapidly devalue, cause wide-scale panic and lead to the complete collapse of an already fragile economy. Quick measures by the Arab and international community diffused this anticipated crisis.

In March 1999, Jordan reached an agreement with the International Monetary Fund on a new three-year financial package, which would replace the current ten-year program. The new package provides Jordan with an extra $150 million per year. In return, Jordan agreed to a number of economic reforms.

In June 1999, leaders from the Group of Eight called on the world community to help alleviate Jordan's $7 billion debt encumbrance. This global pledge to lend assistance to the Kingdom supports Abdullah's foremost priority, namely to create an improved economic climate for the people of Jordan.

Debt relief and forgiveness are of supreme importance for Jordan's feeble economy. The debt ratio in this Arab nation is around 100 percent of GDP, one of the highest rates in the world. In order to illustrate the severity of Jordan's stagnation, debt servicing this year will consume 26 percent of the central government's budget.

Jordan's government is greatly concerned about the impact of the growing level of unemployment, which already stands at between 15-20 percent, and low wages, which have dropped by more than 20 percent during the 1990s. Increasing jobless rate, diminishing per capita purchasing power, spreading poverty and deteriorating farmers' conditions have pushed many Jordanian Parliament Members to demand immediate economic restructuring and clear development strategies in order to save the national economy from a prolonged recession.

**Economic Indicators**

|  | 1999** | 1998 | 1997 |
|---|---|---|---|
| GDP Growth (percent) | 1.0 | 2.2 | 1.3 |
| GDP per capita (US$) | — | 1,551 | 1,514 |
| CPI Inflation (percent)* | 2.5 | 3.1 | 3.0 |
| Unemployment (percent) | 17 | 15 | — |
| Exports (US$bn) | 1.75 | 1.80 | 1.84 |
| Imports (US$bn) | 3.75 | 3.84 | 4.11 |
| Trade balance (US$bn) | –2.00 | –2.04 | –2.27 |
| Budget deficit (excluding grants, US$mn) | — | — | 476 |
| Budget deficit (excluding grants, % of GDP) | — | 10.7 | 7.7 |
| Budget deficit (including grants, % of GDP) | — | 6.9 | 3.1 |
| Foreign debt (US$mn) | — | 7,046*** | 6,452 |
| Foreign Aid (JD million) | — | 183.1 | 134.7 |
| Internal Debt (JD million) | — | 905.0 | 1,600 |

* Inflation figures based on government cost of living index, which includes subsidized items.
** 1999 figures are initial projections
*** 95.3% of GDP

The Jordanian government controls roughly 60 percent of the country's economy and is also the largest employer. Government entities, such as the

Social Security Agency, have large investments in share holding companies. Government regulations and procedures are bureaucratic, although the liberalization of investment laws is expected to ease the red tape.

The government has announced a privatization program but has not made heavy progress. In late 1998, roughly one-third of the Jordan Cement Factories Company was sold to the French Lafarge. The Government also plans to sell its ownership in the Aqaba Railway Corporation, Royal Jordanian Airlines, Public Transport Company, and Jordan Telecommunications Company (JTC). In early 2000, it was announced that the government sold 40 percent of its shares in JTC to France Telecom.

In April 1999, Jordan agreed on a three-year reform package with the IMF. The program's policies envisage economic growth of 3-4 percent by 2001.[1] The scheme stresses private sector participation, in addition to implementing sound fiscal and monetary policies. For the first time, the plan includes improvements in transparency and accountability of government accounts.

In 1996, the government passed a securities law designed at enhancing the efficiency, transparency and overall performance of the stock market and encouraging foreign investment. This was part of the first phase in overhauling the Amman Financial Market (AFM) since its 1978 establishment. The move was part of Jordan's overall economic reform program. The law, drafted with World Bank assistance, will ease the state's grip on the bourse and encourage faster and clearer presentation of company results.

In another step to draw foreign indirect investment, the country put into effect May 17, 1997, a new Securities Law that established an independent Securities Exchange Commission (SEC), a private securities bourse, a private depository and transfer center, and a society for financial professionals licensed to practice in Jordan.

The Jordanian Bourse is linked to the Paris Bourse for automated clearing and settling purposes. It is also connected to other major international exchanges on an on-line basis.

---

[1]    Suleiman al-Khalidi, "Jordan Says New IMF Deal Brings Sustained Growth," *Amman Newsroom*, (April 15, 1999.)

The Securities Law permits recapitalization and abolishes the capital gains tax, which had been set at 15 percent. Approximately 40 Jordanian companies are able to offer tax-free stock dividends to their shareholders.

Under a 1995 law, foreigners may buy up to 49 percent of any of the ninety-eight firms listed on the exchange.

Presently, the AFM combines the running of the stock market with a regulatory role. The new law divides these tasks among three separate bodies: the Amman Securities Exchange Commission, responsible for day to day operations of the market; the Central Depository Body, responsible for settlement and clearing of stock and the centralization of the current manual share settlement, which involves cumbersome paperwork; and a government watchdog, the Securities Exchange Commission to oversee the two previous bodies. The exchange and Central Depository Body both have boards of directors composed of licensed financial brokerage firms.

The new law also regulates Jordan's first mutual funds, with manager accreditation falling under SEC jurisdiction.

At the sectoral level, construction, agricultural and manufacturing sectors have been the main drivers of economic growth in recent years.

## Industry

Jordan's industrial sector includes several major producers in the minerals sector and small to medium scale industries in other sectors. In some major industrial enterprises, the government continues to hold substantial shares.

Leading Jordanian industries are phosphate fertilizers and minerals, petroleum products, food processing, metal products, cement and building materials, cigarettes, animal feed and clothing. Additional industries include furniture, pharmaceuticals, cosmetics, paints, plastics, paper and cardboard.

The country's industrial sectors have continued to grow with the strong minerals industry undertaking ambitious expansion plans. Small and medium scale industries are also expanding growing with record numbers of new industrial companies registering and commencing work. Although Jordan's industrial exports were devastated by the loss of the Iraqi, Kuwaiti and Saudi markets occasioned by the Gulf War crisis, many industrialists have bounced back. They have seized on growing domestic market demand growth in the domestic market led by the returnees and are using more imagination and energy than they had previously in order to look for new markets. In addition, the government itself encourages private industry to diversify and to develop new overseas markets.

Industrial zones have been established at Sahab (south of Amman), Irbid and Salt; while Zarqa and Aqaba have been further developed as industrial centers.

## Tourism

Tourism is a main source of income and foreign currency, contributing more than 10 percent to the country's GDP. Since 1992, this industry has grown at an annual rate of between 6-8 percent. The government is working feverishly with the private sector in transforming the country into a popular tourist destination.

Since the 1994 peace agreement with Israel, 46 new hotels have been built in Jordan, and expansion is continuing. Aggregate tourist number are, however, somewhat disappointing. Official figures show 1.1 million tourists in 1997 versus 858,000 in 1994, although only about one-third of these are estimated to be real tourists.

## Exports

Jordan's Central Bank put exports for 1998 at about US$ 1.80 billion compared to US$ 1.84 billion for 1997. Imports in 1998 stood at US$ 3.84 billion, versus US$ 4.11 billion in 1997.

# Business Environment

## Privatization

The government has set the goal of privatizing most of its public sector enterprises. The Cabinet Committee on Privatization, which was created by the Council of Ministers. The Committee is responsible for setting broad policy and guidelines for the privatization program.

The government of Jordan carries out its privatization program through three distinct methods. The government sells its shares in existing companies; it incorporates existing state economic enterprises as a first step towards their privatization and the eventual sale of their shares; the government also sanctions the licensing of private investment in various activities, mainly utilities that have previously been controlled by government monopolies.

The Telecommunications Law (No. 13 of 1995) created a committee with the authority to license private sector projects. In the electricity sector, the General Electricity Law (No. 10 of 1996) permits the licensing of independent power producers and independent power distributors. The General Electricity Law also allows industrial enterprises to set up their own power generating facilities and allows them to exchange their electricity with other independent power producers.

Jordan's Telecommunications Corporation (TCC) and the Jordan Electricity Authority have both been commercialized. The government has already announced its intention to sell a 26 percent stake in the TCC, and new telecommunications services are open to the private sector. In October 1998, however, the sale of a 40 percent stake to a strategic shareholder was suspended indefinitely, when the Southern Bell Corporation pulled out. The Jordan Investment Corporation (JIC) plans to sell shares in a number of public companies, and has already sold a 33 percent stake in the Jordan Cement Factories Company (JCFC) to the French Lafarge.

There have also been extensive discussions regarding the privatization of Jordan's national airlines, Royal Jordanian. In October 1999, the planned sale of a 49 percent stake to a strategic partner was announced. Banque Paribas, US consultant SHA, and Clifford Chance and Line & Partners, both of the United Kingdom, have been carrying out the airline's financial, legal and technical restructuring since October 1998. Once the airline is privatized, it will remain the sole Jordanian carrier and will retain exclusive rights for all network traffic for four years. It will also maintain exclusive rights for the route it will operate for a further four years.

The JIC functions as the investment arm of the Jordanian government. It has already concluded a number of sales of its shareholding in Jordanian private and public shareholding companies, mostly in the hotel and tourism sector.

## Incorporation

The 1989 Companies Law allows for the transformation of state economic enterprises into public shareholding companies. Initially, such companies are to be owned by the government. They may be sold at a later stage, in whole or in part. A new Companies Law, which took effect in June 1997, helps streamline foreign direct investment in Jordan.

The Jordan Electricity Authority, which was incorporated in the form of a public shareholding company as of September 1996, was the first such enterprise to be incorporated. Next was the Telecommunications Corporation, which was incorporated as of January 1997. Similar plans are underway regarding the Royal Jordanian Airlines, Aqaba Railway Corporation, Public Transport Company, Aqaba Port and Queen Alia International Airport.

## Licensing

In order to license private investments in government controlled sectors, legislative amendments and reforms are required. This task has already been accomplished for the telecommunications and electricity sectors.

## Stock Exchange

The Amman Financial Market (AFM) is a credible and regulated market that is one of the largest Arab stock markets. The AFM is open to foreign investors who may own up to 50 percent of any listed public shareholding company.

Bonds and shares of Jordanian public shareholding companies, government and municipal bonds may be traded on the AFM. Over-the-counter trades, options, futures and other derivative trading, however, are prohibited.

## Major Projects

A number of joint projects with Israel have been proposed (in energy, water, electricity, infrastructure and tourism), although, as yet, none have been undertaken.

During the November 1996 Cairo Economic Conference, Jordan presented 25 national projects in the industry, telecommunications, energy, water, transport and tourism sectors, requiring US$ 3.7 billion in private financing. None of the sectors, with the obvious exception of tourism, are directly affected by the regional political climate.

The industrial projects are concentrated on mineral exploitation, in which Jordan already has experience and a strong track record in attracting private investment. Interest in new telecommunications projects is already running high. Jordan's limited natural energy resources might make energy a rather hard sector to sell to international investors, but the government is not deterred. Its invitation for expressions of interest in building a private oil refinery attracted no less than 17 responses early in 1996. Additionally, the US Enron Development Corporation has reaffirmed its interest in building a liquefied natural gas (LNG) plant in Aqaba, importing the gas from the Gulf.

Tourism is the most vulnerable sector, but it has seen extraordinary growth since the signing of the peace treaty between Jordan and Israel in 1994. Leading international names, including Movenpick, Marriott, Hyatt, Four Seasons and ACCOR are already involved in new projects in Amman and the Dead Sea. The Aqaba Regional Authority has also issued licenses for four new hotels in Aqaba, including one for Jordan's first 100 percent Israeli-owned investment.

The Jordan Rift Valley is also on the agenda as a joint Jordanian-Israeli offering with 12 to 13 projects, with each of the two sides presenting two projects in detail. Israel presented a joint telecommunications project while Jordan has elected to offer the Aqaba/Peace airport and a logistics center for land transport. Jordan will also be involved in the EU-sponsored Regional Economic Development Working Group (REDWG) schemes, which link it with Israel, the Palestinian Authority and Egypt.

The following projects have been proposed in various economic sectors:

**Energy:** Expansion of power generation capacity, refinery expansion and development, oil and gas exploration.

Bids for the construction of Jordan's first major independent power project (IPP) were received in May 1999. The 300-450 MW build-own-operate station will be built at Al-Samra, north of the Zarqa industrial city, and is due to commence operating in 2001.

**Telecommunications:** The installation of new telecommunications services and data networks.

**Tourism:** Development of the Aqaba tourist area and the Dead Sea tourist area.

**Industry and Mining:** Production of magnesium oxide, magnesium metal plant, potassium sulphate, calcium phosphate and potassium nitrate. Glass sand production, gold exploration, copper exploration, kaolin/clay exploration.

## Build Operate Transfer

Jordan is also seeking private investors for the Amman-Zarqa light railway project, which it hopes to see launched as Jordan's first transport scheme carried out on a build-operate-transfer (BOT) or build-own-operate (BOO) basis. Austria Rail Engineering Company has completed a feasibility study for the 42-kilometer line, which would link Zarqa with Amman and may be extended to the Amman suburb of Suweileh. The government is now seeking international financing for the detailed feasibility studies and designs.

The US-based Corporate Holdings of America signed an initial agreement with the Jordanian government in June 1996 regarding the construction of an oil refinery in Jordan. The proposed plant is to have an installed refining capacity of 250,000 barrels per day. The project will also include the construction of a 165 MW power station as well as a 20,000 cubic meter per day desalination plant. The overall cost of the planned undertaking has been estimated at US$ 2.5 billion.

Construction is expected to take about four years to complete, and the concession is to last for a 20-year period effective from the beginning of commercial operations. At that time, a new Jordanian company capitalized at US$ 700 million is to be established upon final agreement. Although local investors will be offered up to a 45 percent equity stake in the venture, American investors will take a controlling interest and will be obliged to cover whatever stake Jordanian investors fail to take-up.

## Franchising

Jordanian businessmen have expressed an increased interest in franchising, especially in industry, services, and fast food although retail and service franchises are rare in Jordan.

## Leading Business Opportunities

| Rank | Sector | Rank | Sector |
|---|---|---|---|
| 1 | Telecommunications Products | 16 | Slaughter House Tender |
| 2 | Turnkey Telecommunications Systems | 17 | Phase Two of Aqaba Thermal Power Station |
| 3 | Electronic Products | 18 | Solar Energy Tenders |
| 4 | Security Products | 19 | Telephone Network Project Tenders |
| 5 | Instrumentation Products | 20 | Dams Tenders |
| 6 | Oil Field, Gas Equipment— Products and Services | 21 | Water Sector Tenders |
| 7 | Mining Equipment and Services | 22 | Industrial Sector Tenders |
| 8 | Agricultural Equipment and Products | 23 | Cars |
| 9 | Environmental Products | 24 | Military Uniforms |
| 10 | Thermal Power Station Contract | 25 | Fiberglass |
| 11 | Solar Energy Turnkey Projects Contracts | 26 | Reinforcements |
| 12 | Ductile Iron and High Density Polyethylene Pipes | 27 | Lubricating Oils |
| 13 | Casing, Screens, Drill Pipe and Drill Bits | 28 | Industrial Chemicals and Additives |
| 14 | Electromechanical Equipment | 29 | Optical Instruments |
| 15 | Sewage Projects, Tunneling, Pipe Jacking and Concrete Structures | 30 | Overhead and Sound Projectors |

## Legal Review

The laws governing business in Jordan have undergone a fundamental change in 1995. This has been in line with government policies to convert Jordan from a consumption- to a production-oriented economy and to open all economic activity to the private sector, both local and foreign.

In recent years, priority was given to new investments, taxation and protection of intellectual property laws. New legislation has also been passed in the areas of labor law and sales tax. Key changes have been introduced in the laws governing major infrastructure enterprises such as the Telecommunications Corporation and the Jordan Electricity Authority as part of an ongoing privatization program, as well as in the laws governing activities of the Amman Financial Market (AFM).

## Judiciary

The Jordanian judicial system is comprised of both civil and religious courts. The religious court system's jurisdiction extends to all matters of personal status, and the civil courts have jurisdiction over all other matters.

### *Religious Courts*

The religious court system has jurisdiction over matters of personal status, including marriage, divorce, inheritance and alimony. Persons of the same religion are subject to the appropriate religious courts, the *Shar'ia* Courts for Muslims and Ecclesiastical Courts for Christians. Persons not of the same religion who do not expressly consent to the jurisdiction of a religious court may bring their dispute to the civil court having appropriate jurisdiction.

### *Civil Courts*

The civil judiciary is a three-tiered system. The lowest courts are the fourteen Magistrates Courts and the seven Courts of First Instance. The Magistrates Courts have expressly defined jurisdiction to hear civil and criminal cases of matters involving small fines of a maximum imprisonment period of two years.

The Courts of First Instance have general jurisdiction in all criminal and civil matters not expressly granted to the Magistrates Courts' jurisdiction. The Courts of First Instance also sit at a court of appeal for judgments of Magistrates Courts.

The next judicial tier is the Court of Appeals, which is presided over by a tribunal of judges. Jurisdiction of the Court of Appeals is geographically based. The Courts of Appeals hear appeals in chambers in chambers of Magistrates Courts' decisions, and decide on appeals from decisions of the Courts of First Instance and the Religious Courts.

The Court of Cassation is the highest level of the judiciary. A full panel of judges hears important cases. A five-judge panel hears ordinary appeals of decisions from the Court of Appeals.

## Business Forms and Structures

A new Companies Law, aimed at encouraging investment, became effective in June 1997. Companies Law No. 22 of 1997 limits routine procedures and facilitates the process of company registration.

The Law introduced the not-for-profit company form as well as the civil company form, which provides for the establishment of companies by professional persons, such as lawyers, doctors or engineers.

Under the new Law, companies are no longer required to pay a 15 percent capitalizing charge, which had previously acted as a barrier to capital reserves. In addition, amendments to the Law allow company founders to adopt the prices they deem appropriate to estimate the value of their fixed assets.

The Law provides for several entity forms under which business may be conducted in Jordan. These are: (1) general partnership; (2) limited partnership; (3) limited liability company; (4) limited partnership in shares; (5) public shareholding company; (6) mutual fund company; (7) offshore company (exempt company); and (8) foreign company (operating and non-operating).

## Companies Law

### Public Shareholding Company

A public shareholding company may be formed by two or more shareholders whose liability is limited to their respective share of the company's equity. The minimum authorized capital is set at a JD 500,000 minimum. The subscribed capital must exceed JD 100,000 or 20 percent of the authorized capital, whichever is greater.

Banks, financial institutions and insurance companies may only be incorporated as public shareholding companies. Companies operating franchises must also be incorporated in this form.

### Offshore Company

An offshore company (or exempt company) is a public company, private company or a partnership limited in shares, which is registered in Jordan, but conducts its business outside the Kingdom. It is an entity that was introduced in order to attract foreign investments.

This entity may not offer its shares for public subscription in Jordan, and it is prohibited for Jordanians to subscribe to its capital. At least 5 percent of the capital of the offshore company must be invested in Jordanian securities. Where the offshore company is engaged in insurance, banking, finance or joint investments, its capital must be at least JD 1,000,000.

### Mutual Fund Company

A mutual fund (joint investment) company may be organized as a public shareholding company. Its objectives are restricted to investing funds on behalf of others by way of dealing in securities.

This entity may take the form of an open-ended fund with variable capital, which issues redeemable shares, the value of which is determined by the value of the company's assets. It may also take the form of a closed-ended fund, whose shares are not redeemable and are traded on the stock exchange.

### Foreign Operating Companies—Branch Offices

This business structure is open to foreigners wishing to engage in business ventures in Jordan. A foreign company that has been awarded a contract in Jordan requiring execution of work therein must register a branch office with the Controller of Companies in the Ministry of Industry and Trade.

Such a company is registered as a foreign operating company for purposes of the contract and for the duration thereof. If the company obtains other contracts in Jordan, then the same registration will be extended so as to cover such new contracts. If the company does not obtain any new contracts, then the branch office should be closed and liquidated upon the completion of the contract in respect of which the registration was effected.

Registration fees payable for a Branch Office are JD 250 if the share capital of the foreign company at its home office does not exceed the equivalent of JD 1 million, and JD 500 if the share capital of the foreign company exceeds the equivalent of JD 1 million.

### Foreign Non-Operating Companies—Regional Offices

Foreign companies are encouraged to set up regional offices in Jordan through tax and customs duty exemptions and provisions for the free movement of foreign currency. A regional office can operate from Jordan and conduct business anywhere in the world, except in Jordan, and may not generate income in Jordan. It may, however, collect information concerning general business opportunities in Jordan or in respect to a particular project. The duration of the regional office is not limited to any period of time or to the completion of a specific project.

The Companies Law does not elaborate on the size or type of foreign company that may register as a regional office in conformity therewith. It is now the policy of the Ministry of Industry and Trade, however, to restrict this facility only to substantial and large companies of international standing in their fields.

A Regional Office enjoys certain exemptions and facilities including the following:

- Neither the foreign company nor its regional office established in Jordan will pay any local taxes, including Income Tax and Social Services Tax;
- The non-Jordanian employees of the regional office are exempted from payment of income tax and Social Services Tax on their salaries;
- A regional office may import its office equipment, furniture and business samples free of customs duties, import fees and all other related charges;

- The non-Jordanian employees of the regional office may import a car every five years free of customs duties upon depositing a bank guarantee for the amount of the duty with the Ministry of Finance and Customs as a guarantee that will be discharged upon exporting the car out of Jordan or selling the car locally after paying the duty thereon;
- A regional office can maintain an account in Jordan in foreign currency or in Jordanian Dinars, provided that deposits of money to such accounts are from foreign sources; such funds may be deposited in the account and withdrawn in order to be repatriated to the foreign parent company without exchange control restrictions;
- No fees are payable upon the registration of, or in connection with the operation of a regional office;
- A regional office is exempted from the requirement of registering with the Chamber of Commerce and all other professional associations, as well as from the payment of any fees in this regard; and
- The non-Jordanian employees of the regional office are granted residence and work permits; however, the number of non-Jordanian employees at the regional office may not exceed that of its Jordanian employees.

### Dissolution of a Company
A company may go into voluntary liquidation in the event that: The period fixed for its duration has expired, the objective for which it was formed has been achieved or proves to be impossible to achieve. Voluntary liquidation may also take place in the occurrence of an event stipulated in the company's Articles of Association or by the adoption of a resolution of the Company's general meeting of shareholders.

A compulsory liquidation may be ordered by the court if the company so resolves, if the company commits a serious breach of law or of its articles of association, if it suspends its business activities for a period exceeding one year, if the number of its shareholders decreases below the legal minimum or if the company is unable to pay its debts.

The company, its creditors, the Controller of Companies or the Attorney General may make an application for the compulsory liquidation of the company.

## Partnerships

### General Partnership

A general partnership is formed by at least two and not more than twenty partners who are jointly and severally liable for the partnership's debts. Only the names of the actual partners may be included in the partnership's name.

A partnership's interest may be transferred with the approval of all partners or in accordance with conditions established in the partnership agreement. The management of the partnership is vested with one or more managers who are individuals and who may or may not be partners in the partnership.

According to the new Law, if the partnership consists of two partners, the withdrawal of one of the partners will not lead to the dissolution of the partnership. Instead, the remaining partner may seek to replace the absent partner with another. Failure to do so within three months of the partner's withdrawal will result in the partnership's dissolution by virtue of law.

### Limited Partnership

A limited partnership consists of two or more partners who are jointly and severally liable for its debts and one or more partners whose liability for the partnership's debts is limited to their contribution to the partnership's capital. The limited partners of the limited partnership may not participate in the management of the partnership or act in its name.

### Limited Partnership in Shares

This form of business entity consists of two or more general partners who are jointly and severally liable for its debts and three or more partners whose liability for the partnership's debts is limited to their respective share of the partnership's equity. Partners are not required to be individuals, and the name of the partnership should include the name of one or more of the general partners and the words, "Limited Partnership in Shares."

The minimum capital permitted in this form of partnership is JD 100,000, which must be divided into negotiable shares of equal value of JD 1 each. Shares may be issued to the public for subscription but must not exceed twice the general partner's capital in the partnership.

The limited partnership in shares shall be dissolved or liquidated in the manner provided for by the company's articles of association. If not provided for, the provisions regarding liquidation of the public shareholding company shall apply.

## Joint Ventures

A joint venture need not be registered in Jordan and, hence, is not governed by the Companies Law. A joint venture is typically regulated by the contractual agreement between the joint venture parties. This does not apply in the event that the parties envisage the establishment of a corporate entity.

## Currency and Banking

### Foreign Currency Control

In accordance with the Foreign Exchange Control Law No. 95, of 1966 and the Foreign Exchange Control Regulations of 1978, as amended in 1979, the Central Bank of Jordan (CBJ) is the ultimate authority for enforcing foreign exchange controls in Jordan. Its foreign exchange controls cover all fields of transactions in the Kingdom including: inflow and outflow of Jordanian and foreign means of payment; dealing in foreign currencies; resident and non-resident accounts in Jordanian Dinars and foreign currencies; lending in foreign currencies; commercial payments; free trade zone payments; invisible payments and capital transfers; guarantees; export earnings' repatriation; commissions on foreign exchange permits; reporting requirements; and auditing and statement of account regulations.

Law No. 95 allows for the free exchange of banknotes, coins and gold. It allows licensed banks, with the approval of the CBJ, to manage foreign currency accounts, as well as to purchase and to sell foreign currencies. According to Article 6 of the Law, foreign residents may open accounts in local and foreign currency and may transfer funds without restrictions.

### Conversion and Transfer Policies

In March 1995, the CBJ announced that the Jordanian Dinar is fully convertible for commercial transaction purposes.

There are no restrictions on transferring funds associated with investments. CBJ Regulations permit non-residents and foreign investors who transferred funds into Jordan to remit their funds abroad in the same or in any other transferable currency.

To transfer funds outside Jordan, a local bank must obtain a permit from the CBJ. Furthermore, before an investment is made, the CBJ must be informed when an investor transfers funds into Jordan, opens a non-resident account at a local bank or seeks to transfer foreign currency funds outside Jordan. CBJ's approval for these transactions is generally granted liberally.

Prior to investing in Jordan, non-residents may obtain explicit regulations governing their specific needs from the CBJ. There are no limitations on the inflow or outflow of funds for remittance of profits, capital gains and royalties regarding intellectual property, as long as a prior authorization from the CBJ has been obtained.

The CBJ is in favor of liberalizing the country's check clearing and current account system. An initiative to automate and modernize the system is currently underway, and will likely be instituted in the near future.

## Banking

The CBJ is the monetary authority of the country. Other financial institutions include approximately 15 foreign and Jordanian commercial banks and specialized credit institutions, such as the Industrial Development Bank. The specialized credit institutions offer equity capital. Banks, both foreign and Jordanian, may be established in a free zone; must deal exclusively in foreign currency and must operate independently of other banking activities in the country.

## Intellectual Property

### General

The Kingdom of Jordan is a signatory to the Paris Convention for the Protection of Industrial Property and a member of the World Intellectual Property Organization.

### Patents

Although Jordan is a member of the Paris Convention for the Protection of Intellectual Property, the international classification of patents is not observed in Jordan. Applications for the grant of a patent are filed with the Patent Office, which examines the applications for compliance with formalities and patentability under the Jordanian Patents and Design Law and may require amendments to applications to achieve conformity.

Appeals by applicants against the requirements of the Patent Office as decided by the Registrar of Patents are made by petition to the High Court of Justice within 30 days of the Registrar of Patents' decision.

Approved applications are published in the Official Gazette. The period during which any interested party may file an opposition is two months from the date of publication. If no opposition has been filed or if the Registrar or court rejects the filed oppositions, a decision granting the patent is issued.

Patents are valid for a period of 16 years from the date of filing the application, provided that registration fees are paid along with the decision to grant the patent and that renewal fees are paid every four years during the patent term.

Patent rights are freely transferable; however, notice of the transfer must be published in the Official Gazette and properly registered with the Patent Office so that they may become valid *vis-à-vis* third parties.

Under the Patents and Design Law, patents are not granted for chemical products relating to medical drugs, pharmaceutical compositions and food. The methods and processes used in the preparations of such products, however, may be the subject of a patent.

The Patents and Design Law requires that the owner of a patent use the patented product or process in Jordan within three years of the date the patent was granted; if this requirement is not satisfied, the law provides for compulsory licensing of the patent.

The Patents and Design Law provides penalties for infringement of patents.

## Trademarks

In August 1999, Jordan's Lower House of Parliament approved a draft to amend its Trademark Law, in an effort to facilitate its accession to the World Trade Organization. In some aspects, Jordanian legislators went beyond the minimum obligations set forth by the Trade Related Aspects for the Protection of Intellectual Property Rights and the Madrid Convention to provide further protection for trademark owners.[2]

The new law protects registered trademarks for a ten-year period, even though TRIPS only stipulates a minimum of seven years. The draft also widened the range of marks that can be protected by the law to include "famous" marks and "group" marks. "Famous" marks are trademarks that become known in the Kingdom through advertising and publicity, even if they are not yet marketable. "Group" marks are used to identify groups regardless of the nature of their work, even if they are not used for commercial purposes.

The new draft annulled the link between the trademark and the trade outlet, so the owner can waive a right to the trademark or rent it without relinquishing the right to the outlet. The draft also increased the period before the owner loses his right to the trademark if it is not used from two to three years.

The international classification of goods regarding trademarks is observed in Jordan, although the Trademarks Law does not adopt the classification for service marks that are recognized worldwide. Applications for registration of a trademark are filed with the Registrar of Trademarks. The Registrar conducts an examination of the application, and, if accepted, the trademark application is published in the Official Gazette. Any interested party may file an opposition within three months of publication.

Oppositions that are not settled by the Registrar or appeals based on the Registrar's decision are brought to the High Court of Justice. If no opposition has been filed or if the Registrar or court rejects the filed oppositions, a decision regarding the trademark is granted and the appropriate certificate is issued.

Based on recent amendments, trademark registration is now valid for a period of ten years beginning on the date the application was filed and is renewable for additional periods of 14 years each.

---

[2]      Dina Hamdan, "Legal experts, officials praise amendments to intellectual property legislation," *Jordan Times*, (September 29, 1999).

Trademarks are freely transferable, but in order for them to be valid *vis a vis* third parties, notice of the transfer must be published in the Official Gazette and properly registered with the Registrar of Trademarks.

The Trademarks Law requires actual use of the trademarks registered. Trademarks of which there was no *bona fide* use or which have not been actually used for a period of three years immediately prior to the submission of an application for cancellation may be annulled.

Unauthorized use or imitation of a trademark registered in Jordan is punishable by law.

## Copyright

In 1992, the Copyright Protection Law No. 22 was enacted. The Copyright Law grants copyright protection to original works of literature, art and science of any type, purpose or importance. It covers works of art as may be expressed in writing, sound, drawing, photography and motion pictures, including books, speeches, plays, musical compositions, films, applied art, three-dimensional works and computer software.

A copyright is filed at the Ministry of Culture. The work protected must be original and involve personal innovation and arrangement. The protection period, for both Jordanians and foreigners, is 30 years after the death of the author. The Ministry of Culture may publish or republish a work subject to copyright protection if the author or the author's heirs have not published or republished the work within six months of the date the Ministry has given notice that the work is to be so published or republished. In the event of publication or republication by the Ministry of Culture, the author or author's heirs are entitled to fair remuneration.

The Copyright Law provides penalties for infringement. Enforcement of the Copyright Law is in the jurisdiction of the civil courts; however, the implementing regulations relating to the law have not yet been promulgated.

In late 1998, an updated Copyright Law was passed, and Jordan acceded to the Berne Convention in April 1999. However, enforcement mechanisms have yet to be established. Jordan is currently on the United States Trade Representative's Special 301 watch list for inadequate intellectual property protection. In negotiations with the US Government, Jordan has agreed to a plan that calls for significant improvement in intellectual property protection over the next several years.

There remains, however, strong resistance to rapid implementation of a modern intellectual property regime in Jordan. Much of this resistance stems from the influential pharmaceutical industry, which profits from unlicensed copying of patented drugs. The majority of videos and software sold in the Jordanian market are also pirated. Jordan's accession to the World Trade Organization will eventually require that the government of Jordan establish a TRIPS-comparable intellectual property regime.

## Taxation

The Jordanian tax law is the Income Tax Law No. 57 of 1985. Several amendments have been issued since then by the tax authorities. The latest amendment adopted is Amending Law No. 14 of 1995, and new tax adjustments contained therein came into effect in 1996.

Taxpayers may determine their own fiscal year. Tax returns are to be filed with the Tax Department within four months after the end of the fiscal year. Taxpayers who pay their tax liability within the first month following the close of their fiscal year are entitled to a 6 percent discount on their taxes due. Similarly, a 4 percent discount and 2 percent discount are available to taxpayers who pay their taxes during the second or third month, respectively, after the close of their fiscal year. In case of late filing of a tax return, a fine of 2 percent per month, but not exceeding 24 percent overall, will be imposed. A fine of 1.5 percent per month is imposed on taxpayers who fail to pay their taxes.

## Income Taxes

The primary types of income taxes levied are corporate income tax, individual income tax, withholding tax and distribution tax. The Income Tax Law of 1985 was recently amended to include provisions of particular benefit for investors. This amendment, which came into effect in 1996, allows higher allowances for individual taxpayers and lower tax rates for individuals.

## Taxation of Companies and Businesses

All companies, local and foreign, operating in Jordan are subject to corporate income tax at the following rates:

| Type | Rate |
|---|---|
| Mining, industry, hotels, hospitals, transportation, contracting and other sectors approved by the Council of Ministers | 15% |
| Banks, financial and finance companies, exchange companies and brokerage companies (in case of banks, financial and insurance companies, the tax payable each year should not be less than 25% of their net income before any distributions are made) | 35% |
| All other companies | 25% |

## Taxation of Individuals

Salaries, wages and other income paid to Jordanian and foreign employees are taxable. The Income Tax Law gives a 50 percent exemption from tax on private sector employees' annual salaries up to JD 12,000 and a 25 percent exemption on amounts above JD 12,000. Foreign employees working for non-Jordanian companies are exempt from paying all income tax. In addition, there are personal and family exemptions given by the Income Tax Law. In the public sector, 50 percent of the salaries and wages of employees are tax exempt.

The taxable income of an individual, not exempted as stated above, is subject to the following tax rates:

| Annual Taxable Income | Rate |
|---|---|
| First JD 2,000 | 5% |
| Next JD 2,000 | 10% |
| Next JD 4,000 | 15% |
| Next JD 4,000 | 25% |
| Next JD 4,000 | 30% |

## Withholding Tax

Ten percent of any payment made by a Jordanian resident to a non-resident should be withheld as payment on account of the tax due and should be forwarded by the Jordanian resident payer to the tax authorities within thirty days from the date it was withheld.

Every employer who pays salaries, wages, allowances or bonuses to employees must deduct from such payments the tax due and forward it to the tax authorities on a monthly basis.

## Distribution Tax

This tax is levied on the distribution of company profits (i.e., dividends) and amounts to 10 percent of the dividends paid out. This tax must be deducted and forwarded by the entity distributing the dividends to the Tax Department within 30 days from the date of such distribution. For purposes of this tax, profits transferred abroad by a foreign company operating in Jordan shall be considered as distributed profits.

## Taxable Income

According to law, income arising or deemed to be arising in Jordan shall be subject to tax. In order to determine a taxpayer's taxable income, all expenses wholly and exclusively made or incurred in the production of income during the year shall be deducted.

Company expenditures on training, marketing, research and development are tax exempt. Profits from the export of goods and services are totally exempted, with the exception of exports of phosphate, potash, fertilizers and other exports that are governed by trade protocols.

## Deductions

The following items are not deductible under Jordanian tax law:

- Revenues and provisions;
- Capital losses (for non-depreciable assets);
- Capital expenditures;
- Head Office expenses for foreign branches in excess of 5 percent of the taxable income of the branch in Jordan;
- Losses or expenses recoverable under an insurance policy or a compensation contract;
- Amounts paid as income tax and social services tax;
- Depreciation expenses in excess of the permissible rates.

## Loss Carry Forward

Losses realized in a particular tax year may be carried forward in order to be deducted from taxable income during the next six consecutive tax years. Losses may be not carried backward and applied to a previous tax year's taxable income.

## Depreciation on Fixed Assets

Fixed assets can be depreciated following an accelerated depreciation method.

## Other Tax Exemptions

According to the Investment Law of 1995, projects approved under that law and established in the Hashemite Kingdom of Jordan are entitled to tax exemptions. The new law offers incentives to investors in the form of tax exemptions that are weighted in favor of less developed areas. Projects in Zone A receive a 25 percent deduction; projects in Zone B receive a 50 percent deduction; and projects in Zone C receive a 75 percent deduction in accordance with the following stipulations:

- For hotels to benefit from the incentives granted by this law, they must be classified as more than three stars in Zone A;
- The shores of the Dead Sea, within a five kilometers depth from the coastline, are classified as Zone A for hotel projects;
- All areas of Jordan are classified as Zone C for the sectors of agriculture, animal resources and maritime transport and railways.

## Other Taxes

### Social Service Tax
A social service tax is due from each individual and equals 10 percent of the taxpayer's income.

### Universities Tax
This tax is payable by shareholding and foreign companies at a rate of 1 percent of net income before taxes and distributions.

## Sales Tax

The taxpayers as defined by the Sales Tax Law are the manufacturers, merchants or service providers whose sales amount to JD 100,000 per annum and importers of any goods or services irrespective of the volume of their imports. The sales tax rate ranges from 0 percent up to 20 percent of the value of goods, and for services, the sales tax is fixed at a rate of 10 percent.

This tax is payable when the sale is completed or the service is rendered. In the case of imported goods, the sales tax is payable at the customs clearance stage, prior to the release of such goods.

## Treaties for the Prevention of Double Taxation

Jordan has signed agreements for the prevention of double taxation with Austria, Bahrain, Belgium, Canada, Cyprus, Denmark, Egypt, France, Iraq, Kuwait, Libya, Malaysia, Oman, Pakistan, Qatar, Romania, Saudi Arabia, Spain, Syria, Tunisia, Turkey, the United Arab Emirates, United Kingdom, the United States and Yemen.

## Investment and Trade Issues

### Encouragement of Investment Law

The Investment Promotion Law No. 16 of 1995 repealed the Encouragement of Investment Law No. 11 of 1987 and Law No. 27 of 1992 Regulating Arab & Foreign Investments. The new law opens the financial markets to all investors and provides for the equal treatment of investors regardless of nationality.

The new law abolishes the distinction between *economic* and *approved economic* projects. Therefore, projects in the following sectors enjoy the special exemptions specified under the law: (1) Industry; (2) Agriculture; (3) Hotels; (4) Hospitals; (5) Maritime Transport and Railways; (6) Leisure and Recreation Compounds; (7) Convention and Exhibition Centers; and (8) any other sectors or its branches that the Council of Ministers decides to add based on the recommendation of the Higher Council for Encouragement of Investment. These sectors are also subject to a revised tax rate of 15 percent under the latest amendments to the Income Tax Law.

In addition, exemptions from taxes and fees extend to all imported fixed assets, imported fixed assets of the expansion of productive capacity over 25 percent, and imported spare parts.

Exemptions from income and social service taxes for a ten-year period starting from the date of production is granted in ranging amounts according to the level of development of particular locales.

The Committee for Encouragement of Investment considers investors' applications from other sectors for inclusion under the Encouragement of Investment Law and makes the appropriate decisions within 30 days from receiving such applications. A rejected application that is returned must include the reasons for the rejection. A new government office is to be established to encourage investment and to speed procedures for registering and licensing new investments. The law also contains a commitment that all investment proposals will receive a response from the Higher Council for the Encouragement of Investment, a body made up of ministers and business representatives, within 30 days of application.

The new law also allows direct entry into the Jordan stock market in order to help attract foreign capital. Furthermore, the law permits foreign investors to buy shares directly, provided that the total foreign ownership in the publicly traded company does not exceed 50 percent at the end of the close of trade on the official market.

## Restrictions on Foreign Investment

Special rules were issued specifying the sectors in which foreign investors are allowed to invest and the proportion of ownership foreign investors may maintain in addition to the minimum capital requirement for foreign investors. Until recently, such minimum capital requirements were set at a minimum of JD 100,000 with the exception of investments in the stock market, where such minimum was set at JD 1,000. On February 22, 1997 the Council of Ministers resolved to remove the minimum investment requirement of JD 100,000. Pursuant to said resolution, Jordanian and non-Jordanian investors are now afforded equal treatment with regard to their investment in Jordanian companies.

## Encouragement of Foreign Investment

The Encouragement of Foreign Investment Regulation of 1995 allows wider foreign ownership and direct entry of foreign nationals and companies into the Jordan stock market. This regulation is intended to enhance the opportunity for substantial foreign investment and, in conjunction with a reduced tax structure, to enhance returns on stock. The Regulation is intended to boost confidence in Jordan as an attractive emerging market and to help attract foreign capital.

The Regulation eliminates the cumbersome requirements requiring prior approvals by the Cabinet and the purchasing of permits through licensed brokers as well as the set limitations on ownership. It also provides tax exemptions for investment in less developed regions in Jordan.

The Regulations for the Promotion of Foreign Investment Law No. 39 of 1997 eliminated the 50 percent ceiling on foreign equity ownership in the Amman Financial Market, transportation, insurance, banking, telecommunications and agricultural sectors. The 50 percent ownership ceiling remains in the construction, trading, trade services and mining sectors. These Regulations also reduced the minimum amount of foreign investment from JD 100,000 to JD 50,000.

During 1997 and 1998, roughly one-third of foreign investment projects benefited from the investment promotion law, compared with one-fifth of projects in 1996.

## Investment Tax Incentives

Exemptions from income tax and customs duties for projects are provided for under the Encouragement of Investment Law. All fixed assets for the project are exempt from customs duties and taxes. Fixed assets include the equipment, machinery apparatus and tools needed for the project. For hotels and hospitals, the definition includes furniture and other material specific to these industries. Imported spare parts for the project will be exempt from customs duties and taxes provided the value of these parts does not exceed 15 percent of the value of their related fixed assets.

Net profits of the projects are exempt from income tax for up to ten years starting from the commencement of commercial production or providing services in accordance with the rates set forth, in the Other Tax Exemptions section above.

Furthermore, additional incentives are granted if the project undergoes expansion, development or modernization resulting in an increase of its productive capacity. Hotels and hospitals may enjoy exemption from customs duties and taxes every seven years for the purchase of new furniture and other materials specific to these industries.

## Dispute Settlement

According to Law No. 16, foreign investors have the rights to seek third party arbitration or an internationally recognized dispute settlement mechanism. The Government recognizes decisions reached by the International Center for the Settlement of Disputes. Jordan's legal system permits the implementation of internationally acknowledged dispute settlement measures.

## Free Trade Zones

In order to encourage export-oriented industry, Jordan has set up a number of Free Zones. The first Free Zone was established at the Aqaba port along the Red Sea. Other free trade zones are located at Zarqa, the Sahab industrial estate and Irbid.

Free Zones come under the supervision of an autonomous body, the Free Zone Corporation and are governed by the Free Zone Corporation Law No. 32 of 1984.

Projects must meet the following criteria in order to qualify for licenses to operate within a free zone area: (1) applying new technology and introducing new industries to the country; (2) using local raw materials or components; (3) raising the level of domestic labor skills; and (4) reducing Jordan's imports. Applications for a Free Zone license are filed with the Free Zone Corporation.

Projects granted a license in a Free Zone enjoy the following privileges: (1) exemption of profits from income tax for a period of twelve years; (2) exemption of non-Jordanian employees from income tax on their remuneration and from the social service tax; (3) exemption for goods imported into or exported from Free Zones from customs duties, import fees and any other fees and taxes; (4) exemption of lands, buildings and properties in free zones from licensing fees and taxes; and (5) freedom to repatriate capital investment and profits earned, subject to prevailing laws and regulation.

Furthermore, importers using the Free Zones to supply the local market avoid import license fees amounting to 5 percent of cargo value, until the goods are actually cleared for release from the Zone.

## Qualifying Industrial Zone

Pursuant to the United States—Israel Free Trade Area Implementation Act of 1995, the governments of Israel and Jordan agreed to the creation of the Irbid Qualifying Industrial Zone (QIZ). This zone is located in the Irbid duty-free zone in Jordan in conjunction with the Israeli side of the border-crossing at the Sheikh Hussein—Nahar Hayarden Bridge. On March 13, 1998, the Office of the United States' Trade Representative designated the first Jordan-Israel "qualified industrial zone" at the Al-Hassan Industrial Park in Irbid, Jordan. According to this special status, goods from the zone that are produced through Jordanian-Israeli commercial cooperation, and which meet certain minimal criteria, are eligible for duty-free entry into the United States. This initiative has already significantly increased Jordanian-Israeli dialogue on commercial issues and has generated notable private sector interest from both countries. More than $140 million worth of new projects have been set up at the Irbid QIZ in 1999. These new investments will bring to $350 million the aggregate value of projects in the zone, whereby most of these factories produce textiles and apparel. In 1998, the United States imported from the QIZ goods valued at approximately $17 million.[3]

The Governments of Israel and Jordan agreed to establish a joint committee with the responsibility of identifying those businesses located within the Irbid Qualifying Zone that involve substantial economic cooperation between the two countries.[4] The parties involved have indicated that they regard this agreement as an important step toward cementing industrial

---

[3]    *Palestine Economic Pulse*, v. IV, no. 2, 1999, p. 10.
[4]    According to the US-imposed conditions, a minimum of 35 percent of the content of goods produced in the Irbid Park must come from Jordan and Israel or the Palestinian Territories. Israel and Jordan agreed that each country must contribute at least 11 percent of this content requirement.

cooperation between Israel and Jordan.[5] This American initiative demonstrates that the future of regional economic cooperation will be determined not just by increases in bilateral trade, but more significantly, by cooperation between entrepreneurs and industries in joint manufacturing and the export of their products to third markets.

Based on the initial success of the Irbid QIZ, the United States announced in March 1999 the creation of a new Israel-Jordanian QIZ, to be located on the Israeli-Jordanian border south of the Beit She'an Valley. Plans for the creation of the new QIZ are moving forward under the direction of the Jordan Gateway Project Corporation, which has reported that a number of Israeli and Jordanian companies have already expressed an interest in joint QIZ ventures.

## Customs

Taxes on imports are the chief source of domestic revenue. All imported goods are subject to custom duty, except those specifically exempted. Rates of duty vary according to the importance of the item to the national economy. Essential commodities and various raw materials attract relatively low rates of duty, while luxury goods attract high rates. As part of its efforts to accede to the World Trade Organization by the beginning of 2000, Jordan has accelerated economic reforms and continued to slash duties on imports. Nevertheless, this bold liberalization program threatens local business monopolies that prospered from the state protection they received during King Hussein's reign.

## Customs Procedures

Customs procedures in Jordan have historically been a major impediment to free trade. Overlapping areas of authority and excessive signature clearances on paperwork of shipments remain unchanged. Actual commodity appraisal and tariff assessment practices often differ from the written regulations. Discretionary decisions are sometimes made about certain cases that are subject to conflicting instructions and regulations.

---

[5] *Agreement between the Government of Israel and the Hashemite Kingdom of Jordan on the Qualified Industrial Zone,* (Doha, November 13, 1997).

It is anticipated that Jordanian customs legislation will be amended in the near future. The amendments provide the Customs Department with more powers regarding violations and confiscation and delegates part of the Minister of Finance's powers to the Director General of the Customs Department.

Under the prevailing Import Tariff Schedules, valid since 1989, a high tariff rate is imposed on luxury goods and on major categories of consumer goods. On automobiles, the tariff rate ranges from 110 percent to 310 percent. To stimulate export production, import tariffs are low on many raw materials, machinery and semi-finished goods. To secure tariff exemptions, businesses must document that the raw materials to be imported will be used in export production, maintaining at least 40 percent Jordanian value-added content.

The Director General of Customs may grant temporary admission status to certain goods, such as heavy machinery and equipment used to implement Government projects, or important projects that have obtained Government approval. Foreign construction companies operating alone or with a Jordanian partner can apply for this temporary admission status.

## Labor Law

The new Labor Law No. 8 of 1996 governs Labor affairs in Jordan. The provisions of the law apply to all employees and employers as defined by Article 2 of the Law.

Maximum working hours are 48 during a six-day week. The seventh day is a paid weekly holiday. Additional hours will be considered as overtime and qualify for compensation of 25 percent over the regular wage. Except in the event of an emergency, an increase in daily work hours is subject to approval by the Minister of Labor.

Employees are entitled to an annual 14-day, fully paid sick leave that may be extended by an additional 14 days if the employee was hospitalized. The Law makes provisions for compensation regarding on-the-job injuries. A worker is also entitled to a one-time 14-day leave to make the pilgrimage to the Islamic holy shrines in Mecca, provided he has worked for the same company for at least five years.

Female employees are allowed ten weeks maternity leave with pay. Employers who employ 20 or more women must provide daycare for all children under four years of age.

The minimum age for child employment under controlled conditions has been raised to 16 years. The new Law places restrictions on the types of jobs minors may hold, as well as on the number of hours they are allowed to work.

The new Law regulates labor unions and employer alliances. Workers are free to join unions without objection from their employers. Strikes and close-downs are also regulated by the new Law. Approximately 30 percent of the total labor force, including government service, is unionized. Labor unions exist in some large industrial firms, in the banking sector, and among engineers, physicians, pharmacists and lawyers.

The current labor Law allows employers to terminate the services of employees if they are forced to undergo reorganization. Article 31 of the Law gives employers the right to reduce the wages of workers or dismiss them for any reason. The Law does not obligate employers to include end-of-service retirements in their employment packages. If the employer has, however, agreed to the end-of-service retirement either through a contractual basis or personnel agreement, this right cannot be dismissed.

A serious shortcoming of the Jordanian Labor Law is Article 20, which grants employees the right to own the intellectual property right of works developed on the job. If their position requires that they research and develop for their employers, the Article provides the employee with a right to 50 percent ownership of the developed work. This provision contravenes all major international laws and discourages investments in industries such as software development, audio and video recording, and pharmaceutical development.

## Environmental Law

Jordan is a signatory to several environmental treaties, among which are the following:

The 1973 Washington Convention on International Trade in Endangered Species of Wild Fauna and Flora. The objective of this convention is to protect certain endangered species from over exploitation via a system of import/export permits. Jordan became a signatory on November 4, 1980.

The 1973 International Convention for the Prevention of Pollution from Ships. The objectives of this convention is to preserve the marine environment by achieving the complete elimination of intentional pollution by oil and other harmful substances and the minimization of accidental discharge of such substances. Jordan became a signatory on March 17, 1975.

The 1951 International Plant Protection Convention. The objective is to maintain and increase cooperation in controlling pests and diseases of plants and plant products, and in preventing their introduction and spread across national boundaries. Jordan became a signatory on April 24, 1970.

The 1972 Convention on the Prohibition of the Development, Production, and Stockpiling of Bacteriological (Biological) and Toxic Weapons, and on Their Destruction. The objective of this convention is to eliminate and to prohibit the development of biological weapons, as a step towards general disarmament for the sake of all mankind. Jordan became a signatory on June 27, 1975.

# KUWAIT

## Recent Political Developments

On May 4 1999, the Emir of Kuwait, Sheikh Jaber al-Ahmad al-Sabah, decided to adjourn his nation's Council (Parliament). While the motives behind his decision were disputed, the event marked the first time that Kuwait's Parliament has been dissolved constitutionally. In general, the people's reaction to this measure was supportive, on the grounds that popular political participation would resume in the summer. Other voices, however, mainly from opposition circles, expressed their concern that this development would be used as a "sword in the neck of the next Council."

| | |
|---|---|
| Population | 2.34 million (1998) |
| Religions | 85% Muslim (Shi'ite 30%, Sunni 45%, Other 10%) Christian, Hindu, Parsi and other 15% . |
| Government | Constitutional Monarchy |
| Languages | Arabic (English is widely spoken) |
| Work Week | Public Sector: Saturday–Thursday 8:30–12:30 Banking: Sunday–Thursday 8:30–12:30 |
| Monetary Unit | Kuwaiti Dinar (KD) |
| Exchange Rate | KD 0.3063=US$ 1 |

Two months after Kuwait's Parliament was adjourned, opposition candidates captured two-thirds of the 50 parliamentary seats in July's 1999 elections, with Sunni Islamist parties recording the most impressive gains. Pro-government parliamentarians now number 16, while Shi'ite Muslims, including two leading anti-corruption Islamists, increased their representation from 5 to 6 seats. The composition of the new cabinet makes it doubtful that legislation approved by the Council of Ministers in Parliament's absence will be ratified.

The virtually unchanged makeup of Kuwait's cabinet has sparked domestic controversy. The retention of key cabinet posts, including that of Prime

Minister by Crown Prince Sheikh Saad al-Abdullah al-Sabah, occurred despite calls from opposition candidates and separate senior political postings from the royal family.

On the domestic front, the issue of women rights is high on the public agenda. Early in 2000, women protested Parliament's November 1999 vote against a bill that would give women the right to vote and run for office in the next elections in 2003. But the mostly Islamist and traditional tribal and all-male body shot the law down by two votes. This was in spite of Emir Sheikh Jabar al-Ahmad a-Sabah's decree in May 1999 after dissolving the parliament that gave women full political rights. It was a decree that received support from Kuwait's western allies and other Arab countries where women have suffrage rights.

At the international level, Iraq continues to pose a threat to Kuwait almost a decade after the invasion. Following a December 1998 US and British attack on Iraq launched from Kuwait, Baghdad verbally berated Kuwait and even questioned the validity of the Kuwaiti border although it officially recognized it in 1994.

The sheikdom is, however, mending relations with Jordan, following the severing of ties due to the latter's support for Iraq following the invasion.


## Recent Economic Developments

The Kuwaiti economy is driven by oil production and related industries. Kuwait holds 10 percent of the world oil reserves, some 96 billion barrels. Oil accounts for more than 90 percent of total exports and the bulk of state revenue. Its oil sector has essentially recovered to pre-Iraqi invasion levels.

Besides oil, the government has substantial overseas investments estimated at between $60-90 billion.

The country's population is just over 2.3 million. Only 700,000 are citizens.

To date, Kuwait has been relatively slow in implementing economic reform and privatization programs. This is in part because many of the decisions will cut into the welfare system and will be unpopular with the public. Thus to offset losses, the government has chosen to use money from the Reserve Fund for Future Generations (estimated $45 billion).

The government has taken some important steps, including creation of a new investment law designed to attract foreign investment by allowing foreign majority ownership of businesses. The law was passed by Amiri decree in June 1999 and is in effect. It can, however, be invalidated by a majority vote of the National Assembly. But the country may have to do more if it wants to overcome other negative aspects affecting foreign investment such as its small market size, poor geographical position and high labor costs to draw investors.

The government approved a $13.912 billion budget for 1999-2000, projecting a $6.645 billion deficit. Expenditures have been cut by 2 percent from the previous year. Oil income is calculated at $10 a barrel, reflecting the collapsed 1998 prices. Prices in the second half of 1999, however, have gone as high as $26 up from less than $10 in December 1998. This is the highest oil prices have risen since the Gulf war.

But the situation was different in 1998 when collapsed oil prices dragged the Kuwaiti economy down 16.3 percent from $30 billion in 1997 to $25.314 billion in 1998. It further helped shrink oil and gas contribution to GDP from 45 percent to 34 percent in that same period. Per capita income declined 18.2 percent from $15,272 in 1997 to $12,151 in 1998.

The lost revenue forced the government to suspended all new projects last year. The Ministry of Electricity & Water's budget was cut by 8 percent, which forced the suspension of plans to build a new power and desalination plant at Al-Zour.

A bright spot in 1998 was the 2.9 percent growth in the non-oil sector, although that was significantly less than the 10 percent growth in 1997. The main driver of this expansion was a return of expatriate workers to pre-invasion levels. Many of the expatriates are non-Arab single males who tend to send most of their earnings home. They have replaced many of the Palestinians who lived in Kuwait with their families before the war.

This labor and demographic change has had significant impact on consumer-oriented businesses that comprise much of Kuwait's non-oil economy since the demand from this portion of the population, more than 60 percent, is now for less expensive items.

This has put the government in a Catch-22 situation. On the one hand, the government is considering to change this by allowing more expatriates to bring their families to Kuwait. Yet on the other hand, the government wants to reduce the country's reliance on expatriates though a policy of "Kuwait-ization". There is public and political pressure on all firms and government ministries to reduce their dependency on non-Kuwaitis. Nearly 50 percent of Kuwaiti nationals are under 15. As this population ages, the need for job creation will increase.

The government's two biggest expenses are its defense spending and public wages. At the end of 1998, the government announced ways to reduce the deficit such as cutting fuel subsidies, taxing consumer goods, gradually eliminating electricity and water subsidies, imposing housing, labor and airport taxes and introducing individual contributions to the social security budget. But because of fear of public reaction, the government has yet to implement any of them.

Changes may occur however with the forming of a new National Assembly and Cabinet in July 1999. Particularly important to the government's objectives will be the National Assembly's approval of proposed Foreign Investment and Intellectual Property Rights laws.

This new law permits for the first time majority foreign ownership of Kuwait-based firms. The law still prohibits foreign investment in the upstream petroleum sector, but does allow investment in joint venture petrochemical projects. The law also permits foreigners to own up to 40 percent of banks and to invest in stocks directly through the Kuwait stock exchange. Property ownership is restricted to other GCC-member states.

In 1993, the government adopted the Difficult Debts Law that should provide sufficient debt relief and a mechanism by which large Kuwaiti investors can recover losses incurred during the Iraqi invasion of Kuwait in 1991 and some losses dating to the 1982 Souk Al-Manakh Stock Exchange crisis. That crash occurred when cumulative trading losses reached US$ 100 billion, US$ 20 billion of which was attributed to approximately 3,000 well-connected Kuwait merchants. In the last decade, the Kuwaiti National Assembly passed bills aimed at forcing debtors to repay, but this legislation has proven ineffective.

## Major Economic Domains

### Oil
The Kuwaiti oil sector is government-owned. Crude oil production is currently under 1.9 million barrels per day (bpd) with a capacity estimated at

## Economic Indicators
### (In billions of Kuwaiti Dinars, unless otherwise indicated)

| | 1999e | 1998 | 1997 |
|---|---|---|---|
| GDP (KD billion by current prices) | | 7.7 | 9.2 |
| GDP Per Capita (US$) | 11,584 | 12,151 | 15,272 |
| GNP (KD billion by current prices) | | 9.5 | 11.1 |
| Inflation | 0.9 | 0.15 | 0.66 |
| Government Spending as % of GDP | 51.8 | 56.9 | 43.4 |
| Unemployment (%) | 0.7 | 1 | 1.3 |
| External Debt (US$ millions) | 137.7 | 244.7 | 425.3 |
| Exports (KD billions) | | 2.9 | 4.3 |
| Oil Exports (KD billions) | | 2.6 | 4.1 |
| Imports (KD billions) | | 2.2 | 2.4 |
| Domestic Debt (KD millions) | | 4.3 | 4.6 |
| Deficit (KD billions) | 2.1 | 1.2 | 0.7 |
| Oil Production | | 2.077 | 2.089 |

2.4 million bpd. Kuwait's refining capacity is currently 895,000 bpd, almost 100,000 bpd above the pre-invasion level. Production is limited to 1.84 million bpd by an OPEC arrangement designed to lift deflated oil prices. The country, however, plans to expand production capacity to three million bpd by 2000 and 3.5 million by 2005.

Kuwait is looking to expand into petrochemicals. There is a $2 billion petrochemical complex in the Shuaiba Industrial Area.

### Non-Oil
It is unclear if the strong growth of 1996 and 1997 can continue without economic reforms. Privatization may promote long-term growth in telecommunications, housing, power generation and health care. So far the government has resisted privatization out of fear of increasing unemployment among Kuwaitis and causing prices to rise if they discontinue subsidizing public utilities.

Kuwait's non-oil economy has been flat since a reconstruction boom which followed the country's liberation after the Gulf War. The poor economic performance can be traced, in part, to the country's changing demographics following the Gulf War. Even now, Kuwait's population is less than 80 percent of the pre-war population.

In general, Kuwait's government presently dominates the local economy. With increased pressure from the business community and the public, however, that role will decline and the country should move towards privatization and rationalization of the economy. Kuwait's economic system, modeled on a welfare state, provides for a large measure of government regulation. These regulations restrict participation and competition in a number of sectors of the economy and strictly control the roles of foreign capital and expatriate labor.

The Kuwaiti government owns interests in many of the private companies in the country including most of the nation's banks. In some cases, the government bought these shares to ameliorate the Souk Al-Manakh stock market collapse in 1982. In other cases, the government ownership was used to provide capital for local industries.

The era of government ownership seems to be coming to an end, however. As a part of ongoing privatization efforts, the Kuwaiti government has begun to relinquish its interest in these companies, generally by offering its shares for sale on the Kuwaiti Stock Exchange. Private foreign investors may participate in this privatization process by purchasing up to 40 percent ownership of Kuwait's national industries, subject to prior Kuwaiti government approval.

Finally, the Kuwaiti government is, by far, the largest employer of Kuwaiti nationals, 93.4 percent of whom work for the government or a government-owned company. Through efforts to "Kuwaitize" its work force, the government of Kuwait, in effect, has guaranteed employment to all Kuwaiti nationals. While this has had a social benefit, at least superficially, it has resulted in many government ministries being over-staffed and under-productive. It has also made it difficult for private companies to recruit Kuwaitis for meaningful, but rigorous, jobs.

### Balance of Payments
Kuwait's balance of payments situation is healthy, with exports exceeding imports by a comfortable margin. Since crude oil and refined petroleum products comprise more than 90 percent of the value of exports, the country's balance of payments is highly susceptible to changes in oil prices. The Kuwaiti government generally takes a conservative pricing position for oil revenue in its budget projections.

In 1998, the country had a $1.97 billion trade surplus and a current account surplus of $2.59 billion. These accounts are expected to remain in surpluses as long as oil prices remain strong.

## Business Environment

### Stock Exchange

At the end of November 1999, the Kuwaiti bourse dropped to a record low of 1,388.6 points. During the first week of December, the stock exchange was at 1,409.3, 16 percent below the year's high and about 51 percent under the all time high set in November 1977.

The Kuwait Stock Exchange (KSE) was reopened after the Iraqi invasion. Presently, the KSE lists stocks of 65 Kuwaiti companies, 10 companies from other Gulf states and Kuwaiti mutual funds. A new law now permits foreigners to own up to 40 percent of banks and to invest in stocks directly through the Kuwait Stock Exchange.

### Major Projects

A new pier at Mina al-Ahmadi refinery is to be built with private-sector involvement. The pier is expected to be up to two kilometers long with four to six berths. It will handle various products, including gas-oil, naphtha, kerosene, butane and propane and vessels of 60,000-300,000 dwt.

A KD 34 million headquarters is being built for the Kuwait Petroleum Corporation. The complex will cover 54,000 square meters and include a 17-story tower for the Oil Ministry, a car park, auditorium, library, prayer hall, training center, grand mosque and conference hall.

Denmark's Haldor Topsoe was awarded a contract last autumn to provide the technology for the planned gas-oil desulfurization (GOD) plant at Min al-Ahmadi refinery. The estimated $125 million project involves building a GOD unit with a capacity of 70,000 barrels a day. The unit will produce low-sulfur diesel oil, sulfur and aromatics and the feedstock will be gas-oil from crude distillate units.

### Build Operate Transfer

The Al-Sharq waterfront project is one of Kuwait City's main attractions. This project, which consists of shops, restaurants, a marina, a cinema and a fish market, was the third phase of a waterfront development project carried out on a BOT basis by the local National Real Estate Company.

The government is now starting with the fourth and fifth stages. The fourth stage has been awarded to a consortium led by Kuwait's only commercial Islamic bank, Kuwait Finance House. The project involves development of a 2.5 kilometer of coastline.

In the fifth stage, the United Real Estate Company is investing about KD 50 million over 24 years to the project, which includes building a commercial space, government offices, a mosque, parking and recreational facilities.

The $350 million Sulaibiya wastewater treatment plant will also be done on a BOT basis. The plant will have a capacity of at least 250,000 cubic meters a day and a reverse osmosis unit to produce non-potable water. The winning consortium will operate the plant for 30 years and power will be charged at 5 fils ($0.016) a kWh with a 3 percent compounded price increase.

## *Franchising*

Although the Kuwaiti market is relatively small, franchising offers profitable opportunities. The population of 2.3 million have high disposable income and a strong inclination to buy foreign and especially American goods. Additionally, labor saving services are in demand. At present, most franchises are in fast food, with McDonald's being a recent arrival.

A local sponsor is required to establish such operations. American firms dominate the fast food sector with the following franchises: Hardee's, Kentucky Fried Chicken, Burger King, Chicken Tikka, Wendy's, Pizza Hut, Subway and Baskin Robbins. Light competition in this sector comes from Pizza Italia and Wimpy. Opportunities exist for franchises in other areas such as: automotive service centers, beauty salons, testing centers, dry cleaning/laundry shops and photocopy stores.

The Kuwait franchise market is characterized as fiercely competitive. Japanese electronics and cars have a strong appeal to the Kuwaitis. Brands like National, Panasonic, Sanyo, Toshiba, N.E.C., Sharp, Toyota, Nissan, Datsun, Honda, and Subaru are examples of the heavy Japanese presence in the Kuwaiti market. Similarly, British and German products and services enjoy a strong positive image in Kuwait.

Another major type of franchise in Kuwait is the car dealership, with almost all known automobile makes represented in Kuwait: Ford, Chrysler, GM, GMC, Cherokee Jeep (US); Volvo (Sweden); Mercedes, BMW, and Audi (Germany); Jaguar and Rolls Royce (UK) as well as the Japanese dealers noted above.

Among clothes franchises, Kuwait has attracted the British firms Mother Care and British Home Store (BHS). The market is ready for foreign franchises in the clothing and lingerie areas.

## Leading Business Opportunities

| Rank | Sector |
|------|--------|
| 1 | Hospital Management Services |
| 2 | Medical Insurance Services |
| 3 | Safety & Security Equipment |
| 4 | Rubber Tires for Cars |
| 5 | Air Conditioning & Refrigeration Equipment |
| 6 | Computer & Peripherals |
| 7 | Automotive Parts & Service Equipment |
| 8 | Medical Equipment |
| 9 | Pharmaceuticals |
| 10 | Pollution Control Equipment |
| 11 | Advertising |
| 12 | Building Products |
| **Best Prospects for Agriculture** | |
| 1 | Corn Oil |
| 2 | Poultry Meat |
| 3 | Frozen/Chilled Beef |

# Legal Review

## Judiciary

### *Common Courts System*

Kuwait's legal code is a combination of original legislation, historical precedent and a civil code drafted by jurists from various Arab countries.

In 1960, Kuwait adopted a unified judicial system that covers all levels of courts.

## Summary Courts

In each administrative district of Kuwait there is a Summary Court, composed of one or more divisions, each presided over by one judge. The Summary Courts deal with civil and commercial cases and leases. The judgment of the Summary Court is final in cases in which the amount involved is less than KD 1,000. These courts also deal with misdemeanor criminal cases for which the maximum penalty is three years imprisonment.

## Courts of First Instance

Courts of First Instance deal with disputes relating to civil, commercial, labor, rent and personal status issues in which the amount involved exceeds KD 1,000. In addition, the Courts of First Instance hear felony criminal cases and appeals from the Summary Courts on misdemeanor cases.

## High Court of Appeals

The High Court of Appeals hears appeals on judgments from the Courts of First Instance. An independent department in the Court of Appeals is the Court of Cassation, which considers cases relating to civil, commercial, labor and personal status issues and certain criminal cases.

## Superior Constitutional Court

The Superior Constitutional Court is the highest level of the Kuwaiti judiciary. The Superior Constitutional Court interprets the constitution and deals with disputes related to the constitutionality of laws, statutes and by-laws. The judgment of the Constitutional Court is binding on all lower courts.

## Business Forms and Structures

### Companies Law

A new law permits for the first time majority foreign ownership of Kuwait-based firms. The new law still prohibits foreign investment in the upstream petroleum sector, but does allow investment in joint venture petrochemical projects. The law also permits foreigners to own up to 40 percent of banks and to invest in stocks directly through the Kuwait stock exchange. Property ownership is restricted to other GCC-member states.

The Commercial Companies Law No. 15 of 1960, as amended, and the Commercial Law No. 68 of 1980, which contains provisions of particular significance to foreigners, regulate the various types of business organizations that can be established in Kuwait.

The following types of organizations are available under Kuwait law: (1) Limited Liability Company; (2) Joint Stock Company; (3) General Partnership; (4) Limited Partnership; and (5) Joint Venture.

With the exception of the joint venture, all these forms of incorporation are endowed with independent legal personality.

Foreigners wishing to conduct business in Kuwait may find it easier to do so following changes to the Commercial Companies Law. This legislation, enacted in 1992 and amended, allows holding companies to be created to hold stock or shares in and to participate in establishing Kuwaiti or foreign limited liability companies. Holding companies are also entitled to grant loans or guarantees to such limited liability companies as well as to manage such companies, hold industrial and intellectual property rights, grant licenses thereto and own moveable and immovable property.

## Limited Liability Companies

The limited liability company is the form of incorporation which most resembles the private limited company of Western terminology. Such a company is simple to establish and to operate and, therefore, is popular with foreign investors. A limited liability company is formed by applying for a Memorandum of Association to be entered into the Commercial Register, a process which may last three months.

The limited liability company acquires legal personality only upon being registered in the Commercial Register. The original life-span of the limited liability company may be up to twenty-five years, but the members may decide to extend its life for an unlimited period. A minimum of two and a maximum of thirty members, of which one must be Kuwaiti, is required. If the members include a husband and wife, however, then a minimum of three members is required. Until recently, all the members were required to be individuals. Law No. 28 of 1995 which amended the Commercial Companies Law allows companies to participate in establishing a limited liability company. The limited liability company may not be used for insurance, finance and banking activities.

The capital is divided into shares of equal value with a minimum of KD 7,500. Shareholders have a right of first refusal over shares offered for sale by other shareholders.

The limited liability company is managed by one or more directors, named in the Memorandum or appointed by the general meeting of shareholders. The directors have full authority to obligate the limited liability company, unless the Memorandum provides otherwise or the shareholders vote to restrict this authority. Holding an office in a rival company or a company with similar objectives as well as entering into transactions which compete with or are similar to the company's business is prohibited unless authorized by the shareholders.

Directors are personally liable to the company, the shareholders and third parties for any mismanagement, breach of law or violation of the company's Memorandum. The directors report to the general meeting of shareholders.

A limited liability company with more than seven shareholders must have a Supervisory Board consisting of at least three members. The duties of the Supervisory Board are to review the company's balance sheet, the distribution of profits and the annual report. The Supervisory Board reports on these matters to the general meeting of shareholders.

The general meeting of shareholders is obliged to require reports from the Supervisory Board and the Supervisory Board must convene a general meeting of shareholders at least once a year. Members holding at least 25 percent of the capital may also convene general meetings. Most resolutions of the general meeting are decided by majority vote, unless the Memorandum provides otherwise. To amend the Memorandum as well as to decrease or increase the capital a special majority of the shareholders holding 75 percent of the shares of the company is required.

A limited liability company is required to have at least one auditor to be appointed by the general meeting of shareholders. The auditor is responsible for the accuracy of the financial reports submitted to the general meeting regarding the company's accounts. The balance sheet must be sent to the Ministry of Commerce where it is open to public inspection.

The dissolution of a limited liability company is obligatory upon any of the following: expiry of the company's term; completion of its stated objectives or purpose; declaration of insolvency; or a court order for winding up.

A shareholder of a limited liability company is liable for the obligations or debts of the company only to the extent of such shareholder's share in the company's capital. If the number of shareholders drops below the statutory minimum at any time, however, the remaining shareholders are liable to the full extent of their assets for the obligations of the company. If the minimum number of shareholders is not satisfied within one month of when the requirement failed to be met, the company shall be deemed dissolved as a rule of law.

## Joint Stock Companies

The joint stock company is the Kuwaiti corporate form which most resembles the public company in Western terms. All shares are negotiable, and shareholders are liable for the joint stock company's obligations only to the extent of the nominal value of their shares. A joint stock company may offer its shares to the public or remain a closed company. If the company deals in banking, insurance or finance activities, foreign ownership may not exceed 40 percent.

A joint stock company whose shares are offered to the public is formed by preparing and submitting a Memorandum and Articles of Association along with an application for a decree authorizing incorporation to the Ministry of Commerce and Industry. At least five founders must be registered. If the decree authorizing incorporation is granted, the company acquires legal personality as of the date of the decree, which must be published in the Official Gazette.

The founders must subscribe for at least 10 percent of the capital, which must be paid for before public subscription starts; a minimum of 20 percent of the capital must be paid for upon incorporation. Subscriptions are conducted through approved banking institutions.

Within thirty days of the completion of the public subscription, a general meeting of shareholders must be held to elect the initial members of the board and approve the founders' report on the corporation. Following this meeting the joint stock company must be entered in the Commercial Register.

A closed joint stock company, the shares of which are not offered to the public, does not require a decree authorizing incorporation. The incorporation documents must contain a declaration that the founders have subscribed for all the shares. The founders are required to pay at least 20 percent of the nominal value of their shares upon incorporation and the remainder within the next five years.

A minimum investment of KD 37,500 is required to establish a public joint stock company, and a minimum of KD 7,500 is required to establish a closed joint stock company. The capital must be divided into equal value shares having a minimum nominal value of KD 1 and maximum nominal value of KD 75. Shares may be issued at a premium but not at a discount. Shares may be sold, pledged or otherwise disposed of, but such transactions are effective only when they have been entered in the company's register of shareholders. Kuwaiti shareholders may not sell to foreigners. Founders may transfer their shares after the lapse of three years from the date of incorporation or after a dividend of at least five percent has been distributed. Other shareholders may transfer their shares at any time after the company has issued its first balance sheet or one year following the commencement of operations. Bearer shares may not be issued.

By resolution of the general meeting, a joint stock company may issue bonds by public subscription, thus entitling the holders to receive fixed interest amounts payable on fixed dates. The subscribed capital of the joint stock company must be paid in full prior to opening subscription of the bonds. The total value of the outstanding bonds may not exceed the subscribed share capital. A general meeting of bondholders must be held for each bond issue in order to safeguard the rights of the bondholders. Representatives of the bondholders' may attend but not vote in general meetings of the shareholders.

The board of directors of a joint stock company must consist of at least three members whose terms of office may not exceed three years but whose appointment may be renewed for successive terms. Directors are required to hold at least 1 percent of the capital. A person may not serve on more than three boards of Kuwaiti joint stock companies or be a managing director or chairman in more than one joint stock company.

Directors are elected by the shareholders by secret vote. Foreign organizations may designate representatives to the board in proportion to their holdings, and such representatives have the same rights as elected directors; the organization which appointed them is held responsible for their acts.

The authority, restrictions and liabilities of the board members of a joint stock company are similar to those of board members in a limited liability company.

Directors are prohibited from having any personal interest in the company's transactions, and they may not take part in the management of a rival company without the approval of the general meeting.

Remuneration paid to directors may not exceed 10 percent of net profits after deducting required reserves, depreciation and a dividend of at least 5 percent.

A general meeting must be convened at least once every year. In addition, the board must convene a general meeting of shareholders upon the request of shareholders holding at least 10 percent of the capital. Quorum at a general meeting is satisfied when shareholders holding at least 50 percent of the capital are present. Resolutions are decided based on simple majority vote.

Certain matters require extraordinary resolutions of shareholders holding at least 75 percent of the shares, such as amending the incorporation documents, selling the entire operation, winding up or merger, and reducing capital.

Other matters such as increasing financial liability of shareholders, increasing the nominal value of the shares, reducing the dividends specified in the Articles, setting new conditions on shareholder participation and voting at the general meeting or restricting the shareholder's right to sue directors require a unanimous vote.

The rules regarding the appointment of an auditor and dissolution are similar to those of a limited liability company.

## Partnerships

### General Partnerships

Two or more persons may form a partnership. Each partner is fully liable for the partnership's debts. The general partnership is established by preparing and registering with the Commercial Registrar a Memorandum and Articles of Association. Amendments to the Memorandum and Articles require unanimous approval of all the partners. The general partnership acquires legal personality only upon registration, but third parties may consent that the partnership existed prior to its registration.

Each partner must contribute to the capital. Transfer of a partner's share is subject to the provisions of the general partnership's Memorandum and Articles or to the consent of all the partners.

The general partnership must have at least one manager whose authority is specified in the Memorandum and Articles. Partners who are not managers may not take part in the management of the partnership, but have the right to inspect the general partnership's books and records.

The partnership is terminated upon the following: its term of existence expires and has not been extended; the objective for which it was established has been achieved; it loses all or most of its assets; court order; unanimous decision of the partners; or the bankruptcy of the partnership or one of its members. If a partner is declared bankrupt, however, the remaining partners may elect to continue the general partnership without the bankrupt partner.

### Limited Partnerships

There are two types of limited partnerships, a regular limited partnership and a limited partnership limited by shares.

A regular limited partnership has at least one general partner, whose liability for the obligations of the limited partnership is unlimited and at least one limited partner whose liability for the obligations of the limited partnership is limited to the extent of his investment in the limited partnership. The regular limited partnership is generally governed by the same rules that apply to a general partnership, subject to the following conditions: limited partners are limited to serving as supervising managers; they can exercise authority within sanctioned limits; and they may advise the management.

Any other format participation in the management by a limited partner may result in his liability to third parties.

The limited partnership limited by shares is governed by similar rules. Additionally, the capital of a limited partnership limited by shares must be divided into shares. Any specific provision in the partnership's incorporation documents may also restrict its activities. The position of the limited partners is governed by the rules relating to shareholders in a joint stock company as described above.

## Joint Ventures

Under Article 59 of the Kuwaiti Company Law joint ventures are a contractual type of partnership relationship between at least two persons, which has no independent legal personality and requires no formal establishment procedures. As a joint venture has no independent legal personality; actions for the joint venture are undertaken by the ventures. Thus, a venturer transacting for the joint venture bears unlimited liability toward third parties for such transaction. The liability of a non-transacting venturer is limited to his share in the joint venture. If the transacting venturer is a non-Kuwaiti, then the Kuwaiti venturer must serve as the non-Kuwaiti's guarantor in that transaction. In the event a joint venture were to deal with third parties in its own name, the effect would be to expose all of the joint venturers to unlimited, joint and several liability, regardless of whether a particular venturer was personally involved in the specific transaction.

# Commercial Agency and Representation

## General

Since foreign businesses may not open branch offices in Kuwait, they must resort to appointing commercial agents or representatives to transact their business in Kuwait unless they choose to cooperate with a Kuwaiti national to establish another kind of corporate entity. Foreign businesses carrying out government work must appoint a service agent or sponsor. There are no express provisions governing service agents or sponsors, however, the rules governing commercial agents are applied by analogy.

## Commercial Agency

Commercial agencies are regulated by Law No. 36 of 1964 or the Regulation of Commercial Agencies, and the Kuwaiti Commercial Code, Chapter 5, Articles 260-296.

Law 36 provides that only Kuwaiti nationals may act as commercial agents in Kuwait. The relationship between the Kuwaiti agent and the foreign principal must be direct, and commercial agencies are not enforceable unless registered in the Commercial Register.

Amendments to this law has been made that allow foreign investors to own up to 40 percent of a bank.

The Kuwaiti law defines three types of agencies:

**The Contractual Agency:** In a contractual agency, the local agent agrees to promote the principal's business on a continuous basis in a specified territory and to enter into transactions in the principal's name in return for a fee. The contract must be in writing and must indicate the territory covered, the agent's fee, the term, the product or service that is the subject of the agency, and any relevant trademarks. If the agent is required to set up showrooms, workshops or warehouse facilities, the term of the contract must be no less than five years.

**The Distributorship:** Under this type of agency, the local agent is the distributor of the principal's product in return for a percentage of the profits.

Only Kuwaiti nationals or Kuwaiti corporate entities may act as distributors. In order for a corporate entity established in Kuwait to be deemed a Kuwaiti corporate entity for purposes of acting as a distributor, it must have Kuwaiti participation of at least 51 percent. The principal must directly enter into a contract with the distributor in a contract which provides for the appointment of the distributor and which limits the distributor's activity to promoting and to distributing the principal's products. Distributors bear their own business expenses. If the distributor is to incur the expense of building special facilities, such as a showroom or a repair and maintenance facility, then the distributorship term must be established for a minimum of five years. Distributorships need not be exclusive as a practical matter.

**The Commission Agency:** This agency is provided for in Articles 287 through 296 of the Commercial Code. In this type of agency, the agent enters into contracts in the agent's own name. The principal's name may not be disclosed without the principal's permission, however, this rule is difficult to adhere to in practice since most manufactured products bear the principal's name.

The following protective legislative measures are designed to protect the local agent:

- Commercial agencies must be registered in order to be enforceable;
- Kuwaiti law is the governing law in matters pertaining to public policy;
- The principal may not terminate the agreement without proving breach of contract by the agent; unless the principal pays compensation to the agent;
- The principal may not refuse to renew the agency agreement when it expires without paying the agent equitable compensation for nonrenewal if the agent proves that he has committed no breach and that his activities led to the successful promotion of the principal's products;
- The agent may sue both the principal and any new agent the latter may appoint in Kuwait if the termination is proved to be the result of their concerted action.

## Commercial Representation

A commercial representative is a Kuwaiti individual or entity engaged by a foreign company pursuant to a "commercial representation agreement," to represent its business interests in Kuwait. The authority granted to a commercial representative is usually more limited than the authority granted an agent. A commercial representative may be paid according to a set fee, a commission or a percentage of profits. Articles 297 to 305 of the Commercial Code govern the commercial representative's obligation. In executing documents on behalf of the foreign company, the commercial representative must sign his name as well as the name of the foreign company and indicate that he is a commercial representative. A foreign company is liable for all of the commercial representative's actions and liabilities, so long as they are conducted or incurred within the scope of representation.

A commercial representation agreement is not registered with the Ministry of Commerce and Industry. The advantage of a commercial representative over an agent is that the representative can be engaged, compensated, and terminated as agreed upon by the parties to the commercial representation agreement, and the representative is not protected by the legal provisions applicable to agencies as discussed above.

**Currency and Banking**

## Foreign Currency

There are normally no foreign exchange restrictions in Kuwait. The Kuwaiti Dinar is freely convertible for all current and capital account transactions. The exchange rate is calculated daily on the basis of a basket of currencies which is weighted to reflect Kuwait's trade flow.

## Banking

The banking system of Kuwait is supervised by the Central Bank of Kuwait. A recently approved law now allows non-Kuwaitis to own up to 40 percent of a bank. In addition to the commercial banks in Kuwait, there are specialized banks which include the Industrial Bank of Kuwait, the Kuwait Real Estate Bank and the Saving and Credit Bank.

Kuwaiti banks have established banking relationships throughout the West. Full correspondent relationship, which include deposit account services, are more limited and concentrated in large regional banks.

Several American banks provide a wide range of correspondent services. In addition, many non-US banks also share firm correspondent relationships with Kuwaiti banks.

## Commercial Banks

Kuwait has seven commercial banks of which one, the Bank of Bahrain and Kuwait, is a foreign joint venture bank. Apart from this exception, foreign banks are not allowed to operate within Kuwait or to hold shares in Kuwaiti banks.

## Other Financial Institutions

Kuwait has a number of specialized banks. The Kuwait Finance House is a commercial bank that carries out Islamic financial transactions. The Industrial Bank of Kuwait and the Kuwait Real Estate Bank function much like American investment banks.

## Intellectual Property

In April 1998, Kuwait was placed on USTR's Priority Watch List. In 1999, new copyright and patent protection laws were passed that greatly improve the situation. During the first half of 1999, the Ministry of Information raided and seized pirated software and videocassettes and fined the violators.

### Patents

A new amendment to Law No. 4 of 1962 is designed to bring Kuwait into compliance with WTO criteria. Protection is now available for patented inventions and know-how for up to 20 years. The patent, however, must be renewed every four years. Patent infringement is punishable by a maximum jail term of one year and/or a fine of no more than $16,500.

The Kuwait Patent Office is located in the Ministry of Trade and Industry. Once an application is filed with the Registrar of Patents, no further action is taken by the Patent Office since it has not yet started the process of conducting examinations of patent applications. Opposition actions are not available in Kuwait.

Law No. 4 of 1962 provides for the registration of patents and industrial models in Kuwait. Although the Patent Law was enacted in 1962, the Patent Office in Kuwait was opened only in 1995, after a resolution adopted by the Gulf Cooperation Council (GCC) states calling for a unifying of the patent registration systems of the member countries.

The Kuwaiti government is presently preparing a draft law for the protection of patents to replace the current law discussed above. The draft, if adopted, would, *inter alia,* narrow the definition of a patent and lengthen the validity period to twenty years.

### Trademarks and Service Marks

Kuwait has effective trademark laws but weak enforcement. In general, Kuwait follows the international classification of trademarks with a few exceptions. In accordance with Islamic mores, the Trademark Law does not protect trademarks or service marks in classes 32 and 33 relating to alcoholic beverages and pork. Following the filing of an application to register a trademark, the application is examined as to registrability. The law allows an opposition to be filed by any interested party. An opposition requires the applicant for the registration to submit a counter-statement in order to maintain the application. In the absence of any opposition or the rejection of any filed oppositions, the trademark is registered.

A trademark registration is valid for ten years from the date of filing the application. The trademark registration is renewable for additional periods of ten years each. A trademark which lapses because of non-renewal may be registered in the name of a third party three years following the lapsed registration.

Use of the trademark in Kuwait is not a prerequisite for registration or for maintaining its validity. A trademark is vulnerable to cancellation, however, if a party convinces the court that the trademark was not actually used in Kuwait for five consecutive years or that no *bona fide* use of the trademark was made.

Assignment of a trademark is effective with regard to third parties only after the assignment has been entered in the register and published in the Official Gazette.

Unauthorized use or imitation of a registered trademark are offenses punishable by law.

## Copyright

The country's new copyright law protects computer software, video and music tapes, cassettes or CDs. It also protects, cinema, drawings, original books, translations and scientific papers. The new law issued in 1999 includes KD500 fines and/or a imprisonment for a one year maximum. Repeat offenders can face stiffer penalties. On December 7, 1999, the Kuwaiti Parliament approved the law.

## Taxation

### Tax Basis

There is no tax liability imposed on individuals and wholly owned Kuwaiti businesses. Tax is imposed only on foreign corporate bodies, including foreign partnerships, that conduct business in Kuwait directly or through an agent. Income tax is imposed on net profits of the foreign corporate body which is connected with or related to operations within Kuwait as well as on capital gains. Furthermore, the foreign corporate body is subject to tax on that proportion of the net profits of a Kuwaiti corporate entity, partnership or a joint venture, which may be attributed to it such as royalties, management fees, technical service fees or interest.

Conducting business in Kuwait may include: (1) the purchase and sale in Kuwait of properties, goods or rights and the keeping of a permanent place of business; (2) operation of any industrial or commercial project in Kuwait; (3) rental of properties; or (4) provision of services. A foreign corporate body for the purpose of taxation is defined as an association that has a legal existence completely separate from its members. Certain foreign partnerships, which in their country of origin may not be defined as a separate legal entity, may also be included in the term. In the event that there is more than one corporate body in a Kuwaiti entity or joint venture, each one is taxed separately.

The tax is imposed on profits. In calculating taxable profits, the following can be deducted: (1) expenses incurred; (2) depreciation; (3) head office and overhead expenses at specific rates; and (4) commissions to agents, up to a limited percentage.

Income gained by activities outside Kuwait is not taxable provided the activities are not connected to operations within Kuwait.

Losses can be deducted from profits in subsequent taxable years, indefinitely, but may not be carried back.

### Tax Rates

The income tax is imposed at a fixed rate determined by a graduated schedule ranging from 5 percent for income in excess of KD 5,250 up to 55 percent for income in excess of KD 375,000. Tax is calculated as the lower of: (1) the whole profit taxed at the highest applicable tax rate; or (2) the profit amounting up to the upper limit of the previous tax bracket at the rate applicable to that bracket plus the excess profit over the upper limit of the previous bracket.

Deductions are allowed for business expenses, depreciation of assets and loss carry forwards. A small percentage of revenues may be deducted for office overhead expenses.

## Tax Administration

The taxpayer must submit its tax return within three and one half months of the end of the tax period. Upon a taxpayer's request, the Director of Income Taxes can modify the taxpayer's tax year.

The tax return and supporting documentation must be certified by a recognized firm of accountants approved by the Director of Income Taxes.

There is no administrative appeals process over the Director's decisions, and both sides may challenge such decisions in civil court. The tax is payable in four equal installments on the fifteenth day of the fourth, sixth, ninth and twelfth month following the tax period, unless modified by a decision of the Director of Income Taxes.

## Investment and Trade

Recently, Kuwait adopted Law No. 56 of 1996 (Effective 15.1.97), creating an independent entity called the Industrial Authority, and abolishing the Shaubia Industrial Authority and the Industrial Committee. All industrial projects in the emirate, including those now in operation, will have to be licensed by the new authority.

## Investment Laws

Kuwait's new investment law authorizes tax holidays for up to 10 years. Incentives include grants, tax deferrals, special access to credit and import quota exemptions.

A variety of incentives are offered to new manufacturing businesses under the investment laws. Industrial enterprises which are eligible to receive such investment incentives must first obtain a permit from the Minister of Commerce and Industry prior to being established. Prior to effecting any change in its capacity, location, or business, an approved industrial enterprise must obtain a modified permit from the Minister of Commerce and Industry. Eligible enterprises are businesses run by Kuwaiti individuals or companies established in Kuwait.

Approved industrial enterprises must provide the Ministry of Commerce and Industry with their annual financial statements and records of goods imported duty-free under the incentives program. The work force of an approved industrial enterprise must be composed of at least 25 percent Kuwaiti nationals, unless waived by the Ministry of Commerce and Industry because of the unavailability of sufficient qualified Kuwaiti labor.

## Trade Agreements

Kuwait is a member of the GCC and, as such, is subject to the GCC trade agreements. These agreements are described in the section on Trade Agreements in the chapter on Bahrain.

Kuwait has been a member of GATT and has signed the WTO agreement.

## Customs

Only Kuwaiti nationals and entities in which Kuwaitis hold at least a 51 percent interest are permitted to import goods into Kuwait. Foreign business entities are required to use a Kuwaiti import agent. Customs duties is 4 percent on average, which is applied to the cost, insurance and freight value of goods. There is also a customs clearance and inland transportation that is usually charged $175 per container. Some items which are competitively produced in Kuwait are subject to an elevated customs duty of 15 percent.

Imports that compete with locally manufactured goods of "infant industries," the Ministry of Commerce and Industry may impose protective tariffs of up to 25 percent. In these situations, tariffs are imposed on a case-by-case basis.

Since July 1, 1997, the Council of Ministers approved imposing a 70 percent customs duty on cigarettes and tobacco products in lieu of the previously approved 100 percent. The Kuwaiti government may also raise tariffs in order to increase revenue and "harmonize upward" with tariffs in other GCC states.

## Public Sector Procurement

Procurement by the Kuwaiti Government and its agencies is governed by Law No. 37 of 1964 as modified by Law Nos. 13 and 31 of 1970 and 1977, respectively concerning Public Tenders (hereinafter, the "Tenders Law"). The Tenders Law provides that any procurement made by the Kuwait Government with a value in excess of KD 5,000 must be conducted through the Central Tenders Committee procedures in order to ensure competitive pricing.

Article 5 of the Tenders Law provides that a bid for a government contract may be made by a Kuwaiti merchant, individual or company which is registered in the Register of Commerce in the Chamber of Commerce and Industry of Kuwait. A foreign entity may act as a government contractor only through a Kuwaiti entity in which it has an ownership interest or by acting directly but with the assistance and support of a Kuwaiti agent or commercial representative. The tenderer must be registered in the Classification List of Contractors and Suppliers.

The two exceptions to the application of the Tenders Law are Ministry of Defense procurements and other specialized procurements by the approval of the Central Tenders Committee.

## Labor Law

Kuwaiti nationals have the right to join and to establish unions. Expatriate workers are allowed to join unions after a five-year residency term but only as non-voting members. Kuwaiti law forbids the establishment of more then one union per "functional area".

Kuwaiti workers have the right to organize and to bargain collectively. The right to strike is recognized but is limited by Kuwait's labor law, which requires compulsory negotiations followed by arbitration. The constitution prohibits forced labor except in cases specified by law with just remuneration. The minimum age for employment, both full and part time, is eighteen years of age. There is no minimum wage for the private sector and in the public sector the minimum wage is KD 226 a month for Kuwaiti bachelors and KD 301 a month for married men.

General working conditions are established by Kuwaiti law for both the public and the private sector, with the oil industry treated separately. The work week is limited to forty-eight hours with one day of rest per week and a minimum of fourteen days of vacation annually.

The law governing the oil industry provides for a forty hour work week, over time pay, and thirty days annual leave. Women are promised equal pay for equal work.

Employers are responsible for maintaining a safe working environment.

Foreigners wishing to work in Kuwait must obtain a work permit before entering the country. Such permits are granted by the Ministry of Labor and are generally limited to sectors in which there is a need for expatriate labor such as tourism, industry, banking and private education.

Foreign contractors are obliged under Decision No. 694 (26.7.92) to take part in a counter-trade offset program if the accumulated value of contracts in which they are engaged is equal or greater than KD 1 million.

The offset may reach up to 30 percent of the monetary value of the said supply contract and can be performed by counter-trade, training or investment programs. The offset obligations must be settled within eight years.

### Environmental Law

The Gulf War resulted in serious environmental damage. Iraq's mass destruction of oil wells, the huge oil spills caused by allied air strikes and the use of heavy tracked vehicles in the desert by both sides triggered an environmental catastrophe, resulting in frequent sand storms, the destruction of marine wildlife, and high levels of poisonous by-products in the air from the 1991 oil fires.

Kuwait is a member of several treaties concerning the preservation of the environment.

As of Feb. 27, 1975 Kuwait has been obliged under the International Convention for the Prevention of Pollution of the Sea by Oil, to *inter alia,* limit the size of oil tankers and to regulate oil tankers arrangements.

As of March 29, 1975, Kuwait has been obliged under the Convention Concerning Protection Against Hazards of Poisoning Arising from Benzene, to, *inter alia,* protect workers from hazards arising from benzene by using substitutes, providing adequate means of personal protection and taking all necessary measures to prevent the escape of benzene vapor into the air.

As of July 1, 1979, Kuwait has been obliged under the Kuwait Regional Convention for Cooperation on the Protection of the Marine Environment from Pollution to take all measures to prevent abate and combat pollution of the marine environment caused by ships, aircraft, land-based sources, exploration of the sea bed and other human activities. The convention also provides for a system of research and cooperation between the gulf states. Under an enclosed protocol to this convention, the gulf states have established the Marine Emergency Mutual Aid Center in order to combat sea pollution caused by oil.

Kuwait is a signatory to two treaties prohibiting the development and use of weapons modifying the environment, namely bacteriological toxin and nuclear weapons. Furthermore, Kuwait has ratified, *inter alia,* the following international environmental agreements: the 1977 UN Environmental Modification Convention (ENMOD); the 1983 FAO International Undertaking on Plant Genetic Resources; the 1967 Outer Space Treaty; Annex 16 on Environmental Protection to the 1944 Chicago Convention on International Air Aviation; the 1969 Brussels Convention Relating to Intervention on High Seas in case of Oil Pollution Casualties and its 1973 protocol; the 1982 UN Convention on the Law of the Sea; and the 1971 Brussels Convention on the Establishment of an International Fund for Compensation of Oil Pollution Damage.

# LEBANON

## Recent Political Developments

A large post-civil war political shake up occurred in Lebanon when Prime Minister Hariri chose to resign in 1998, following a power struggle with the new President and former army Chief of Staff, Emile Lahoud.

Hariri is attributed with having steered his country out of the Civil War and into better economic times. His main emphasis was rebuilding the infrastructure, something he accomplished while racking up a huge debt in the process.

While his resignation did usher in a period of uncertainty, the transition to the new Prime Minister, Selim al-Hoss, seems to have progressed smoothly. Hoss, who possesses a doctorate in economics and served as Prime Minister during the Civil War, is trying to steer the economy away from the public to the private sector.

| | |
|---|---|
| Population | 4.00 million (1999) |
| Religions | Muslim, Christian |
| Government | Democratic Parliamentary Republic |
| Languages | Arabic; (French, English and Armenian are widely spoken) |
| Work Week | Government: Monday–Friday 8:00–14:00 Saturday 8:00–13:00 Banking: Monday–Friday 8:00–12:30 Saturday 8:00–12:00 |
| Monetary Unit | Lebanese Pound (L£) |
| Exchange Rate | L£ 1,507=US$ 1 |

But many wildcards still exist in Lebanese politics. Syria, the main power broker in the country, controls Lebanon's political system. Syria's reach became clear when the former army's chief of staff, Lt.-Gen. Emile Lahoud, met with Syrian officials in November 1998 to ensure his election as the country's president. Without Syria's approval, Lahoud's chances would have been negligible.

Besides Syria's role in the election, it has made inroads into other areas. There are currently 35,000 Syrian troops stationed in Lebanon. High-ranking officers have created economic empires in certain parts of the country, where they have come to control trade in the area. Furthermore, more than 700,000 Syrian workers work in Lebanon and take at least $2 billion out of the country each year.

The structure of Lebanon's political system has in the past and continues to create predicaments. The government's structure is based on a complicated compromise by the three main religious factions: the Maronite Christians, the Sunni Muslims and the Shi'ite Muslims. According to the arrangement agreed upon in 1943, the leaders of these factions assume the roles of President, Prime Minister and Speaker of the Parliament respectively. The three political figures are also known as the "Troika". Tension and rifts generally characterize the relationship among the Troika. At present, Lahoud is the Maronite President, Hoss, the Sunni Prime Minister and Nabi Berri the Shi'ite Speaker of the Parliament.

On Lebanon's southern border, the threat of confrontation with Israel continues to create a tense atmosphere. While most clashes between Lebanese and Israelis occur inside the security zone, they have spilled deeper into the country at times. In June 1999, Israel launched its most serious attack since 1996. At least seven were killed, and 50 wounded. The attack also targeted Beirut's rebuilt infrastructure.

Israel's new Prime Minister Ehud Barak has promised to withdraw the Israel Defense Forces from Lebanon by July 2000. The sudden resumption in Israeli-Syrian peace talks in December 1999 raised new hopes for Lebanon as well. Any comprehensive peace agreement will inevitably include as Israeli withdrawal from Southern Lebanon. Initially, Lebanese officials expressed outrage over the perceived Syrian neglect of their interests in negotiations with Israel. Lebanon has since appointed Interior Minister Michel Murr as the head of his country's negotiation team, and is expected to participate in future talks. Despite the prominence of the Lebanon factor in any comprehensive solution, the Lebanese government is certain to remain Syria's subordinate throughout the negotiations.

## Recent Economic Developments

The Lebanese economy that is emerging nearly a decade after the end of the Civil War is characterized by competition, open-market commercial orientation and the region's most liberal banking program.

Still, Lebanon is picking up the pieces of its battered economy. The delicate internal and external predicaments in which the country is caught impose constraints on both the political and economic environments.

Externally, the primary factor is Syria, the country's true power that has stationed troops inside Lebanon since 1989. On another front is Israel, which has maintained a "security zone" in southern Lebanon to combat threats to its northern border. Israel demonstrated its ability to affect Lebanon's economy when it launched its strongest attack in years against the nascent infrastructure in June 1999, destroying highways, bridges and badly damaging Beirut's power stations.

Internally, the country's policies are affected by political struggles between various religious groups, each of which holds powerful constitutionally guaranteed positions within the political system. This internal dynamic came to a head in 1998 when a power struggle between Prime Minister Hariri and the newly elected President and former army chief of staff, Emile Lahoud, led to Hariri's resignation.

Hariri's departure brought to a close the opening chapter in the country's economic comeback. During his tenure, which lasted from 1992 to 1998, the economic goal was to rebuild the country's infrastructure as quickly as possible, regardless of the accrued costs. Hariri, a billionaire construction tycoon, was viewed as the right man for this job because of his international stature and close relationship with Gulf countries, which allowed him to secure loans from the oil-rich region. He is credited with stabilizing Lebanon's currency, which was in the process of collapsing before he took office. Also under his term, the Lebanese lira rose in value against the dollar, and Lebanon received its first long-term foreign debt rating from S&P, Moody's and others.

On the down side, Hariri's rebuilding policies led to massive budget deficits and borrowing. The ratio of public debt to GDP, which in 1993 was 50 percent, grew to 113 percent in 1998. It was estimated at 130 percent by the end of 1999. The weight of debt, which ballooned to $22 billion by the end of 1999, and budget deficits, began to wear down the economy. Growth slowed to an annual average of 3 percent from 1995 to 1998 versus its peak of 8 percent in 1994. By 1999, it had regressed to less than 1 percent. The large-scale government borrowing also crowded out private-sector borrowing and pushed up interest rates, making it difficult for private capital investments.

In the relatively calm year of 1991, industrial production, agricultural output and exports showed substantial gains. Further rebuilding of the war-ravaged country was delayed in 1992 because of resurgent political wrangling, but in October 1992, al-Hariri was appointed Prime Minister, and under his leadership, Lebanon embarked on the road to economic recovery. Efforts centered on currency stabilization, budget deficit reduction, an ambitious reconstruction program, attracting foreign aid and investment and regaining Lebanon's role as the banking, trading and entertainment center of the Middle East.

The recovery program led by former Prime Minister Hariri was aimed at constructing a modern, competitive economy that would take advantage of Lebanon's educated and entrepreneurial population. Al-Hariri has developed a two-stage development program, known as Horizon 2000 (the original target date), comprising a short-term emergency reconstruction phase (1993-1995) and a medium-term recovery phase (1996-2003). The program's estimated cost is US$ 11.67 billion, and it boasts the ambitious goal of doubling per capita GDP by the end of the period. Infrastructure projects in the program included the construction and repair of electricity stations, the country's telecommunications network and water and sewerage facilities.

The implementation of al-Hariri's plan has suffered several setbacks. In April 1996, for example, clashes between Israel and the Shi'ite guerrilla movement, Hizballah, severely damaged homes, businesses and infrastructure, costing the economy an estimated US$ 400 million.

Hariri's successor is Selim al-Hoss, a former Prime Minister who served at different times during the Civil War. Hoss, who possesses a doctorate in economics, aims to usher in the country's new economic phase – that of structuring the economy around the private sector as the main driver of growth.

Lebanon's public finances, its yawning trade deficit, and its high rates of unemployment (up to 20 percent of the work force) and underemployment are not encouraging. In addition, an influx of Syrian labor has increased unemployment and placed a heavy burden on Lebanon's social security system. As a result of this influx, Lebanon is transferring at least US$ 2 billion a year to Syria.

It must be recalled, however, that while Lebanon remains a tiny economy, much of the trade imbalance is caused by imports of machinery. Capital is flowing in from expatriate Lebanese and other Arabs (albeit mostly for speculative property deals), and gold reserves are ample. As long as stability lasts and the economy remains on course, the horizon appears reasonably promising.

Premier Hoss faces a large task in front of him. His government aspires to replace the public sector with the private as the main engine of growth. He is seeking to reduce public debt to 85 percent of GDP by 2003. The 1999-2000 budget forecasts $3.31 billion in revenues and $5.54 billion in spending, creating a deficit of 40 percent, or 13 percent of GDP.

In order to generate additional revenue and to reduce the deficit, the government is raising corporate taxes from 10 percent to 15 percent, doubling the bracket of personal income tax to 20 percent and adding $0.066 per liter of gas, in addition to other hikes. These measures were expected to raise roughly $400 million in extra revenue. But some of these hikes may be offset by other developments. For instance, the gas increase was consumed primarily by a 70 percent rise in world oil prices and is not expected to yield the projected revenue.

Furthermore, Lebanon is receiving economic resources from elsewhere. The World Bank announced in February 1999 that it would extend $600 million more for reconstruction and budgetary support measures. This matches an initial $600 million offered in 1993. The country is also receiving money from the Gulf as well as repatriation of between $6 billion and $7 billion a year by Lebanese living abroad. This money is sufficient to cover the country's trade deficit, which has dropped to its lowest level since 1993. A gradual rise in exports and drastic fall in imports have combined to reduce the country's trade deficit to $5.05 billion for the first 11 months of 1999. During this period, total exports rose by 6 percent to $630 million, up from $594 million in the corresponding period of 1998, and total imports fell by 13.7 percent to a record 5-year low of $5.7 billion.

During the first 11 months of 1999, Lebanon's fuel bill rose to $443 million, compared to $416 million for the entire year of 1998. Precious metals and jewelry, worth $86 million, maintained its position atop the country's export list, comprising 13.7 percent of total exports. Chemicals, valued at $75 million (11.9 percent) placed second. In third place were metals, which amounted to $71 million, or 11.3 percent of the total. The leading imports were machinery and mechanical appliances worth $837 million, 14.7 percent of the total. Vehicles worth $561 million and mineral products valued at $551 million followed in importance.

A successful $540 million Eurobond issued in February 1999 attracted roughly $200 million more than the government expected. Lebanon issued Eurobonds worth a total of $1.2 billion in 1999. Despite their popularity and parliament's authorization for a $2 billion borrowing program, Lebanon's Finance Minister is opposed to issuing more Eurobonds, so as not to further exacerbate the debt situation.

While the end of the Civil War and greater stability spurred economic growth, the economy began a relative slowdown beginning in 1996 that continued through 1999. The real annual growth rate, which peaked at 8 percent growth in 1994, declined from 3.5 percent in 1997 to less than 1 percent in 1999. Forecasts for 2000 set GDP growth at 1.8 percent.

In 1999, the government designed a five-year plan for economic reform in an attempt to alleviate the economic problems facing the country. The core elements of the plan are privatization, tax system reform, and restructuring Lebanon's debt. The scheme aims to reduce the budget deficit to 5 percent of GDP from the current level of 15 percent by 2003. This plan will supplement an administrative reform program aimed to eliminate the bureaucratic corruption that many believe is the root of the country's economic tribulations.

## Main Economic Domains

### Telecommunications
This is one sector in which the Lebanese are quickly catching up to the rest of the world. In 1998, the size of this market was estimated at around $4 billion and contracts for landlines and mobile phones are plentiful.

The inadequate and unreliable infrastructure led to tremendous demand for mobile services. As late as 1996, nearly 15 out of every 1,000 Lebanese

## Economic Indicators

|  | 1999 | 1998 |
|---|---|---|
| GDP Growth (percent) | 0.8 | 3.0 |
| External Debt (US$ billions) | 5.5 (as of October 1999) | 4.18 |
| Public Debt (US$ billion) | 20 | |
| Budget Deficit (percent of expenditure) | 42.5 | 43.8 |
| Imports (US$ billion) | 5.2 (YTY to October 1999) | 5.9 (YTY to October 1998) |
| Exports (US$ million) | 563 (YTY to October 1999) | 537 (YTY to October 1998) |
| Balance of Payment (US$ million) | 32 (as of April 1999) | −487.6 |
| Total Bank Assets (L£) | | |
| Foreign Exchange Net Reserves (US$ billion) | 4.4 (as of October 1999) | 3.7 (as of October 1998) |
| Foreign Exchange Gross Reserves (US$ billion) | 7.6 | 6.4 |
| Beirut Stock Exchange Market Capitalization (US$ billion) | — | 2.4 |
| Beirut Stock Exchange— Average daily traded volume ($ million) | 0.2 (as of November 1999) | 1.37 |
| Inflation (percent) | 1.0 | 4.0 |

had phone lines. There were no public phone lines and 200,000 people used mobile phones. Today, 580,000 citizens, roughly 15 percent of the population have mobile phones and talk for an average of 750 minutes a month, amounting to 620 minutes longer than the global average.

Contracts have been signed with Ericsson, Siemens and Alcatel for the supply and installation of digital exchanges. These agreements consist of installing 972,000 new lines throughout Lebanon at a cost of $80 million. A further 250,000 lines were awarded for the provision of the local network in suburban and rural areas. The Ministry of Post and Telecommunications targets a penetration ratio of 35 percent by the end of 2000.

Internet and e-mail services are available and quite reliable. Lebanon's two Intersat and two Arabsat earth stations are undergoing rehabilitation and upgrade works.

## Industry

The main industries in Lebanon are food processing, textiles, cement, chemicals, oil refining, furniture, jewelry and some metal work. Virtually all industry is privately owned and much of the manufacturing capacity is located in East Beirut.

Before Lebanon's industrial sector can realize its true potential the government must develop a clear and integrated policy, including regulatory and customs reforms. Without these reforms there is little chance that industry can contribute much to private-sector growth and, thus, overall GDP growth.

The country has taken steps in this direction with plans to build industrial parks, reduce customs duties charged on some imported raw materials and the decision to pay a 5 percent interest rate subsidy on loans to industry.

The industrial sector is still trying to recover from the impact of the fifteen-year Civil War. The lack of adequate infrastructure, rising costs of services and scarce bank credits are slowing recovery, although imports of industrial machinery have started to pick up.

## Agriculture

Agriculture accounts for about one-third of GDP. Thirty percent of total land is cultivated arable or utilized forest. The most fertile areas are located along the coastal strip and in the Beka'a valley. The main crops are wheat, barley, corn, vegetables, potatoes, citrus fruit, hemp (hashish), olives and tobacco. The primary livestock are sheep and goats.

The agricultural sector suffers from labor shortages, lack of banking facilities and rising costs of services. The government subsidizes sugar beets, wheat and tobacco and has succeeded in reducing the lucrative but illegal drug production in West Beka'a and Ba'albek—Hirmil. Several multinational donors are financing agricultural and livestock projects.

## Construction and Real Estate

1999 was a disappointing year for contractors. Few projects were initiated and a number that were scheduled never began. The bottleneck has been the government's continued attempts to redraft the scope and activities of the public bodies charged with carrying out the reconstruction program, primarily the Council for Development & Reconstruction and the Investment Development Authority of Lebanon.

A $550 million project to develop the coast between Beirut and Antelias was postponed in April after investors feared the risks were too great. Another project to build 10,000 housing units has been postponed and a design-build-operate-transfer free trade zone and industrial zone at Quleaat has also been delayed.

This construction downturn is in contrast to the early 1990s when the sector performed well, particularly between 1993-1995. During those years, both engineering construction permits and cement deliveries rose dramatically despite a moderate rate of construction.

## Tourism

Lebanon was a major tourist center prior to the outbreak of the Civil War, and its scenic beauty, sunny climate and historic sites attracted some two million visitors annually. In 1974, tourism contributed about 20 percent of the country's income.

Today, $500 million is being injected into the hotel industry to return and restore Beirut's famed hotels to their former glory. There is also significant construction of new hotels, with a goal of creating 18,000 rooms by the end of 2002. Continued stability has convinced many internationally famous hotels, restaurants and clothing stores to reopen in Beirut, including the Marriott, the Intercontinental Vendome, Hard Rock Cafe, Henry J. Benas, Pizza Hut, Hardee's, Kentucky Fried Chicken and Baskin Robbins. The famous Casino Du Liban reopened in 1996.

There are currently nearly 400 hotels in Lebanon, most of them are in the Beirut area. The Ministry of Tourism estimates that there are some 3,000 restaurants, nightclubs, and cafes in Lebanon, compared to a pre-war figure of more than 5,000. There are about 650 travel agencies.

With the quieting of the political situation, the private Arab business sector has begun to show renewed interest in investing in Lebanon. Thus, in discussions with the government, Lebanese entrepreneurs now occasionally raise the possibility of improving infrastructure facilities and access roads to tourist sites in the country. During 1993-1995, a number of requests were presented for the speedy repair of the Tyre-Sidon road, which bears a heavy traffic load during the summer months, despite having been severely damaged during the Civil War. Other tourist sites in Lebanon where road infrastructure is inadequate are located in the Ba'albek, Kar'oon Lake, Anjar and Byblos areas.

## Public Finance

As noted, the government's budget deficit remains one of Lebanon's most important and pressing economic problems. The budget has been in chronic deficit throughout the last decade as the government continued to pay its employees and to supply goods despite its inability to collect sufficient revenues. Borrowing from the banking sector has financed the deficit.

The government has taken a number of practical measures to reduce the deficit and to maintain a stable budget since 1992. These include the regulation of public expenditure and various steps to increase internal revenues.

The huge structural imbalance in Lebanon's trade has also restricted growth. The manufacturing sector is not sufficiently developed to provide an alternative to imported consumer goods or production input. The result is that economic activity remains almost entirely dependent on imports.

| 1993–2003 Budgetary Allocations | | | |
|---|---|---|---|
| Transportation | US$ 2,969 billion | Water Supply | US$ 930.0 million |
| Electricity | US$ 1,645 billion | Government Buildings | US$ 270.0 million |
| Education | US$ 1,530 billion | Solid Waste | US$ 180.0 million |
| Housing and Resettlement | US$ 1,050 billion | Tourism | US$ 188.7 million |
| Telecommunications | US$ 715.0 million | Social Affairs | US$ 130.0 million |
| Agriculture and Irrigation | US$ 650.0 million | Management and Implementation | US$ 150.2 million |
| Public Health | US$ 500.3 million | Private Sector Services | US$ 100.6 million |
| Wastewater Treatment | US$ 500.3 million | Information | US$ 50.0 million |
| Industry | US$ 394.9 million | Environment | US$ 35.0 million |

## Business Environment

### *Privatization*

The government under Hoss is working to reduce public debt. The 1999–2000 budget seeks to reduce public debt to 85 percent of GDP by 2003 and plans a major privatization program. But many believe that the state-owned enterprises are not in condition to be placed on the market. For example, the power sector, which posts losses of roughly $200 million a year because of low collection rates, would in its present state be an unattractive proposition for a private operator. In fact, of all of the state-owned businesses, the public telecommunications authority, Ogero, is one of the few revenue-generating parts of the state sector.

The Lebanese government has been taking fairly modest steps towards privatization. One project that seems likely to get off the ground is the expansion and management of the port of Sidon. Consideration is also being given to the private management of the port of Beirut. Privatization of some state assets, including the loss-making carrier Middle East Airlines, is being seriously considered, but faces stiff opposition from many politicians.

### *Stock Exchange*

The Beirut Stock Exchange (BSE) was reopened in the beginning of 1996 after more than eleven years of inactivity. The BSE is considered to be an important financial tool that will assist in stimulating the Lebanese economy by attracting capital to the country. Currently, there are only a few securities traded on the BSE, and it does not meet international stock exchange standards. By the end of 1998, the BSE had a market capitalization of $2.4 billion with 12 companies listed. In 1998, the bearish mood that dominated most emerging markets, coupled with high interest rates on government paper, burdened the BSE with the market index losing 27.8 percent on the year. In 1999, the daily average trading volume dipped sharply to $200,000, versus $1.36 million in 1998 and $2.61 million in 1997.

The Lebanese government intends to increase the level of trade on the BSE by developing its exchange standards, enhancing technological support, and offering attractive tax rates and liberal currency regulations to foreign investors.

## Major Projects

The Council for Development and Reconstruction (CDR) currently has US$ 1.6 billion in projects underway, including the Beirut Airport project, the beltway road system around Beirut, modernization of the telecommunications network and improvements to the energy sector. International funding for these projects is vital to the success of the program. Of the grants and loans committed thus far about 85 percent come from Arab or European sources and the World Bank, with Italy being the major individual source of foreign financing. Thus, for example, the US$ 190 million contract for the new Beirut University, to be undertaken by a consortium comprising Ed Zueblin of Germany, Turkey's Tekser, the local Arabian Construction Company and Milne & Nicholls of Canada, will be financed by Saudi Arabia and Oman. Direct US financing is negligible. European firms such as Ansaldo and Siemens, and American corporations such as Motorola and MCI Communication are already deeply involved in Lebanese reconstruction projects.

Nevertheless, US hesitation to invest in Lebanon has given Europe a distinct edge in the Lebanese market. The undeveloped relationship and commercial obstacles, manifested, for example, by restrictions on direct flights between the US and Lebanon, is reflected in mutual trade figures; the US imports less than 10 percent of all Lebanese exports.

The reconstruction of Beirut's City Center is being undertaken by Solidere, which is listed on the Beirut Stock Exchange. Work on infrastructure, which includes office and housing projects as well as land reclamation and archaeological parks, began in the summer of 1994.

As part of its reconstruction program, the Lebanese government plans to build five free trade zones in several locations throughout the country. Three are already in operation, including the Tripoli Port and Selaata Free Zone (in northern Lebanon).

The first to be built, the Beirut Port Free Trade Zone, was inaugurated in late 1995. This zone, which will eventually encompass approximately 100,000 square meters, replaces the former free trade zone destroyed during Lebanon's Civil War. The government is implementing a US$ 130 million project to upgrade Beirut's port facilities in an effort to recapture its pre-civil war status as one of the main ports of the eastern Mediterranean. So far, two buildings with a total area of 24,000 square meters have been constructed at a cost of US$ 6.5 million.

With regard to other free trade zones, the government commissioned a British company to conduct research and to assist in the establishment and operation of free trade zones in Lebanon. The purpose of the research is to determine suitable locations and to provide appropriate recommendations for management and operation of the zones. The government intends to develop the infrastructure and to build large storage facilities in the zone areas. It does not intend to sell areas in the zones but, rather, to lease them to companies for a period of twenty-five years.

In an effort to restore confidence in Lebanon, US President Bill Clinton sponsored the Friends of Lebanon Conference. The conference concluded with attendees pledging US$ 1 billion in financial assistance to all sectors in Lebanon for 1997 and a total of US$ 2.2 billion to be delivered by the year 2000. Other conference participants announced immediate contributions while some countries pledged to send technical delegations to Lebanon to work on specific programs and projects.

## Build Operate Transfer

The lack of reserves available for the financing of Lebanon's development, reduction in foreign aid and the hesitation shown by international financial institutions to finance projects in the face of the country's increasing debt have meant that Lebanon is increasingly turning to private funding, particularly BOT's, to promote large infrastructure projects. Nevertheless, the BOT arrangement is still rare in Lebanon, and only few such projects have been implemented.

Two BOT franchises pertaining to global standard for mobiles (GSM) networks were awarded in August 1994. This type of financing is unusual in this sector because of its sophisticated high-tech nature, which is subject to rapid change and to difficulty in predicting prices. Three companies, France Telecom, Mobile Liban and LibanCell (FTML) have already begun operating the network under twelve-year concessions. Mobile Liban is 67 percent owned by France Telecom and 33 percent owned by the local company Mikati, and already has over 56,000 subscribers since starting services at the end of January 1995. LibanCell, which is owned by a group of local companies, and Telecom Finland (14 percent), has attracted over 50,000 customers since launching operations in April 1995. Both digital cellular operators plan to increase their network capacity to keep up with demand.

## Franchising

Commercial representation companies are subject to law number 34/67 on exclusive rights for commercial representation, distributorship and franchising. Such companies can be either limited partnerships or joint-stock corporations. Two thirds of the board of directors must be Lebanese. Both types of companies must have a majority of Lebanese partners or shareholders holding capital and a Lebanese manager.

**Major Business Opportunities**

| Rank | Sector |
|------|--------|
| 1 | Telecommunication Equipment |
| 2 | Trucks, Trailers/Buses |
| 3 | Transportation Services |
| 4 | Computers/Peripherals |
| 5 | Medical Equipment |
| 6 | Healthcare Services |
| 7 | Construction Design and Management |
| 8 | Durable Consumer Goods (Appliances) |
| 9 | Motor Vehicles |
| 10 | Franchising |
| 11 | Hotel Services |

## Legal Review

Lebanon is a democratic republic with a parliamentary system of government. Confessional groups and traditionally powerful clans dominate Lebanese politics. An informal system of power sharing among Lebanon's officially recognized religious groups pervades all aspects of civil society.

The Prime Minister, nominated by the president in mandatory consultation with the speaker of the Chamber of Deputies, is subject to the Chamber's vote of confidence. Lebanon has universal adult suffrage, and voters elect

128 representatives for a four-year term. The Chamber is made up of an equal number of Christians and Muslims.

Since the end of the Lebanese civil war in 1990, the government has consolidated its authority in many parts of the country. Some militias, including Hizballah and its allies in the south, have not yet been disarmed however.

## Judiciary

The Lebanese legal system is a mixture of Ottoman Law, Canon Law, the Napoleonic Code and Civil Law. There are four courts of cassation in the country; three that deal with civil and commercial disputes and one with criminal matters. There is also a judicial review of legislative action in Lebanon.

## Business Forms and Structures

### Companies Law

The Lebanese Code of Commerce provides for the following types of business associations: unlimited partnerships, limited partnerships, co-partnerships, joint stock companies, limited partnerships by shares, limited liability companies and companies with variable capital.

The most common forms are the joint stock company and limited liability company. Foreign investors may also be interested establishing branch offices of foreign companies.

### Joint Stock Company

A joint stock company is an association of funds contributed to by three or more persons. A joint stock company should have a minimum authorized capital of L£ 30 million. Ownership of shares in the company entitles the shareholder to membership in the company, a right to participate in management and a right to vote. These shares are negotiable or transferable. The liability of each shareholder is limited to the value of the shares held. The Board of Directors must set aside 10 percent of net profits to create a statutory reserve fund until such time as this reserve fund becomes equivalent to one-third of the capital of the company. A joint stock company must appoint an auditor.

Lebanese law does not provide for direct limitations on foreign interest in joint stock companies. The only indirect limitation is that the Board of Directors must have at least three Lebanese members out of the maximum twelve allowed. Another limitation is confined to joint stock companies whose object is the acquisition of and trading in real estate in Lebanon. In this case, Lebanese nationals must hold 50 percent of the capital.

## Limited Liability Company

A limited liability company has between three to twenty members. It cannot issue shares, debentures or bonds, nor can it invite the public to subscribe for ownership in the company. The trade name is usually anonymous, but it must be followed by the initials SARL and may include the names of the partners. The legal incapacity or bankruptcy of a member does not entail dissolution of the company. Shares in a limited liability company are not negotiable and cannot be transferred to third parties without the prior approval of members representing at least 75 percent of the capital. The capital must be fully paid up and must appear on the letterhead or any other printed documentation of the limited liability company. The liability of each partner is limited to the value of shares held. The legal reserve of such a company must be equal to 50 percent of the capital. The capital must be fully deposited in a bank under the company's name.

Management may be entrusted to one or more partners, and a manager cannot conclude on the company's behalf any deal in which he has a direct or indirect interest, unless prior authorization is granted. Limited liability companies may not pursue the objects of banking, financial operation and insurance. The company must be formed with the mutual consent of the members embodied in a memorandum of association.

## Branch Offices

Local branch offices are used frequently by foreign companies doing business in Lebanon. To set up a branch office, the foreign company's Board of Directors must execute a power of attorney in favor of a person residing in Lebanon granting authority to register the company in Lebanon, to represent it in court and to sign documents on its behalf. The representative must be given a copy of the company's articles of association or incorporation, and a copy of a resolution of the company's Board of Directors authorizing the opening of the branch, nominating its representative, and issuing the power of attorney.

## Commercial Representation

Commercial representation is governed by a Legislative Decree of 1967, according to which a commercial agent may negotiate for the conclusion of sales or the supply of services on behalf of his principal. The agent can act, according to the decree, in the name of and for the accounts of the principal.

An agreement granting exclusive representation or distributorship to a person is considered an agency agreement and may be granted only to Lebanese nationals, unless the foreign agent is a national of a country that assures reciprocal treatment to Lebanese nationals.

The decree stated some mandatory provisions, based on public policy reasoning, dealing with the termination of agency agreement and the consequences thereof. For instance, the termination of the agency agreement entitles the agent to compensations, notwithstanding any agreement to the contrary.

The Decree states, *inter alia,* that exclusive jurisdiction regarding any dispute arising from the agreement is given to the local court in the area where the agency agreement is carried out.

### Currency and Banking

## Foreign Currency

Trade barriers and obstacles are minimal in Lebanon. Foreigners may invest freely in many industries and sectors. Lebanese nationals are allowed to quote prices or to agree to pay in foreign currencies. In general, there are no foreign exchange restrictions, and Lebanese nationals are free to transfer abroad any amount they want in any currency. It is notable that this freedom regarding foreign currency does not apply to certain areas, including commercial agency agreements.

## *Banking*

Improving economic and financial conditions have led to more favorable monetary and banking activity; the consolidated balance sheets of commercial banks and customer deposits have increased considerably; and bank deposits are being de-dollarized. The exchange rate for the Lebanese Pound remains stable and the Lebanese Pound deposits carry high yields. The Central Bank of Lebanon (CBL) and many commercial banks (representing over 80 percent of Lebanon's banking activity) joined the SWIFT (Society For World Interbank Financial Transfer) network. Monetary authorities are working on developing financial markets and instruments in order to channel savings into productive sectors.

Banking secrecy was introduced in Lebanon to attract capital from other countries in the region. The secrecy laws made banking Lebanon's major economic sector and the one that most successfully withstood the Civil War. Banking secrecy, within limits of public policy, is absolute. It applies to banks, bank personnel, financial companies and client transactions. Violation of banking secrecy triggers criminal and civil liability. The Bank Secrecy Law of September 3, 1956 allows banks to open secret bank accounts where the account holder is known only to the manager. Such accounts may be referred to by a number only. No account is to be divulged to third parties, including legal authorities, and no seizure or attachment can be made without written consent of the account holder.

Banks in Lebanon have generally been performing well, and their profitability is among the highest in the Middle East. However, a large percentage of their income is generated from their heavy investment in Lebanese Treasury bills. At the end of 1998, T-Bills accounted for 35 percent of the total banking sector deposits, which was were equivalent to approximately four times banks' capital and reserves.

## Intellectual Property

Lebanon is a signatory to the Paris Convention (London text), the Madrid Agreement for the Repression of False or Deceptive Indications on Goods (London text) and the Nice Agreement for the Classification of Goods and Services.

Violation of intellectual rights, however, remains a serious problem in Lebanon, especially in the areas of unauthorized copying of imported books, videotapes, cassettes and computer software. The government does a poor job of enforcing the law, and protection must be sought in the courts.

## Patents

Patents are granted for fifteen years from the date of filing. A patent application should be filed before the invention has been used or published in Lebanon or abroad. Applications are not examined as to novelty, and there are no opposition provisions. Pharmaceutical formulas or compounds are not patentable.

A patent may be declared void unless the invention has been worked in Lebanon within two years from the date of grant, three years for nationals of convention countries. There is no provision regarding the grant of a compulsory license in the absence of working. To be effective, assignments must be registered with the Patent Office.

## Trademarks

Trademark laws in Lebanon are old and rudimentary. The laws date from the beginning of the century and have not been updated to take into account economic developments and changes.

A trademark application can include goods in any number of classes. An application for the registration of a trademark is examined as to whether it offends public order and morals or represents natural or foreign decoration. If the application is accepted, a certificate of registration will be issued and is effected by publication in the Official Gazette. There are no opposition provisions, but any interested party may bring forward action for cancellation at any time during the term of protection on grounds such as lack of distinctiveness and improper registration.

A trademark is valid for fifteen years from the date of filing and is renewable indefinitely for similar periods. Assignment of a trademark must be recorded with the Trademark Office in order to be effective against third parties. Assignment may be with or without a business concern. Use of a trademark is not compulsory in order to file an application for registration or to maintain registration.

Infringement of the trademark laws is punishable by fine and imprisonment. Civil remedies are also available in the form of injunctions and damage awards. In the case of trademark imitation, the courts look for a general resemblance from the consumer point of view in determining whether the trademark is violating a protected mark.

## Designs and Industrial Models

Designs and industrial models are may be registered for an initial term of five years from the date of filing. Registration may be extended as long as twenty-five years. Designs and industrial models should be distinguishable from those previously known. Advertising prior to filing applications, even by way of sale of the relevant products, does not preclude registration. There are no provisions for opposition to the registration of designs and industrial models. Assignment of designs and industrial models is allowed. Working of designs and industrial models is not required, and compulsory licensing is not applicable. Damaging a validly registered and published design or industrial model knowingly is punishable by fine.

### Taxation

Income tax in Lebanon is levied on all persons or entities, whether or not residing in Lebanon, on income or profits derived in Lebanon. Income tax applies to income or profits derived from trade, commerce, industry and vocational activities. Profit consists of the gross taxable income after deduction of expenses and charges necessary for the carrying out of the trade, industry or business. The corporate income tax was raised from 10 to 15 percent recently. The individual marginal tax rates range between 2 percent to 28 percent. Bodies such as hospitals, schools, cooperative societies and trade unions are entitled to tax exemption. Also, there are special exemptions for agricultural and industrial activities as well as special tax rates for industries located outside of Beirut. Special rules apply to foreign companies that hail from countries with which Lebanese taxpayers enjoy reciprocal treatment.

**Investment and Trade**

## Barriers to Trade and Investment

Lebanon is a country of free trade. There are certain goods, however, such as computer hardware and software, and firearms and munitions that require an import license. Lebanon adheres to the Arab League boycott of Israel and therefore, the import of goods from Israel is officially prohibited, although this ban is not fully enforced.

## Customs

Lebanon levies most customs duties on an *ad valorem* basis, the average being 25 percent calculated on the CIF value of the goods converted to local currency by reference to the official dollar rate. Special low rates apply to certain imports from member countries of the Arab League, and many agricultural products are exempt from customs duties. Importation of a few specified commodities requires an import license that must be obtained prior to shipment. Free zones offering facilities for re-packaging and processing merchandise, assembling and manufacturing are located in the Beirut Port and the Tripoli Port.

## Work Permits

To reside and work in Lebanon, a foreigner is required to have a work permit issued by the Ministry of Social Affairs and a residence permit issued by the Ministry of Interior. In addition, foreign nationals that wish to carry on business in Lebanon must have a commercial register. Broadly speaking, work permits are granted to persons having skills not readily found in Lebanon and to management personnel (usually up to three people on the management staff of foreign firms).

**Environmental Law**

Lebanon entered into a number of international environmental agreements including the Convention concerning the Protection of Workers against

Ionizing Radiations (Geneva, 1960); the Agreement for the Establishment of the General Fisheries Council for the Mediterranean (Rome, 1949); the Convention for the Protection of the Mediterranean Sea against Pollution (Barcelona, 1976); the Outer Space Treaty and related instruments (1967); and Annex 16 on Environmental Protection to the 1944 Chicago Convention on International Civil Aviation.

# MOROCCO

## Recent Political Developments

After ruling for 38 years, King Hassan died in July 1999 from a heart attack. Immediately after his death, his son, Crown Prince Sidi Mohammed, 37, was anointed the new king.

The new king has not had much time to settle into his job. There are critical political and economic issues confronting the country that need to be addressed.

One such problem is the disputed Western Sahara region, in which the kingdom has been at odds with its neighbor, Algeria. Morocco claims this former Spanish colony is under its sovereignty, while Algeria backs the Polisario guerrillas who are seeking independence.

| | |
|---|---|
| Population | 29.1 million (1999 estimate) |
| Religions | 99% Islam; less than 1% Jewish |
| Government | Constitutional Monarchy |
| Languages | Arabic (official), French (business), Berber dialects, Spanish (in North) |
| Workweek | Monday–Friday 8:30–12:30; 4:00–18:30 |
| Monetary Unit | Dirhams (MD) |
| Exchange Rate | MD 9.8=US$ 1 |

In early November, the new king publicly offered proposals for ending the dispute, including holding elections for a royal advisory council in the disputed territory. He also affirmed the country's commitment to a UN-sponsored peace plan, in which a referendum will be held to determine the region's future. His main condition was that all potential voters must be able to participate. Differing views regarding voter eligibility have already caused long delays in the referendum, now scheduled for July 2000.

The new king must also try and pick up where his father left in trying to mend relations with Algeria. Problems arose in 1994 after Algerian gunmen attacked a Moroccan hotel. Before his death, King Hassan was due to meet the Algerian president to try and reconcile differences.

Morocco is one of few Arab countries to have good relations with Israel. And while not especially central to the Arab-Israeli peace process, Hassan II unreservedly supported and instigated moves towards Israeli-Palestinian reconciliation.

While facing tough economic situations, the new king is working with a much healthier economy because of reforms implemented by his father. In early September 1996, Moroccans voted almost unanimously for the King's plan to create a powerful upper-house of parliament and to strengthen economic development efforts as well as Morocco's regional influence. According to official results, 99.56 percent, or more than 10.15 million of the 12.35 million eligible voters, voiced approval for the plan.

The plan called for the division of the existing 333-seat parliament into two houses. The lower house, the New House of Representatives, will seat members elected directly by the public. The upper-house, the Chamber of Counselors, will be elected indirectly, mainly through local councils, professional bodies and trade unions, and the Chamber will have the power to force votes of no-confidence and to topple the government.

The changes will assist the government in developing Morocco's rural areas, where half of the population now resides. Direct elections to the second house should spread influence to rural areas that have traditionally had little voice in political matters. Despite the poverty in rural Morocco (a population of 1.5 million with a per capita income of just over US$ 200), and the high illiteracy rate, the rural areas contribute significantly to the national economy, mostly through the export of agricultural products.

## Recent Economic Developments

King Hassan died in the summer of 1999 bequeathing to his son, Sidi Mohammed a much more economically healthy kingdom.

The new king is continuing on the road to economic reform, which his father began in the early 1980s with the support of the IMF and World Bank. These reforms, which have included overhauling the banking and tax systems and easing import restrictions, have led to decreased inflation, increased per capita income and more healthy government financial accounts. The government is continuing with its privatization program and has placed a priority on developing infrastructure.

Morocco has many economic strengths, including the world's largest phosphate reserves, a diverse agricultural sector, a sizable tourist industry, a growing manufacturing sector (especially in the clothing industry), and considerable inflows of funds from Moroccans working abroad. Most of Morocco's trade is with Europe, with France alone accounting for about a quarter of Morocco's imports and a third of its exports.

But the country also has weaknesses. One such weakness is rainfall as the agricultural production comprises more than 16 percent of GDP. Economic output can vary widely from year to year depending on the amount of rainfall. Another serious problem facing the new king is job creation as unemployment nears 20 percent.

Parliament approved a MD 140.9 billion budget for fiscal 1999-2000. The budget forecasts total resources of MD 125.6 billion, a 5.8 percent increase over the year before. The budget deficit is to increase to MD 15.9 billion from 13.8 billion and state spending will increase by 3.4 percent to MD 63.4 billion. GDP is expected to grow by 8.4 percent up from around 0.2 percent in 1999.

The Moroccan government has pursued an economic reform program supported by the International Monetary Fund (IMF) and the World Bank since the early 1980s. It has restrained government spending, revised the tax system, reformed the banking system, followed appropriate monetary policies, eased import restrictions, lowered tariffs and liberalized the foreign exchange regime.

These reforms and changes have paid off. Per capita income, for example, has risen; inflation decreased and stabilized and there is narrower fiscal and current account deficits. Further indication is the increased amount of foreign investment, which rose 424 percent between April 1998 and April 1999 from MD 207.7 million to MD 1.0627 billion.

Still, the IMF is calling on Morocco to do more faster. The organization is urging the authorities to reform the civil service, abolish food subsidies and speed up privatization.

Additionally, the IMF wants Morocco to extend tax coverage to agriculture and to broaden and harmonize value-added taxes and excises. The organization did praise the country's creation of six commercial courts for resolving business conflicts, a development that will increase Morocco's attraction in the eyes of investors.

One of the country's economic Achilles heels is rainfall. Agricultural production constitutes more than 16 percent of GDP, and a large part of the Kingdom's revenues come from agricultural exports. Thus, years with plentiful rainfall will be reflected positively in GDP and years where there is drought will have negative effects. In 1995, for example, drought led to a four percent decrease in GDP, while 1996 rains raised that figure to 11 percent. In 1998, massive floods led to a 2 percent drop in Morocco's output. Excluding agriculture, however, the economy grew by 3.1 percent.

Job creation is another serious problem for this nation where more than 70 percent of the population is under age 25. Despite creating 50,000 new jobs since March 1999, Morocco's unemployment still approaches 20 percent. Further exacerbating the situation is that a large population segment lives below the poverty line. These realities pose serious social and political threats to the regime's stability.

The government has recently begun to use revenue generated from its privatization program to address social problems. In August 1999, the government announced an initiative to funnel revenues from a GSM license into a fund that would be used to combat unemployment and bureaucratic red-tape that is repelling some potential investors. Additionally, the fund will concentrate on housing projects in remote areas, upgrading the country's infrastructure and tourism sector.

The government has also placed a priority on developing the country's infrastructure. Large projects are being carried out on the kingdom's telecommunications and transportation infrastructure.

The government is continuing with its privatization program. The parliament recently passed a privatization law intended to accelerate the sale of state-owned enterprises, including approval to sell the government's stakes in more than 100 enterprises. The government hopes such steps will reduce the mounting debt, which in December 1998 was $18.3 billion.

## Fiscal Policy

The Moroccan government has reduced its role in the economy during the last decade. In particular, it ceased direct credit and foreign exchange allo-

## Economic Indicators

| | 2000(F) | 1999(E) | 1998 |
|---|---|---|---|
| GDP Growth (percent) | 8.4 | 0.2 | 6.5 |
| GDP (MD bn) | 391.4 | 364.6 | 346.9 |
| GDP per capita (US$) | 1,361 | 1,277 | 1,249 |
| Agriculture (% of GDP) | 16.3 | 15.5 | 16.2 |
| Non-Agricultural GDP growth rate | 4.2 | 3.9 | 3.4 |
| Inflation (%) | | 1.1 | 2.7 |
| Exports (%GDP) | 24.2 | 23.8 | 22.5 |
| Imports (%GDP) | 32.2 | 31.7 | 30.6 |
| Households Consumption (% GDP) | 67.3 | 67.4 | 68.0 |
| Imported Services Growth (%) | 2.2 | 2.8 | 2.5 |
| Exports Growth Rate (%) | 2.2 | 2.5 | 0.9 |
| Gross Investment (%GDP) | 22.7 | 21.9 | 21.9 |
| Gross Domestic Saving (%GDP) | 21.1 | 20.4 | 20.2 |
| Government Revenue (budget)** (MD bn) | 125.6 | 118.3 | |
| Government Expenditure (budget)** (MD bn) | 141.5 | 132.1 | |
| Overall Deficit (budget)** (MD bn) | 15.9 | 13.8 | |
| Deficit as % GDP (budget) | (F) 2.0 | 2.3 | |

cation, reduced trade barriers, restrained government spending, lowered taxes and embarked on a privatization program.

The government has sought to reduce its deficit. In 1995, it rose above 5 percent of GDP, decreasing to roughly 3-4 percent in the late 1990s.

## Monetary Policy

Morocco has managed to keep inflation in check during the last decade, averaging less than 3 percent a year.

## Balance of Payments

Morocco's chronic merchandise trade deficit is generally offset by receipts from tourism, workers remittances and foreign investment. But a widening gap between deficit and revenues has begun to put pressure on Morocco's foreign exchange reserves. Many economic gains in one sector have been offset by losses in others. For example, foreign investment in 1997 jumped 2.5 percent from $235 million in 1996 to $800.9 million in 1998, but revenues from tourism and worker remittances both decreased by 1.3 percent. In 1997, exports grew 7 percent and imports increased 4.1 percent, but exports remained only 59 percent of imports.

## Business Environment

### *Privatization*

The government approved a law in 1999 that would accelerate privatization plans, covering the sale of stakes in more than 100 companies. The government in the summer of 1999 sought an advisor to help with privatizing the state telecommunications company, Ittisalat al Maghrib. In the first round, between 20 percent and 30 percent of the company will be sold. The country's airlines, the Royal Moroccan Airlines, is also to be opened to the private sector as is the Public Bank.

Morocco was one of the Middle East's first countries to begin a privatization program. In 1989, a law was passed calling for the privatization of 112 firms by the end of 1995. The law was amended in 1994 to add two more firms and extend the deadline to 1998. By mid-1998, some or all of its stakes in 34 firms and 18 hotels had been sold.

More recently, the Moroccan parliament passed a privatization law intended to accelerate the sale of state-owned enterprises. The approved legislation calls for the sale of stakes in more than 100 companies, including the telecom utility, Ittsalat al-Maghrib.

Morocco boasts what many have termed the Arab world's most ambitious privatization program, with 112 firms worth US$ 2 billion mandated for sale by mid-1996. As a result of a rough economic performance in 1995, however, the government raised less than half the US$ 400 million that had been forecast from selling state-owned assets that year.

### *Stock Exchange*

In the beginning of 2000, the Casablanca Stock Exchange will move action from the trading floor to the computer, allowing brokers anywhere to trade directly in the Moroccan market. There are 55 companies and 84 mutual funds traded on the Casablanca exchange, with daily volume running at about $10 million. This relatively small capitalization makes this exchange unattractive for big investors. In May 1998, the volume of transactions reached MD 18.1 billion versus MD 27.6 billion a year earlier. During that same period the market capitalization dropped from MD 148.3 billion to 134.3 billion.

While the exchange performed relatively well, particularly before the Asian crisis in 1998, it has slumped since. One of the biggest issues facing the exchange is convincing more local companies to go public. Many, however, are family owned and resist making their finances available.

## Major Projects

### Telecommunications

In 1997, parliament adopted a new telecommunications law that has changed the industry. The law divided the "ONPT" monopoly into two independent entities: "Ittissalat Al Maghrib," the telecommunications operator, and "Barid Al Maghrib," the postal service operator. Furthermore, the law opened the way for private firms—local and foreign—to compete in telecommunications.

Today, the telecommunications market is rapidly growing. The government has sought to increase the number of main lines to 2 million to a teledensity of 10 percent. The government also wants to install fiber optic inter-urban networks connecting most major cities and extending telecommunications services to 1,600 rural locations, possibly with a fixed wireless technology.

Mobile phone use is also rapidly growing. The number of users is expected to grow at an annual rate of 16 percent, from the current 15,000 to 6 million by the end of 2014. In July 1999, the government awarded a $1.1 billion contract to Medi Telecom-Telefonic of Spain to operate the country's second mobile telephone system.

### Power Generation

The National Office of Electricity (ONE) has launched a program to meet growing electricity demand and to bring electricity to rural areas. The office is using solar power to electrify the most remote areas, where approximately 40,000 villages are without basic water and electrical services.

*Roads and Highways*

Approximately 60,000 km of roads covers Morocco, reaching all parts. The government plans to add an additional 1,000 kilometers of 4-lane highways by 2004 to reduce congestion and improve safety. The number of cars on the road and traffic has been increasing. In 1995, there were 1.4 million registered motor vehicles, with that number growing by 6 percent a year.

*Railway*

The Office National des Chemins de Fer (ONCEF) is planning two major projects. The first is 120 km of new tracks from Taourirt to Nador. The second 1,000 kilometers of new tracks form Marrakech to Laayoune.

## Franchising

The franchising market is expected to grow at an annual average rate of 30-50 percent during the next 4 years. Opportunities exist in fast food, hotels and motels, auto repair, toys, convenience stores, dry cleaning, printing and business equipment and services.

In 1992, Pizza Hut became the first franchise to open in Morocco. Most franchises are in fast food, clothing, furniture and cosmetics.

In addition to McDonald's and four Pizza Huts, which have had successful openings in Morocco, Dairy Queen has opened a restaurant in Rabat. A Moroccan franchisee has signed a contract with Subway Sandwiches. There appears to be an ample market for additional fast food chains. Hotels and motels, automotive parts and services, dry cleaning business equipment and services offer additional franchising opportunities in Morocco.

### Leading Business Opportunities

| Rank | Sector |
|------|--------|
| 1 | Telecommunications Equipment |
| 2 | Electrical Power Systems |
| 3 | Environmental Equipment & Services |
| 4 | Water Resources Equipment & Services |
| 5 | Engineering Services |
| 6 | Franchising |

# Legal Review

## Judiciary

There are six components to the Moroccan judicial system. The majority of legal matters fall within the jurisdiction of Regional Tribunals, which decide cases of personal property damages. Such judgments, excluding minor offenses punishable by a small fine, may be appealed to the Court of Appeals. The Court of Appeals also has a separate civil and criminal division. Despite previous announcements, the new Commerce Law, passed on May 18, 1996, did not establish special commercial courts. Courts of First Instance adjudicate crimes punishable by up to five years imprisonment and civil, personal status, or commercial cases. Monetary judgments of small amounts are not subject to appeal.

The decisions of all courts and tribunals may be reviewed by the Supreme Court. There is also the High Court of Justice that has jurisdiction over criminal and felonious matters allegedly committed by government officials. In addition, there are specialized Labor Tribunals which settle disputes by means of conciliation.

## Business Forms and Structures

### Companies Law

Under Moroccan law, the primary types of corporate structures available are: limited liability companies; private limited companies; limited partnerships with shares; general and limited partnerships; and joint-ventures, all of which generally conform to Western company forms of the same nomenclature. The two most widely used are the SA and the SARL, as described below.

### Limited Liability Company

Limited liability companies (SA) must have a minimum of five shareholders who can be either legal entities or individuals. As with traditional limited liability companies, the shareholders' liability is limited to the amount of share equity the shareholders hold. Upon incorporation of the limited liability company, a quarter of the equity capital must be paid in advance if paid in cash contributions. If it is paid in contributions in kind, it must be fully paid upon incorporation. Both bearer and registered shares may be issued by the limited liability company. The minimum share value is MD 50. The company has no corporate name but a trade name, and there are generally no restrictions on the sale and transfer of shares to third parties.

## Private Limited Company

The private limited company (SARL) is an intermediate type between associations of persons and of capital, bearing resemblance to both partnerships and share companies. It is always a trading company, regardless of its corporate name and its minimum equity capital is MD 10,000. It may be formed by two or more members who are only liable to the amount of their share of the equity capital in the company. Unlike a general partnership, members of a private limited company do not need to be registered merchants. The private limited company must file a memorandum of association as part of its incorporation process. The capital stock has to be fully described and paid up as the company is formed. Stocks shall have the same face value and are not negotiable; they may be transferred only through contracts. "Parts Sociales" may be transferred to third parties outside the company only with the co-associates' consent.

## Partnerships

### General Partnerships

In a general partnership, the partners are jointly and severally liable, without limitation, for the debts of the partnership. Partners may be individuals or corporations, however, they do have to be registered as merchants. There is no restriction on participation by foreign individuals or corporations in general partnerships.

### Limited Partnerships

In a limited partnership at least one partner must have unlimited liability while the others have limited liability. A partner whose liability is limited may not take part in the management of the partnership. Limited partnerships are relatively rare in Morocco.

## Limited Partnership with Shares

This corporate form is essentially a joint stock company wherein the capital is divided into shares to be held by active and inactive partners. There must be at least one active partner who has unlimited liability with regard to the debts of the entity, and three inactive partners who are liable only to the extent of their shares in the equity capital. The limited partnership with shares is operated by the active partners or by external managers. The governing body is a board of trustees composed of at least three of the inactive partners.

## Joint Ventures

A joint venture does not have a separate legal personality, and its existence is not normally disclosed to third parties, except to the tax authorities. Joint ventures are used for financial syndicates or to undertake specific construction contracts.

## Branch Offices

The branch affiliate or subsidiary of a foreign corporation is regarded as a separate legal entity. The Moroccan branch, however, has to disclose certain details regarding its parent-company, its representatives and its delegated powers. When registering a branch in Morocco, the foreign parent-company must submit its articles of incorporation along with the incorporation documents of the branch.

## Sole Proprietorships

Foreigners may establish in Morocco sole proprietorships. In a sole proprietorship, the business is conducted under the responsibility of an individual personally liable for the debts of the business to the extent of all business and personal assets. The business must be registered with the Commerce Registry and with the tax authority.

# Currency and Banking

## Foreign Currency Control

The Moroccan government has made the Moroccan Dirham (MD) convertible for an increasing number of transactions over the last few years. As of February 1993, the MD was made convertible for all current transactions and for some capital transactions, notably, capital repatriation by foreign investors. Foreign exchange is routinely available through commercial banks for such transactions upon presentation of documents. The Central Bank sets the exchange rate for the MD against a basket of currencies of its principal trading partners. The rate against the basket has been steady since a 9 percent devaluation in May 1990, with changes in the rate of individual currencies reflecting changes in cross-rates. In a further move, the Ministry of Finance recently decided that private enterprises are allowed to access international financial markets directly.

International financial transactions are subject to the control of the Moroccan Exchange Office, which retains the authority to act in a balance of payments or liquidity crisis.

The liberalization of the exchange control has removed all barriers for international trade transactions, foreign investments, income transfer, foreign technical assistance and tourism. Remittances of capital and related income to non-residence are guaranteed. No limitations are imposed on the time or amount of profit remitted. Loans, however, must be authorized by the Office of Exchange. Another important decision gives the banks the possibility to freely conduct investment operations in international capital market sites and, also, to engage in hard currency accounts or in any other amount of capital deposited by foreign entities.

## Banking

The Moroccan banking system is similar to that of France, but not quite as sophisticated. It is composed of a Central Bank and about fifteen other commercial banks that provide a comprehensive range of services. Financing is available from quasi-state and from private institutions.

The banking industry is highly regulated. Central Bank regulations deal with minimum capital requirements, liquidity, solvency and legal lending limit ratios. In 1991, credit ceilings were substituted with indirect monitoring by way of changes in reserve requirements and controlled access to the Central Bank rediscount window. The legal lending limit of 7 percent of net capital funds is regarded by the profession as constraining. This situation has been mitigated by the recent five-fold increase in the legal lending limit for credit guaranteed by OECD-based banks.

The Banking Law of April, 1967 dealing with banking and credit practices was replaced by a law of July, 1993. Among other things, the new Banking Law also covers finance companies and other credit institutions and defines in detail the kinds of transactions that can be undertaken by credit institutions. The law also creates a national council of surveys and cash, as well as a committee on credit institutions.

## Commercial Banking Services

There is no clear-cut distinction between commercial and merchant banks. By and large, all commercial banks provide commercial and saving services, with merchant banking as an accessory service. The four largest commercial banks are: Credit Populair du Maroc (or Banque Populaire), Banque Commerciale du Maroc, Banque Marocaine du Commerce Exterieur and Wafabank.

Moroccan banks offer a broad range of regular banking services, including depository services and trade and credit services. Several banks now offer electronic banking services for corporate clients and a wide array of consumer banking facilities such as credit cards, ATMs and telephone banking services. Most banks are linked to the SWIFT global payment system, enabling them to quickly execute foreign currency and convertible MD transactions to non-residents, including transactions involving the repatriation of earnings of foreign companies. Moroccan banks, however, are still not in the position of offering a complete spectrum of modern services in terms of foreign exchange, money and capital markets and corporate finance activities. In order to ameliorate this situation, the Moroccan monetary authorities are working on regulatory changes which would promote additional modernization of the industry.

## Offshore Banking

An offshore bank is a legal entity or individual regardless of nationality whose headquarters are based in an offshore financial location and whose activities consist of dealing in convertible foreign currency deposits and undertaking with these same currencies any credits, exchange or financial activity. Currently, there are two offshore banks in the Tangier Free Trade Zone. Offshore banks are not obliged to repatriate any income or foreign revenues and have total exchange freedom with regard to their transactions with non-resident entities. These banks have free access to investment activities in Morocco and to capital participation operations in local corporations. They are exempt from registration fees, VAT, patent and urban tax as well as all import duties and taxes and TPA on distributed dividends.

## Special Purpose Banking

A number of financial institutions, mainly those that are government-controlled, have been established to serve special purposes, including providing finance to the agricultural industry, to hotels and other property and to investment considered as contributing to the economic development of Morocco. Notwithstanding the special purposes allocated to those institutions, they are increasingly involved in ordinary activities of commercial banks.

## Other Financial Institutions

The few companies dealing with leasing are usually owned by larger institutions in the industry. Venture capital is hardly used for financing, and there are no specialized venture capital companies in Morocco. With regard to investment institutions, there are over twenty insurance companies in the country governed by special regulations.


## Intellectual Property

Morocco has a relatively comprehensive regulatory and legislative system for the protection of intellectual property. Intellectual property rights, however, must be registered in both Casablanca and Tangier in order to be protected in Morocco.

Morocco is a member of the World Intellectual Property Organization (WIPO) and party to a number of other international agreements and conventions dedicated to the protection of intellectual property, including the Bern Copyright, Paris Industrial Property and Universal Copyright conventions, the Brussels Satellite Convention, and the Madrid, Nice and the Hague Agreements for the Protection of Intellectual Property.

Morocco was considering enactment of a new law on industrial property protection in a bid to stop unlicensed use of international brands or makes by local companies. Although Morocco is under various obligations due to its membership to GATT since 1994, the new Commerce Law of May 13, 1996 did not include any provisions strengthening intellectual property rights.

## Patents

Any individual or legal entity may file an application for a patent with the Moroccan Patent Office in Casablanca. The Patent Office examines applications with regard to form only and not with regard to novelty or merit. The particulars of the application are published in the Official Gazette. No opposition procedure is provided, and patents issued are valid for twenty years. Universal novelty of the invention is required by law to grant a patent, and working of patents issued is required by law to maintain the patent. Patents rights may be freely transferred to third parties, however, the transfer must be registered with the Patent Office in order to be effective against third parties.

## Trademarks

The international classification of goods is followed in Morocco. Trademark applications are examined by the Trademark Office only with regard to form. Registered trademarks in the preceding year are published in a special trademark supplement of the Official Gazette. No opposition procedure is provided. A registered trademark is valid for twenty years from the date of registration renewable for additional twenty years periods.

Transfer of trademark rights must be registered with the Trademark Office within three months in order to be valid against third parties. Infringement of a registered trademark may be punishable under either the penal or civil laws of Morocco.

## Copyright

Moroccan law provides copyright protection for the literary or artistic expression of an idea, and there are no registration requirements to invoke such protection.

A copyright confers upon the author two principal rights: a property right and an ethical right. The property right gives the author the exclusive right to exploit the copyrighted work for pecuniary gain. This right extends throughout the author's lifetime, and, thereafter, it is transferred to the benefit of the author's heirs for a period of fifty years.

The ethical right protects an author's non-pecuniary interest in the literary or artistic work, which includes the protection of authorship and integrity. This right is perpetual, inalienable and remains with the author until death, and thereafter, with the author's heirs. Authors may sell all or part of their property rights, or the right to perform or reproduce the work, without forfeiting their ethical rights.

## Taxation

The Moroccan taxation system consists of direct and indirect taxes. Indirect taxes provide a greater source of tax revenue than the direct taxes. The system is statutory-based and has been recently updated in part with effect from 1/1/1996 by the Investment Charter (Law No. 18/95). There is virtually no case law on taxation, and tax-issues hardly come before the courts. In general, the tax authorities do not issue advance rulings on taxation matters.

### Taxation of Companies

Moroccan corporations are subject to a unitary tax system. The corporate tax (impet sur les societes or IS) rate has been reduced to 35 percent in 1996. Corporations are taxed under a special tax regime, which covers limited liability companies, limited partnerships by shares, general and limited partnerships in which at least one partner is a corporate entity, civil companies, branches of foreign corporations, public sector companies having profit-oriented activity and joint ventures having business-oriented activity. General partnerships and limited partnerships in which all partners are individuals may elect to be taxed under the corporate tax regime. The same applies to joint ventures in which all parties are individuals.

Foreign corporations are subject to taxation on income arising in Morocco if they have or are deemed to have a permanent establishment in Morocco. Taxation of corporations is the same irrespective of ownership, and foreign owned corporations are essentially regarded as Moroccan corporations insofar as they are incorporated in Morocco.

The corporate tax regime is based upon territoriality. Net profits earned by foreign subsidiaries and establishments of Moroccan companies are not taxable until profits are actually repatriated and distributed to shareholders.

Taxable income is based on receipts and accruals from products delivered, services rendered and work carried out and accepted by customers. Interest, royalties, income and service fees are subject to corporate income tax at the rate of 36 percent. Dividends received by corporate shareholders from taxable entities incorporated in Morocco are not taxable. This exemption does not apply, however, to foreign investment income, which is taxed after deducting foreign withholding taxes.

Morocco exempts certain types of income from corporate taxation. The first is income derived from agriculture which is exempt until the year 2020. The second concerns income of companies set up in the Western Sahara. There are also specific tax incentives exempting some companies from corporate tax for specified periods. In addition, Moroccan corporations can distribute tax free dividend of common- stock pro rata to all common-stock shareholders.

All expenses incurred for the purpose of the business are normally deductible, including salaries and wages, depreciation, rent and representation expenses. Only 75 percent of the amount paid for purchases of raw materials and products, start-up expenses, donations and other general expenses equal to or exceeding MD 10,000 are deductible, unless the payment is made by a non-assignable crossed check, bank transfer or bill of exchange. Except for the corporate tax (IS), taxes are deductible.

Expenses incurred outside Morocco by a foreign company having permanent activity in Morocco require adequate justification and documentation before they may be deducted. Losses may be carried forward and deducted from taxable profit for a period of four years.

A minimum amount of corporate tax is payable by companies other than foreign companies (cotisation minimale or CM), irrespective of the company's profits or losses. The CM is based on turnover, income from interest, subsidies, bonuses or donations received. The CM is levied at a rate of 0.5 percent of income, and is not payable by companies during their first thirty-six months of operation.

## Registration Fees

Morocco imposes a registration fee at a fixed rate of 0.50 percent on the forming or increasing of company capital. This rate is reduced to 0.25 percent for deeds of partnership or capital increase of investment banks and companies the main purpose of which is either stocks and shares management or application for other companies on joint account.

## Subsidiaries of Foreign Companies

Subsidiaries set up in Morocco by foreign companies are treated as local companies, independent of their foreign parent-company for legal and taxation purposes. Inter-company transactions must be on an arm's length basis. Expenses must be incurred in the furthering of the subsidiary's objectives and not those of its parent-company.

Dividends paid to non-resident shareholders are subject to a 15 percent withholding tax. Interest, royalties and service or management fees paid to non-residents are subject to a 10 percent withholding tax. These rates may be reduced or waived under prevention of double taxation treaties.

## National Solidarity Levy

Companies subject to corporate tax must pay a levy called National Solidarity Levy (PSN). The base used to asses this levy is equal to the base chosen for the assessment of corporate tax, and it is calculated by applying a 10 percent rate to the amount of the corporate tax. If a company is fully exempt from corporate tax, PSN has to be paid in an amount of 25 percent to a theoretical corporate tax. The PSN cannot be less than MD 1,500 for a yearly turnover of less than MD 1,000,000 and not less than MD 3,000 for a turnover of more than MD 1,000,000.

## Capital Gains Tax

Morocco instituted a tax on the proceeds from stocks and company's shares and comparable income (TPT), distributed by companies based in Morocco and paying taxes on corporations. The tax of 15 percent is collected at the source and applies to:

- Dividends;
- Capital interest;
- Profit percentages;
- Special allowances or the payment of fees and other compensations allotted to members of the board of directors (except for the fraction of these compensations considered as salary and subject to personal income tax -IGR);
- Sums levied on profits to repay capital produced to stockholders or to buy over stocks;
- Beneficiary/founder's shares;
- Surpluses from winding up augmented by reserves built up over at least ten years ago;
- Profits made in Morocco by establishments whose home office is located abroad, as these profits are made available to such companies abroad.

## Taxation of Individuals

Individuals, regardless of nationality or activity, who have their habitual residence in Morocco are subject to a personal income tax (impet general sur le revenue or IGR) on their worldwide income on a progressive scale between 13 and 44 percent. Individuals not having their habitual residence in Morocco are subject to tax only on Moroccan-source income. Habitual residence status is established by reference to one of the following: (1) place of permanent abode; (2) center of economic interest; and (3) duration of stay in the country exceeding 183 days within any period of 365 days. The issue of double taxation is partially addressed by tax treaties or unilateral relief in the form of tax credit.

Generally speaking, there are no concessions for foreign nationals working in Morocco, but the cost of home travel is exempt from tax every two years, and a substantial reduction in tax on pensions received from other countries is granted. In addition to employment income, tax is levied on professional and business activities, investments and rent.

All compensation paid to employees is taxable, including salaries and wages, allowances, pensions, annuities, reimbursement of taxes and all benefits derived from employment. Taxable benefits include the furnishing of an automobile for the employee's private use, housing benefits and profit sharing or retirement plans paid by foreign companies.

An individual taxpayer can deduct from taxable income any necessary traveling and entertainment expenses, provided they are incurred in the performance of that individual's duties, and are justified by the nature of the profession.

## Other Taxes

### Value Added Tax

The Value Added Tax (VAT) is a non-cumulative tax levied at each stage of the production and distribution cycle. Thus, suppliers of goods and services must add VAT to their net prices. Where the purchaser is also liable for VAT, input VAT may be offset against output VAT. The standard VAT rate is 19 percent and applies to all suppliers of goods and services, except those taxed at other rates or those who are exempt. A reduced rate of 7 percent applies to specific items such as banking and credit services, leasing, gas, water and electricity. A reduced rate of 14 percent applies to building and construction activities and to the transport and the hotel industries.

Two types of exemptions from VAT are provided. The first is an exemption with credit, equivalent to the zero tax concept, which applies to exports, agricultural material and equipment and fishing equipment. The second is an exemption without credit, i.e., the seller receives no credit for input VAT paid. This exemption applies to basic foodstuffs, newspapers and international transport services.

### Business Tax

A business tax, or patente, is levied on individuals and enterprises that habitually carry out business in Morocco. The tax consists of a tax on the rental value of business premises (rented or owned) and a fixed amount depending on the size and nature of the business. The tax rates range from 5 percent to 30 percent and pro rata reimbursements are granted for businesses which commence or cease activities during the tax year.

### Patent Tax

The Patent Tax is to be paid by individuals involved in commercial activities who are not exempted by special decree (dahir). The tax includes a proportional tax which averages 10 percent of the rental value of industrial establishments and a variable tax which depends on the number and kind of pieces of equipment owned by the business entity.

## Stamp Duty/Notarial Tax

Corporate stocks, founder's shares and bonds issued by companies are free from both stamp duty and formalities. A notarial tax is imposed based on the capital stock, in the amount of 1 percent for stock up to MD 5,000, 0.5 percent from MD 5,000 to 10,000 and 0.2 percent for over MD 10,000.

## Urban Property Tax and Municipal Tax

Owners of real estate are subject to urban property tax on the rental value of the property. The same applies to owners of machines and appliances that are integral parts of the establishment producing goods or services. The general urban property tax rate is 13.5 percent of the rental value. It is 3 percent for lots and 4 percent for structures and fittings as well as for machines and appliances.

The tenants of rented property are subject to a municipal tax on the value of the property. The rate is 10 percent of the normal rental value of the buildings located within the urban areas and 6 percent of the normal value on peripheral zones of urban communes.

## Tax on Interest

Tax is imposed on individual or corporate residents in respect of interest earned on bonds and other loan securities, fixed and current account deposits, loans and advances, and various loans conducted through banks or financial institutions.

## Customs Duties

All goods and services may be imported; Goods deemed to have a negative impact on national production, however, may require an import license. Most products imported are subject to import duties, the rates of which vary between 2.5 percent and 10 percent for equipment, materials, spare parts and accessories. Some materials and products, however, are exempted, especially those imported under the investment charter, imported under customs economic systems and those using renewable energies. Value added tax is also payable on goods imported into Morocco.

## Import Tax Levy

The Import Tax Levy (PFI) is imposed on imported commodities at a fixed rate of 15 percent. It is reduced or eliminated, however, as follows:

- A rate of 12.5 percent for pharmaceuticals or raw materials used in the manufacturing of pharmaceuticals;
- Exemption for the import of material subject to customs duties;
- Exemption for enterprises which engage in research activities involving mineral substances;
- Exemption for materials using renewable energies;
- Exemption for fertilizer products;
- Exemption for certain antibiotic medical products.

There is also a para-fiscal tax of 0.25 percent that applies to imported commodities.

## Treaties for the Prevention of Double Taxation

Since a Moroccan resident is taxed on worldwide income, the Moroccan tax system provides relief from foreign taxes paid on such worldwide income by means of a foreign tax credit. This foreign tax credit cannot exceed the Moroccan tax otherwise payable in respect of the foreign-source income.

The Moroccan government is eager to encourage foreign investment. This is reflected by the territoriality principle for taxation applicable to corporations mentioned above. In addition, Morocco has concluded about seventeen treaties for the prevention of double taxation, mainly with developed countries. Morocco's list of treaty-partners include Belgium, Canada, France, Germany, Italy, Luxembourg, the Netherlands, Norway, Romania, Spain, Sweden, Tunisia, the United Kingdom and the United States.

Most of the tax treaties are based on the OECD model and do not contain specific anti-abuse provisions. Reduced withholding tax rates vary from one treaty to another, and in the case of the treaty with Sweden, the rate is zero. Of special interest is the treaty with France which offers advantages involving self-employed foreigners and payments for technical assistance and contracts (e.g., imported supplies).

## Investments and Trade

### Investment Charter

Resident or non-resident foreign nationals are entitled to invest freely in Morocco and no investment operation in Morocco requires any prior authorization from the Control Exchange Office. Prior to 1996, Morocco offered foreign investors a package of investment incentives contained in various investment codes in different areas of business such as exports, tourism, industrial, mining, maritime, handicraft and real estate investments. Those codes have been replaced by a new Investment Charter, promulgated by Decree No.1-95-213 of November 8, 1995. Effective as of January 1996, the new Charter set up as a framework the main objectives regarding the promotion and development of investments in Morocco within the next ten years. It also codified several existing regulations some of which have been implemented through their inclusion in the Corporate Tax Law in 1996. Further, the Charter establishes that benefits for investors under previously existing laws will be maintained until expiration of their term and of the conditions for which they had been granted.

## Investment Incentives

The Charter gives the same preference to all sectors except for agriculture. The top five sectors Morocco is trying to develop are: banking, industry, holdings, real estate and trade. Special incentives have been made available to attract these industries, these incentives differentiate between the installation phase and the operational phase of a company.

Incentives offered for the Installation Phase are:

- Exemption from formalities for land acquisition;
- Application of a registration fee of 2.5 percent for acquisition formalities for land;
- Application of 0.5 percent registration fee for inputs in capital formation of companies or increases in capital;
- Reduced import dues (between 2.5 percent and 10 percent maximum ad valorem);
- Exemption from import tax levy (PFI);
- Patent tax: suppression of the variable tax and exemption during first five years of operation;
- Exemption of urban tax for first five years after the completion or installation of new buildings;
- Exemption of reimbursement of VAT for equipment, material and tools acquired locally or imported.

Incentives for the Operational Phase are:

- Profits and income liable to corporate tax are not subject to the National Solidarity Contribution (PSN);
- Profits and income completely exonerated from corporate tax pay a contribution at a rate of 25 percent of the normal corporate tax;
- Exemption from corporate tax for exporting enterprises for five years;
- 50 percent reduction in corporate tax or income tax during the first five years thereafter;
- Enterprises are allowed to create an annual investment reserve free of tax;
- Application of sliding scale amortization for equipment;
- Exemption from real estate profits tax when premises are first ceded for use as accommodation.

In addition, special incentives are available to encourage companies to comply with environment protection laws or to install environment protection equipment.

## Administrative Proceedings

Apart from serving as an outline for various changes in tax law, the Charter also promotes facilitation and reduction of administrative procedures involving the carrying out of investments. To that end, a special administrative body for the promotion of investments was instituted and charged with assisting investors. In addition, in all cases where approval of an administrative authorization for the granting of advantages proves to be necessary, this authorization is deemed to be granted when the administration has kept silent regarding the result of the request during a period of sixty days after the date the request has been filed.

## Public Sector Investment Contracts

The Charter also offers special contracts with the state to enterprises whose investment programs are important due to their size, the number of stable jobs created, the region in which they will be carried out, the technology they transfer or their level of environmental protection. Under these contracts, the state can grant a partial exemption from the following expenses:

- Costs of purchasing the land necessary for carrying out the investment;
- Costs of external infrastructure;
- Costs of professional training.

The Charter explicitly mentions that these contracts can include provisions, stipulating that the method regarding the settlement of disputes arising between a foreign investor and the Moroccan state will be in accordance with international agreements ratified by Morocco with respect to international arbitration.

## Investment Promotion Fund

The Charter creates an Investment Promotion Fund, a special appropriation account designed to be used for the operations relating to the responsibility of the state for the cost of advantages granted to investors under the framework of the investment contract regime. The Charter, however, does not stipulate how the fund will be financed.

## Foreign Trade

As a member of GATT, Morocco has gradually removed most restrictions for imports originating from other member countries. According to the law of November 9, 1993 relating to foreign businesses, all goods and services can be imported without a licensing requirement. In the event that imports are deemed to have a negative impact on national production, however, an import license may be required. In addition, the following duties can be imposed:

- Compensatory duties, in the event that the product imported benefits from manufacturing or export bonuses or subsidies in its country of origin;
- An anti-dumping duty, in the event that the import value is lower that the normal value of the item.

In order to import into Morocco, some documentation procedures are required. A person or entity must be registered in a register of importers and must obtain the authority to import from the Ministry of Commerce and Industry. An import registration form (engagement d'importation) should be obtained from a Moroccan Schedule A Bank for all imports into Morocco. This form facilitates both custom formalities and the payments of the invoice.

In recent years, export regulations have undergone a substantial amount of liberalization. Export licenses are not required, and export sales are not subject to export tax. The sole obligation on the part of the exporter is the repatriation of export benefits. The repatriation should be performed in a 120 day period, however, the deadline can be extended in case the trade obligations require do so. Settlements relating to exports can now be made in foreign currency, and the exporter is no longer required to produce the customs declarations justifying the import of foreign currency. Similarly, the financial regulations pertaining to investment operations are now directly handled at the level of the banking institutions.

## Free Trade Agreements

In 1995 Morocco entered into a Free Trade Agreement with the European Union which gives preferential treatment to Moroccan goods exported to the EU. Under the agreement, industrial products can be exported to the EU duty-free without quantitative restrictions. Only for agricultural products, some quotas and restrictions remain.

Recently, the country has signed an additional trade agreement with Ministers from four EFTA States (Switzerland, Norway, Iceland and Liechtenstein). Whereas the EFTA members will eliminate all restrictions on imports of industrial products, processed agricultural goods, fish and other marine products, Morocco has agreed to phase out tariffs and quotas over twelve years, while retaining the right to introduce restrictions to protect nascent or restructuring industries.

Morocco has also signed free trade arrangements with members of the Maghreb Arab Union (UMA). For all practical purposes, however, the UMA is dormant, and regional economic integration has been stalled. Another bilateral free trade arrangement has been established with Saudi Arabia.

## Free Trade Zone

There is a Free Trade Zone in Tangier which is open to both Moroccan and foreign companies. The sixty-five companies located in the zone may import goods duty-free and are exempt from other taxes. The only requirement is that all local workers be paid directly in foreign exchange, which they are then obliged to exchange for MD at Moroccan commercial banks operating in the zone.

## Labor Law

The employment contract binding the employer to each of his employees is governed by the Royal Decree dated August 13, 1913, which lays down a code of obligations and contracts. Such contract may be written or oral.

A decree of October 23, 1948 sets out a specimen contract applicable to all industrial and commercial establishments. It defines the reciprocal rights and duties of employer and employees. An employer, however, can make more favorable arrangements in his establishment, subject to agreement with the Minister of Labor.

Workers have the right to join together in unions for the protection of their rights and to strike in defense for their collective interests. Nevertheless, the Inspectorate of Labor endeavors to settle disputes by mediation. At the same time, if both parties agree, arbitration may avoid recourse to strike action or legal action before the Tribunal of First Instance.

There is no legal requirement for employees to be involved in the management of companies or to be represented on the board of directors. Although there is no legislation requiring participation by labor in the profits of a business, a number of companies have implemented profit sharing plans.

The work week is limited to forty-eight hours, with no more than ten hours worked per day. Every employee is entitled to a weekly day of rest and a number of statutory paid holidays.

## Salaries and Wages

There are no legislated wage controls in Morocco other than the minimum wage. Therefore, wages and salaries can be freely contracted between employees and employers. Apart from agreed pay increases, an indexing system enables the government to raise by decree all wages and salaries effectively paid when the Central Commission for Prices and Wages records an increase of at least 5 percent in the cost of living.

Wages, whatever the method of remuneration (time rates, piece rates or job rates) must be paid at least twice a month, at a maximum of sixteen days' interval. Salaries must be paid at least once a month.

## Health and Safety

The provision of medical services is compulsory in every firm employing more than fifty persons. Employers must provide the services of a doctor; alternatively, they may set up a joint service with other firms, supervised by a chairman. The operation of such health service is subject to inspection.

Every firm must observe standard safety regulations. Certain forms of work considered as dangerous are covered by special regulations, including, *inter alia,* employment of women and children. The Inspectorate of Labor ensures that these regulations are observed.

## Termination of Employment

Dismissal of personnel may take place for a number of reasons, such as reduction of jobs in the particular branch, incapacity owing to age or insufficient aptitude or as a disciplinary measure owing to a serious offense. Except in the case of a serious offense, the worker is entitled to notice, which varies according to his seniority in the firm and the nature of his work. Such a dismissed worker is also entitled, after a year's service, to compensation proportionate to the length of his service with the firm.

## Social Benefits

Membership in the social security system (Caisse nationale de Securite Sociale or CNSS) is compulsory for all employers, and they are required to register all their workers. CNSS pays industrial and commercial workers family allowances and daily allowances in cases of illness, accident or occupational diseases not covered by workers compensation, allowances in case of death, disability pensions, old-age pensions and survivors' pensions.

All employers and employees are covered by the social security system. Foreign workers coming to take up employment in Morocco participate on the same basis as Moroccan nationals.

## Environmental Law

Morocco faces various environmental problems, including several arising from natural hazards. The main difficulties arise from Morocco's dependency on water and the economy's vulnerability to climatic change. Morocco is now defined as a "water-stressed" country. Per capita supplies and water quality are declining, rural areas are poorly served with water, and there are substantial losses in both irrigation (which currently accounts for 85 percent of water use) and drinking water systems in urban areas. In addition, the country suffers from oil pollution of its coastal waters.

In attempting to solve these difficulties, Morocco has made some progress toward defining a national environmental action plan, but overall institutional awareness and coordination are weak. Morocco is, however, a party to various international agreements regarding environmental protection issues such as biodiversity, climate change, endangered species, marine dumping, marine life conservation, nuclear test ban, ozone layer protection, protection of world cultural and natural heritage and the protection of the wetlands. It has also signed agreements for the establishment of a General Fisheries Council for the Mediterranean and of a Commission for Controlling the Desert Locust in the Near East. In addition, Morocco has signed but not ratified further agreements on desertification, environmental modification and the law of the sea.

Some exemption from taxes and other duties have been made available for persons and entities promoting or implementing environmental protection.

# OMAN

## Recent Political Developments

The Sultanate of Oman is a monarchy which has been ruled by the Al Bu Sa'id family since the middle of the eighteenth century. It has no political parties or directly elected representative institutions. The current Sultan is Qaboos Bin Sa'id Al Sa'id who acceded to the throne in 1970. Although the Sultan retains firm control over all important policy issues, he has brought tribal leaders and other notables into the Government. In 1996, the Sultan presented the "Basic Statute of the State," Oman's first written constitution, which guarantees various rights within the framework of Koranic and customary law.

In accordance with tradition and cultural norms, much decision-making is by consensus among these leaders. In 1991, the Sultan established a fifty-nine seat Consultative Council, or *Majlis Ash-Shura,* which replaced an older advisory body. The Government selects council members from lists of nominees proposed by each of the fifty-nine *wilayats* (regions). After the country's first national census in 1993, the Sultan expanded the member-

| | |
|---|---|
| Population | 2.4 million (1999), including approx. 600,000 expatriates |
| Annual Population Growth Rate (estimate) | 4.9 percent |
| Religion | Islam |
| Government | Constitutional Monarchy |
| Languages | Arabic (English is widely spoken) |
| Work Week | Public Sector: Saturday–Wednesday 7:30–14:30 Private Sector: Saturday–Thursday 8:00–13:00 Banking: Saturday–Wednesday 8:00–12:00 Thursdays 8:00–11:00 |
| Monetary Unit | Omani Rial (OR) |
| Exchange Rate | OR1=US$ 2.6 |

ship of the new Council to eighty seats. The Council has no formal legislative powers, but may question government ministers and recommend changes to new laws on economic and social policy.

Oman has been an active participant in the Middle East peace process. It participated in the Multilateral Working Group and has played an active role in the Working Group on Water Resources. Oman was the first Gulf country to host an official Israeli delegation and in 1996 Israel and Oman opened trade mission offices in each other's countries.

## Recent Economic Developments

Oman is one of the smallest oil producers in the Gulf region, although its strategic location on the Strait of Hormuz leading into the Gulf necessitates 40 percent of the world's oil supply to cross through its waters. Based on current reserve estimates and production rates, the country's oil resources are expected to last 20-25 years. This is significant in Oman, where oil revenue in 1998 comprised 69 percent of government expenditure and 30 percent of GDP, which was $14.1 billion.

Whether this total depletion becomes reality, the Omani government is preparing for the worst by developing other revenue-generating industries, particularly in the area of gas. It is also seeking to privatize government-owned enterprises and replace the public sector with the private as the main engine of economic growth.

Since 1970 Oman has used its modest oil revenue to make impressive economic progress and to improve public access to health care, education and social services. In recent years the Omani government has sought to diversify the economy and to stimulate private investment.

As a result of the large number of foreign workers, the government is attempting a policy of "Omanization" to introduce more Omanis into the work force.

Estimates of the population growth rate vary, but most fall within the range of an increase of 4.9 percent each year. Virtually all Omanis are Muslim. Half are adherents of the Ibadhi sect, the others are Sunni with a small number of Shi'ites in the country as well. The Shi'ites are particularly prominent in commerce. Expatriates follow a variety of Indian and Western religions, and there are places of worship for their faiths in Oman.

Since 1973, the Omani government has invested its oil revenues in building a modern infrastructure. The latest major government project is a $2.4 billion liquefied natural gas (LNG) project in Sur, which will be exported LNG to Korea, India and Japan. Planning has begun on an industrial free zone to attract foreign multinationals and to develop Salalah as an air-sea cargo hub.

The most successful recent major project is Port Salalah, a $250 million container transshipment port, which opened in November 1998. Since then, the port has undergone steady growth in shipping traffic and has the potential to generate rapid industrial development in southern Oman.

There are many characteristics of the Omani economy that are enticing foreign investors, including the country's free market economy and unrestricted foreign exchange or capital flows. The country is also attractive because of its private-sector based development strategy, renewed emphasis on privatization, favorable credit ratings from overseas lenders, customs duties exemptions, and overall atmosphere of stability and moderation.

Furthermore, the country's attempt to gain membership to the World Trade Organization by 2000 means it must take measures to meet requirements in intellectual property protection, market access and customs valuation.

There are, however, some constraints to engaging trade and investing in Oman. They include the country's small, undeveloped, high value domestic consumer market as well as a business sector that is risk averse and its bureaucratic processes.

Another significant constraint is the government tender practice. Tender Board guidelines stipulate that an Omani bid receive a 10 percent price preference. Thus, a bid by an Omani company that is 10 percent higher than a bid from a foreign company will be viewed as equal.

Companies seeking to invest in Oman also need to be aware of the country's Omanization program, in which the government sets quotas regarding the number of Omani nationals each company must hire. This program is becoming increasingly important considering the country's demographic trends. Expatriates comprise roughly 25 percent of the population, which is growing at 2.5 percent annually. More than 69 percent of Omani nationals are 25 or younger, meaning that roughly 20,000 secondary school graduates are entering the job market each year, most of whom are unable to find adequate work. The country is seeking to remedy the situation by emphasizing job training and employment creation.

The government, which operates under five-year development plans, is trying to diversify its economy away from oil. To achieve this, the government has opened the country to foreign participation in the economy, particularly in the form of joint ventures and, especially, in the industrial field. Although bureaucratic processing of commercial licenses can be cumbersome and time-consuming, the government does promote a free market economy. There are no restrictions on the flow of capital, whether in terms of salaries or the repatriation of corporate profits.

Nationalization of foreign enterprises is unknown in Oman and the government is beginning to privatize some of its state-owned companies. In addition to the oil and gas sectors, the areas with the greatest commercial opportunities, there are other sectors in Oman that offer significant potential. These include water saving technologies for agriculture, equipment for the treatment of wastewater, medical equipment, telecommunications, joint ventures in light industry, training and vocational education and development of an infrastructure for increasing tourism to the Sultanate.

The major obstacle to doing business in Oman is the country's small population and resulting small domestic market. Exacerbating this problem is the lack of a modern, high value consumer market, particularly beyond the capital area. In addition, other Gulf state producers typically offer higher subsidies for industry than Oman, creating similar industries and making competition difficult. Oman's trade and investment regime reflects fiscal, social and other priorities which sometimes conflict with industrialization.

Oman's economic dependency on oil means that its economic health fluctuates with oil prices. In 1998, depressed oil prices reduced the country's GDP by 10.2 percent, cutting oil revenue by 29 percent that year. Despite this, oil revenue comprised 69 percent of government revenue and 30 percent of overall GDP.

The affect of oil price fluctuation can also be seen in per capita GDP. In 1996 this figure stood at $6,486 rising to $6,848 in 1997 and dropping to $6,163 in 1998.

**Economic Indicators (in OR millions, unless otherwise indicated)**

| | 1998 | 1997 | 1996 |
|---|---|---|---|
| GDP at current prices (OR bn) | 5.46 | 6.08* | 5.87 |
| Total Government Revenue (OR bn) | 1.85 | 2.27 | 1.99 |
| Oil & Gas as % of Government Revenue | 70.6 | 79.6 | 76.8 |
| Total Government Expenditure (OR bn) | 2.22 | 2.31 | 2.25 |
| Current Account Balance (OR mn) | −1.134* | −22 | 131 |
| Average Daily Production of Oil (1,000s of barrels) | 899 | 904 | 885 |
| Average Oil Price ($ per barrel) | 11.92 | 18.62 | 19.42 |
| Total Exports (OR bn) | 2.12 | 2.93 | 2.82 |
| Non-Oil Exports (OR bn) | 0.19 | 0.20 | 0.17 |
| Trade Balance (OR mn) | −122 | 938 | 1,004 |

Furthermore, the price fall caused the Sultanate to experience its first trade deficit of $174.3 million since 1970. The value of its major export, crude oil, dropped by 37 percent that year to $3.6 billion. Non-oil exports decreased by 2 percent to $517.7 million.

On a brighter side, non-petroleum activities increased by 4.6 percent in 1998 with an 11.2 percent increase in transport activities, attributed mostly to Port Salalah.

To recover some of the lost revenue, the government announced a host of spending cuts and tax increases for FY 1999. The government announced that overall government spending would be reduced 7 percent. The budgets of most ministries, including defense, were cut between 5-10 percent, except the ministries of education and health, which were increased slightly. Salaries – which total roughly 68 percent of government spending – were untouched. Other revenue-generating measures included raising net corporate tax on Omani companies from 7.5 to 12 percent, increasing customs duties on imported cars with engines above 2500cc from 5 to 10 percent and from 5 to 15 percent for cars with engines above 2500cc. The government also increased duties on imported luxury goods from 5 to 15 percent and duties on imported alcohol and pork products increased from 100 to 200 percent.

These measures achieved their intended goal. Despite a 13 percent increase in aggregate expenditures, Oman forecasts a sharply reduced fiscal deficit of $906 million.

## Oil and Gas Sector

With the possibility looming that the country's oil supply will be depleted within the next 25 years, the Sultanate is looking to its 25 trillion cubic feet of proven gas reserves as its future economic savior. The government believes that number will rise to 40 trillion during the next few years.

As of mid-1999, the $2.4 billion liquefied natural gas project was nearly finished. The project, which includes pipelines, a plant and collector facility, is expected to yield 6.6 million tons a year. This output has already been sold to Korea, India and Japan. The first deliveries are scheduled for March 2000.

Earnings from the LNG project are set to fundamentally change the structure of Oman's revenues from the exploitation of its natural resources. Yet oil will continue to be the driving force of the economy and every effort is being made to maximize the potential of Oman's oil resources.

The country's main producer, Petroleum Development Oman (PDO), is 60 percent owned by the state and 34 percent by Shell Petroleum Company. Other producers in Oman are Occidental of Oman, Japan Petroleum Exploration Company (Jape), Elf Petroleum Oman and International Petroleum Bukha.

The government plans to increase production to 1 million bpd by the year 2000 was thwarted with the oil price crisis. To help raise prices, oil exporters agreed to cut production. Production dropped slightly in 1998 to 896,000 bpd from 1997 levels.

## Non-Oil Sector

The fifth five-year plan (1996–2000) concentrates on creating a stable economic framework and human resource development. With plans to raise the contribution of the industrial sector to the domestic product from 5.2 percent (the current percentage) to 15 percent by the year 2020, the Sultanate looks to the next century with great confidence and determination.

Non-oil activities increased 4.6 percent in 1998, including an 11.2 percent increase in transport activities, primarily occurring in Port Salalah.

The port is 40 percent owned by Omani investors, 30 percent by the government, 15 percent by US Sea-Land and 15 percent by Maersk. It is located 150 km from major east-west shipping lanes, and is already handling more than 60 vessels a month. It has become a leading container port on the Indian Ocean Rim.

The government announced plans in June 1999 to establish a industrial free zone at the port, which can potentially attract multi-national manufacturing and processing operations, as well as becoming a major air-sea cargo hub.

Additionally, the Oman is looking to develop a lucrative tourism industry. The government wants tourism's contribution to GDP to increase from 0.05 percent now to 5 percent by 2020. First, the country needs to develop a tourism infrastructure, including roads and hotels. Hotels are beginning to open, including a $23 million Hyatt Regency, which opened in 1998. Tour groups are also coming, particularly from Germany, Austria and Scandinavia. Still, most of the country's estimated 35,000 tourists in 1998 were there on business.

## Business Environment

The government's emphasis on income diversification has opened the country to foreign participation in the economy, particularly in the form of joint ventures. Oman is actively seeking private foreign investors, particularly in light industry, tourism and power generation. Those investors who allow technology transfer and provide employment and training for Omanis are particularly welcome. The government established in 1997 the Omani Centre for Investment Promotion and Export Development (OCIPED) to attract foreign investment and make it as easy as possible to form business and develop private sector projects.

Oman's labor law and the Oman tax law also affect a foreigner's ability to do business in Oman. Since there is no complete body of regulations codifying these laws and many government decisions are made on an *ad hoc* basis, investors should consider engaging local counsel. Recent changes in the tax law have, for the first time, required Omani companies to pay taxes on profits. The taxes levied on foreign companies and joint ventures were recently changed, and companies with foreign ownership of less than 90 percent are subject to the same tax as Omani firms.

Foreign investment in Oman is allowed only through joint stock companies or joint ventures. In both forms, majority Omani ownership is generally required, although joint venture industrial projects may be up to 65 percent foreign and up to 100 percent in special cases.

## Privatization

Since 1998, the government has emphasized privatization of its power, telecommunications and air transport sectors. Merrill Lynch is advising the government on its privatization plans for the General Telecommunications Organization at a still-unannounced date. Credit Suisse/First Boston is doing the same for the planned privatization and expansion of Muscat's Seeb International Airport, scheduled for 2002.

Besides these big plans, the government is allowing private investment into some of its smaller holdings, including a flour mill and Muscat port services.

Royal Decree 42/96, which became effective on June 15, 1996, authorized the creation of a Privatization Committee charged with the task of establishing a privatization program, particularly with respect to service and utility sector businesses. The Foreign Capital Investment Law applies to the participation of foreign investors in the privatization of such entities.

The Decree acknowledges that the government has set a course of slow and careful privatization in order to encourage economic growth. Priority is to be given to the service and utility industries, and special considerations must be made with regards to environmental protection in implementing privatization plans. The Decree encourages investment from abroad. Foreign investment, however, must be licensed according to the Foreign Capital Investment Law.

Oman also intends to initiate the selling of existing state assets, including holdings in a number of banks, the General Telecommunication Organization (GTO), Gulf Air and possibly the Oman Mining Co. As GTO is the second highest government revenue earner, it will not be easy for the government to let it go.

## Stock Exchange

The Muscat Securities Market (MSM) lost more than 50 percent of its value in 1998. In 1997, it had been the world's best performing securities market before dropping from a high of 509 points in February 1998 to 228 points in December 1998. As of mid-1999, the MSM showed little sign of recovery despite the government's injection of liquidity by creating a OR 100 million National Investment Fund. Observers have attributed the MSM crash to speculation and over-valued offerings combined with the impact of the Asian financial crisis and the oil price slump.

The Muscat Securities Market was established in 1989 pursuant to the Law of Muscat Securities Market and Amendments (Royal Decree 53/88) and Ministerial Decision 112/88. The Exchange was modeled after exchanges in Taiwan, Malaysia and New York. The framework of the statute and regulation is rather comprehensive and sets out provisions regarding members, brokers, dealers, administrative organization, market finance, disclosure, control, disciplinary actions and the like. The Muscat Securities Market is active and sophisticated. It has acquired a good reputation in terms of management and administration. A well-known fund-raising exercise associated with the National Bank of Oman was conducted through the Muscat Securities Market, and local companies have raised funds through that market. Modifications to the Law adopted in 1994 allow foreign investors to invest in approved investment funds, up to 49 percent of the shares, and such investment funds are treated as 100 percent Omani entities and can freely invest elsewhere in the economy as such.

Oman's Royal Decree No. 80/98 established a Capital Market Law, governing activity on the Muscat Securities Market.

## Build Operate Transfer

In 1996, Oman became the first Gulf country to employ exclusively the build, own, operate and transfer (BOOT) method to a major power project, a 90 MW plant in Manah. The government has announced four new BOO power projects, including a 200 MW power project in Salalah; a 400 MW power/desalination plant at Barka; a 200 MW power plant at Sharkiya; and a 190 MW extension of the Rusayl power plant. As of mid-1999, these power projects remained in different stages of tender writing and issuance.

## Leading Business Opportunities

| Rank | Sector |
|------|--------|
| 1 | Petroleum and Gas Sectors Technology and Equipment |
| 2 | Electrical Machinery and Mechanical Equipment |
| 3 | Prepared Foodstuffs, Beverages & Tobacco |
| 4 | Health Care Products |
| 5 | Water Saving Technologies |
| 6 | Tourism |
| 7 | Telecommunications & Rural Electrification Projects |
| 8 | Power Plant Construction, Power Generation Equipment, Power Plant operations and Process |
| 9 | Training Programs & Other Educational Services |
| 10 | Franchising |

# Legal Review

On November 6, 1996, by Royal Decree 101/96, the Sultan established the current Constitution of the Sultanate of Oman, known as the "White Book" in the form of a basic law. The Constitution provides that Oman is an Islamic State and that Islamic *Shar'ia* Law forms the basis of the legislative enactments of the Sultanate. Legislative power resides with the Sultan, and the Oman Council is an advisory body. Notwithstanding the Islamic sources of Omani law, over the past twenty years, a large body of commercial statutes, largely drawn from French and Egyptian statutes, have been enacted.

## Judiciary

Civil and criminal legal jurisdiction is exercised by the *Shar'ia* Courts. Appointments of judges, or *kadis*, to these courts are made by the Sultan. Appeals are made to the *Shar'ia* Chief Court in Muscat, and subsequent appeals are made directly to the Sultan who determines matters brought before him in accordance with his own notions of justice.

## *Arbitration and Dispute Resolution*

Oman belongs to the International Center for the Settlement of Investment Disputes (ICSID). The country's Commercial Court handles most tax and labor cases and the government is insisting that foreign suppliers accept this court for arbitration.

Royal Decree 47/97, which went into effect in 1997, is Oman's first law governing arbitration. The new law regulates any arbitration conducted in Oman or abroad if the parties expressly agree that this law should govern. Under the new law, parties may agree upon a procedure for the resolution of disputes between them. The Commercial Court will only intervene if the applicant party shows good grounds for intervention. Although the law preserves the rights of parties to agree on procedural maters, in the absence of agreement, the law imposes certain rules. In addition, proceedings must be held in Arabic. Enforcement of the arbitration judgment is vested with the Commercial Court, and, although arbitration judgements are not subject to appeal, an application can be made to the Court to nullify judgements.

## Business Forms and Structures

## *Companies Law*

Foreign participating Omani enterprises is governed by the Foreign Business and Investment Law of 1974 as well as the Commercial Companies Code of 1974, the Commercial Register Law and the Commercial Agencies Law as amended by Royal Decree 73/96.

The Foreign Business and Investment Law allows foreign companies to: (1) incorporate a local company; (2) establish a branch office; (3) establish a consultancy; or (4) appoint a commercial agent, provided the foreign company is engaged only in providing goods or services to be imported into Oman. Such enterprises must be approved by the Foreign Capital Investment Committee in the Ministry of Commerce and Industry. Ordinarily at least one member of the enterprise must be an Omani national and at least 35 percent of the profits and capital of the enterprise have to be owned by Omani nationals. In the public transportation, utilities and real estate sectors, at least 51 percent of the shareholdings must be held by Omani nationals.

Foreign persons or companies may participate in four types of business associations defined under the Commercial Companies Law, as follows: (1) General Partnerships; (2) Limited Partnerships; (3) Joint Stock Companies; and (4) Limited Liability Companies. The Commercial Companies Law also defines a Joint Venture.

## General Partnerships

A general partnership is an association of at least two persons and whose members are jointly and severally liable to the obligations of the association to the full extent of their personal wealth. There is no maximum limit to participation. All general partnerships must be registered in the Commercial Registrar. The agreement that sets out the relationship among the partners, as well as any subsequent agreements must be filed with the Commercial Registrar. The name of the partnership must consist of the name of one or more of the partners together with an indication that the partnership exists. Management devolves upon all partners, unless otherwise is indicated in the partnership agreement. Managers may perform all acts necessary to accomplish the objectives of the partnership, subject to limitations arising under the partnership agreement and limitation arising by operation of law. Dissolution may take place where the term of the partnership expires, the partnership accomplishes its objects, all interests are transferred to one person, bankruptcy, loss of all or most of the capital, and the creation of a members contract to dissolve the partnership. In addition, the partnership may be dissolved upon the death, insanity, bankruptcy or withdrawal of a general partner, unless the partnership contract indicates otherwise.

## Limited Partnerships

A limited partnership has two types of members: general partners who are involved in the management of the partnership and limited partners who merely contribute capital to the partnership. The general partners are liable to the obligations of the partnership to the full extent of their personal wealth. The liability of limited partners to the obligations of the partnership is restricted to the amount of capital contributed by the limited partners, provided the limited partners do not participate in management of the partnership or otherwise act in the partnership's name. A limited partnership must have at least two participants, and there is no maximum limit to participation. All limited partnerships must be registered in the Commercial Registrar. The partnership agreement and any subsequent agreements must be filed at the Commercial Registration. As with general partnerships, the name of a limited partnership must include the name of one or more of the partners together with an indication that the partnership exists. Managerial structures are similar to those that exist in general partnerships save for the restrictions imposed on the limited partners to engage in management. Hence, management is confined to and exercised by the general partners. The dissolution of limited liability partnerships is based on the same principles governing the dissolution of general partnerships, but it must be emphasized that the death, insanity, bankruptcy or withdrawal of a limited partner does not warrant dissolution.

## Joint Stock Companies

A joint stock company is a business association with fixed capital divided into negotiable shares and is approximately equivalent to an English public company. The minimum capital requirement is OR 25,000. Shares may be made available for public subscription. Shares of different classes are permitted. Subject to certain conditions, a joint stock company may issue debentures as well. It is important to note that the Muscat Securities Market Law requires that all Omani joint stock companies be members of this Market. Additionally, a 1989 amendment to the Commercial Companies Law states that where a joint stock company under establishment has capital in excess of OR 500,000 or where a joint stock company increases its capital above that amount, at least 40 percent and no more than 70 percent of the shares must be offered to the Omani public. A joint stock company must have at least three shareholders. The liability of shareholders is confined to the nominal value of their shares in the registered capital.

All joint stock companies must be registered in the Commercial Registrar and must have the prior approval of the Minister of Commerce and Industry. Articles of association and other incorporation documents must be filed in the Commercial Registrar. The name of a joint stock company must not be misleading as to the objectives of the company and must include an indication of limited liability.

The management of a joint stock company is vested in the Board of directors, comprising of three to twelve members. Joint stock companies are bound by all acts of their directors acting within the scope of their registered powers within the legal restrictions. The directors are liable to the company, the shareholders and third parties for any fraud, negligence or illegality in their acts as well as for failure to act as prudent persons in the relevant circumstances.

Dissolution may take place where the term of the company expires, the company accomplishes its objects, all interests are transferred to one person, bankruptcy, loss of all or most of the capital and the creation of a members contract to dissolve the company.

## Limited Liability Companies

A limited liability company is a business association with fixed capital divided into negotiable shares. It is similar to an English private company, and, more so, to a French SARL and is particularly suitable for foreign participation. The minimum capital requirement is OR 10,000. A limited liability company must have at least two shareholders and no more than thirty shareholders. The liability of shareholders is confined to the nominal value of their shares in the registered capital.

All limited liability companies must be registered in the Commercial Registrar and must have the prior approval of the Minister of Commerce and Industry. Articles of association and other incorporation documents must be filed in the Commercial Registrar. In practice, a standard form of constitutive contract is required for all limited liability companies, and members possess preemptive rights on the transfer of shares by other members to third parties. The name of a limited liability company must not be misleading as to the objectives of the company and must include an indication of limited liability.

The management of a limited liability company devolves upon one or more managers who may not be members of the company. The managers' authority to act on the company's behalf is limited by their registered powers and is confined to restrictions arising by operation of law. As in joint stock companies, all authorized acts performed by the managers bind the company, and the managers are liable to the company, the shareholders and third parties for any fraud, negligence or illegality in their acts or for failure to act as prudent persons in the relevant circumstances. The dissolution of limited liability companies is dictated by the same principles governing dissolution of joint stock companies.

## Joint Ventures

A joint venture is a business association which establishes a legal relationship among its members without affecting third parties. Since there is no legal relationship with third parties, members of a joint venture incur no liability unless the joint venture discloses the existence of the joint venture to a third party who is thereby induced to enter into an agreement with the joint venture or one of its members. In such a case, the liability of the joint ventures is to the full extent of the ventures' wealth.

A joint venture must have at least two participants, and there is no maximum limit to participation. Joint ventures are not subject to registration requirements. The agreement that sets up the joint venture must define the objectives of the joint venture, the rights and obligations of its members and the distribution of profits and losses.

Dissolution of joint ventures may take place where the term of the venture expires, the venture accomplishes its objects, all interests are transferred to one person, bankruptcy, loss of all or most of the capital and the creation of a members contract to dissolve the venture.

## Commercial Agency

As discussed below in the section on Investment Incentives, foreign entities are required to retain an Omani agent in order to conduct business in Oman, unless working on a government contract. Agents must be Omani citizens, and agencies must be majority Omani-owned and controlled. Agents must also be members of the Omani Chamber of Commerce and Industry. Commercial agency relationships must be registered, and a principal place of business must be maintained in Oman.

Royal Decree 73/96 amended the Commercial Agencies Law. The amendment became effective September 25, 1996. The amendment eliminated the requirement of territorial exclusivity.

These amendments affect the legal claims of the agent *vis-à-vis* the principal. Ordinarily, unjust termination of an agreement for both limited and unlimited duration agency places liability upon the terminating party who is required to pay suitable compensation. The right of the agent to claim compensatory damages for breach of contract remains unchanged. In light of the new amendments, however, the principal is able to appoint other agents, and the agent is unable to prevent the registration of such appointment. Consequently, the agent's claims for compensatory damages for a breach of contract may be reduced.

Principal-agent disputes are arbitrated by the Authority for the Settlement of Commercial Disputes. Certain classes of goods require a special license (e.g. firearms, alcohol, narcotics). Documents in English and Arabic must include a certificate of origin signed by the Chamber of Commerce or another authorized body.

## Currency and Banking

### Foreign Currency Control

Oman's exchange system is free of restrictions on payments and transfer for international transactions, and the Omani trade system may be regarded as virtually fully open.

### Banking

The financial institutional framework of Oman is mainly composed of banks, money exchanges companies, insurance companies, pension funds, hire purchase and leasing companies and the Muscat Securities Market. The banking sector is the major component of the financial system and is comprised of the Central Bank of Oman, 17 commercial banks of which seven are locally incorporated and three specialized banks. The banking industry is regulated by the Banking Law of 1974.

### The Central Bank

The Central Bank of Oman (CBO), which was established in 1975, has taken several measures to strengthen its supervisory role and to ensure the soundness of the banking system and the economy. These measures include the raising of the maximum limit on investment in Government Development Bonds, encouragement of mergers within the financial system and the issuance of regulations governing investment banking activities. The CBO requires that commercial banks maintain minimum capital holdings of OR 10 million for locally incorporated commercial banking institutions and OR 3 million for foreign incorporated commercial banking entities.

## Oman Development Bank

The Oman Development Bank provides loans and guarantees for financing development expenditure for manufacturing, tourism and service projects in designated sectors of the economy. The loans and guarantees may amount to 100 percent of the paid-up capital. In addition, the Oman Development Bank may participate in the share capital of the company or underwrite an issue of shares to the public up to 51 percent of the capital of the company. The government may bear 3 percent of the interest for projects located in Muscat, and 5 percent for projects located outside Muscat. The term of such loans may range between three and ten years. As to security, the Oman Development Bank may require that mobile and fixed assets be mortgaged in its favor, and, in certain cases, personal guarantees may be necessary.

## Intellectual Property

The Sultanate joined the World Intellectual Property Organization in September 1996. The sultanate is also applying for membership in the WTO, which would require a signing a number of agreements, including one on protection of intellectual property rights.

## Trademarks

In 1996, the country enacted a copyright protection law but did not begin enforcement until 1999, when the government destroyed pirated cassettes. In its attempt to gain acceptance to the WTO, the country is working to become TRIPS compliant.

The Omani trademarks regimes consists of Royal Decree 68/87, Decree Law No. 635/1991 and Royal Decree 33/91. Registrable marks consist of distinctive shapes consisting of words, signatures, letters, drawings, symbols, headings, seals, pictures, engraving or any other distinctive mark or combination. With the exception of alcoholic goods of Class 33, Oman has adopted all forty-two classes of the International Classification. Prior to registration, marks are published in the Official Gazette and in one daily paper. Opposition may be filed within thirty days from the date of publication in the Official Gazette. Upon registration, a ten year period of protection is granted, renewable for similar periods, and exclusive ownership of the mark is given. Marks which have not been used for five years or more may be challenged for lack of use. Marks unlawfully registered or which have not been effectively used for five consecutive years can be canceled upon a petition filed by the Registrar or any interested party. Violation of the law triggers criminal penalties including fines, imprisonment or both.

## Copyright

In 1996, Oman enacted a new copyright law by Royal Decree 47/96. Under this law, the authors of original works of art in literature, science (including computer programs), arts and culture in general enjoy the protection of the law irrespective of the value, type, manner of expression or purpose of those works. The copyright is the sole right of the author unless proved otherwise. Such rights include the right to translate, abridge, publish, financially exploit and reproduce the work. Certain exploitations of such works are allowed for, e.g. teaching purposes, use by public libraries, personal use and the like. The Commercial Disputes Settlement Committee may make orders regarding unauthorized publication or display, which include stopping publication, display or manufacturing and attaching the revenues made by virtue of the breach of the author's rights. The right to financially exploit the work lapses after fifty years from the death of the author or the death of the last author in case of joint works. A protection period of twenty-five years from the date of publication applies to movies, applied-art works, photographs, works belonging to private or public corporations, works firstly published after the author's death and works published under a pseudonym or without bearing the author's name.

Authors possess the right to transfer all or part of their rights in the work free of charge. Publications of literary, artistic and scientific works which are published in Oman by means of reproduction, shall first be filed with the Ministry of Commerce and Industry, and the works will be also published in the Official Gazette. Violation of the provisions of the Royal Decree 47/96 triggers criminal penalties including fine and imprisonment.

### Taxation

The Omani tax regime has been considered to be both reasonable and pragmatic in its dealing with taxpayers. The tax system has undergone important changes reflecting the government policy of opening up the economy to foreign investment, and more changes are forthcoming. By and large, taxation is moderate because many of the government's revenues are oil revenues. Therefore, Oman levies no personal income tax, estate tax or gift tax. All entities, both foreign and locally owned, are taxable in Oman.

## Taxation of Companies

The most important tax in Oman is the tax on business income, which is based upon the Corporate Income Tax Law of 1981 and subsequent Royal and Ministerial Decrees. Taxable entities are entities that have a permanent establishment in the country, so that any entity that has personnel present in Oman is taxed. Taxable income includes business profit, interest, royalties and capital gains, and is computed on the net income arising in Oman or deemed to have risen in Oman after deducting all ordinary expenses, such as expenditure incurred in producing the gross revenue, bad debts, auditors' fees, depreciation, head office expenses, sponsorship fees and certain donations. Losses may be carried forward for up to five years.

Beginning in 1999, the government no longer required minority foreign-owned joint ventures to include a publicly traded joint stock company listed on the national stock exchange.

The tax rates vary in accordance with the amount of taxable income and the percentage of Omani ownership. Tax holidays granted under the investment incentives laws also provide a reprieve.

Minority foreign-owned joint ventures are taxed at the national corporate rate of 12 percent. Majority foreign-owned joint ventures with Omani participation are taxed at a maximum 25 percent. And wholly foreign-owned companies are taxed at maximum of 50 percent.

## Tax Incentives

The government offers foreign investors various incentives, including a five-year tax holiday for companies engaged in industry, mining, tourism, fishing, agriculture, and public utilities; national tax treatment and an income tax reduction for joint ventures with at least 51 percent Omani ownership.

In October 1996, by Royal Decree 87/96, the Law of Income Tax on Companies was amended by Royal Decree 87/96, and the Law of Profits on Tax on Commercial and Industrial Establishments (applicable to Omani companies in which there are foreign participants) was amended by Royal Decree 89/96. These amendments, among other things, substantially reduced the tax rates applicable to Omani mixed public joint stock companies, as follows:

| Amount of Taxable Income | Approximate Tax Rate Before Amendments | Tax Rates After Amendments |
| --- | --- | --- |
| The first OR 30,000 | Between 0–10% | Exempt |
| The following OR 30,000 | Up to 30% | 5% |
| Any amount in excess of the above | Up to 50% | 7.5% |

To qualify for these reduced tax rates, at least 51 percent of the share capital of the mixed entity must be held by Omani nationals, and at least 40 percent of the share capital must have been offered to the public. The amendments provide that the shareholdings of foreign companies' branches are to be included in the calculation of Omani shareholding, thus encouraging foreign companies to hold shares in Omani public joint stock companies.

In entities other than public joint stock companies in which there is foreign participation of not more than 90 percent, the amendments provide the following tax rates shall apply:

| Amount of Taxable Income | Approximate Tax Rate Before Amendments | Tax Rates After Amendments |
| --- | --- | --- |
| The first OR 30,000 | Up to 10% | Exempted |
| The following OR 30,000 | Up to 25% | 15% |
| The following OR 150,000 | Up to 30% | 20% |
| Any amount in excess of the above | Up to 50% | 25% |

Omani companies having foreign participation which is in excess of 90 percent are subject to the prevailing tax rates prior to the enactment of the amendments.

Royal Decree 89/96 amended the Profits Tax on Commercial and Industrial Establishments Law that is applicable to Omani companies in which there is no foreign participation. The amendment provides that, under certain circumstances, those tax rates will continue to apply to the entity even if some of the shares are held by a branch of a foreign company, a foreign company or a mixed Omani company established under the Foreign Business and Capital Investment Law.

The amendment also grants a tax exemption to entities owned or used by Omani nationals. To qualify for the exemption, the entity must be engaged in certain sectors of business activity or organized under the Law on the Organization and Encouragement of Industry, and the exemption is valid for five years from the date production commences unless renewed for an additional period of not more than five years.

## Withholding Tax

As of the 1996 tax year, certain payments made by Omani businesses to foreign companies that do not have a permanent establishment in Oman are subject to a withholding tax, introduced by Royal Decree 87/96. The withholding tax applies to payments such as royalties, management fees, machinery and equipment rentals, payments for the transfer of technical expertise or for research and development. The withholding tax is levied at a rate of 10 percent of the gross payments made.

## Tax Holidays and Tax-Related Incentives

Foreign investment projects are exempt from tax on profits for a period of five years, effective from the date of establishment. An additional five-year income tax exemption may be granted. Moreover, foreign investment projects may be exempt from customs duties on imports of machinery and equipment required for their establishment. Raw materials required for the production of products unavailable in Oman are also exempt from customs duties. The exemption from customs duties on such products is given for five years from the production date and may be renewed once more for another period of five years.

The above exemptions are also applicable to new extensions in projects. The Capital Investment Law defines "extensions" as the increase in capital which is utilized for adding new fixed capital assets which results in increase in the production capacity of the project and which aims at producing or providing new activities or services.

## Levies and Duties

Oman imposes other taxes as well. These include:

**Labor Levy:** This levy is applicable to all business entities. Rates up to 6 percent of Gross Employees' salaries.

**Social Security Levy:** This levy is applicable to all business entities employing Omani nationals. The employers contribute 9 percent of gross employees salaries, the employees contribute 5 percent of gross employees' salaries.

**Customs Duties:** These duties apply to all importers. Mostly, they are of 5 percent of CIF value charged for most goods. Certain essential goods are exempt (e.g. gold, silver bullion, seeds, live plants, refined petroleum products, books, various foodstuffs). Special 100 percent duties apply to alcoholic beverages, tobacco and pork products. With a few exceptions, goods produced in GCC states enter Oman duty-free.

**Investment and Trade**

## Foreign Investment Requirements

The Foreign Capital Investment Law of 1994 provides the legal framework within which foreigners may invest and carry on business in the Sultanate of Oman. The following address procedural requirements and investment vehicles of which prospective investors should be aware.

## Licensing Requirements

Foreigners cannot conduct any commercial, industrial or tourist business or otherwise participate in an Omani company unless a license is obtained from the Ministry of Commerce and Industry. A license is granted upon the fulfillment of the following conditions:

- The business must be conducted by an Omani company with a capital of at least OR 150,000;
- The foreign share therein must not exceed 49 percent of the company's total capital, unless authorization to increase participation up to 65 percent is given by the Minister of Commerce and Industry. In instances where the project contributes to the development

of the economy, the project's capital exceeds OR 500,000 and an approval is given by Development Council, foreign participation may be increased up to 100 percent.

Exemptions from the above requirements may be granted under the following circumstances:

- The company conducts a business under a special contract with the government or a contract established pursuant to a Royal Decree;
- The company conducts a business which is declared by the Cabinet as necessary for the country.

The following information and certified documents must accompany a license application:

- The objects of the proposed business;
- Articles of association or constitutive agreement;
- Details of each proposed shareholder or partner;
- The aggregate interest in the capital to be owned by foreigners;
- A certificate from the Commercial Registrar Secretariat of the Ministry of Commerce and Industry that no other company is engaged in Oman under the proposed name;
- Power of attorney to at least one individual;
- Financial reports;
- The foreigner's major activities and projects;
- Approvals from other government departments where relevant;
- Operation through a Branch of a foreign Company or through a Commercial Agency.

It is possible for foreigners to carry on business in Oman without direct Omani participation in ownership and management. For example, foreigners may set up a branch office to perform specific contracts awarded by the government or by an oil company holding a concession granted by the government. Registration of such a contract with the Ministry of Commerce and Industry and the appointment of an Omani agent allows lawful performance of the contract, including ancillary activities, without the need to set up a company of the types described above. In addition, certain professional consultants, in areas where there is a critical shortage, are allowed to set up a branch office in Oman subject to the satisfaction of certain requirements.

## Investment Incentives

Investment incentives granted by the Ministry of Commerce and Industry are provided pursuant to Royal Decrees and the Foreign Capital Investment Law of 1994:

## Government Loans

Under Royal Decree 40/87, foreign investors may be eligible for interest-free soft loans from the Ministry of Commerce and Industry, provided that not more than 25 percent of the equity in the company is owned by non-Omani persons. Such attractive loans are given for the following purposes:

- Acquisition of fixed assets for new projects;
- Acquisition of machinery and equipment for expansion of existing projects;
- Infusion of finance into a 'failing' industry, provided that the entity has been in existence for at least one year, losses have not been caused by mismanagement and that it can be established that the loan would convert the entity into a viable enterprise.

The granting of such loans is linked to priority areas as determined by the Ministry of Commerce and Industry. There are two priority areas which are encouraged in the Sultanate. The first concerns the following industrial projects or entities:

- Export-oriented projects;
- Food processing industries;
- Projects using at least 20 percent local raw materials;
- Projects employing at least 35 percent Omani employees;
- Joint stock companies with at least 40 percent of public subscription.

The second priority area concerns the following tourism projects or entities:

- Projects outside the capital area assisting in regional development;
- Projects involving a new tourism activity;
- Projects with at least a 30 percent Omani work force;

- Projects with foreign investment that will transfer management techniques to Oman;
- Projects that promote traditional industry or that market their products;
- Joint stock companies with at least 40 percent of public subscription.

The amounts of the loans are determined in accordance with the following guidelines:

- Up to 100 percent of the paid-up capital for projects in the capital area;
- Up to 125 percent of the paid-up capital for projects in other areas;
- Joint stock companies may be granted a loan not exceeding OR 3 million;
- Non-joint stock companies may be granted a loan not exceeding OR 250,000;
- Tourism projects may be granted a loan not exceeding OR 500,000.

Loans given for new and expansion projects can be repaid over fifteen years, with the first installment paid after a grace period of five years. For tourism projects and 'failing' industries, the repayment period is thirteen years, with a grace period of three years. Delayed installments may attract an annual 10 percent interest charge, calculated for the period of delay. As to securities, all fixed assets of the project are mortgaged under a first priority charge to the government for the term of the loan.

## Other Incentives and Provisions

Tax-related incentives and government loans are the major incentives given to foreign investors. Additional incentives and provisions are provided under Royal Decrees and the Foreign Capital Investment Law.

Foreign investors are specifically allowed to resolve disputes with third parties by way of local or international arbitration. The importation of any production materials, machinery, parts, and the like does not require to registration in the Importers Registrar. Foreign investors are free to conduct the licensed activity and to transfer abroad the imported capital along with the profits accrued in the project. Their projects may not be confiscated or expropriated unless for the public interest and against equitable compensation. Foreign businesses may be entitled to preferential allocation of government land. They may be given a free survey of industrial investment opportunities, a reduction in charges for electricity, and priority in government purchases.

Other incentives include the following:
- Low interest loans from the Oman Development Bank;
- Subsidized plant facilities and utilities at the industrial estates;
- Exemption from customs duties on equipment and raw materials during a project's first ten years;
- Significant incentives, including subsidies and tariff protection, are mostly available to joint stock companies.

## Investment from Gulf Cooperation Council States

Oman is a member of the Gulf Cooperation Council States (GCC) that includes Saudi Arabia, United Arab Emirates, Bahrain, Qatar and Kuwait. Under the United Economic Agreement of the GCC states of 1981 and the resolution of the Supreme Council of GCC states, Oman permits GCC nationals to conduct certain economic activities in specified fields in the Sultanate upon the same terms and conditions as applicable to Omanis. The fields are determined periodically by the Ministries of Commerce and Industry and of Finance and Economy. Activities currently permitted include industry, agriculture, animal resources, fisheries, construction, management of hotels and restaurants, retail and wholesale trade, law, medicine, accountancy, engineering, pharmaceutical, craft and computer programming.

## Public Sector Procurement

The government carries out most major infrastructure and commercial projects and at times it may carry out a project as a party to a joint venture. Design, engineering, construction, operation and maintenance contracts may be awarded separately. In order to monitor these contracts and ventures, a Tender Board was set up to handle all large governmental projects. Certain bodies, however, have their own tender boards: the Ministry of Defense, the Royal Oman Police, the General Telecommunication Organization, and the Petroleum Development Oman.

For contracts the value of which is higher than OR 100,000, the Tender Board sets the terms of bidding, issues invitations and selects the winners. In general, there is no formal pre-qualification process. Nonetheless, bidders must comply with the procedure set out in the Law and Regulations for Government Tenders (Royal Decree 86/84). For example, bidders are required to have an Omani sponsor or partner and must be registered with the Tender Board as well as with the Ministry of Commerce and Industry. Bidders are generally required to submit a deposit equal to 2 percent of the tender's value in the form of a bank guarantee. The main factor taken into account by the Tender Board is the price, in addition to past performance, financial capacity, compliance with procedure and the like. Within fifteen days of receiving the award, the winner has to submit a bank guarantee amounting to 5 percent of the value of the contract.

**Labor Law**

The Labor Law of 1973 governs the area of industrial relations in Oman. The law reflects the government's policy regarding the 'Omanization' of the work force, which presently includes a significant numbers of foreign nationals. Therefore, the Labor Law states that foreign nationals may not be employed as technical assistants, guards, light vehicle drivers, Arabic typists, agricultural workers, forklift or mixer operators and public relations officers. If no Omanis are available, an employer may be allowed to bring foreign workers into the Sultanate. Foreign employees need to obtain a labor permit signed by their prospective employers. There are also entrance requirements, applying to all foreign visitors, which must be complied with.

The government sets wage guidelines in the private sector. Employers may pay additional taxes on salaries paid to foreigners. Fringe benefits for employees can be generous in the Sultanate. Most entities pay a housing and utilities allowance of up to 50 percent of the basic salary. The maximum work week is forty-eight hours, longer than that of most industrial countries. Annual leave is fourteen days. Severance pay is mandated at fourteen days pay for each year of the first three years of employment and thirty days for each year thereafter. There are also provisions concerning sick leave and maternity leave.

Disputes regarding employment conditions may be refereed to the Ministry of Social Affairs and Labor, and arbitration of disputes may be conducted by the Labor Welfare Board that hears disputes involving industrial relations matters. An entity with fifty or more employees must prominently display its procedure for settling grievances. No employee may be fired for filing a grievance.

## Environmental Law

Oman has a developed body of law governing environmental matters. Efforts to consolidate the laws recently have been undertaken. Of primary importance is the Law on the Protection of the Environment and Prevention of Pollution (Royal Decree 10/82). It addresses offenses against the environment, which is defined broadly to include "air, water, soil, land life, marine life and factors and natural materials with which man deals in his place of work."

Oman has laws and regulations governing waste management, including hazardous waste and chemical waste and protecting the marine environment. Civil remedies are also available to persons harmed by offenses against the environment.

Environmental issues of pressing importance for Oman include the rising rate of soil salinity, beach pollution, particularly from oil spills, and the limited supply of fresh water resources. Oman is a signatory to several international environmental conventions, including: the Law of the Sea, Marine Dumping, Ship Pollution and Whaling.

# PALESTINIAN AUTHORITY

## Recent Political Developments

Since Ehud Barak was elected Israeli
Prime Minister in the spring of 1999,
the Palestinians have realized several
significant achievements. Subsequent
to the September Sharm El-Sheikh
Accord, Israel released scores of Palestinian prisoners, transferred land to
Palestinian control, and permitted development of the Gaza Port to commence.

| | |
|---|---|
| Population | 2.98 million (1999) |
| Religions | 75% Muslim; 25% Christian and other |
| Government | Self-Governing Autonomy |
| Languages | Arabic; Hebrew, English (spoken at senior business and government levels) |
| Work Week | Saturday–Thursday |

Practically, the most important event was the opening in October 1999 of
the long-anticipated "safe passage" zone through which Palestinians could
travel between the West Bank and Gaza Strip. This 44-kilometer corridor,
which extends from the Erez checkpoint (Gaza Strip) to Tarqumiyah near
Hebron, holds significant symbolic value for the Palestinians, since it forms
both demographic and geographic unity between Gaza and the West Bank.

Besides this, the passage answers criticism directed at Israel that it has prevented Palestinians in the separate autonomous areas from visiting friends
and family. Inaugurating the safe passage aims to improve the Palestinians'
social and economic plight. It may also have the effect of alleviating Palestinian trade obstacles and easing the sense of isolation that is especially
prevalent in Gaza, whose 1 million residents could until now only leave the
Strip with permits that were difficult to obtain.

The World Economic Forum at Davos during January 2000 provided an opportunity for Yasser Arafat and US President Bill Clinton to discuss timely
political issues (Israeli Prime Minister Ehud Barak made a last minute deci-

sion not to attend). Still, the Palestinian and Israeli leaders understand they have to accelerate efforts to reach a peace settlement. Both sides have expressed serious doubt about meeting the February 13, 2000 deadline for a framework agreement; negotiations over lagging Israeli withdrawals from West Bank territory remain deadlocked.

Not all news on the Palestinian front is discouraging, however. Earlier this month, the Palestinian National Authority announced policy changes, which include a new financial management body and assurances that tax revenues and public accounts would be the responsibility of the Finance Ministry. Michael Camdessus, head of the International Monetary Fund, has publicly welcomed these proposed reforms. The designed measures come in response to international criticism regarding a lack of transparency and high levels of perceived corruption throughout Palestinian public institutions, which may threaten future streams of foreign donor aid.

## Recent Economic Developments

The economic growth that many predicted would come to the Palestinians following the 1993 Oslo agreements has yet to materialize. The PA economy is presently in shambles. Population growth is exceeding the limited economic growth and thus GDP per capita is declining. Yasser Arafat and the Authority continue to face serious challenges to their economic and political development, such as high unemployment, rampant corruption, a continued fundamentalist threat and dependency on the Israeli economy.

In contrast to real growth in the 1970s and early to mid-1980s, Palestinian GDP has stagnated or declined since the late 1980s due to several factors. These factors include the Intifada, the loss of remittances from Palestinians expelled from Gulf countries following the Gulf War, the reduction in work permits issued by Israel and the impact of Israeli border closures.

Although Israel and the Palestinians continue to negotiate their separation, the Palestinian economy in many ways continues to be defined by its relationship with Israel. Israel, for example, currently purchases almost 85 percent of West Bank/Gaza exports. And realistically, much of the Palestinian economy, and many Palestinians' livelihood, will depend on Israel for the foreseeable future.

Despite the economic hardships and obstacles, there are significant investment opportunities in the Palestinian Authority, including Infrastructure
development, private housing construction, manufacturing and industry,
agriculture and tourism. And despite official statistics showing a recent economic slowdown in the West Bank and Gaza, there has been a substantial
increase in imports of consumer goods, particularly small electronic appliances, clothing and shoes.

But there are also many obstacles to investment. The Palestinian Authority
has been accused of widespread corruption and a lack of transparency. So
acute has the problem become, that many donor countries who have
pledged millions of dollars in aid have thus far refused to meet their obligations fearing that the money will be misused.

But there are some worrisome signs that the PA plans to own different parts
of the economy. For example, the PA has signed monopoly deals that grant
government control of sales of fuel, cigarettes and cement.

Further cause for concern is the critical role the PA, including Chairman
Arafat and various ministers, play in the approval process for private commercial projects. Several ministries are often responsible for major projects
and foreigners interested in investing must speak to representatives from
each. Additionally, a new investment law requires special approval of new
investments that seek incentives, such as tax holidays. Some investors believe this system to be tainted and many proposals submitted by Israeli investors have not been approved. Other foreign investors have chosen not to
invest in the PA fearing that the region may not be as politically stable as its
leaders purport it to be. The PA, however, is working to amend this investment law in a way that will be more attractive to investors.

An additional factor that has further exacerbated the economic problems is
the vast corruption among most of the higher echelons of the Palestinian
government. Many "donor countries" that have pledged economic aid packages have become concerned by the corruption and lack of transparency
and have refused to release the funds.

In 1998, gross national product (GNP) in the West Bank and Gaza rose to
$4.509 billion from $4.235 billion the previous year. Gross domestic product (GDP) rose 2 percent, and amounted to roughly $3.9 billion. The dis-
crepancy between GNP and GDP levels (GNP tends to run about 25-30

percent higher) stems from repatriated wages and other funds from Palestinians living abroad.

But when these figures are converted into GDP per capita, the results are far less encouraging. Due to natural population growth of approximately 4 percent, GDP per capita actually declined by 2 percent to $1,380 in 1998 from $1,430 in 1997.

**Economic Indicators (in US$, unless otherwise indicated)**

|  | 1998 | 1997 |
|---|---|---|
| GNP (billions) | 4.5 | 4.2 |
| GDP per capita | 1,380 | 1,430 |
| GDP Growth (percent) | 2 | 0.8 |
| Workers in Israel (thousands) | 45 | 35 |
| Donor Aid Received (millions) | 400 | 550 |
| Unemployment (percent) | 14.4 | 20.3 |
| Budget Deficit (millions) | 153 | 37 |

Recently released indicators also reveal enhanced economic conditions in the PA. The foremost of these is a decline in the official unemployment rate to 13.8 percent in the middle of 1999, versus 15.6 percent a year earlier. During the first half of 1999, 47,100 net new jobs for Palestinian workers were created. More than 60 percent of these jobs were located within the Palestinian economy (as opposed to Israel), of which 38.2 were in the private sector. The total value of projects approved under the Palestinian Law for the Encouragement of Investment in the first half of 1999 was $107.6 million compared to $161.0 million for all of 1998. Foreign investment projects accounted for $15.1 million, or 14 percent of the total.

Still, donor aid disbursements amounted to merely $268.3 million in 1999, versus levels of $364.1 million, $475.1 million and $541.9 years in 1998, 1997 and 1996 respectively. As alluded to earlier, major donors, particularly the European Union and the United States, have grown increasingly frustrated with the lack of accountability for past disbursements of assistance.

The Palestinians and Israel signed an economic accord as part of the Gaza-Jericho Agreement in May 1994. Known as the Paris Protocol, this and other follow-up agreements grants the PA responsibility over most key spheres in the Gaza and Jericho economies, including trade and investment. The West Bank and Gaza market, with a total population of nearly 3 million, is approximately 5 percent the size of the Israeli economy.

The West Bank/Gaza economy remains linked and heavily dependent upon the Israeli market. Israel currently purchases almost 85 percent of West Bank/Gaza exports, and the Palestinian Authority, which does not have its own currency, uses the New Israeli Shekel (NIS) as legal tender. (The Jordanian Dinar is also legal tender in the West Bank but the NIS is more widely used). As the Palestinians assume greater control of their economy, however, the strong economic ties between Israel and the Palestinians may gradually weaken, particularly in terms of trade sources. Discussions are underway at several levels regarding the final status economic relationship between Israel and a Palestinian state (i.e. free trade, customs union).

But no matter what the outcome of these talks is, realistically, Palestinian labor, and much of the Palestinian economy, will remain dependent on Israel for the foreseeable future. Commercial development in the territories, even at an optimistic pace, cannot occur overnight. Furthermore, closures will remain an obstacle to the mobility of Palestinian labor and Palestinian economic growth in general.

In fact, the years since peace negotiations with the Palestinians began in the early 1990s have been some of the harshest in terms of economic growth in the Palestinian territories. In contrast to real growth in the 1970s and early to mid-1980s, Palestinian GDP has stagnated or declined since the late 1980s due to several factors. These include dislocations caused by the Intifada (uprising), starting in December 1987; the loss of tangible Gulf remittances (with the expulsion of Palestinians from Gulf countries following the Gulf War); the reduction in work permits for Israel from a high of over 100,000 before 1990 to about 50,000 in December 1996; and since 1993, the impact of Israeli border closures on the economy.

The impact of closures itself can be seen in the improved economic growth in 1998 during which there was a sharp drop in the number of border closures with Israel from an estimated 14.5 days, compared with four times that figure in 1997. According to Labor Ministry and UN Special Coordinator Office (UNSCO) estimates, 1998 Israeli work permits averaged 44,000 per month. But at least as many workers are thought to have crossed illegally to Israel.

The Palestinian Central Statistics Department reported that the rate of unemployment in Palestinian territories dropped to 14.4 percent in 1998, compared to 20.3 percent in 1997. The highest rate of unemployment was among the young from both genders in the 15-24 year age bracket. The unemployment rate was 22.6 percent in this age bracket, 22.0 percent among males and 27 percent among females.

Workers in Palestinian lands in 1998 were distributed as follows: 53.8 percent in the West Bank, 24.5 percent in the Gaza Strip, and 21.7 percent in Israel and the settlements. The report showed that roughly one quarter of the Palestinian work force (27.1 percent) work in services and 18.2 percent are employed in business and trade and in the restaurant and hotel industries.

Despite official statistics showing a recent economic slowdown in the West Bank and Gaza, there has been a substantial increase in imports of consumer goods, particularly small electronic appliances, clothing and shoes. This may be due to a growing "gray" market with unreported income, and to increasing ties between Palestinians living in the West Bank and Gaza and expatriate Palestinians.

Moreover, since the beginning of reconciliation between Israel and the Palestinians in 1993, expatriate Palestinians have begun to transfer funds to the area for investment and residential/commercial construction.

One area where investments has remained strong since the 1980s is in housing accounting for 20 percent of GDP compared to 7 percent in similar economies. Gaza and Ramallah in the West Bank have witnessed a boom in housing construction since the signing of the Declaration of Principles in September 1993.

Most housing construction is privately financed and benefits the middle and upper classes as well as many expatriate Palestinians. Availability of affordable housing remains a serious problem for the lower-middle and lower classes, particularly in Gaza. Land prices, especially in urban areas, have skyrocketed since September 1993, primarily because of the scarcity of land available for development in the West Bank or Gaza.

While a number of Arab banks have already established offices in the West Bank and Gaza, the financial services market remains relatively undeveloped. Correspondent and other international banking relationships are developing. Because the PA permits holding foreign currency accounts, some observers believe that areas under Palestinian Authority control for banking services will show strong growth in offshore banking facilities.

## Leading Growth Sectors

### Infrastructure Development

Both publicly and privately financed infrastructure development projects will be a major growth sector in the West Bank and Gaza during the next five years. Construction of the Gaza port, for which France and the Netherlands are providing $60 million, is scheduled to begin shortly. Palestinian officials have indicated that this contribution must be revised as the project's cost has risen.

During the past five years, there have been measurable improvements in the physical and institutional infrastructure in Palestinian-controlled areas. Between 1994 and 1998, the Palestinian Economic Council for Development and Reconstruction (PECDAR) implemented projects to improve 783.5 kilometers of roads throughout the West Bank and Gaza, with major attention focusing on municipal and village roads. Another 154 kilometers of roads are being renovated with financial backing coming from the European Investment Bank (EIB). Furthermore, hundreds of schools and clinics have also been renovated and expanded, and two new hospitals recently built.

The water and sanitation sector has received considerable attention, with $315 million being disbursed to 112 projects during 1994-98. Of this, roughly 80 projects were designed to increase water quantities available to Palestinians to 28.6 million cubic meters a year through network expansion, rehabilitation and new source development.

This target has not been reached, primarily because Israel, which continues to control water resources in the West Bank and Gaza, has refused to issue the necessary permits. Nevertheless, tangible improvements have been made, and access to piped water has increased throughout the areas.

In the power sector, the first independent project (IPP) is now underway with Enron International of the US and the Palestine Electricity Company (PEC). The two bodies have signed an agreement with the Palestinian Energy Authority to supply electricity from a planned $140 million, 136-MW combined cycle power plant to be built south of Gaza. It is scheduled to be operational by mid-2000. PEC shareholders include Athens-based Consolidated Contractors International Company (CCC), Palestine Development & Investment Company (PADICO), Arab Bank, Arab Palestine Investment Company, and the PA.

### Private Housing Construction

Private housing construction is also expected to be a strong-growth sector as demand for low and lower-middle income housing is expected to remain high. Much of this demand can be met by local builders and engineers at comparatively low prices. Still, innovation in low-cost, multi-family housing construction is needed from outside sources. There is a growing trend, particularly in Gaza, of building large commercial and residential towers rather than one or two story buildings. Companies that can produce low-cost construction inputs in high volume should consider marketing and distribution options in the West Bank and Gaza.

### Manufacturing and Industry

Expansion is expected in light industry and low-tech electrical assembly, such as car dashboards and electronic goods assembly, and in the manufacturing and export of processed foods, pharmaceuticals, textiles and shoes, hardware, wood and cane furniture, plastics and housewares. Construction inputs, such as cement and steel products, also will be in heavy demand. The relatively high education level of the work force compared with Jordan's and Egypt's should give the West Bank and Gaza a competitive advantage in industries requiring technical expertise.

### Agriculture

The agricultural sector employs more than 14 percent of the West Bank and Gaza workforce and accounts for 30 percent of West Bank's and 25 percent of Gaza's GDP. The sector possesses excellent growth potential, particularly for providing inputs for the local food processing industry. Local entrepreneurial talent, climate and a sound technological base are strategic advantages in the sector. The ultimate growth potential of the agricultural sector, however, depends in part upon the willingness of Israel and neighboring countries to lower agricultural trade barriers or to at least allow the transit of Palestinian agricultural goods to Europe and the Gulf.

### Tourism

Tourism in the West Bank and Gaza is also expected to grow, but expansion depends heavily on security issues and, in areas of the West Bank where Israel remains in control, on certain administrative matters. Expansion of the tourism sector also depends on obtaining land and building permits from the Israelis.

## Business Environment

### Stock Exchange

PADICO, a consortium of Palestinian businessmen, and Samed, a PLO-owned business conglomerate have invested US$ 2 million in the Palestine Securities Exchange (PSE), which opened in Nablus in late-February 1997. The Exchange is a private Palestinian company owned by the Palestinian private sector (70 percent), the PA (20 percent) and public share holding companies (10 percent). Shares are listed in Egyptian pounds, Jordanian dinars, or Israeli shekels.

At the opening, 21 Palestinian public holding companies obtained quotation on the PSE. In June 1997, the number had dropped to 13. As of July 1999, 20 companies were trading on the exchange. An average of six firms trade actively during the PSE's three weekly sessions on Mondays, Tuesdays, and Wednesdays.

To obtain a quotation, a company should be a public share holding company with a capital of at least US$ 750,000, at least 250 shareholders and at least 25 percent of the shares should be owned by the public. Most importantly, the publicly traded companies must disclose its assets and gains or losses. Generally, public share holding companies in the PA are not required by law to be quoted on the stock market and, thus, do not have to disclose their finances. So far, this has prevented many of Palestine's existing public share holding companies, a substantial number of which are believed to fulfill the current requirements, to apply for a quotation. This situation, however, might change as Jordan, who until recently followed the same rule, made it now obligatory for its public share holding companies to be quoted.

### Donor Assistance

From 1994-1998, donors committed $3.821 billion and disbursed $2.639 billion in aid to the Palestinian Authority and Palestinian non-governmental organizations. Of this total, some $1.56 billion went to public investment projects by September 1998. On November 30, 1998, the international donor community pledged another $3.3 billion over five years to support Palestinian development efforts.

Although domestic revenues have risen recently, the economy remains heavily dependent on foreign aid, with donors financing the entire capital budget and pledging $700 million in grants, soft loans and guarantees for 1999. On a recent visit to Jerusalem, Kemal Dervis, World Bank vice-president for the Middle East & North Africa, advised the Palestinians not to become too dependent on foreign aid. Dervis warned that aid would start to decline after the next two-three years. Any real move toward Palestinian self-sufficiency requires a change in the political and security situation that would encourage higher private inflows and allow greater freedom of movement for Palestinian goods.

A report by the United Nations Representative Office in the Palestinian Authority revealed that the total aid provided by donor countries to the Palestinian Authority in 1998 amounted to $399.8 million. This reflected a 27.4% fall compared to 1997, during which donor countries' aid equaled $550.6 million. Through September 1999, the PA had received $174 million out of the $524 million pledged. The perceived high levels of corruption throughout Palestinian institutions may threaten future streams of foreign donor aid.

## Major Projects

### Build Operate Transfer
New developments in areas such as power generation and telecommunications are planned as build-operate-transfer (BOT) operations. If the interest of foreign investors is to be secured, however, it will require a concerted effort from the sponsors of the peace process to receive guarantees from Israel that contractors will be able to secure permission for their equipment and staff.

### Franchising
Because the Palestinian Authority offers only a relatively small local population, the best franchising potential exists in sectors where specific dietary, language or usage patterns differ from those in neighboring countries. For example, food and computer items and office supplies may be best mar-

keted in the West Bank and Gaza with Arabic markings, rather than using Hebrew as required inside Israel.

The fast food business is booming in Israel, and Palestinians enjoy eating American hamburgers, pizza and other popular food items. Fast-food franchises may want to consider lowering the cost of fast foods as a first step to entering the Palestinian market. Opportunities exist for pizza, ice cream, and competitively priced hamburger and chicken meals.

Western consumer brands ranging from household cleaning items to snack foods have an excellent reputation in the West Bank and Gaza. Palestinians are willing to pay for good quality and internationally recognized names. In addition, good opportunities exist for snack foods, cereals, sauces and other foods which do not need refrigeration during transit.

Sales of office products and supplies offer an excellent opportunity as the Palestinian Authority and Palestinian municipalities expand operations and as local businesses grow. Most Palestinian businesses and official offices currently purchase their supplies through office supply stores in Tel Aviv.

Automotive supplies, hardware parts and service equipment offer good sales opportunities. Extensive construction and a likely increase in Palestinian auto sales over the next five years will spur a need for a wide range of automotive parts and equipment. Of particular interest to the local market are refurbished engines and parts and good quality automotive items such as motor oil.

Franchising and distributorships are becoming increasingly popular, with the best prospects in hardware, computers, electronics and office equipment, fast food, amusement and theme-parks, and small business services such as copying and printing.

While a number of Arab banks have already established offices in the West Bank and Gaza, the financial services market remains relatively undeveloped. Correspondent and other international banking relationships are developing. Some observers believe that areas under Palestinian Authority control for banking services will show strong growth in offshore banking facilities, due to the fact that the Palestinian Authority allows holding foreign currency accounts.

## Legal Review

While business people want to conduct business and are less concerned with the legal intricacies involved in doing business, lawyers are more concerned with proper appellation, codes and structures. Since negotiations between the Palestinian Liberation Organization and Israel, commenced in 1993, changes have been taking place in almost every aspect of day-to-day life for the Palestinians. Therefore, the nomenclature, the laws and the formalities change along with the latest current events, and they are not always immediately disseminated. Thus, there is a real risk of uncertainty in the Palestinian Authority, although policy makers assure continuity and consistency in the transfer of powers and subsequent law making as the Palestinian Authority takes control.

The primary documents to which Israel and the Palestinian Authority are parties, which affect the changing status and nature of the Palestinian Authority, are the Declaration of Principles on Interim Self-Government Arrangements, signed in Washington, DC on September 13, 1993 (hereinafter, the DoP); the Israeli-Palestinian Interim Agreement on the West Bank and Gaza Strip, signed in Washington, DC on September 28, 1995 (hereinafter, Oslo 2); and the Protocol on Economic Relations, signed in Paris, France on April 29, 1994 (hereinafter, the Paris Protocol). There have been numerous other forum discussions, official and non-official committee meetings and conferences at which papers were presented and adopted which have some bearing on the changes taking place in the Palestinian Authority.

Certain geographical areas and substantive areas of law have been delineated as within the control of the Palestinian Authority. Not all areas of law that are within the substantive jurisdiction of the Palestinian Authority may be applied or enforced in all areas under its geographical control. The various documents defining the process of moving to self-rule have delineated areas as follows: Area A covers urban areas which have autonomy, such as Gaza and Jericho. The Palestinian Authority is responsible for the administration and enforcement of laws on all levels in Area A, including civilian and police power. Area B covers rural areas in which the Palestinian Authority has civilian jurisdiction but no police powers. Area C includes Jewish settlements, military areas and open areas. All powers and authority in Area C are administered and enforced by the Civil Administration. Certain of the agreements defining the transfer of powers to the Palestinian Authority have provided interior measures until a final resolution is reached. For example, special provisions in Oslo 2 allow for the transfer of taxes collected from Palestinians located in Area C by the Civil Administration to the Palestinian Authority.

## Background

A brief legal history of the area is essential to understanding the complexity of the issues facing the Palestinian Authority in gaining a unified system of laws. There are several sources of law that control various legal matters in different parts of territory known as Gaza and the West Bank. These sources include Ottoman civil law, which was applied to the Palestinian territories during the Ottoman Empire's rule between 1517 and 1917. The Ottoman civil code, Al Magella, is still the applicable rule of law in the West Bank and Gaza with regard to matters in which no subsequent laws have been adopted by any later controlling authority.

The British occupied Mandatory Palestine from 1917 until Israeli establishment in 1948, during which time its occupation was formalized as a Mandate under the direction of the League of Nations (from 1922 to 1948). Many aspects of commercial law, among other areas, were subject to decrees issued by the British High Commissioner during the Mandatory Period. Mandatory law and British legal principles are still widely applicable in Gaza today as a result of the lack of any subsequent legal authority until recently. In contrast, the West Bank has replaced most of the British Mandate laws with Jordanian laws.

Since in 1948, the control and administration of the areas of Gaza and the West Bank have been diverse and not uniform. This has resulted in a dichotomous legal system, which is being addressed by the Palestinian Authority.

## Gaza

Following Israel's establishment in 1948, Egypt administered the Gaza Strip until June 1967. Egypt never made any territorial claims over the Gaza Strip and merely undertook its administration. During the Egyptian administration, Egypt applied certain administrative regulations (hereinafter, the Egyptian Regulations) in order to implement the law, which were issued by the General Governor and Administrative Governor. While a legislative body was created called the Palestine Legislative Council, British Mandatory law remained mainly intact.

## The West Bank

In contrast to the Gaza Strip, Jordan formally annexed the West Bank in April of 1950. Thus, the applicable law in the area up until that time was modified and replaced as necessary to bring it in accordance to Jordanian law. Since June 1967, the West Bank has been controlled by Israel, and administered by the Israeli Defense Forces and, specifically, by the Israeli Civil Administration since 1981. Jordanian law continues to be applied in the West Bank, as modified by military orders issued by the Israeli military or Civil Administration (hereinafter, Military Orders). In the absence of Jordanian law, reference is still made to Ottoman civil law.

## Israeli Administration of Gaza and the West Bank

The Israeli Defense Forces has administered the Gaza Strip and the West Bank since June 1967. With the exception of Israel's formal annexation of East Jerusalem, the territories under its administration continued to be controlled by the laws previously applicable to the specific area, as modified by Military Orders issued by the Israeli military and relating primarily to matters of security. Areas that have obtained autonomy under the ambit of the Palestinian Authority apply laws enacted by the Palestinian Authority, and in matters where no new law has been enacted they continue to apply the rules of law that were applicable to those areas prior to autonomy. Thus, in the autonomous West Bank town of Jericho, laws enacted by the Palestinian Authority are applicable, but in their absence Jordanian law, modified by Military Orders (if such orders were not revoked by the Palestinian Authority) is applied. Similarly, in Gaza, in the absence of laws enacted by the Palestinian Authority, British Mandatory law, as modified by Egyptian Regulations and by Military Orders (if such Military Orders have not been revoked by the Palestinian Authority), is applied.

## The Basic Law Draft

The Palestinian Authority is currently in the process of adopting a temporary Basic Law (Draft of the Basic Law for the Palestinian National Authority in the Transitional Period—The First Reading). The law was drafted by a team of lawyers to serve as a provisional constitution for the Palestine State in formation. The Basic Law has passed the first reading and is yet to be put into final form. It can only take effect, however, after a joint Palestinian-Israel committee determines it does not exceed the PA's rights under the Agreement on the Gaza Strip and the Jericho Area. So far, the Basic law contemplates a broad array of citizen rights and establishes a three-pillar system of a reformed judiciary with extensive power as well as provisions for the legislative and the executive bodies. Its norms are superior to legislation or administrative decrees, and it also incorporates the most important treaties on international human rights.

## Judiciary

Currently, there are still two court systems in the Palestinian Authority. One system is in effect in Gaza and the other in the West Bank.

### Gaza

In Gaza, the judiciary is divided into three levels, in accordance with the system installed during the British Mandatory period: the Magistrates Courts, the Central Courts and the High Court.

The Magistrates Courts are authorized to decide civil suits where the amount of the dispute is valued at less than US$ 8,300. The Central Court hears civil suits where the amount in controversy exceeds US$ 8,300. Matters relating to the enforcement of Magistrates Court judgments are submitted to the jurisdiction of the Central Courts.

The High Court sits in two capacities, either as the High Court of Appeals or the High Court of Justice. In its capacity as the High Court of Appeals, the High Court hears appeals from decisions issued by the Magistrates and Central Courts. In its capacity as the High Court of Justice, the High Court hears cases that challenge laws or regulations as being contrary to public policy. It also hears administrative law matters in disputes involving administrative agency decisions, orders or regulations.

Judgments obtained in Gaza are valid for a period of fifteen years. Enforcement of judgments that are not voluntarily paid is carried out by the Department of Execution, which issues an order to the judgment debtor to pay and is enforced by the police.

## The West Bank

The judiciary in autonomous areas of the West Bank is in the process of becoming fully functional. In other areas of the West Bank, the judiciary is less than fully functional.

The judicial system for the West Bank is modeled after the Jordanian system and is composed of Magistrates Courts, Courts of First Instance, Appeals Courts and a Court of Cassation. The Magistrates Courts have jurisdiction to hear cases involving claimed disputes not exceeding 250 Jordanian Dinars. Cases involving claims exceeding that amount are submitted to the jurisdiction of the Courts of First Instance. The Courts of First Instance have some limited appellate review functions over decisions of the Magistrates Courts. Appeals from judgments of the Courts of First Instance and the Magistrates Courts are heard by the Court of Appeals.

While the judicial system ostensibly calls for a Court of Cassation, a Supreme Court, none has operated in the West Bank since 1967. Therefore, decisions of the Appeals Courts are final and not subject to appeal.

The lack of a court of last resort, the long delays involved in scheduling court hearings as well as the lack of a police force capable of executing judgments (except in the autonomy areas), are the primary reasons stated for the reportedly high out of court settlement rate of cases filed in the trial courts in the West Bank.

Enforcement of court decisions in the West Bank is regulated by the Jordanian Enforcement Law of 1952 and the Jordanian Enforcement of Foreign Decisions Law of 1952. Before the establishment of a Palestinian police force in the West Bank, court decisions of civil courts were practically unenforceable. The introduction of Palestinian police following the re-deployment of Israeli Military forces is believed to gradually increase the likelihood that decisions will be enforced.

The enforcement of foreign judgments in the West Bank under the Jordanian Law of 1952 remains generally problematic as the law gives the local courts the discretion to refuse to enforce the foreign decision if the foreign country's laws do not reciprocate. Also, foreign decisions relating to land disputes are generally not enforceable.

As of January 1999, the Palestinian judiciary consisted of 65 judges, 30 in the Gaza Strip and 35 in the West Bank. 12 Judges sit on the High Court, nine of whom are based in the Gaza Strip, while the remaining three are in the West Bank. A further 21 judges preside over cases in the two district courts and six magistrate courts in the Gaza Strip, while 32 judges preside over similar cases in the West Bank. In the Gaza Strip, for example, more than 75,000 cases were processed in Magistrate (or trial level) courts in 1998—an estimated 61,000 criminal cases and 14,000 civil cases. Members of the judiciary regularly complain about the low number of judges relative to the number of cases.

## Alternative Dispute Resolution Mechanisms

Both in Gaza and in the West Bank, alternative dispute resolution is widely used for resolving commercial and business disputes. During a period of political and legal instability, alternative dispute resolution mechanisms were thought to provide greater convenience and predictability than the court system. Mechanisms presently used are arbitration, mediation and other less common forms of dispute resolution. Arbitration laws exist both in Gaza (Palestine Arbitration Ordinance of 1929) and in the West Bank (Jordanian Law of Arbitration of 1953) providing for enforcement of arbitration agreements and awards. In Gaza, institutionalized arbitration is available through the Palestinian Chamber of Commerce.

### Business Forms and Structures

## Companies Law

The administration of the relevant laws governing companies was transferred to the Palestinian Authority under the terms of Oslo 2. To date, the Palestinian Authority has not issued any decrees or other regulations that significantly alter the pre-existing legal frameworks prevailing in the areas that are now autonomous. As a result, two separate Palestinian Authority ministries are responsible for registering companies and administering the applicable companies laws in Gaza and the parts of the West Bank that have attained self-rule.

In Gaza, the prevailing legal framework for registering a company is the British Mandatory Companies Law, No. 18 of 1929, as amended. The Palestinian Authority Ministry of Justice now administers registration of companies in Gaza.

In areas of the West Bank that have attained self-rule, the Jordanian Companies Law No. 12 of 1964 is the prevailing framework for registering a company. In Jericho and in other areas where the Israeli Defense Forces have withdrawn, the registration process for registering a company is now administered by the Controller of Companies located in the Palestinian Authority's Ministry of Economy, Commerce and Industry. In other areas, the duties of the Registrar of Companies are handled by the Civil Administration.

Two types of companies are recognized under the prevailing legal frameworks in both Gaza and the West Bank: private stock companies and public stock companies. Companies established in Gaza may only issue one class of shares, in contrast to companies established in the West Bank, which are entitled to issue different classes of shares.

## Private Stock Companies

A private stock company must have a minimum of two shareholders and a maximum of fifty shareholders. Such companies are prohibited from offering their shares to the public. Furthermore, private stock companies may impose restrictions on the transferability of their shares. Liability of a shareholder in a private stock company is limited to the value of the shares such shareholder holds in the company.

## Public Stock Companies

Public stock companies must have at least seven shareholders. Public stock companies may not restrict the transferability of their shares. Liability of a shareholder in a public stock company is limited to the value of the shares such shareholder holds.

The amount of share capital, expressed in Jordanian (JD) or Israeli (NIS) currency must be divided into shares of equal nominal value of not less than JD 1 and not more than JD 10. A shareholding company, from the date of its registration, becomes a corporate body bearing the name that is stated in the by-laws and articles of association.

In both Gaza and the West Bank, the general partners of a public stock company must subscribe to a minimum of 10 percent of the shares. The remaining shares are to be offered for public subscription by means of a notice published in at least two daily newspapers one week prior to the subscription's commencement.

If the total value of the project exceeds JD 50,000, and among the general partners there is a foreigner, the general partners may not cover more than 75 percent of the shares and the remainder of the shares must be offered to the public.

## Registration and Fees

In the mid-1990s, the PA standardized company registration fees for both Gaza and the West Bank. Companies are now required to pay 0.5 percent of the company's stated capital, plus minor additional charges such as a service fee of 285 NIS, a per shareholder fee of 84 NIS, a fee for the registrar's notarization of signature of 74 NIS, and a 13 NIS fee for stamps. There appears to be no additional fees for foreign companies. For purposes of registration, however, local companies must submit a completed company's registration form, plus two copies of the company's articles of incorporation and by-laws.

## Foreign Companies

A foreign company (including subsidiaries, representatives and branch offices) that wishes to conduct business in the Palestinian Authority must fulfill the identical registration requirements as a locally established company. The foreign company must file copies of its certificate of incorporation, memorandum and articles of association, authenticated by the registrar of companies located in the place of its incorporation. These documents must also be translated into Arabic. The documents should include the nationality, age, address and initial stock holding of each of the founding shareholders of the company, as well as the amount of the company's authorized share capital upon its establishment.

In addition to its registration application, a foreign company must provide a letter stating the names, addresses and nationalities of the directors of the company and of others who have been granted signatory rights on behalf of the company. A company representative and attorney must be appointed in order to register the company. In the autonomous Palestinian areas, a power of attorney authenticated before a notary public is sufficient. In other areas of the West Bank, authentication must be carried out by an Israeli foreign consular official.

The fees for registration of a foreign company are not equal to those applicable to locally established companies. Foreign companies registering in Gaza must pay a registration fee of approximately US$ 100. In the West Bank, as of April 1995, a foreign company whose initial capital upon incorporation in its country of origin was less than US$ 1.666 million had to pay a registration fee of US$ 1,870. A foreign company whose initial capital upon incorporation in its country of origin was more than US$ 1.666 million must pay a registration fee of US$ 3,740. There are also certification and publication fees and stamp duties that are applied to the registration of a company.

Where the Civil Administration is still responsible for administering the registration of companies, additional requirements are imposed, including applications for work permits for non-resident shareholders. These additional requirements result in extended delays of up to six months in the registration of companies. In contrast, registration of companies within the autonomous areas may be completed in a week to ten days.

## Partnerships

Partnerships in the Palestinian Authority are divided into two categories: General and Limited Partnerships. The law recognizes a partnership when two or more people work together to operate a for-profit business. In the General Partnership, all partners are jointly and severally liable for all the obligations of the firm that are incurred while serving as a partner. The name of at least one of the partners must be indicated in the title of the general partnerships. Limited Partnerships are required to have at least one general partner who is personally responsible for the liabilities of the company and at least one limited partner whose liability is limited to the amount of capital invested. The latter may not participate in the management of the company. The shares in a partnership are to be divided in accordance with the shareholders' agreement.

Partnerships must register with the Companies Registrar, in accordance with Law No. 12 of 1964 in the West Bank and the Companies Ordinance

No. 18 of 1929 in the Gaza Strip. They are subject to a flat fee of 493 NIS, service fees of 285 NIS, a fee per shareholder of 74 NIS and a stamp fee of 13 NIS.

## Sole Proprietorships

One of the most common forms of business found in the PA areas is the sole proprietorship. This is typically a small, often family-owned enterprise which has a license to operate but is not a registered business or formal entity. Sole proprietorships are not recognized as a company and, thus, do not enjoy the benefit of limited liability. Bank accounts and tax records have to be registered in the name of the owner and not in a company's name.

## Commercial Agency and Representation

As of January 1997, the PA began to enforce a law in effect since March 1996, which requires the appointment of direct dealers/agents for all goods entering the PA areas. The law requires all foreign companies distributing goods in the PA areas to appoint a direct agent who is to register with the Ministry of Economy and Trade in accordance with the prevailing rules and regulations. The agency rights are deemed to cover the entire area of the PA (West Bank and Gaza). To protect direct agency rights, the Ministry will prevent the import, entry or distribution of goods into the Palestinian market unless authorized by the agent. Direct agents may also authorize primary, sole or more distributors in the PA areas in order to facilitate delivery of goods to and between the West Bank and the Gaza Strip. Individuals and companies that already have direct agency agreements for the PA areas must register as agents (individual and/or company) and register the agency agreement itself with the Ministry. If business is conducted in areas where agents are not used in the ordinary cause of business, foreign companies may qualify for an exemption from the Ministry whereby they may distribute through distributors and middlemen who have to register at the Ministry's Registrar of Distributors and Middlemen.

The law further stipulates that agents for special category goods including cigarettes, electrical appliances, pharmaceuticals, cars, certain foodstuffs and agricultural items are forced to comply with the technical requirements of the concerned ministries and departments of the PA prior to registering with the Ministry.

## Foreign Currency and Banking

### Foreign Currency Control
In areas of the West Bank under the control of the Civil Administration, the Controller of Banks regulates currency transfers that are in line with the currency control laws applicable in Israel. Furthermore, while bank accounts may be held in any of three currencies - US dollars, Jordanian Dinars or New Israeli Shekels - withdrawals from accounts located in the West Bank under the control of the Civil Administration may be made only by converting the amount into either NIS or JD.

### Banking
In accordance with Oslo 2, responsibility for banking has been transferred to the Palestinian Authority. The Paris Protocol contains significant provisions that will affect Palestinian banking when implementing legislation and regulation is effected.

The Paris Protocol authorized the creation of the Palestinian Monetary Authority (PMA), which enjoys the powers of most central banks, with the notable exceptions that it cannot issue a Palestinian currency and it cannot apply for state membership status at the International Monetary Fund. The PMA supervises fiscal policy in the Palestinian Authority and manages official reserves. It also reviews proposed legislation that will regulate banking in the future.

Regular savings accounts and interest bearing checking accounts in dollars may be opened in the West Bank and Gaza. Accounts may be held in U.S. dollars, Jordanian Dinars or New Israeli Shekels, and all three currencies are used for conducting business in the Palestinian Authority.

In the absence of a Palestinian currency, banks operating within the jurisdiction of the Palestinian Authority have to compete for deposits with banks located elsewhere. This competition is mostly for local residents' deposits. Unlike Israeli banks, local banks are generally not allowed to offer inflation-indexed savings accounts or foreign currency-dominated accounts, which places them at a relative disadvantage in competing for the accounts of large Palestinian firms and international organizations.

While many financial institutions are now operating in the Palestinian Authority, two of the most active banks are the Arab Bank and the Cairo Amman Bank. As Palestinian banking is still in its infancy and the banks that operate in the Palestinian Authority are unable to assess credit risk and worthiness, mid- and long-term financing is often difficult to obtain. It is anticipated that this will change as experience is gathered by the lending institutions as well as the promulgation of regulations and guidelines by the PMA.

As of 1997, there were 17 commercial banks with 69 branches operating in the PA-controlled areas of West Bank and Gaza, including one foreign bank (ANZ Grindlays). The largest institution is the Arab Bank, which currently has 17 branches worldwide, including two in New York.

Banks in the PA area generally offer only short-term credit such as overdrafts, LC's and bank guarantees. Average interest rates on loans in Israeli Shekels are 20-25 percent and 13 percent on loans in Jordanian Dinars. In 1996, the Arab Palestinian Investment Bank (APIB) started conducting business in the Palestinian areas. It was established by the Arab Bank (55 percent of shares), the International Financial Corporation, the private investment arm of the World Bank (25 percent of shares), the German Investment and Development Company (DEG), which belongs to the German Government (15 percent of the shares) and the Enterprise Investment Company, owned by Palestinian businessmen (5 percent of the shares).

### Bilateral Banking Agreements
Israel, Jordan, Egypt and the Palestinian Liberation Organization have concluded several bilateral agreements, some of which affect banking matters.

The Central Bank of Jordan (CBJ) and the Israeli Controller of Banking (ICB) reached an agreement allowing Jordanian banks to open branches in the West Bank, after first seeking the approval of the CBJ and ICB. This agreement will be valid until superseded by action of the PMA.

The Arab Land Bank reopened its branches in the West Bank pursuant to the terms of an accord reached between Egypt and Israel in May of 1993, subject to the supervision of the CBJ, ICB and the Central Bank of Egypt.

## Intellectual Property

The Jordanian laws concerning trademarks, patents and designs are applicable in the West Bank, with the exceptions that publication requirements are fulfilled by publishing notices three times in a local newspaper and that registration offices are located in the cities of Ramallah and Jericho. Copyrights are protected under Law No. 16 of 1924. In addition, autonomous cities are also governed by the Intellectual Property Laws of the West Bank.

In Gaza, the Palestinian Trademark and Patent Laws No. 35 of 1938, adopted during the British Mandate, are still applicable. The registration system under those laws is very similar to those prevailing in the West Bank under Law no. 33 of 1952. Despite the different authorizing legislation, the substantive differences between the laws governing intellectual property matters are minimal.

Furthermore, a side letter to the Paris Protocol provides that the parties to the agreement will hold discussions regarding mutual recognition and protection of patents, designs and trademarks, in addition to other intellectual property.

## Patents

In both Gaza and the West Bank, patent protection is granted for a period of 16 years from the date of filing the patent application. Furthermore, both systems allow for the compulsory licensing of a patented product if the "reasonable requirements" of the public under the applicable law have not been met.

In Gaza, the novelty requirement for patents may be met if the invention has not been previously published or used in the Palestinian territories. Likewise, the novelty requirement in the West Bank is met if there has been no prior publication, use or sale in the West Bank.

## Trade and Service Marks

Trademark protection is available for registered trademarks up to a period of seven years, a term that may be extended for additional periods of 14 years each. The prevailing laws in both Gaza and the West Bank prohibit the registration of a trademark that is contrary to public morals.

It is now possible to register service marks in Gaza and the West Bank. The Palestinian Minister of Justice in September 1996 issued a decision that amended Appendix No. 4 of the Implementation Regulations of the Trademarks Act of the Year 1940. Service marks can now be registered under the registration system applicable in Gaza. The International Classification of goods and services (classes 35-42) is used to classify services by enumerating the classes and class headings eligible for expanded registration.

## Designs

New and original designs that have not yet been published may be protected under the laws of both Gaza and the West Bank. Both applicable legal systems prohibit the registration of designs that are contrary to morality or to the public order. In Gaza, a registered design may be compulsorily licensed under certain circumstances. Compulsory licensing of designs is not permitted in the West Bank.

## Taxation

The Agreement on the Gaza Strip and the Jericho Area, signed in Egypt on May 4, 1994 (hereinafter, the Gaza-Jericho Agreement), which incorporated the Paris Protocol into its provisions, authorized the transfer of power and authority relating to taxation to the Palestinian Authority. Oslo 2 also includes provisions on taxation and allows both Israel and the Palestinian Authority to levy personal or individual taxes.

Under Article V of the Gaza-Jericho Agreement, the right to tax residents of Gaza and the West Bank is territorially based. Area A covers the urban areas populated by Palestinians, such as Gaza, in which the Palestinian Authority has full power over all aspects of government, including taxation. Area B covers the rural areas in which the Palestinian Authority has civilian (as opposed to police powers) jurisdiction, including powers of taxation. Area C includes areas within the West Bank that are the subject of negotiations and in which there are Jewish settlements, military areas or open areas. The Palestinian Authority has no jurisdiction to tax Jewish settlements and military areas. With regard to open areas in Area C, however, the Palestinian Authority has limited civilian powers, including the power to tax Palestinian residents located therein. The Palestinian Authority's power to enforce the tax laws in Area C is limited. In the event that Palestinian taxpayers are located in Area C, their taxes will be levied by the Civil Administration and transferred to the tax authorities of the Palestinian Authority.

The Palestinian Authority has delegated taxation powers to the Ministry of Finance, which, in turn, has created a Tax Department. The Tax Department has issued a personal income tax regulation that became effective January 1, 1995 and is applicable to Palestinian residents of the West Bank and Gaza. Since no other regulation, directive or legislation regarding taxation has been adopted by the Palestinian Authority, Jordanian Income Tax Law No. 25 of 1964, as amended by Military Orders, remains applicable in the West Bank, and the British Mandatory Income Tax Law No. 13 of 1947, as amended by Military Orders, rules in Gaza, with regard to all other taxes, including corporate income tax. The Ministry of Finance, however, has issued a large number of regulations to supplement the existing laws.

The PA has taken steps to stimulate investment with an April 1999 decision to cut income taxes. Company tax rates were slashed to 20 percent from 38.5 percent, while personal rates for higher incomes dropped to 20 percent from 48 percent, and low-income rates were reduced to merely 5 percent.

## Taxation of Companies

The controlling tax laws in the West Bank and Gaza define a company as any public or private shareholding company incorporated or registered in accordance with the prevailing law. Thus far, no distinction has been made between local and foreign companies for the purposes of taxation.

A territorial approach regarding the source of income is applied in order to determine taxable income. In Gaza, all revenue from any of the sources listed in the British Tax Law "accruing in, derived from, or received in" Gaza is considered taxable income. In the West Bank, taxable income is defined as all revenues from any of the sources provided in the Jordanian Tax Law "accruing in or derived from" the West Bank. Taxable income may be reduced by permissible deductions and exemptions as provided under the relevant law. Thus, any company, whether local or foreign, which earns revenues that are accrued in or derived from the Palestinian Authority (and in the case of revenues in Gaza which are received in Gaza), are subject to taxation.

Business losses can be carried forward from year to year, provided that the carry over does not exceed four years and as long as not more than 50 percent of taxable income is carried over for each of the four years and that the carry over is not for a loss, other than from the source originally stated. The appropriate tax authority must authorize all carry overs.

Tax incentives are available for approved investment projects, which include exemptions from VAT and other duties and taxes. These incentives are discussed at greater length in the section on Investment Incentives below.

## Dividends

Dividends distributed in the Palestinian territories to shareholders of a foreign company are subject to 25 percent withholding, whereas dividends distributed to shareholders of a Palestinian company are not taxed, regardless of the nationality or the place of residence of the individual shareholder. Only dividends paid from profits are taxable; dividends paid after redistribution of capital are exempt from taxation. Retained earnings are taxable under the Investment Law unless they are re-invested.

An automatic deduction of 25 percent is withheld at the source from companies that own stock in another entity, unless these companies obtain a Deduction at the Source Certificate, which grants a reduction of up to 5 percent. Applications for these certificates are available from the district tax offices.

## Withholding Taxes

The intertwined nature of the Palestinian and Israeli economies creates a complicated situation regarding withholding taxes on transactions between Israelis and Palestinians who are subject to tax under the separate jurisdictions.

The Paris Protocol, as amended, provides that when a Palestinian remits payment to an Israeli, no tax shall be withheld at source on income from the sales of goods from areas under Israeli tax jurisdiction that are not supplied by means of a permanent establishment (such as a branch, office or factory) in the areas under Palestinian tax control. Where income from the sale of goods is attributable to a permanent establishment in areas under Palestinian tax responsibility, tax may be withheld at source, but only on such income as is attributable to such permanent establishment.

289

No tax shall be withheld at source on income derived by an Israeli from transportation activities, if the point of departure or the point of final destination is within the areas under Israeli tax jurisdiction.

When an Israeli remits payment to a Palestinian on income accrued or derived in the West Bank or Gaza, no tax shall be withheld at source on income from the sale of goods from areas under Palestinian tax responsibility that are not supplied by means of a permanent establishment in the areas under Israeli tax responsibility. Where income from the sale of goods is attributable to a permanent establishment in the areas under Israeli tax responsibility, taxes may be withheld at source, but only on income that is attributable to such permanent establishment.

No tax shall be withheld at source on income derived by a Palestinian from transportation activities if the point of departure or the point of final destination is in the areas under Palestinian tax responsibility.

Each of the parties to the Paris Protocol undertook to provide that certificates of non-withholding be provided as proof that payments made were not subject to withholding tax requirements. If appropriate certification is not provided, taxes are to be withheld at source by the payer, according to applicable law.

Each party to the Paris Protocol will grant its residents tax relief for tax paid on income accrued in or derived in the areas under the tax responsibility of the other party. The parties also committed to establish a committee to review procedures regarding tax issues, including measures concerning double taxation.

## Indirect Taxes

The Palestinian Authority is empowered under the Paris Protocol to set certain indirect taxes, such as a value-added tax and import duties. The Palestinian Authority collects these revenues, and if they are still collected by the Civil Administration, the revenues are transferred by the Civil Administration to the Palestinian Authority.

## Value Added Tax

Under the terms of the Paris Protocol, the Palestinian Authority's ability to determine a value added tax for Gaza and the West Bank is limited by the restriction that the rate may not be under 15 percent. At present, value added tax is charged at a rate of 17 percent in both Gaza and the West Bank, the same rate prevailing in Israel.

Exceptions are applied to tourist services, fruits and vegetables and products that are ultimately exported (including all raw materials and component parts). Further, companies and institutions whose annual sales do not exceed NIS 36,000 are also exempt from paying VAT. Companies can apply for refund of VAT payments on all business start-up costs and on goods that are exported.

The Palestinian tax authorities have accounts in all foreign and domestic banks in the Territories, so VAT taxes may be deposited in any of these banks. Payments must be made monthly or bi-monthly, depending on the classification of the business.

A special VAT is applied to financial institutions, including banks and insurance companies (provided they are not non-profit organizations), which is levied at a rate of 17 percent on employee salaries per month and on profits.

## Import Duties

The Paris Protocol provides that the Palestinian Authority may charge import duties, provided that, with regard to certain products, the rates charged must be the same as the Israeli tariffs.

## Real Property Tax

Property taxes in Gaza and the West Bank vary between localities and are generally applied using two separate systems: one for municipalities and another for villages. The village system of property tax applies only to irrigated land, and each village maintains its own schedule of rates. The tax paid depends on what type of crop is grown and on the land area in cultivation.

For municipalities there are two categories of property—buildings and vacant land (including agricultural land). Assessments determine the base for municipal property tax. Vacant land is taxed using the assessed value of the land as a basis. For buildings, the rental value is assessed, depending on actual rental value, location and type of structure. Although the rates vary, the tax rates for buildings in the West Bank are generally 13.6 percent of the assessed rental value. For vacant land, the assessed rate is 0.6 percent of the assessed land value. In Gaza, the rate for buildings is 15 percent of the rental value, 9 percent of that total is assessed to the tenant, the other 91 percent assessed to the owner. For vacant land, the rate is 15 percent of the imputed production value of the land.

## Investment and Trade

### Investment Incentives

The Palestinian Authority's Ministry of Economy and Trade and Ministry of Industry promulgated the Law on the Encouragement of Investment of 1995, enacted on April 29, 1995 (hereinafter, the Investment Law), which authorizes the establishment of the Palestinian Higher Agency for the Encouragement of Investment (hereinafter, the Investment Agency) to implement the provisions of the Investment Law.

The Investment Agency board of directors is composed of fifteen private and public sector members and is chaired by the Minister of Economy, Trade and Industry. Decisions are made by majority vote of the board of directors, and, in case of a tie, the chairman casts the deciding vote. The board of directors appoints auditors to audit the Investment Agency's account in conformity with generally accepted practices and to submit a report to the President of the PA every six months.

The Investment Law is aimed at encouraging investment in all sectors of the economy and developing export oriented businesses. Certain categories of investment projects are exempt from taxes and customs duties under the Investment Law provided the investment project fulfills certain criteria.

To be eligible for the exemptions available under the Investment Law an investment project must meet the following criteria:

- The investment project must have paid-up capital of more than US$ 500,000 and/or be a project that permanently employs at least twenty-five Palestinian workers. The projected business plan of the investment project must be for at least ten years. Projects answering these criteria are entitled to an exemption from income taxes and duties for the first five years.

- The investment project must have paid-up capital of more than US$ 150,000 and less than US$ 500,000 and/or be a project that permanently employs at least 15 Palestinian workers. The projected business plan of the investment project must be for at least six years. Projects answering these criteria are entitled to an exemption from income taxes and duties for the first three years.
- The investment project must have paid-up capital of more than US$ 100,000 and less than US$ 150,000 and/or be a project that permanently employs at least 10 Palestinian workers. The projected business plan of the investment projects must be for at least five years. Projects answering these criteria are entitled to an exemption from income taxes and duties for the first two years.
- The Investment Law allows the Agency to grant additional special exemptions to projects that have paid-up capital of more than five million U.S. dollars and/or which permanently employ at least fifty Palestinian workers.
- Additional exemptions may be granted for both export-oriented products and projects that will benefit the Palestinian economy.

The Investment Law, however, does not define what is considered to be paid-up capital for its purposes, nor does it define Palestinian workers. Also, the law gives no indication at what point after approval an investor must satisfy the criteria in question. This is especially problematic in light of the Investment Agency's right to cancel its approval and demand repayment of all taxes and dues (see below).

## Application Procedure

Applications for approval of a foreign investment project in areas under the full civilian jurisdiction of the Palestinian Authority (i.e., Areas A and B) are filed with the Palestinian Authority Ministry of Economy, Commerce and Industry.

All investors must receive the approval of the Investment Agency. The application has to be supported with a technical and economic feasibility study of the project. Further, it is required that investors obtain all necessary licenses and permits from political authorities before the Investment Agency will approve a proposal. The Investment Agency has between 30 and 60 days from the date of the application to provide an answer that should include the reasons supporting the decision. Following approval, the investor must present an action plan detailing the steps to be followed to complete the project. The project must be started within six month of the date of approval.

The Agency has the power to cancel investment licenses in advance or retroactively at any time if it finds they do not comply with the Investment Law itself or with the conditions of the license. Investors whose licenses are superseded or canceled have no recourse to judicial review or to independent arbitration to challenge the decision; they can only appeal the decision before the President of the PA. The Investment Agency may also approve all asset transfers in connection with investment projects. The criteria for such approval are not stated in the Law, except for the provision that priority must be given to Palestinian purchasers.

The Investment Law does not stipulate clearly whether investors who do not wish to obtain benefits under the Investment Law are required to obtain the approval by the Authority in order to carry out their project.

## Protections for Foreign Investors

Foreign, non-Palestinian Arab and expatriate Palestinian investors who invest in approved investment projects may repatriate their capital and profits after paying applicable taxes. The Investment Law also grants them the right to permanent residence status and provides guarantees against nationalization, expropriation or confiscation.

With respect to protection against nationalization, the law states that no investment, irrespective of the investor's nationality shall be nationalized in whole or in part without the investor's consent. This rule, however, is subject to the exception that expropriation is conducted in compliance with a final judgment handed down by a competent court according to Palestinian law.

Investors do have the right to transfer capital and profits after having paid the dues prescribed by Palestinian law. The nature or level of these dues, however, is not mentioned in the Investment Law.

Finally, according to the Investment Law, all disputes between investors and the PA are to be settled by Palestinian courts according to applicable Palestinian law. Independent arbitration does not seem to be a possibility, although in its official summary, the PA states that the Investment Law "admits the possibility of dispute resolution through arbitration" without citing a provision that contains direct or indirect reference to arbitration.

## Trade Issues

The Paris Protocol addressed many of the sensitive trade issues affecting the intertwined Palestinian and Israeli economies. In particular, the Paris Protocol determined significant measures with regard to agriculture, industry and tourism. The Palestinian Authority is entitled to market its agricultural and industrial products externally (i.e., outside of Israel), without restriction under the terms of the Paris Protocol, provided Palestinian certificates of origin are issued for the product designated for export.

## Imports

All imports into the areas ruled by the PA must comply with a specific list of sanctioned imports and meet certain quota and standards requirements, as agreed to by the PA and Israel. The list is available at the Ministry of Economy, Trade and Industry. It is expected that this list will be expanded and that the quota limits will be increased in the near future.

Licensing is required for specified imports into PA territory, including health products, food, transportation and fuel. Also, imports generally need to comply with PA standards and requirements, as well as with environmental standards.

The documentation procedures required for imports include:

- a certificate of incorporation if the importer is a duly registered company;
- a certificate of good standing from the appropriate Chamber of Commerce;
- a certificate of foreign trade dealings obtained from the Ministry of Economy Trade and Industry;
- a pro-forma invoice with the estimated value of the goods imported;
- import licenses for goods that are on the specified list.

To facilitate the importing process, the required documentation must be presented to the Customs Department. Obtaining an import license takes approximately 10 to 15 days following the submission of the completed application to the Customs Department. Licenses are valid for a period of six month to a year, depending on the product.

## Agriculture

The Paris Protocol determined that there would be free movement of agricultural products, free of customs and import taxes, between Israel and the Palestinian Authority, subject to certain exceptions and limitations regarding veterinary certification and international codes for livestock. The agricultural section of the Paris Protocol temporarily restricts market access between the two parties for poultry, eggs, potatoes, cucumbers, tomatoes and melons.

## Industry

The Paris Protocol establishes free movement of industrial goods between the two sides to the Protocol. Such goods will be free of any restrictions, including customs and import taxes. The Protocol provides that the Palestinian Authority may employ incentives and adopt encouragement measures, including measures similar to those in force in Israel, to encourage and to promote the development of industry in the Palestinian Authority. With regard to industrial goods, each party agreed to take steps to prevent environmental damage to territory of the other party.

## Tourism

Each of the parties to the Paris Protocol agreed to allow the entry of tourist buses and other transportation authorized by the other party to enter its jurisdiction. Access to tourist sites and places of religious and national significance in both jurisdictions will be open for visitation to all tourists at reasonable hours. Each party is committed, under the Paris Protocol, to protect and to ensure the proper maintenance of historical, archaeological, cultural and religious sites. The Paris Protocol also calls for the establishment of a Palestinian Tourism Authority, which will be responsible for, among other things, regulating, licensing, classifying and supervising tourist services, sites and industries.

## Product Labels

The Palestinian Authority issued a regulation requiring, as of March 30, 1996, that products intended for sale in the West Bank and Gaza be labeled in Arabic and that the Arabic characters should be larger than those used for a second language, if any. The content of the second language version should correspond exactly to the Arabic version.

The law also provides that the label is to include specific details such as the name of the product, the trade name, the grade of the product, name and address of the importer if the product is imported, the place of production, name and address of manufacturing company, date of production and expiration date, basic ingredients that make up the product, storage directions and quantity in numbers, length or area as applicable.

## Trade Agreements

The Palestinian Authority has finalized trade agreements with the European Union, Jordan and Egypt. Products originating in the PA thus gained preferential status for import into the EU. All industrial products and some agricultural products are granted duty-free access, for some agricultural products reduced restrictions apply.

In October 1996, following the obtaining of beneficiary status under the Generalized System of Preferences (GPS), the PA entered into an agreement with the United States gaining duty-free access for certain Palestinian products.

## Real Estate Property

Under Oslo 2, the Palestinian Authority is responsible for land registration, planning and zoning. Zoning regulations and building and safety codes are in effect in both Gaza and in the West Bank. The Palestinian Authority has not yet issued any legislation in the area of real estate ownership. Therefore, the Ottoman and British Mandatory law regarding real property governs in Gaza, and the Ottoman law as amended by British Mandatory and Jordanian law and modified by Military Orders, regarding real property governs in the West Bank.

In Gaza and the West Bank, registration of land is effected in the Department of Land Registry. In Gaza, foreign entities may purchase land. Real estate development companies, however, must first obtain approval of the President of the Palestinian Authority before registering purchased property. In the West Bank, in accordance with Jordanian law, foreigners may only purchase property which is located within municipal boundaries, subject to obtaining the permission of the Civil Administration in accordance with Jordanian law, unless a special exception is made (such as for an approved investment project).

In 1967, the Civil Administration took title to all property owned by absentee landowners. Such property cannot be conveyed by the absentee owner, regardless of whether the owner has a valid title under Jordanian law. Under Oslo 2, the Palestinian Authority is responsible for absentee property but is obligated to safeguard the rights of Israelis in such property.

## Collateralization of Loans

Land is often a preferred collateral security for loans. Only about 35 percent of the land in the West Bank and about 50 percent of the land in Gaza has been registered. The remainder is unregistered, and ownership is determined based on family and community records and evidence. The lack of a formal land registration system and the dearth of clear evidence of title in real property often raises questions regarding boundaries and legal succession. These factors and the uncertainty regarding whether it is possible to foreclose on collateral security in the event of default on a loan, make the banks, especially foreign banks, unwilling to grant collateralized loans. Reportedly, many local banks require numerous cosigners, and they resort to extended family members of the borrower to recoup bad debts.

In the past, the Civil Administration was responsible for enforcement of foreclosure on land used as collateral for a loan. As a result, lenders refrained from resorting to foreclosure on land, in order to avoid having to resort to the Israelis to enforce such measures. Furthermore, the Civil Administration was reluctant to become involved in such civil matters and, therefore, enforcement, if requested, was slow to come. Now that the Palestinian Authority has the police powers necessary to enforce the civil laws in Area A, it remains to be seen whether enforcement and implementation of foreclosures will take place and become routine. The question of enforcement is not merely an issue of adequate and authorized police, but also one of social mores. Palestinian society has a strong taboo against evicting a person from his home. For this reason, the courts may be reluctant to order foreclosure and eviction since it would not be well received in the community.

While the Jordanian Collateral Lending Law No. 46 of 1953 is applicable in the West Bank, it is outdated. It does not provide for giving written notice to the borrower of the lender's intent to foreclose prior to commencing foreclosure proceedings, and it does not include a statutory redemption period during which the borrower, after having received notice of foreclosure, may redeem the loan and avoid foreclosure. Furthermore, no parallel law is applicable in Gaza. A modern collateral lending law, applicable throughout the Palestinian Authority, which addresses the societal concerns regarding foreclosure and eviction, and which is enforceable by the courts and police in the autonomous areas, would greatly enhance the economy by reducing the lending institutions' risk. The reduction of risks is crucial to bringing down the costs of lending and to making loans more widely available. Collateral security is merely one area in which the lack of a unified, modern legal system with practical experience in enforcement and implementation can deter investment and hinder growth in the Palestinian Authority.

## Environmental Law

The Palestinian Authority is not presently a signatory to any international or regional environmental treaties. In addition, there is no specific legislation regarding the environment in the PA. The Palestinian National Council, however, is considering drafts to such laws. Environmental provisions are included in laws such as the criminal code and import standards.

# QATAR

## Recent Political Development

The 1990s has been a dynamic decade in the politics of Qatar. In June 1995, Sheikh Hamad bin Khalifa al-Thani, the eldest son of Emir Sheikh Khalifa bin Hamad al-Thani, toppled his father in a bloodless palace coup. Although Sheikh Khalifa had vowed to regain power "at any cost" and was alleged to have supported an unsuccessful coup in early 1996, a truce was reached in October of that year. Furthermore, the former emir returned US$ 2 billion of missing state funds claimed by the government in worldwide lawsuits following an out-of-court settlement in 1997.

But that did not end the family drama. In October 1999, a cousin of the ruling Emir of Qatar went on trial, charged with masterminding the failed 1996 coup attempt against the Emir, Sheikh Hamad. The defendant, Sheikh Hamad bin Jassem bin Hamad al-Thani, is alleged to have plotted with unnamed foreign powers to overthrow the present Emir. Sheikh Hamad was once Qatar's Economy Minister and chief of police. The alleged coup was foiled when Qatari troops overpowered a band of mercenaries on the border with Saudi Arabia.

Sheikh Hamad has made moves towards democracy by encouraging public debate, ending press censorship and abolishing the Ministry of Informa-

| | |
|---|---|
| Population | 0.54 million (1999) |
| Religion | Islam |
| Government | Constitutional Monarchy |
| Languages | Official: Arabic (English is widely spoken) |
| Work Week | Public Sector: Saturday–Wednesday 7:00–13:00 Private Sector: Saturday–Thursday 7:30–13:00; 16:00–18:00 Banking: Saturday–Wednesday 7:30–11:00 Thursdays 7:30 –11:30 |
| Monetary Unit | Qatari Riyal (QR) |
| Exchange Rate | QR 3.64=US$ 1 |

tion. He has broken with the Gulf's male-dominated tradition by appointing a woman as under-secretary at the Education and Culture Ministry.

He has also scheduled municipal elections to foster grassroots democracy. It is speculated that he may order voting to fill certain seats on a thirty-five member advisory council and give it more powers to oversee the government.

In mid-July 1999, the Qatari Emir established a 32-member committee to draft a permanent Constitution for his state. The new Constitution will be geared to establishing an elected Advisory Council (Parliament) to replace the current one, which comprises 30 members appointed by the Emir. The current 30-year old Constitution falls short of the Qatari people's aspirations and provides scant opportunity for them to play a role in the decision making process.

In foreign relations, Qatar has always conducted an independent policy. As such, they have restored full ties with Gulf War foe Iraq and befriended radical Shi'ite Iran. During the decade, it has had disputes with its Bahraini neighbor after the latter discovered in December 1996 a network of Qatari spies operating in Bahrain. Recent events as of January 2000, however, point towards a possible cooling of tensions and eventual rapprochement between the two Gulf states. During the first week of January, the Emir of Bahrain, Sheikh Hamad bin Isa al-Khalifa, visited Qatar in what was interpreted as a new step toward improving relations between the two neighbors. The Bahraini Emir and his Qatari counterpart, Sheikh Hamad bin Khalifa al-Thani, met and discussed the long-standing territorial row. Following several rounds of official talks, the leaders vowed to enhance links in the economic, investment, trade and media fields.

Elsewhere, Doha established special relations with Western nations by giving the Pentagon a weapons depot on its soil, and providing France and Britain with lucrative arms deals and business contracts. US and French companies now dominate Qatar's oil and gas sector, which was once the exclusive domain of British Petroleum Co. Plc. and Royal Dutch/Shell Group.

# Recent Economic Developments

Although Qatar is one of the smallest Gulf countries in terms of geography, it has the third largest supply of natural gas in the world as well as a large supply of petroleum.

Qatar believes its future economic security lies in its North Field, the world's largest concentration of natural gas at more than 500 trillion cubic feet (14 trillion cubic meters). The development of this field is expected to cost a total of US$ 30 billion.

Qatar is governed by the ruling Al-Thani family through its head, the Emir. The Emir holds absolute power that has been influenced by consultation with leading citizens, rule by consensus and the right of personal appeal to the Emir. The Emir considers the opinions of leading citizens, whose influence is institutionalized in the Advisory Council, an appointed body that assists the Emir in formulating policy.

The State owns most basic industries and services, but the retail and construction industries are held in private hands. The government's plan for the immediate future is to maximize revenues, minimize the growth in expenditure and encourage the private sector to play a greater role in the economy.

Qatar's 120,000 native population enjoys high per capita incomes (about US$ 17,000), mainly from oil sales. But several years of low oil prices forced the country to become more economically prudent. Citizens, for example, must now pay for basic health services and driving licenses. The only services that Qataris receive free of charge are water and electricity, and even this may not last much longer.

This year's projected budget deficit is estimated at nearly $1 billion, equivalent to 10 percent of GDP. In an attempt to reduce this gap, the government has begun implementing austerity measures and is systematically withdrawing the numerous privileges it has distributed to nationals at the peak of the oil boom.

Despite the large projected deficit, the government has promised the International Monetary Fund to balance its budget by 2000. The government is hoping that higher oil output, coupled with rising prices will help close the gap. Qatar receives about 70 percent of its state revenue from oil sales and the rest from hydrocarbon-base industries.

In 1998, Qatar's balance of trade surplus declined to QR 1,307 million (roughly US$ 358 million) from QR 3,164 million (US$ 867 million) in 1997. This contraction is primarily the result of two factors: reduced rate of exports combined with an increased rate of imports. On the export side, Qatar's oil exports expanded in volume, but yielded less revenue due to last year's price slump.

Qatar is banking its future prosperity and political profile on its North Field; the world's largest single concentration of natural gas at more than 500 trillion cubic feet (14 trillion cubic meters). The development of this field is expected to cost a total of US$ 30 billion.

But the investment should be worthwhile. In 2002, gas sales are anticipated to reach 10.8 million tons, up from 3.6 million tons in 1999. Total LNG revenues in 1999 are projected to double to almost $2,200 million, as Ras Laffan Natural Gas Company (Rasgas) commences its operations and Qatar Liquefied Natural Gas Company (Qatargas) expands production. In August 1999, Rasgas cemented an energy deal with India's Petronet, consisting of the annual purchase of 7.5 million tons of LNG for 25 years, beginning in July 2003. Rasgas has also bid to acquire a 26 percent stake in the two Indian LNG terminals.

In addition, the signing of preliminary agreements to supply gas to the UAE's Offset Group under the Dolphin Gas Project will further boost Qatar's industry in several ways. Dolphin will help Qatar develop the regional market for gas that it has eagerly sought. Furthermore, if plans for a multi-billion dollar undersea pipeline to Pakistan and India materialize, the financial rewards from tapping these markets will be lucrative. Nevertheless, these plans will not be realized in the near future. Pricing and legal obstacles have blocked the project since 1993, while Pakistan has stated that it would not provide any financial support, since it prefers that the project be financed by the private sector.

The Qatar Central Bank successfully launched the state's first local Treasury bond in July 1999. The enthusiasm with which the local bond issue was received was mainly due to strong foreign interest in the offering, which closed approximately 100 percent oversubscribed. The attraction to foreign banks was that interest paid on the bonds is non-taxable. The issue also represents a government attempt to diversify its borrowing options, and follows official indications that Qatar will reduce its activity on the international project finance market.

## Economic Indicators

| Indicators: | 1997 | 1998 | 1999e |
|---|---|---|---|
| Real GDP (US$bn) | 10.8 | 12.0 | 12.2 |
| Real GDP growth (%) | 10.5 | 0.3 | 1.5 |
| Fiscal deficit (% of GDP) | −6.5 | −10.3 | −10.4 |
| Annual Inflation (%) | 2.9 | 1.5 | 3.0 |
| Exports (fob, US$bn) | 5.36 | 4.25 | 4.35 |
| Imports (fob, US$bn) | 4.71 | 4.37 | 4.70 |
| Trade balance (US$bn) | 0.65 | -0.12 | −0.35 |

e = forecasts

While the government is focusing its energies on meeting the increasing economic expectations of the population, its success will be linked to the relatively higher rate of oil production (and prices) from both on and off-shore fields, as well as oil prices.

The government's plan for the immediate future is to maximize revenues, to minimize the growth in expenditure and to encourage the private sector to play a greater role in the economy. Difficulties in the gas and oil sector have prompted the Qatari government to turn to other economic channels in an effort to boost revenues. In December 1998, a partial floating of telecom provider Q-Tel took place. During this public offering, 45 percent of Q-Tel's interest was sold to the public, while the government retained control over the remaining 55 percent of the company.

A key policy objective is to rejuvenate the oil sector, which appeared to be in terminal decline until a change of policy brought in foreign companies, new technology and new investment. In the spring of 1996, oil production surged to a ten year high of 470,000 barrels per day (bpd). Further output gains are on the way, as the Government forecasts oil production of 850,000 barrels per day in the year 2000. However, this increased production, even if coupled with higher oil prices, will not alleviate the Government's financial difficulties and budgetary deficits in the near future.

The government is raising new revenues elsewhere. A departure tax is now payable at Doha international airport and draft legislation is being prepared for new health cards and fees.

## Business Environment

The government encourages foreign investment, particularly joint ventures with Qataris. As long as a company has a local agent or sponsor, Qatari law permits fully foreign-owned companies. Foreign-owned firms and the foreign-owned portions of joint ventures are subject to taxes of 5 percent to 35 percent of net profits. Qatari and GCC nationals and business concerns are exempted from the income tax provisions.

Foreign investors are forbidden from expanding investments beyond legal limits unless approved by Emiri decree. Transfer of technology, management and marketing, as was the case in establishing steel, fertilizers and petrochemical industries in the 1970s, were taken as part of the foreign equity (20 or 25 percent).

### *Privatization*

Although Qatar has implemented a privatization policy, it will not become fully effective until the country revises laws relating to foreign investment in business associations. The establishment of the stock exchange is expected to facilitate privatization. As mentioned, the first significant privatization of a state-owned enterprise occurred in December 1998, when 45 percent of the telephone provider Q-Tel was offered to the public.

### *Stock Exchange*

The Doha Stock Exchange (DSE) was established in 1995 under law no. 4/1995. This law regulates securities transactions, such as bonds and shares of Qatar shareholding companies, government or quasi-government (bonds and negotiable instruments and other securities which are authorized for trading). The DSE is an autonomous entity indirectly overseen by the Finance, Economy and Trade Ministry.

Operations began in the first quarter of 1997. Currently, only Qatari nationals can participate. The exchange membership includes the Qatar Central Bank and all licensed commercial banks. Several trading activities are limited to brokers, and there are licensing rules applicable to brokers.

It was officially disclosed that in the second year of the stock exchange's operation (1999), the value of traded stocks grew by 162.5% to QR 1.3 billion, compared to QR 500 million in the first year. The market value of stocks increased by 100% in the first year to QR 12 billion, and by 60% in the second year, reaching QR 19.4 billion. A total of 30 companies reportedly trade on the stock exchange. (QR3.64=$1).

## Leading Growth Sectors

The contribution of non-oil sectors to GDP usually ranges between 63 to 69 percent. Agriculture and fishing, electricity and water, building and construction, and communications have all increased their share of GDP while manufacturing industries and services have decreased.

Since the early 1960s, foreign participation in the Qatari market primarily consisted of providing a wide range of products, including automotive and spare parts, as well as oil field supplies. More recently, however, American technology, products and services are being imported into fields, such as electricity and water, oil and natural gas development and enhancement of recovery of these resources.

## Major Projects

The Ras Laffan field and other liquefied natural gas (LNG) and hydrocarbon projects have attracted billions of dollars in foreign investment.

Qatar has also been working on a $18 billion phased project to improve and develop its gas production and export infrastructure as well as boost crude oil exports. Phase 2 of involves constructing a gas liquefaction plant and port at Ras Laffan by state-owned Qatargas.

A recent Qatari banking study revealed that the overall investment in local gas liquefying projects is estimated at $8.5 billion. These projects are presumed to overcome the current financial difficulties and to stimulate economic growth. This study, which was prepared by the Qatar National Bank, showed that these investments consist of establishing two gas liquefying projects in the North field, in addition to building a seaport to ship LNG to external markets. The total production capacity of both projects is estimated at 11m t/y, most of which will be exported to Japan and other Asian markets. These projects are being implemented by Qatargas, Rasgas, in addition to the Ras Laffan Port. This port, which costs $1 billion, will serve Rasgas, and will commence production in 2000.

The city of Doha will be faced with a 400 Mw power shortfall in the next couple of years if no additional generating capacity is installed. As a result, the state-owned Qatar General Petroleum Company (QGPC) has proposed to undertake the Ras Laffan independent water and power project. In doing so, QGPC in September 1999 awarded a letter of intent to Germany-based Electrowatt Engineering Services regarding a consultancy contract for the agreement.

## Project Finance

To drive its infrastructure expansion plans, Qatar regularly taps the international money markets. Even though the national debt is equivalent to 77 percent of GDP, international financiers are still lining up to lend substantial sums.

At the end of March 1999, the Qatari government faced an aggregate debt burden of $6.4 billion, or 69.4 percent of nominal GDP. Of this total, $3.4 billion was in the form of internal debt and $3 billion constituted external obligations. The increase in Qatar's internal government debt during the past year was caused primarily by an expansion in short-term debt (where maturity is under 12 months), which offset a reduction in medium-term debt (with a maturity between 1-7 years).

Following Law No. 1 of 1998 for Public Debt, Qatar's Central Bank is now authorized to issue treasury bills and government bonds on behalf of the government. To date, there are no detailed proposals for the issuance of either treasury bills or government bonds, but such a move would provide the Central Bank with an additional tool for managing domestic liquidity. Since 1994, the government's total debt has risen by 120 percent.

The majority of Qatar's external debt has accrued to finance its budget deficit and for infrastructure projects. Moreover, the Qatar General Petroleum Corporation (QGPC) and its subsidiaries incurred much indebtedness to finance the development of LNG projects and other industrial enterprises. While some of these obligations have received government guarantees, QGPC has provided its own guarantees for the obligations of relevant subsidiaries, up until the project's completion date.

Qatar enjoys high credibility in the international markets because of its impressive portfolio of project financing deals over the past number of years. Its economic prospects over the medium-to-long term are bright, given the revenue forecasts for Qatargas and Rasgas.

## Distribution and Sales Channels

The Government of Qatar is presently in the process of significantly modifying the current laws and regulations that relate to the marketing of foreign goods and services in the Qatari market. The modifications will ease restrictions on local agent/sponsor clauses and foreign equity participation and foreign investments in certain sectors.

Foreign firms interested in marketing their products and services in Qatar must adhere to provisions of Law No. 4 (1986), which deals with local agency arrangements, and Law No. 25 (1990), which relates to foreign equity participation. Each of these laws outlines the necessity of having a local agent or representative as a sales channel for distributing goods and services in the Qatari market.

## Use of Agents/Distributors

Local agents or representatives must be a Qatari citizen or a company with at least 51 percent Qatari ownership. Only a holder of an import license may import goods for sale in Qatar. Changing a local agent or representative is both a difficult and time-consuming process.

Therefore, selection of agents should be given serious consideration. An effective agent in Qatar will have extensive contacts in both the government and private sectors, thus enabling him to obtain valuable information on upcoming government tenders. A local agent should possess the ability to introduce products or services of his foreign supplier to key government officials.

It is common practice in Qatar and other Gulf States to appoint an exclusive agent or representative as a sales channel. This practice may, however, involve some risk in the case of services, and foreign firms are thus advised to choose local agents for their services on a project-to-project basis, since a local representative may be well connected in several specific areas. Foreign firms are also advised to avoid appointing one regional agent for a number of countries. Qataris prefer to meet senior officers of foreign firms, and believe that the amount of interest displayed by a foreign firm through frequent visits can ultimately make the difference between winning or losing a major contract.

Local agency law prohibits the importation and sale of brand name food products by anyone other than the principal agent. In the case that a local agent increases his prices or fails to stock certain items, such as spare parts, the Ministry of Finance, Economy and Commerce is entitled to authorize importation of these products to a local merchant or company other than the designated agent.

## Establishing an Office/Joint Venture

The Qatari Government has not yet promulgated a branching law that allows establishment of a wholly owned branch of a foreign firm in the local market. The local agent requirement applies to foreign firms wishing to establish a branch in Qatar for a foreign parent company, as well as to those foreign firms entering into a joint venture on the basis of up to 49 percent foreign equity. The foreign firm and local agent should apply for official registration of the agency, joint venture or branch office with the Ministry of Finance, Economy and Commerce's Commercial Registration Department.

The establishment of a majority or wholly owned firm in Qatar is extremely rare, and has generally been restricted to firms and specific development projects in the oil and gas sector. Such arrangements can only be made by the issuance of a ministerial decree, after a judgment that the foreign firm brings technical expertise or financial assets that are unavailable in Qatar. A local agent is still required for such arrangements.

Until mid-1995, Law No. 25 (1990) stipulated that the above-mentioned decree should be issued by the country's Emir. This law was modified and the right to issue the decree was allocated to the Minister of Finance, Economy and Commerce. The aim of this amendment was to hasten the establishment of foreign enterprises.

**Best Business Prospects**

| Rank | Sector |
|------|--------|
| 1 | Machinery and Transport Equipment |
| 2 | Manufactured Goods Classified Chiefly by Materials |
| 3 | Miscellaneous Manufactured Goods |
| 4 | Food and Live Animals |
| 5 | Chemicals and Related Products |
| 6 | Beverages and Tobacco |
| 7 | Inedible Crude Materials, Except Fuel |
| 8 | Mineral Fuels, Lubricants and Related Materials |
| 9 | Animal and Vegetable Oils; Fat and Waxes |
| 10 | Others |

# Legal Review

Islam is Qatar's official religion, and Islamic jurisprudence, the Shar'ia, is recognized as the basis of the country's legal system. Civil legislation is based upon codification. As stated in the provisional Constitution, Qatar is a monarchy with full powers vested in the Emir as the Head of State.

## Judiciary

Several courts administrate Justice: the Higher Criminal Court, the Lower Criminal Court, the Commercial and Civil Court, the Labor Court and the Court of Appeal. In addition, the Shar'ia Courts determine matters regarding the personal status of Muslims and civil cases where the parties submit themselves to the jurisdiction of the Shar'ia Courts. The jurisdiction of the Civil Court covers all civil and commercial disputes. There are no monetary limitations regarding the referral of disputes to the Civil Court to be heard by a single justice. Judicial independence is guaranteed by the Provisional Constitution.

## Business Forms and Structures

The Companies Law No. 11 of 1986 recognizes five types of business associations that may be formed and registered in Qatar. These are: (1) General Partnerships; (2) Limited Partnerships; (3) Limited Partnerships with Shares; (4) Limited Liability Companies; and (5) Joint Stock Companies.

Recently, the Qatari government began reviewing a legislative proposal concerning commercial law that would allow foreigners, both individuals and entities, to hold more than 50 percent of the equity of a Qatari joint venture in partnership with local partners. Currently, as discussed in the section on Foreign Investment, foreign investors are barred from holding more than 49 percent of a local entity. This legislative initiative is intended to further the goals of privatization, encouraging foreign investment and developing small-sized industries.

## *Companies Law*

### *Limited Liability Companies*
A limited liability company must have between 2 and 30 members. Its minimum capital cannot be below QR 200,000. The capital is divided into shares of not less than QR 1,000 each. The articles of association must provide details of the company's trade name, members, head office, objects, capital amount, number and classes of shares, transfer of shares conditions, the company's duration, managers, and methods of distribution of profits and losses. If the number of members exceeds ten, a control council of at least three members must be appointed. An auditor must be appointed if the capital is higher than QR 500,000. The company must keep a register of members. The liability of members is restricted to the nominal value of their shares in the registered capital. The management of the company is entrusted to one or more managers who may or may not be members. The articles of association, as restricted by law, determine their authority. Liability of managers is governed by the same rules determining liability of directors in a joint stock company.

### *Joint Stock Companies*
A joint stock company is comprised of at least five members. The minimum capital required is QR 500,000, and QR 200,000 in a private joint stock

company. The capital is divided into equal nominal shares of not less than QR 100 and not exceeding QR 1,000. The creation of a joint stock company requires the drafting of a memorandum and articles of associations to be presented to the Minister of Economy and Commerce, signed by at least five founders. The incorporation is subject to authorization by decree, which must be published in the official gazette. Founders must produce to the Companies Control Department in the Ministry of Economic and Commerce a bank certificate proving subscription to at least 10 percent of the capital and not more than 20 percent thereof prior to any invitation to public subscription. The corporation's documents must provide details regarding the company's trade name, head office, objects, details of members, capital value, number and classes of shares, duration and assessment of establishment expenses. The company must appoint at least one auditor. The liability of members is restricted to the nominal value of their shares in the registered capital.

The management of the company is entrusted to a board of directors comprising five to eleven directors, each appointed for a period of three years. The board's chairman represents the company *vis-à-vis* third parties and may transact business on their behalf. The chairman is responsible for the implementation of board resolutions. The articles of associations and operation of law restrict the authority of the board. The directors are liable to the company, the shareholders and third parties for any fraud, misuse of authority, non-compliance with the articles of association and with the law and any mismanagement. Non-Qataris may own shares in such a company only under certain circumstances, as discussed below in the section on Foreign Investment.

## Partnerships

### General Partnerships
A general partnership is an association of two or more persons that carry on business under a specific name. A general partnership agreement must specify the partnership's trade name, head office, set objects, details of partners, name of manager, capital value, the share of each partner and methods of distribution of profits and losses. The partners are jointly and severally liable for the obligations of the partnership to the full extent of their assets. The management of the partnership is determined by the partnership agreement and devolves on the partners, unless management is specifically

entrusted to one or more designated managers by an agreement filed with the Commercial Resister.

### Limited Partnerships

A limited partnership is comprised of two types of partners. The general partners handle the management of the business, and the limited partners contribute to the capital of the partnership. A limited partnership agreement must comply with the requirements of a general partnership agreement. Additionally, it must indicate who the general partners are and who the limited partners are. The general partners are jointly and severally liable for the obligations of the partnership to the full extent of their assets. The limited partners' liability is confined to the amount of their capital contribution, provided they do not participate in the management of the partnership or allow their names to be used in the partnership's trade name. The management of the partnership is determined by the partnership agreement and devolves on the partners, unless management is specifically entrusted to one or more designated managers by an agreement filed with the Commercial Resister.

### Limited Partnerships with Shares

In a limited partnership with shares, the number of limited partners may not exceed ten and the number of general partners may not be less than three. The capital of a limited partnership with shares is divided into equal negotiable nominal shares and cannot be less than QR 200,000. A limited partnership with shares' agreement must comply with the requirements of a general partnership agreement. In addition, it must provide details of the control council composed of at least three members and must appoint an auditor if the capital exceeds QR 500,000. The management of the partnership is determined by the partnership agreement and devolves on the partners, unless management is specifically entrusted to one or more designated managers by an agreement filed with the Commercial Resister.

### Emiri Decrees

While the Law Regulating the Investment of Non-Qatari Capital specifically denies the right of non-Qataris to engage in commercial agencies and import businesses (see section on Commercial Agency), investment by non-Qataris in any project and field which aims at enhancing economic development in the countries, or to facilitate public services, or to realize a public benefit, may be made under an Emiri Decree. Such Emiri Decrees may also allow non-Qataris to import materials and equipment required for such projects if unavailable locally. Applications supported by documents for issuing Emiri Decrees are made to the Minister of Finance, Economy and Commerce. If the application is approved, the Emiri Decree will be issued within sixty days.

## Dissolution of Business Associations

The business associations discussed above may be dissolved upon the occurrence of any of the following: (1) expiration of the entity's term; (2) accomplishment of the entity's stated objectives; (3) adoption of a resolution of the entity's members to dissolve the entity; or (4) issuance of a court judgment of dissolution.

There are several specific grounds for dissolution of partnerships, which include: (1) the incapacity or bankruptcy of a general partner; and (2) a substantial loss of the partnership's capital. In addition, there are specific grounds for the dissolution of limited liability companies and joint stock companies.

A limited liability company may be dissolved upon the recommendation of its managers, or of its members representing at least 75 percent of the limited liability company's capital, made in the event the limited liability company lost at least half of its capital. In the event more than 75 percent of the company's capital is lost, the recommendation of the company's members only requires a majority of 25 percent to pass. Additionally, if the company's capital falls below QR 200,000, any one shareholder may obtain dissolution of the company.

In a joint stock company, in the event the company loses at least 50 percent of its capital, the board of directors is required to call a general meeting of the shareholders that would vote to dissolve the company, to decrease the company's share capital or to take any other action deemed necessary. If the board of directors fails to call such a general meeting, any member of the company is entitled to petition the courts to issue a dissolution order for the company.

## Commercial Agency

The Law 4/1986 Concerning the Regulation of Activities of Local Commercial Agencies and their Foreign Principals includes Guidelines for Execution, which were re-issued unaltered in 1994 by the Ministry of Finance,

Economy and Commerce. This law provides that the commercial agent is permitted to distribute and sell the goods or to provide certain services in return for profit commission. The principal has no right to be supported by more than one agent for the same commercial business included in the agency. An agent is not allowed to practice the commercial agency on behalf of a principal who has another agent in the same area running the same business. Compensation for any damage that may be caused by isolation or termination in critical time without a justified reason is compulsory. An unlimited contract may not be terminated by any of the chartered parties, unless one of them commits a malpractice justifying termination. All commercial agency relationships must be registered, and the principal may withdraw at the end of a fixed period upon the execution of a new termination agreement or with the Ministry's approval.

## Currency and Banking

### Foreign Currency

The Qatari Riyal is freely convertible on world financial markets. Currency exchange is regulated by Law No. 4/1982, which controls and sets licensing. In June 1980, the Riyal was pegged to the US dollar at a rate of US$1=QR 3.64, which remains unaltered. The Riyal maintains a floating rate against all other currencies.

Restrictions exist on activities dealing with currency exchange, traveler's checks, precious metals and personal transfers.

### Banking

#### Central Bank

The Qatar Central Bank (QCB) was established in 1973 as the Qatar Monetary Agency. In addition to supervising, coordinating and controlling the banking sector, the QCB also regulates insurance and controls the circulation of currency. The QCB sets interest rates for deposits and credit facilities maintained in Qatari Riyals (QR). The Central Bank adheres to conservative policies aimed at maintaining steady economic growth and leading to a stable banking sector.

## Commercial Banks

There are 14 commercial banks, with a total of 39 branches, operating in Qatar. These include two Islamic banks that were licensed in recent years. Six of the banks are Qatari-owned, two are Arab, and six are foreign banks.

A banking license may be issued to a banking entity whose paid-up capital is at least QR 5 million. If the banking entity is a foreign subsidiary, it must maintain that amount of retained or operational capital in Qatar. Banking entities are required to retain a reserve of 100 percent of their paid-up or operational capital in Qatar. Deposits and credit facilities in foreign currency are subject to variable interest rates determined by the banks in accordance with prevailing market terms.

Credit facilities are provided to local and foreign investors within the framework of standard international banking procedures. QCB guidelines require banks operating in Qatar to grant priority to Qataris and to public development projects in their financing operations. Banks operating in Qatar are also discouraged against foreign stock market operations.

## Intellectual Property

Qatar is not a member of the World Intellectual Property Organization (WIPO) nor does it belong to the Paris Convention for Protection of Intellectual Property. Within Qatar, therefore, owners of trademarks and copyrights and holders of patents are dependent on Qatar's own national laws and regulations for protection.

## Patents and Designs

In the early 1990s, Qatar adopted a Patent Law that was drafted by the General Secretariat of the Gulf Cooperation Council (GCC) in Riyadh, Saudi Arabia. This law has not, however, been enforced. Caveats and cautionary notices may be published in both the Arabic and English language press and appropriate periodicals. While the publication of a cautionary notice does not affect a registration of the invention or design, it is intended to put the public on notice of the interests of its owner and to prevent potential infringement.

## Trademarks

Law No. 3 of 1978, Administrative Decision No. 47 of 1986, and Ministerial Decree No. 17 of 1987, govern the Qatari trademark regime. Names of distinctive features, signatures, words, letters, numbers, designs, pictures, symbols, stamps, seals, vignettes and any other sign or combination of signs having a disjunctive character may be registered as a mark. Marks without distinctive features, expressions, designs and signs of immoral character or contrary to public policy, portraits or emblems of individuals without their permission and marks likely to deceive the public are among the things that cannot be registered as a mark.

With the exception of the alcoholic goods of Class 33, Qatar adopted all 42 classes of the international classification system. Application and registered marks are published in the Trademark Gazette. Opposition may be filed within four months from the date of publication. Upon registration, the mark is protected for ten years, and the protection is renewable for similar periods. The rights confer exclusive ownership of the mark. Lack of use of a mark in Qatar for five consecutive years is a ground for challenge. Violations of the law may give rise to criminal penalties.

## Copyright

The Law for the Protection of Copyright No. 25 of 1995 became effective on January 23, 1996. Under this law, authors of literary, artistic, and scientific works may benefit from protection regardless of the work's value, kind, purpose or media. Protection covers works expressed in writing, sound, drawing, image or motion, creative titles and computer software. Also protected by the law are those who obtain the permission of the original author to translate the work or those who summarize, modify, explain or comment on the work to produce a new form of the work without infringing on the rights of the original authors. The protection extends to the rights of the author and the right of those who translate a work into a foreign language for three years from the date of publication.

Protection is granted to Qatari authors whose works are published inside and outside the country, the works of non-Qatari authors published in Qatar for the first time and the works of authors of any other foreign country that treats Qatari authors on a reciprocal basis. A literary work may be licensed for publication, display or circulation upon meeting the following legal stipulations: (1) The work must be accompanied by a certificate of origin showing the author's name or the name of the person who surrenders the right of usage; (2) The work must be accompanied by a permit from the supplier or owner for display or circulation, showing the geographic areas where the display or circulation, showing the geographic areas where the display and circulation is licensed; (3) The work must be accompanied by a supplier's certificate showing that the publishing rights are covered whether through paying the charges of putting the work to use by the public or by making copies of the work for distribution.

Once granted copyright protection, the author is entitled to attribute the work to himself and to apply his name to all the copies produced from it whenever the work is put to public use, except when the work is mentioned accidentally on a radio or television presentation of current events. This right is inalienable and is not abolished with the lapse of time. The author also has the right to decide on publishing the work, recording or displaying it and to determine the relevant terms. The author has the right to use his work, on condition that the right was not surrendered to another person. Yet, it is forbidden to use any work through transferring it to the public in Qatar except by written, authenticated permission from the author or the author's representative or successor in the event of death.

The author has a vested right to modify or to translate a work into another language; heirs, too, can exercise this right. Only the author has the right to publish his letters and to transfer the financial rights that the work entails, according to the provisions of the law, to another. The author has the right to defend against any violation of his rights and has the right to prevent any elimination, addition, change or deformation of the work.

Even following the death of the author, the rights provided for in the law are all or partly alienable, whether through inheritance or by law. The law stipulates that in cases of joint production of works where it becomes impossible to determine the exact share of each one in the joint work, all participants will be considered equal partners in its ownership, unless otherwise agreed.

Qatar's Ministry of Information and Culture established a Censorship Bureau to enforce Intellectual Property Law No. 25. The abolishment of the Ministry of Information and Culture in October 1996 has prevented proper implementation of this law. The Censorship Bureau, however, has not been abolished. In March 1997, more than 3,000 unauthorized videotapes were voluntarily destroyed by one of Qatar's largest video store in the presence of a representative from the censorship bureau. This incident demonstrates that the government is serious about enforcing the copyright law.

## Taxation

Qatar Income Tax Law No. 11/1993 became effective as of January 1, 1993. It imposes income tax on the taxpayer (natural persons and corporate bodies) arising from activities in Qatar, including profits from any contract executed in Qatar, profits realized from the sale of any asset of an establishment, agency commissions (regardless of whether the contract with respect to which a commission is due is executed inside or outside of Qatar), consultation fees, amounts from the sale, rent or concession of intellectual property rights, bad debts collected by the taxpayer, and net profits upon dissolution of a company.

Taxable income is determined after allowable deductions are made for interest payments, rentals, salaries and bonuses, taxes and fees (other than income tax), depreciation, losses from the sale of assets and humanitarian or scientific donations.

Revenues relating to projects in Qatar, even if executed outside of Qatar, are declared for Qatari tax purposes. Evidence that the work was implemented outside of Qatar is necessary to avoid tax liability with respect to the profits of the project.

Salaries, wages, personal bank interest and other forms of personal income are not subject to tax.

Tax is calculated on a progressive scale rising to a maximum rate of 35 percent on taxable income above QR 5 million. The tax rates are listed below.

Qatar's corporate income tax law is applicable to foreign firms operating in the Emirate, in addition to foreign equity participation in Qatari enterprises. While it is unusual for foreign equity in a Qatari business concern to be exempt from corporate income tax provisions, wholly owned foreign firms operating in Qatar may receive tax holidays.

| Amount of Income | Tax Rate |
|---|---|
| Less than QR 100,000 | exempt |
| QR 100,001 to QR 500,000 | 10% |
| QR 500,001 to QR 1,000,000 | 15% |
| QR 1,000,001 to QR 1,500,000 | 20% |
| QR 1,500,001 to QR 2,500,000 | 25% |
| QR 2,500,001 to QR 5,000,000 | 30% |
| QR 5,000,001 and above | 35% |

In order to receive an exemption from paying corporate income tax of up to 35 percent of net income, a foreign firm must first negotiate this issue with the relevant government department prior to signing a contract. If it is in the government's interest, the department will raise the matter with a country's higher authorities and endorse a request. However, tax exemptions can only be granted by Emiri decree.

Regarding Law No. 11 for the year 1993, Qatari joint stock companies are not exempt from income tax provisions. The government has, however, been issuing decrees every three years that exempt Qatari joint stock companies from paying income tax. The most recent exemption was issued in 1995.

## Investment and Trade

### Foreign Investments

The Law Regulating the Investment of Non-Qatari Capital in Economic Activities No. 25 of 1990 governs the area of foreign investment in Qatar. Under this law, non-Qataris are allowed to engage in trade, industry, agriculture and services under the condition that the non-Qatari investor must have one or more Qatari partners whose share in the business capital is at least 51 percent and that the business relationship with the Qatari partner must be carried on through a commercial company incorporated according to the Companies Law No.11 of 1986 (see section on Business Forms and Structures). The law does not permit non-Qataris to own shares in a joint stock company unless the shareholder is a national of an Arab country that has reciprocal agreements with Qatar or if there is a need for foreign capital or experience, and a license to that effect is obtained from the Minister of Finance, Economy and Commerce.

Non-Qataris meeting the above requirements may also carry on contracting business upon fulfillment of additional conditions. A special license from the Minister of Finance, Economy and Commerce must be issued following consultation with relevant government authorities. This requires that an application be submitted to the Minister, supported by all relevant documents. If 30 days elapse without a reply from the Minister, the application is presumed to have been rejected. Applicants whose applications were rejected may appeal to the Minister within 30 days. The decision in the appeal is final.

In determining applications, one of the factors considered is the demand for the type of business for which an application is made. Businesses engaging in fields for which there is a high demand in Qatar include businesses with high technology expertise.

In 1997, Qatar finalized legislation to abolish the requirement of 51 percent Qatari ownership. This step is aimed at attracting foreign investment in small and medium scale businesses. The new legislation will come into effect pending Emiri approval. As of 1999, this has yet to happen.

## Trade Agreements

Qatar became a member of the General Agreement on Tariffs and Trade (GATT) in 1996. Prior to that time, it participated in GATT as an observer. As a member of the Gulf Cooperation Council (GCC), Qatar participates in the GCC's free trade arrangements. Qatar also became a member of the World Trade Organization (WTO) in 1995.

Qatar has been engaged, through the GCC, in trade and investment negotiations with the United States, the European Community and Japan. The dialogue initiated among them is ongoing. In addition to the GCC Economic Agreement (1983) signed among member states of the GCC, Qatar has also signed economic/commercial agreements with Egypt and Tunisia.

## Import and Export Restrictions

### Imports
Goods and commodities imported into Qatar are subject to customs tariffs as follows:

| Item | Tariff |
|---|---|
| General goods and commodities | 4% |
| Reinforced Iron Bars, Steel and Cement (similar to local manufacture or equivalent) | 20% |
| Ammonia (similar to local manufacture or equivalent) | 30% |
| Cigarettes and Tobacco Products | 50% |
| Essentials and Personal Items (such as foodstuffs, machinery and raw materials for industrial projects) | Exempt |

Imports into Qatar require an import license, which may only be issued to Qatari citizens. Agents and agency agreements are subject to the Law Concerning the Regulation of Activities of Local Commercial Agencies and Their Foreign Principals 4/1986, as discussed in the above section on Commercial Agencies.

In accordance with Islamic tradition, the importation of pork and pork products is prohibited. Also prohibited are firearms, ammunition, immodest prints and pictures, narcotics and artificial pearls. Alcohol and alcohol products are discouraged by the imposition of heavy customs duties.

Goods from other Gulf Cooperation Council countries are given preferential tariff rates. According to a reciprocity agreement among the GCC states, products of GCC origin are exempted from customs duties. Except for steel, along with tobacco and cigarettes, all general merchandise is subject to 4 percent customs duties. The current rate of customs duty for steel is 20 percent, 10 percent for hi-fi equipment and 100 percent for tobacco and cigarettes.

*Exports*
There are no export charges on goods or commodities exported from Qatar.

## Public Sector Procurement

In Qatar, the government is the main end-user of a wide range of products and services. The government's procurement policy is based on standard tender procedures. In order for foreign firms to participate in those tenders, they must obtain a local agent.

In general, The Qatari government does not award turnkey contracts, preferring to award separate contracts to consultants. The government announces invitations to pre-qualify in local and/or foreign papers and periodically through Qatari embassies abroad. Law No. 8 of 1979 also provide for classification of contractors by a committee operating under the Central Tenders Committee (CTC). This process is based upon the firm's financial standing, business reputation and experience. Preference is usually accorded to the lowest bidder that meets all specifications.

## Labor Law

Labor Law No. 3 of 1962 (as amended) governs industrial relations in Qatar. Under the Labor Law, priority in employment is granted to Qataris, then to nationals of Arab countries and, finally, to other non-Qataris. Non-Qataris can be employed only if they obtain a work-permit from the Department of Labor in the Ministry of Labor and Social Affairs. The applicant must have a valid passport and a resident permit and must be of good conduct and reputation. Generally, permits are valid for two years.

There are no fixed minimum wages in Qatar, and no pension schemes are available for non-Qataris. There are no labor unions in Qatar, and strikes, lockouts and slowdowns are prohibited. Workers are entitled to one day off per week and to other benefits such as holiday on the occasion of Ramadan, annual paid leave of fourteen days, illness pay and severance pay. The Department of Labor in the Ministry of Labor and Social Affairs resolves all industrial disputes, after which the matter may be referred to the Labor Court for a final decision.

## Environmental Law

Qatar is a signatory to a number of international environmental conventions, including: The Convention of the Prohibition of the Development, Production and Stockpiling of Bacteriological (Biological) and Toxin Weapons, and their Destruction; International Convention for the Prevention of Pollution of the Sea by Oil, 1954 Concerning the Protection of the Great Barrier Reef of Australia (and amendments thereto); Agreement for the Establishment of a Commission for Controlling the Desert Locust in the Near East; Kuwait Regional Convention for Cooperation on the Protection of the Marine Environment from Pollution; and the Treaty on the Prohibition of the Emplacement of Nuclear Weapons and other Weapons of Mass Destruction on the Sea Bed and the Ocean Floor and in the Subsoil Thereof.

# SAUDI ARABIA

## Recent Political Developments

King Fahd's ailing health has essentially made him the country's leader in name only. Poor health is presumed to have kept him from attending the funeral of his son, Prince Faisal, in August 1999. Running the palace and country for the last several years has been the king's half-brother, Crown Prince Abdullah bin Abdul-Aziz al-Saud, who appears to be the next in a recent spate of young sons to assume power from their long-reining fathers. His succession to the throne is anticipated to be a smooth transition.

In a short period, the Crown Prince, who appears to be popular with the public, has already begun to leave his mark, particularly on economic matters. His influence was noticeable in the Saudi-designed OPEC agreement to cut oil production by a further 1.7 million barrels a day to help raise slumped oil prices. He is also behind a drive for economic reform, efforts to cut the royal family's spending and the introduction of greater accountability.

| | |
|---|---|
| Population | 20.2 million (1999) |
| Population Growth Rate/yr. | 3.4 percent |
| Religion | Islam |
| Government | Monarchy and a Council of Ministers |
| Languages | Arabic (English is widely spoken) |
| Work Week | Business: Saturday–Wednesday 8:00–12:00; 16:00–20:00 Thursdays 8:00–13:00 Public Sector: Saturday–Wednesday 8:00–14:30 Banks: Saturday–Wednesday 9:00–12:00; 17:00–19:00 Thursday: 8:00–13:00 |
| Monetary Unit | Saudi Riyal (SR) |
| Exchange Rate | SR 3.75=US$1 |

The Crown Prince has also been bolstering foreign relationships. He has traveled overseas twice in an official capacity, visiting South Africa, Italy, Libya, Egypt, Syria, Jordan, Morocco, London, Paris, Washington, Tokyo, Beijing, Seoul and Karachi.

Thus far, the Crown Prince has been able to focus most of his attention on economic rather than sensational terrorist matters. There have been no further bombings of American facilities in the Kingdom since the two in 1995 and 1996. The US government is continuing to assist in these investigations and continues to receive reports of other possible attacks on US interests.

The first attack was November 13, 1995, against an American compound in Riyadh. Toward the end of April 1996, Saudi authorities announced that they had succeeded in apprehending the perpetrators, identified as four Saudi nationals. During their interrogation, the four claimed to be veterans of the war in Afghanistan and that the attack in Riyadh was part of a "*jihad*" (holy war) directed against the Saudi royal family and against the leading government-appointed religious clerics in the Kingdom.

The other attack occurred June 25, 1996, when a truck packed with explosives exploded alongside the US military compound in Dhahran on the eastern coast of Saudi Arabia. Nineteen US soldiers were killed. It is believed that Islamic fundamentalists, most likely Saudi nationals, were behind the bombing, although no group has claimed responsibility.

The funding behind these attacks stems from a network of Muslim millionaires, many of whom are also implicated in funding and equipping Muslim fighters in Afghanistan, Bosnia and Chechnya and in financing terrorist operations in Egypt, Algeria and Israel.

The Saudi government officially supports a comprehensive peace in the Middle East but refuses to establish normal relations with Israel until matters such as the Palestinian, Syrian and Lebanese situations are resolved. As the vanguard of Islam's holiest sites, it also takes special interest in the final status of Jerusalem.

Of all the major players in the Arab world, Saudi Arabia's attitude towards the regional process has probably been the most ambivalent. On one hand, King Fahd was quick to endorse the December 1994 Alexandria declaration that called on fellow Arab states to refrain from improving their relations with Israel, at least until a full Israeli peace accord with Syria had been reached. At the same time, the Saudi administration has made it clear that it fully supports recent steps towards Israeli-Palestinian reconciliation and in this spirit has expressed its willingness to jettison its long-standing position that Israel is an enemy state. The peace process, it seems, may not be in Saudi Arabia's immediate economic interest.

## Recent Economic Developments

Saudi Arabia has the largest economy in the Gulf and is the world's largest oil producer and exporter. It has the world's greatest proven oil reserves, 25 percent, equaling some 261.5 billion barrels. The Kingdom has about 25 percent of the GDP of all Arab states, between US$ 130–140 billion. Saudi Arabia has 60 percent of the population of the Arab Gulf states, just over 20 million people, and 50 percent of the population is less than 18 years of age.

The government continues to try and wean the country off of its reliance on oil. There are signs of greater private sector productivity, increased industrial investment, continued positive performance in banking and a higher level of returns on investment. This has been accomplished in an economic environment of price stability, free enterprise, an open economy and an exchange system free of any restrictions.

The Saudis also intend to alter the foreign capital law in order to introduce more incentives that will lure foreign investors. There is also concern, however, that the oil revenue may diminish the perceived need for continued economic reform. In a major policy change, the government early in 1995 began to cut subsidies and to impose charges for public services, belatedly hoping to trim its chronic budget deficit, to heal the erosion of foreign assets and to strengthen public finances.

A growing labor force and an unexpected 35 percent drop in oil prices in 1998 forced the Saudi government to begin implementing various economic reform programs that will place the private-sector as the main engine of economic diversification and growth as well as job creation.

With 70–75 percent of the government's income dependent on oil revenues, the kingdom's overall economic health can rise or fall with oil prices. And in 1998 a drop in prices deflated nominal GDP by 10.8 percent to $130.1 billion, caused a 20 percent deficit in expected revenues to $38.1 billion and pushed the fiscal deficit to $12.3 billion, two-and-a-half times expected. The reduction in oil prices also pushed per capita GDP to $6,600, its lowest level of the 1990s, reversing a three-year growth trend. Per capita GDP has fallen significantly from its peak in 1980, when it reached $15,700, $2,500 more than the US figures. That reversed with US per capita GDP at the end of 1998 of $31,500 dwarfing the kingdom's by $24,900.

For short-term compensation of the lost revenue the government implemented stringent measures and reforms. All unsigned government procurements were suspended, hiring of almost all new government employees halted and operations and maintenance contracts were cut by 10 percent. Of cuts to the budget, defense spending took the biggest hit with an estimated 22 percent reduction. Social services, such as health and education, were reduced by 6 percent. Other revenue-generating steps included extending payment to contractors and increasing gas prices by 50 percent, which can yield an extra $1 billion a year. While the government remains committed to economic reform, the rise in oil prices in 1999 may reduce the incentive to reform and slow the process.

Over-reliance on oil is not the kingdom's only problem. It also faces series job shortages. According to 1997 data, only 2.5 million of workers in a labor force of 7.2 million were Saudi citizens. Half the Saudi population, which is growing at a 3.4 percent rate, is under 18-years-old. This means hundreds of thousands of citizens enter the workforce each year. The government has introduced some measures to address the problem in the short-term, such as requiring firms to increase the number of nationals it hires.

It also doubled to SR 2,000 ($533) the cost of work permits for foreigners. This hike can increase government revenues by several hundred million dollars and simultaneously create jobs for Saudis. The government also made it more expensive for foreigners to enter and leave the country, raising visa prices to SR 500 ($133).

These measures, however, will only create jobs in the short term. The long-term solution—like the solution for economic growth and diversification—rests in restructuring the economy with the private sector at its heart. The strategy for doing so includes privatizing government-owned industries and revising both a 30-year-old law on foreign direct investment and a code that taxes foreign corporate profits up to 45 percent. Other important steps include its negotiations to join the World Trade Organization and opening its capital markets.

In late 1999, the government announced a conservative budget for 2000, with a deficit of $7.467 billion. Revenues for the year are projected at $41.867

billion, an augmentation of approximately $2.667 billion on actual 1999 revenues. Expenditures in 1999 amounted to $48.3 billion.

## Economic Indicators

|  | 1999* | 1998 | 1997 |
|---|---|---|---|
| Real GDP Growth (percent) | 1.6 | 1.6 | 3.0 |
| Per Capita GDP | $6,500 | $6,600 | $7,600 |
| Consumer Price Inflation (percent) | 1.5 | −0.3 | −0.2 |
| Budget Balance (percent of GDP) | −8.8 | −9.4 | −3.8 |
| Current Account Balance (% of GDP) | −3.2 | −12.9 | −0.2 |
| Exports (US$bn) | 35.00 | 42.25 | 59.68 |
| Imports (US$bn) | 23.00 | 24.00 | 26.15 |
| Trade Balance (US$bn) | 12.00 | 18.25 | 33.53 |
| Balance on Goods & Services (US$mn) | −2,000 | 2,250 | 12,537 |

* Estimated

Every five years for the last three decades, the government releases a 5-year strategic plan outlining economic objectives. During the current plan, the government's 6th, which concludes at the end of 1999, the government had hoped to erase its deficit. While it did not accomplish this, the government successfully reduced the budget by 25 percent from $111 billion (five years earlier) to an estimated $28 billion. Furthermore, the government's budget revenues are expected to reach $250 billion, up from $167 billion five years ago.

The focus of the recently unveiled seventh-five year plan is further economic diversification and privatization. Special attention is also placed on human resource development, increasing employment and replacing foreign workers with Saudis.

During the last decade, the Saudi economy has stood on three main pillars: the oil sector, comprising 36 percent, the private sector, also 36 percent, and government spending, 26 percent.

Private sector growth during that period grew at an average rate of 4.1 percent a year, never declining. The non-oil private sector growth dropped from 4.4 percent growth in 1997 to 2.1 percent in 1998.

Oil comprises roughly 75 percent of the government's revenue and despite the price collapse, the proportion dropped only to 70 percent. The collapse did, however, deflate the oil portion of GDP by 34.8 percent.

The oil price reduction also pushed the current account balance into a deficit following two years of surpluses. The 1998 current account deficit was $13.1 billion, compared with a surplus of $254 million in 1997 and $681 million in 1996. In an effort to raise oil prices OPEC cut production, reducing the kingdom's daily production quota to 7.438 million barrels.

In 1999, total government spending is expected to reach $51 billion, up $600 million from the previous year but not near its 1997 level of $56 billion. In 1998, government expenditures was the fastest growing GDP component, rising an estimated 8.8 percent. Much of the spending went toward schools, hospitals and other projects needed to keep pace with a fast growing population. Although the Saudi government has committed itself to economic reform it does not desire to do as such at the expense of social services.

The government has financed some spending through loans. Its 1998 loans marked the 17th consecutive year of borrowing and pushed its public debt burden to 110 percent of GDP.

The Central Bank was busy in 1998 protecting the Riyal from speculators. The currency has been pegged to the dollar since 1986 and has remained since at SR 3.7450 to $1. Inflation has not been a problem. In 1998 and 1997 there was deflation of 0.4 percent and 0.2 percent respectively. Inflation of 1-2 percent is expected in 1999 however. There have been calls in late 1999 to allow the market to determine the currency's value, claiming that it will add stability to the Saudi economy.

Saudi Arabia's budget deficit is structural in nature. Petroleum continues to be the critical source of revenue, averaging 70-75 percent of all revenues over recent years, with customs duties and investment receipts comprising much of the remaining government revenue.

The income and profits of Saudis are not taxed with the exception of a voluntary 2.5 percent annual religious donation. The government grants tax holidays to many foreign investments and, therefore, receives limited fiscal benefit from the growing private sector. At the same time, the government continues to spend on a broad social support program, which includes free or heavily subsidized basic utilities, social services and agricultural products. Spending on these services, on both a recurrent and capital basis, is increasing because of the rapid population growth.

## Principal Economic Sectors

### Industry
Saudi industry continues to grow, raising the number of workers, factories and value. In 1998, there were more than 31,000 factories with a $61.9 billion value and employing 282,000. Some local business leaders believe that the country's abundance of gas, oil and minerals, financial and other resources make the kingdom ripe for industrial development.

Major products of Saudi Arabia's manufacturing sector include refined petroleum, petrochemicals, plastics, processed food, clothing, fertilizer and cement. Manufacturing grew considerably during and after the Gulf War, as many firms took advantage of subsidies and soft loans from the government.

### Mining
Mineral mining has been identified as an important sector the country should target for economic diversification. The kingdom's exportable minerals include iron ore, phosphates, bauxite, copper and other precious and non-precious metals. Forty-two fields containing large mineral deposits have been located in the country's western and central regions.

The government-owned Saudi Arabian Mining Company, Ma'aden, plans to consolidate all projects in which the government is involved. It obtained rights to mine three sites for gold and silver as well as to search the entire country for minerals.

The government is also attempting to use this sector as a lure for foreign investors. It offers 5-10 year tax exemptions and 30 year extraction concessions.

The Saudi Ministry of Petroleum and Mineral Resources is spearheading an initiative to develop new mines to produce iron, phosphates, bauxites and precious metals. The Ministry has started negotiating contracts with Western mining companies.

## Food and Agriculture

Saudi Arabia's long dependence on food imports has turned agriculture into a key sector for development. Limited water resources—primarily irrigated lands near oases—leaves the country with less than 1 percent of farmable land.

Responsibility for establishing agriculture policy rests with the Grain Silos and Flour Mills Organization (GSFMO). This government agency sets production targets, distributes grain quotas to farmers and determines import and export policy.

One GSFMO policy explicitly bans wheat imports and implicitly bans exports. Imports are forbidden and farmers have been issued guidelines to produce only what is needed to meet domestic consumption. There is speculation, however, that the ban on wheat imports will end if the government privatizes its 17 flourmills, something currently under discussion with IMF officials.

Saudi Arabia's leading crops are wheat, watermelons, dates and tomatoes. Other major crops are sorghum, onions, grapes and citrus fruit. Furthermore, the kingdom is the world's leading importer of barely that is primarily used for feeding livestock.

Corn, soybean meal, rice, processed fruits and vegetables, snack foods and breakfast cereals have been identified (in that order) as the Best Business Prospects the agricultural sector. Corn and soybean meal exports from the U.S. in 1998 and 1997 averaged more than $200 million each year.

A growing population and their increasing demands are driving demand for imported processed and packaged food items. The popularity of Western-style supermarkets continues to grow with the number exceeding 250. Also growing is the number of domestic and international food processing companies that manufacture such products as snack foods and fruit juices.

Food processing has started significant growth, but remains modest. Investment in food processing, handling and storage equipment is continuing. Saudi agriculture has shown rapid growth in production over the last several years, while food processing has only recently begun significant expansion. The growth in agricultural output has been led until recently by wheat, but notable increases have also taken place in livestock, vegetables and fruits.

Much of the expansion has relied on imported technology and production inputs. Wheat production is now declining, but output continues upward for most other crops and livestock. Thus, the prospective demand for inputs is mixed, with a weak near term outlook for large machinery and irrigation equipment, but likely growth in demand for inputs related to the livestock or fruit and vegetable segments. Imports of most food and bulk agricultural products, other than a few items such as wheat, eggs and dates, are continuing at a strong pace.

Livestock and poultry farming are also growing fields. An expansion project of the country's two largest poultry producers led to a 30 percent increase in poultry output in 1999 versus 1996. The country, however, remains a large importer of frozen poultry.

### Banking
Saudi banks control approximately one-third of total Arab capital. Several significant developments occurred in 1998 and 1999 in the Saudi banking system, a sector that has been among the country's strongest.

The most significant development was the July 1999 merging of Saudi American Bank (SAMBA) and United Saudi Bank (USB). Their combined assets totaled roughly SR 80 billion ($21 billion). SAMBA'S management will control the assets of the larger institution, which will benefit from the USB's reputation for cost control. Moody's, however, did not believe the banks complement one another, nor that there exists many opportunities for synergy. The company issued a financial strength of C+ to SAMBA, the highest classification ever issued to a Saudi bank; USB received a D rating.

Another development, this one with regional implications, was the agreement by Gulf Cooperation Council members to open their countries to one another's banks.

In general, the Saudi banking system has been strong. This sector is the most actively traded on the Saudi stock market. It also showed the strongest performance of the private sector during the oil-price collapse. Profitability in the country's 11 commercial banks rose more than 10 percent in 1998 to $1.63 billion from $1.48 billion in 1997.

### Electricity
The electric power needs of Saudi Arabia are large and growing fast. Demand has been rising at an average annual rate of 10.5 percent from 1985-

1995, far exceeding the Kingdom's average GDP growth rate. The country is expecting a doubling in demand for electricity during the next 20 years.

In 1998, the government announced plans to streamline all regional electric companies into a single entity, the Saudi Electric Company. This move is seen as the first step toward privatizing this industry.

Demand for electricity is projected in the Sixth Development Plan (1995-2000) to rise at an annual rate of 6.4 percent reaching 5,081 kwh by the turn of the century. This necessitates an additional generating capacity of 9,000 MW in the next five years at a total cost of US$ 8.8 billion or US$ 1.6 billion annually.

The main challenge facing the electricity sector in Saudi Arabia is to put in place the required power generation capacity needed. Because of budgetary constraints and the ongoing public sector retrenchment, the government can no longer be expected to provide all the required investment. The private sector will be called upon to participate in financing power projects. For that to happen, the electricity sector needs to be restructured and electricity tariff rates to be adjusted further.

## Foreign Trade

Oil comprises more than 85 percent of the country's exports. Non-oil exports, including petrochemicals, accounted for 14 percent of total exports in 1997, the last year for which data is available.

Exports in 1997 totaled nearly $60 billion, creating a $33.53 billion trade balance. In 1998 exports declined nearly $20 billion over the previous year, reducing the trade balance to $12 billion.

In 1996, the country had it first surplus in 13 years at $187 million. Low oil prices and reduced oil production are expected to drive down export figures 35 percent between 1998–2000 from 1997 numbers.

Saudi imports of cars have increased, along with spare parts and other transportation equipment. These imports rose 47 percent to SR 15.7 ($4.2) billion during the first 9 months of 1998 compared to the same time period in 1991.

Imports of consumer goods have decreased—foodstuffs by 2.5 percent and medicines by about 1 percent. Jewelry imports declined by about 14 percent during the first nine months in 1998 compared with an 87 percent rise in

1997. Imports of jewelry declined to SR 5.8 ($1.5) billion in 1998 versus SR 6.9 ($1.8) billion during the same period in 1997.

The US is Saudi's leading trade and investment partner as well as top supplier of services and defense equipment. In 1998, the kingdom imported more than $10.5 billion in goods, a 25 percent increase over 1997 figures. Major imports from the US are parts for airplanes, motor vehicles, industrial machinery, electrical and electronic goods, medicines, foodstuffs, furniture and household appliances.

## 1998 Industry Trade Figures*

|  | Total Market Size | Total Local Production | Total Exports | Total Imports |
|---|---|---|---|---|
| Telecommunications | 108 | 3 | 0 | 105 |
| Electrical Power Systems | 1,104 | 104 | 12 | 1,012 |
| Water Desalination Equipment | 357 | 70 | 17 | 304 |
| Computer Software | 440 | 21 | 0 | 419 |
| Auto Parts & Service Equipment | 613 | 87 | 54 | 580 |
| Computers & Peripherals | 257 | 0 | 0 | 257 |
| Medical Equipment | 265 | 18 | 0 | 247 |
| Pollution Control Equipment | 46 | 6 | 0 | 40 |
| Security & Safety Equipment | 102.9 | 0.0 | 0.0 | 102.9 |
| Apparel | 906 | 75 | 13 | 844 |

*Source: US and Foreign Commercial Service and US Department of State

Saudi firms are now incorporating export plans into their business strategies. They are driven by the need to reduce their dependence on the domestic market, which, though fundamentally strong, is prone to a swing in response to periodic government spending cuts.

Although the Gulf states are the main foreign markets for Saudi goods, some Saudi exporters compete in the sophisticated European markets. Main destinations of exports outside the Gulf are Japan, the United States, South Korea, Singapore, France, the UK, Netherlands, Germany, Italy and India.

## Business Environment

### Foreign Investment

Foreign direct investment in Saudi Arabia reached an estimated $15 billion in 1997, with $7 billion coming from the US. Other countries with FDI in the kingdom are: Japan, Britain, Switzerland, France and Germany.

The total volume of foreign investment in Saudi Arabia reached US$ 22.5 billion in 1995, and the greatest number of investments came from the United States, Japan, France, Britain, South Korea, Taiwan, the Arabian Gulf countries, Syria and Lebanon. Most of the investments were made in petrochemicals, airport services, electrical and electronic manufacturing, and the food and beverage industries.

### Privatization

Saudis have traditionally resisted privatization, referring to it as "private sector participation." But the collapse of oil prices forced the Saudis to take privatization seriously. The government created in 1998 two joint stock companies—Saudi Telecommunications Company and the Saudi Electric Company—to help attract local and international investors to buy, finance or manage these utilities. Both these companies are expected to be privatized.

The government has also contracted private corporations to operate most of the kingdom's seaports. Furthermore, there has been speculation that the government is considering privatizing water, roads and Saudi Arabian airlines.

### Saudization

Both the sixth and seventh Saudi Five Year Development plans have emphasized job creation as a national priority through a strategy of "Saudiization." Part of this strategy calls for reducing the number of foreign workers.

The need to create jobs has become increasingly important as the population, growing at yearly 3.4 rate, puts hundreds of thousands of new workers into the labor force each year. (Unemployment figures are unavailable.)

A large majority of the labor force is comprised of non-Saudis. At the beginning of 1996, there were 6.25 million expatriates from 190 different nations in the Kingdom. These workers are concentrated in the construction trades, and as cashiers, accountants, purchase managers and warehouse officers. Currently, 4.7 million workers of the 7.2 million labor force are non-Saudi nationals.

Partly because of this ratio and partly because of reduced oil prices, the government doubled the cost of work permits for foreigners to $533. The increase may raise several hundred million dollars and create jobs for Saudis. Moreover, the government also made it more expensive for foreigners to enter and leave the country, raising visa prices to $133.

Saudi Arabia's rapid development during the past two decades has been the main justification in allocating such a large number of jobs to non-Saudis. Huge infrastructure projects required extensive labor, but local work ethics made imported workers more desirable.

Traditionally, the Saudi private sector has been unwilling to pay Saudis the salaries they demand, preferring instead to hire expatriate labor. Even now, salary levels provide little or no incentive for Saudis to work in positions typically held by expatriates, a trend that is expected to continue.

The Saudi private sector employment constitutes only 16 percent of the total work force. The rate of Saudi employment in the industrial sector stands at 4 percent and in the services sector at 12 percent. In contrast, their share in the public sector stands at 79.2 percent.

To increase Saudi presence in the private sector, the Saudi authorities are considering establishing a minimum Saudi wage, limiting the work day to eight hours and creating social insurance and pension plans similar to those available in the public sector.

The al-Saud ruling family's push for "Saudiization" is motivated by a desire to eliminate possible threats from the Saudi middle class, a reality which has preoccupied the royal family in recent years. In the past, the Saudi middle class received public sector jobs and benefits and in return backed the al-Saud ruling family's monopoly over the Kingdom's economy, finances and politics. But over the last two years, budgetary constraints have left government ministries and agencies unable to provide the same level of jobs and benefits. It is estimated that 20 to 30 percent of Saudi Arabia's university graduates are unemployed.

## Stock Exchange

A significant development regarding the stock exchange occurred in late 1999 with the government opening the market to foreign investors. Non-Saudis are now allowed to invest through funds run by Saudi banks. Many foreign investors had previously demanded to enter the Saudi Stock Exchange, which has 73 listed companies and a total market capitalization of SR 195 ($52) billion.

The 13-year-old market is the region's largest in absolute terms. But it amounts only to 33 percent of GDP, a relatively small ratio. The market is also highly concentrated. SAIBIC comprises 18 percent of the market capitalization and five other companies make up 50 percent.

The Saudi securities market is not highly developed. Under the Banking Control Law, trading in shares is conducted through a department in the Saudi Arabian Monetary Agency (SAMA). Joint stock companies are the vehicle permitting ownership by a large number of public shareholders, and the formation of such companies has been encouraged by the government through its privatization policy.

## Major Projects

The kingdom is working to upgrade and expand its telecommunications infrastructure. The Saudi Telecommunications Company hopes to have a total of 7.5 million phone lines operational by 2005: 6.5 million fixed lines and one million mobile.

Western Region Electricity Corporation started in late 1999 the first stage of an infrastructure project in which 144 new electricity sub-stations are being installed for new residents in Jeddah. In addition, 29 stations are being installed to ease the volume on existing stations.

The country is also investing in roads. The government budgeted $1.22 billion for road projects that will span more than 2,000 kilometers. A series of road projects that will connect Saudi Arabia to Oman, Qatar and the United Arab Emirates have been opened for private-sector involvement.

The Saudi Arabian Railways Organization (SARGO) is also expanding. It intends to spend $4.5 billion between 2000-2005 to construct links between the Red Sea city of Jeddah and Dammam on the Persian Gulf. Other scheduled projects include links to military installations and connecting mining sites and seaports.

The kingdom is also increasing its potable water output with the addition of new water desalination facilities. Currently, the kingdom can produce 726 million cubic meters of potable water, 70 percent of the country's drinking supply. That output will rise to 800 million following the completion of several projects. In 1998, the Shuaiba facility began providing 25 million gallons per day to Mecca and Ta'if. The estimated $1.07 billion second phase is to produce 60 million gallons a day for Jeddah.

The country also plans to spend $4 billion on projects that will provide water to all regions by 2008. The most important projects now are a second station at Shuaiba, a station at Yanbu and one at the Al-Khobar plant.

## Best Non-Agricultural Prospects

### Goods and Services

| Rank | Sector |
|------|--------|
| 1 | Telecommunications Equipment |
| 2 | Electrical Power Systems |
| 3 | Water Desalination Equipment |
| 4 | Computer Software |
| 5 | Auto Parts & Service Equipment |
| 6 | Computers and Peripherals |
| 7 | Medical Equipment |
| 8 | Education & Training Services |
| 9 | Oil & Gas Equipment & Services |
| 10 | Pollution Control Equipment |
| 11 | Franchising |
| 12 | Security & Safety Equipment |
| 13 | Mining Equipment |
| 14 | Apparel |
| 15 | Insurance |

## Franchising

Franchising has become a popular and growing approach for local firms to establish additional consumer-oriented business in Saudi Arabia. This has become a popular sector for Saudis who want their own business and appreciate western business practices. This sector's growth is expected to occur at a 9-10 percent yearly rate for the next two years.

Boutique retail outlets have recently begun to emerge. Branded apparel boutiques are also appearing especially for French and Italian designers.

Opportunities exist in the business service, apparel, laundry and dry cleaning services, telecommunications, automotive parts and servicing, mail and package service, printing and graphic design, courier services, hotels and motels and convenience stores. Non-food franchises comprise 55 to 65 percent of the market, estimated at $274 million in 1997. Success is often associated with franchiser and location.

Fierce competition exists between foreign, local and businesses from developing countries in car rental agencies, laundry and dry cleaning and auto maintenance.

Success in the Saudi market is often attributed to finding the appropriate franchiser and location. Usually, fast food franchises are situated near shopping centers or areas of high traffic flow. Non-food franchises account for 55 percent to 65 percent of the franchise market.

The large expatriate work force in Saudi Arabia patronizes franchises as a way of obtaining the same quality and level of services received at home. Franchising has expanded in the Saudi market at a phenomenal rate, more than 10 percent annually, outpacing other industry sectors.

Franchisers should realize however, that the culture and religious background of the Saudi people might make it necessary to modify some franchise concepts before they can be successfully introduced and operated in Saudi Arabia. These mores include the separation of the sexes and a general prohibition on photos or advertising that would be considered only mildly suggestive in the West.

## *Advertising*

The importance of advertising has grown with recent lifting of a ban on television commercials. Now companies use the full range of advertising mediums to gain market share and increase retail sales. Some televised commercials are broadcast on Saudi's two channels for limited times each day.

Bright colors (red, blue, green, black) are popular, while soft colors (pink, cream) are not. All commercials are screened to ensure compliance with moral and religious standards. The female form is usually not permitted in the media.

Saudi Arabia is the largest advertising market in the region, accounting for 40 percent of all advertising expenditures in the GCC alone. The Saudis, with their relatively high per-capita income and market-oriented economy, have become the prime target of producers of consumer goods and thus, the prime targets of the best international advertising firms.

Print media assumes the bulk of advertising expenditures in the Kingdom, with newspapers accounting for 61 percent of the pie, magazines 23 percent and television just 16 percent. Television was not legalized until 1963 and faced stiff opposition from conservative Islamic forces who termed the medium a "device of the devil."

## Legal Review

The Saudi Arabian legal system is based on Islamic law, the *Shari'a*, with the Koran providing the most important source of law. Nonetheless, Royal and Ministerial Decrees are periodically issued to meet the complexities of modern life and commercialized business transactions. Such Decrees are only valid, however, if they do not conflict with *Shari'a* law. Also, the use of settlement or arbitration for deciding conflicts is becoming more common.

## Judiciary

The main court is the *Shari'a* Court, which operates within the Ministry of Justice and deals with family, real estate and criminal matters. Appeals are made to the *Shari'a* Court of Appeals, and subsequently to the Custodian of the Two Holy Mosques.

The Ministry of Justice addresses disputes regarding commercial and labor matters. All cases concerning commercial disputes are dealt with through the Ministry's Board of Grievances. The Commission for the Settlement of Labor Disputes deals with labor disputes and criminal violations of the Labor Law. The Government Administrative Judicial Committees decide matters concerning insurance disputes, unlicensed foreign capital investment and violations of customs duties.

The Board of Grievances administers disputes between Saudi Arabian government bodies and private parties as well as other matters provided for by special codes such as bribery, forgery and trademarks. Most cases are decided on their individual merits, and judges are therefore not bound by legal precedent.

## Commercial Dispute Settlement

Historically, Saudis have not used commercial contracts that provide for arbitration or adjudication mechanisms outside of such mechanisms within the Saudi government. Saudi Arabia, however, has recently enacted an Arbitration Law and Regulations. As a result, the arbitration of disputes is no longer uncommon in the Kingdom.

Prevailing procedures are more time consuming than those in Europe and the United States and can cause personal inconvenience to foreigners. For example, a letter of no-objection is required from the Saudi sponsor of a foreign employee whose employment has terminated before the Government will issue an exit visa. Unfortunately, this requirement could be used to coerce or to intimidate people in certain business situations. Foreign business passengers traveling on a business visa do not require a letter of no-objection to leave the country.

The Saudis maintain, however, that they have made tremendous progress in resolving the backlog of commercial disputes, almost to the point of complete elimination. Moreover, the government no longer requires exclusive applicability of Saudi law in the resolution of private commercial disputes. In practice, however, Saudi courts tend to apply Saudi law in commercial disputes litigated in the Kingdom, even when the relevant contract contains a foreign choice of law provision and provides for a foreign forum to have jurisdiction. Business-to-business arbitration assistance, although expensive, is available from local chambers of commerce for some types of disputes.

## Business Forms and Structures

Business associations are governed by the Regulations for Companies (issued in 1982, and amended in 1992). The Regulations list business forms and structures, of which joint stock companies and limited liability partnerships are the most attractive to foreign investors. Additionally, there are certain business forms and structures, such as liaison and technical/scientific offices, which are not specifically dealt with by the Regulations but are nevertheless subject to them.

Establishments, or sole proprietorships, although required to register with the Ministry of Commerce, are not subject to the Regulations. Such enterprises are of marginal interest to foreigners since a foreigner is not allowed to conduct business in Saudi Arabia as a sole proprietor. In addition, Saudi law forbids foreigners from engaging in business in the Kingdom under the name of a Saudi national.

Although not provided for in the Companies Law, the Ministry of Industry and Electricity and the Ministry of Commerce have issued administrative fiats that have allowed the creation of wholly foreign-owned branches. Such branches do not require a local sponsor and may enter into contracts and do business in Saudi Arabia under their own names.

## *Companies Law*

The Regulations define a company as a joint undertaking to participate in an enterprise with a view to profit. Thus, a registered company is deemed to be a commercial entity, whatever its objectives may be. Upon registration, the company acquires legal personality. If it is not fully owned by Saudis it may not enjoy certain rights but would still be regarded as a Saudi company.

Every industrial or commercial establishment must be registered in the Commercial Register. Saudi participants in foreign companies and foreign branches need to obtain the consent of the Foreign Capital Investment Committee prior to registration.

## Joint Stock Companies

A joint stock company is owned by five or more individuals or entities. Capital is apportioned into negotiable shares of an equal amount, and shareholders are liable only to the extent of the value of their holdings. The minimum capital requirement is two million Saudi Riyals (SR) or no less than SR 10 million if its shares are offered for public subscription. The par value of each share cannot be less than SR 50, and upon incorporation, its issued paid-up capital must be no less than one-half of the authorized capital. A recent change to the Regulations allows a joint stock company to issue non-voting preferred shares in an amount up to 50 percent of its capital.

Prospective joint stock companies involving businesses such as mineral exploitation, administration of public utilities, banking and finance require authorization by Royal Decree prior to incorporation.

The management is composed of a board of directors. This board, appointed by the shareholders, must have a minimum of three members. Directors must own at least 200 shares of the joint stock company.

## Limited Liability Companies

Generally, a company with foreign participation would incorporate as a limited liability company, meaning a privately held company used to set up industrial, agricultural, contracting or services projects having Saudi and foreign partners. Limited liability companies are specifically not permitted to conduct banking, insurance or savings operations. These entities may not offer subscriptions to the public to raise capital, and partners cannot transfer their interest without the unanimous consent of the other partners.

Limited liability companies may also be established in the form of partnerships limited by shares, in which the limited partner is liable to the partnership's debts only to the extent of his capital contributions reflected in fully tradable share certificates. In practice, partnerships limited by shares are relatively rare.

A limited liability company must be registered under the Regulations for Companies as well as under the foreign capital investment regulatory regime. The various regulations do not specify minimum capital requirements for regular limited partnerships. A minimum capital of SR 1,000,000, however, is required for the establishment of a partnership limited by shares. Contribution stipulations, as well as other mandatory information, must be registered with the Ministry of Commerce.

## Partnerships

### General Partnerships

A general partnership is an association of two or more persons who are jointly liable for the debts of the partnership to the extent of their personal fortunes. As a separate legal entity it can transact business in its own name. Partners are forbidden to transfer interests without the unanimous consent of the other partners. No minimum capital is required, and contribution terms are set forth in the partnership agreement which must be registered with the Ministry of Commerce.

### Limited Partnerships

Limited partnerships are composed of general partners who are liable for the partnership's debts to the extent of their personal fortunes and limited partners who are liable for partnership's debts only to the extent of their investment. Participation by limited partners in the management of the partnership might expose them to joint individual liability with the general partners. Registration requirements are the same as for general partnerships.

The name of the firm must include the name of at least one general partner. For reasons of liability, limited partners should avoid having their names included in the firm name.

### Professional Partnerships

As of 1991, foreign 'free professionals' such as lawyers, engineers and medical practitioners, may establish joint practices with partnerships that are locally licensed. The establishment of a professional partnership requires approval from the Ministry of Commerce, which sets conditions that concern the reputation of the foreign firms, the transfer of interests and minimum participation of Saudi partners (25 percent). Profits of foreign partners from such professional partnership will presumably be taxable, unlike salaries earned by foreign professionals working for local firms.

## Joint Ventures

Foreign investment in joint ventures with Saudi partners has advantages. While foreign partners in a joint venture entity may hold 100 percent of the equity in some Gulf Cooperation Council (GCC) countries, there are advantages in having a local Saudi partner own 50 percent of the equity or more. For example, if a Saudi holds 50 percent of the equity in a joint venture company it enables the company to obtain an interest-free loan for up to 50 percent of the project cost, which is repayable over a period of ten years. In addition, majority Saudi-owned joint ventures are entitled to preference after wholly Saudi-owned companies in the allotment of government contracts. Trading and marketing activities aimed at Saudi individuals or wholly Saudi-owned companies, however, are forbidden to mix Saudi-foreign joint ventures by Royal Decree M/11 of 1962.

## Branch Offices

Foreign companies carrying out industrial or contracting works essential to the goals of economic development in Saudi Arabia may apply to the Foreign Capital Investment Committee for a license to establish a branch in the Kingdom. Upon receiving the license, the company may complete its registration process under the Regulation. It may be noted that, unlike a limited liability joint venture, a branch of a foreign entity is not entitled to a tax holiday. In practice, foreign companies have issued relatively few branch licenses, consistent with a general government policy of insulating the local market from direct competition.

In recent years, however, the concept of branches has been expanded to cover companies that are not involved in industrial and contracting works although the granting of such licenses is rare.

## Saudi Service Agents

Foreign companies operating exclusively for the purpose of implementing government contracts are required to obtain temporary commercial registration. Such registration is available only to contractors operating in the public sector. If a foreign contractor is engaged in a governmental contract and does not have a Saudi partner, it must engage a Saudi national as an agent. In cases of certain military contracts an exception to this general rule may sometimes be made. Agents may receive compensation not exceeding

5 percent of the contract value. The agency agreement should be submitted to the Ministry of Commerce along with the application for temporary commercial registration within 30 days of signing the contract.

## Currency and Banking

### Foreign Currency Control

There are virtually no currency exchange restrictions in Saudi Arabia. Exchange for payments abroad may be obtained freely, and there are no taxes or subsidies on purchases or sales of foreign currency. Officially, the Saudi Riyal (SR) is pegged to the International Monetary Fund's Special Drawing Rights. Since 1981, however, the Saudi Arabian Monetary Authority has instead chosen to peg the SR to the dollar. In order to minimize exchange risks for the private sector, to facilitate long term planning and to encourage repatriation of capital from abroad, the Saudi Arabian Government has maintained the exchange rate at SR 3.75=US$ 1 since 1987.

The depreciation of the dollar relative to other world currencies such as the Yen and the Deutsch Mark have the effect of making US imports even more competitive in the Saudi market. This depreciation has led to talks within the GCC countries concerning the possibility of moving their currencies to a trade weighted unit that would reflect Western European and Japanese imports. GCC finance officials met again in 1992 to discuss this issue but have apparently postponed any changes.

### Banking

Banking in Saudi Arabia is regulated by the Banking Control Law of 1966. The Saudi Arabia Monetary Agency (SAMA), established in 1952, is the country's central bank. Among other things, SAMA issues and controls currency, regulates the money supply, regulates and monitors commercial banks (including deposits, loans and investments) and manages foreign assets. The Banking Control Law provides for state owned and private banks.

### Public Banks

Under the Banking Control Law there are nine public banks in addition to SAMA. The distribution of government subsidies and grants of loans to public and private sector projects are funneled through specialized public funds or banks.

For example, Saudi Industrial Development Fund, which is linked to the Ministry of Industry and Electricity, is aimed at encouraging Saudis to establish small and medium size industrial projects in the private sector. The funds provide loans and advice on marketing, technical and financial matters.

The Saudi Arabian Agricultural Bank, which is affiliated with the Ministry of Agriculture and Water, grants subsidies and makes loans to farmers for the purchase of machinery, feed and livestock. It also finances joint ventures in agricultural projects with foreign participation.

The Real Estate Development Fund offers loans to Saudi individuals and entities for private and commercial housing projects.

The Public Investment Fund, which is controlled by the Ministry of Finance, is used as a medium to long-term financing vehicle for the petrochemical industry, and it acquires equity in companies and banks in order to subsequently sell the equity to low-income groups.

## Private Banks

There are twelve commercial banks operating in Saudi Arabia, three of which are fully Saudi-owned and the remainder of which have a minimum 60 percent Saudi participation. Modern banking in the Kingdom began with branches of foreign banks. As of the mid-1970s, a process of "Saudi-ization" of foreign banks was undertaken that was completed in the early 1980s. Currently, foreign banks cannot operate directly through branches in the Kingdom and must rely on Saudi banks. Cooperation between foreign and Saudi banks may result in the foreign bank providing international offices, training and access to international networks. Under certain conditions, a foreign bank may issue bonds and guarantees certified by a Saudi bank.

## Islamic Banking

Generally speaking, Islamic law forbids the charging of interest. Many Saudi businesspersons who conduct their activities in accordance with Islamic law, use a profit-and-loss sharing arrangements allowed under Islamic law to finance commercial projects. Banks in the Kingdom, therefore, generally provide facilities enabling finance by way of such arrangements.

## Financing Through Financial Institutions

Saudi banks finance Saudi as well as non-Saudi entities. Saudi entities may also borrow from non-Saudi banks and often employ the services of offshore banking units in Bahrain, which is a major banking center for financing countries in the Gulf.

## Import Payment Process

Most Saudi imports are received on the basis of an irrevocable letter of credit (L/C), although other arrangements such as open account, cash in advance and documentary collection are also permitted. Imports do not require mandatory, maximum or minimum credit terms. Typical turnaround time in local credit transactions ranges from three to four months.

## Intellectual Property

Saudi law protects the rights of nationals and foreigners in the field of intellectual property. Every natural or legal person that suffers injury resulting from trademark law infringement may claim damages. Expert proceedings regarding the infringement are permissible, and damages for trademark and patent infringements are punitive and provide compensation for the injured.

Intellectual property rights are also indirectly protected by the provisions of the Regulations for Combating of Commercial Fraud, which enable Saudi authorities to impose numerous sanctions for the production of counterfeit products or unlicensed copies of products, that include seizure and destruction of such products and imposing monetary fines up to SR 100,000 for violation of the provisions of the regulations.

The burden of proof in intellectual property cases lies with the plaintiff, and it is an onerous responsibility, unless the unlawful products are seized. Under Saudi law, documentary evidence does not supplant oral evidence, but the two combined may support each other. In trademark cases, discovery may provide the injured party with material and documentary evidence which alleviates the burden of proof.

349

Orders are enforced in respect of payment of money by effecting seizure against the party losing the case. With regard to prohibitory injunctions and writs of mandamus, orders are submitted to civil right directorates of the Interior Ministry to execute. Non-compliance with such orders may result in the imprisonment of the offender and the seizure of his assets.

## Patents

The Saudi Patent Regulations of 1989 established a patent registration system, covering any new article, methods of manufacture (including improvements in either of them) and product patents. In 1996, the Saudi Patent Office granted its first patents since its establishment in 1990.

A patent may be granted to either Saudi or foreign citizens, including companies. Upon compliance with the registration formalities, the application receives a filing number and the filing date is secured. Patents are valid for fifteen Hijri years (a lunar year under Islamic precepts) as from the date of grant and may be extended for an additional period of five years.

The rights to a patent belong solely to the inventor, who may assign these rights with or without consideration. An industrial patent must be exploited within two years as from the date of grant, and if reasonable grounds are provided, this period may be extended for another period not exceeding two years. Failure to exploit the patent within the relevant period of time entitles the Patent Office to grant a compulsory license for exploiting the patent to any person capable of fully exploiting it.

Patent cases are heard by an administrative commission that has legal competence. This commission sits in the City of King Abdul Aziz for Science and Technology. Decisions concerning patents may be contested by third parties within ninety days of the announcement that a patent has been granted.

## Trademarks and Service Marks

Trademarks and service marks registration is governed by the Trademarks Regulation of 1984. Saudi Arabia follows the International Classification of goods and services, but is subject to various limitations. For instance, trademarks for certain alcoholic goods are not registerable. Additionally, registration applications may be rejected if the trademark offends or is contrary to public morality.

A trademark/service mark application accepted for registration is published in the Official Gazette (*Ummulqura*). If no opposition is filed within three months, the owner would have an incontestable right to use the trademark/service mark for ten Hijri years as of the date of filing the application. The registration of the trademark/service mark can be renewed for additional periods of five Hijri years each. Use of trademarks in not compulsory for purposes of registration or keeping registration in force. A trademark/service mark may be canceled if it was not used for a period of five successive years.

Unauthorized use of a registered trademark/service mark, an imitation applied on goods or with respect to services of the same class, storage, sale, exhibiting for sale or using the trademark/service mark in the course of unauthorized promotion are offenses punishable under Saudi law by fines and imprisonment.

Infringement proceedings in relation to trademarks are heard by the Grievance Board. Forged and imitated goods may be seized by the Commerce Ministry or its branches. If civil proceedings in a trademark case are not initiated before the Grievance Board within 10 days, however, the precautionary proceedings shall become void. A public case must be heard within three years of the alleged offense having been committed. There is no such limitation for private cases.

Decisions of the Trademark Office can be challenged through administrative judiciary channels in the Commerce Ministry and legally before the Grievances Board. Applicants or third parties that have an interest in objecting to a registration have the right to challenge such decisions.

## Designs

Saudi Arabia does not have a statutory design registration system in force. Protection is thus limited and the only available means of protection is through publication of cautionary notices in the *Ummulqura* or in local newspapers. These notices define the owner's interest in the property, announce the ownership thereto and alert the public against any possible infringement. Since cautionary notices are not covered by regulations and are not registered with any government department, it is advisable to republish such notices at frequent intervals.

## *Copyright*

Following pressure from the US Special Trade Representative Office, Saudi Arabia issued its Copyright Regulations in 1989. These Regulations are fairly limited in scope in that they fail to protect foreign copyrights. Also the Regulations do not address enforcement or registration procedures.

Saudi copyrights are generally protected for the life of the author plus fifty and twenty-five years with respect to books and sound and audio visual works respectively. As to computer software, while its protection seems explicit, the Regulations do not specify the protection duration.

## Taxation

A *zakat* or income tax (a religious wealth tax) is assessed on the taxable income of most business organizations. Since only Saudis and GCC nationals are subject to *zakat*, foreigners pay an income tax in proportion to their equity interest. Foreign employees are not taxed on their salaries or wages. There is no sales tax. Capital gains fall under the same umbrella as ordinary income. Taxable net income is fairly consistent for all types of business organizations, foreign or resident.

## *Corporate Income Tax*

Corporate income taxes are levied on the profits of foreign shareholders in a mixed company and the net profits of branches of foreign companies. Company tax rates, which are applicable to limited liability and joint stock companies, are taxed between 25 to 45 percent depending on profit. Petroleum and other hydrocarbon producing companies, however, are subject to a flat tax rate of 85 percent of net operating income.

## *Tax Holidays*

Foreign companies entering into joint ventures with Saudi companies that have been recognized as developing projects by the Foreign Capital Investment Committee may receive a five year tax holiday. The exemption only applies to the particular project for which the Foreign Capital Investment Committee approval is granted. Other income may be held to fall outside the exemption, and therefore, be taxable. Manufacturers of agricultural products may be granted a ten year tax exemption.

## Deductions and Losses

In general, all necessary business expenses incurred in Saudi Arabia are tax deductible except for specific types of expenses which may not be deductible. Expenses of the later type include doubtful debts, termination benefits and general administrative costs of the head office. Other types of expenses may be deductible only if certain conditions are met (e.g., agency fees). Statutory maximum rates have been set with regard to depreciation.

Saudi law has no provision allowing tax losses to be carried forward or back.

## Taxation of Partnerships

A general partnership is taxed in a manner similar to that of a resident company. Non-Saudi and non-GCC individuals and corporate partners, however, are taxed upon their allocated share of profit at the applicable individual corporate tax rates.

## Taxation of Individuals

### Income Tax

Saudis and GCC nationals are not subject to income tax. Self employed foreigners who are resident in Saudi Arabia are not taxed on income from non-Saudi sources but only on Saudi-source income. Foreign employees are not taxed on their wages and salaries. When applicable, income tax is levied by reference to the following table:

| SR | Tax Rate |
|---|---|
| 0–6000 | 0-5%* |
| 6001–16,000 | 5% |
| 16,001–36,000 | 10% |
| 36,001–66,000 | 20% |
| over 66,001 | 30% |

* If the period which the foreigner stays in the Kingdom exceeds one year, the first SR 6,000 of income will not be taxed.

## *Zakat Tax*

*Zakat* is the religious wealth tax imposed on Saudis and GCC nationals, and on companies entirely owned by them. In case of mixed participation, *zakat* is assessed by reference to the proportion of Saudi or GGC participation. *Zakat* rates are 2.5 percent of capital which is not invested in fixed assets or long term investments or which relate to deferred pre-incorporation expenses.

## *Withholding Tax*

Withholding tax is imposed on payments made to non-residents and to persons not registered with the tax authorities for activities within the Kingdom. Tax must be withheld based on deemed minimum profit of 15 percent of the payment. Certain management fees, license fees and royalties are taxed assuming a 100 percent profit. Companies must withhold tax on payments to non-residents including foreign shareholders regardless of any tax holiday granted to the company.

## *Treaties for the Prevention of Double Taxation*

The only double tax treaty signed in Saudi Arabia is with France. Similar treaties have been negotiated with Britain and with Germany. Countries, including Britain, Germany, Japan, and the United States, allow taxpayers to take a credit against their taxable income in such countries for any Saudi Arabian income tax paid.

## Investment and Trade

## *Investment Incentives*

The Foreign Capital Investment Regulations provide for a number of investment incentives to foreign companies and individuals wishing to conduct business in Saudi Arabia.

The Saudi Industrial Development Fund makes interest-free loans to industrial companies of up to 50 percent of the total cost of the project. Project costs includes agreed pre-operating costs, investment in fixed assets and working capital. A 50 percent loan requires Saudi participation which is not less than 50 percent. If Saudi participation is lower, the loan is reduced proportionally. Soft loans are repayable in five to ten years after a one or two year grace period from the date of production. Although the loans are interest-free, an administrative fee of 2.5 percent is normally charged.

All commodities entering the Kingdom for industrial production are exempt from import duty, including spare parts and all plant and equipment required to set up companies.

In addition, industrial facilities are allowed to rent at low to nominal rental fees. They also pay reduced rates for water and electricity. The following five categories of development qualify for foreign investment:

- Industrial development including raw material into manufactured or semi-manufactured products, transferring semi-manufactured products into fully manufactured products and packaging fully manufactured products;
- Agricultural development including the cultivation of fruits, vegetables, nurseries, greenhouses, animal resources and fisheries;
- Health development including building, maintenance, operation and management of hospitals, clinics and health centers;
- Services relating to industries such as tourism, training, technology, environment protection, shipping and information systems; and
- Contracting.

## Other Incentives

Saudi Arabia imposes no exchange control regulations on the entry and repatriation of funds, profits and salaries paid to foreigners employed in the Kingdom. Saudi law prescribes no specific debt-to-equity ratios as a prerequisite to doing business in Saudi Arabia, but certain investment incentives may require specified debt-to equity ratios to be satisfied.

## Trade Agreements

Saudi Arabia is a member of the GCC, and as such, is subject to the GCC agreements regarding trade. These agreements are described in the section on Trade Agreements in the chapter on Bahrain.

## Imports and Exports

### Customs
Many items are free of customs-duties, including food, heavy machinery and raw materials. The basic duty is 12 percent, although certain protected industries, favored under the Regulations for the Protection and Encouragement of National Industries, enjoy a 20 percent protective tariff against competing imports.

In accordance with the Unified Economic Agreement among the GCC states, products manufactured in any one of the member states will be exempt from customs duties when exported to any of the GCC states provided that 51 percent of the factory equity is owned by a GCC national.

### Imports
Only Saudi nationals and 100 percent Saudi-owned companies may import goods. Importers must be licensed by the Ministry of Commerce and must consult the appropriate ministry about the goods or materials to be imported.

Standard measurements, packaging, ingredients and safety standards should comply with the rules established by the Saudi Arabian Standards Organization. In order to enter the country, imports must have certificates of origin. Any product deemed contrary to Islamic law, e.g., pork products and alcoholic beverages, may not be imported.

### Exports
Other than antiques, Arabian horses, livestock or subsidized goods and materials which are in short supply, most goods can be exported from Saudi Arabia. Exporters may need an industrial or an agricultural license.

### Protective Tariffs and Non-Tariff Trade Barriers
Saudi tariff protections are moderate, but have been increased over the years. A number of Saudi "infant industries" now enjoy 20 percent tariff protection as compared to the general rate of 12 percent. Non-tariff barriers are also increasing and include preferences for national and GCC products in government procurements. Presently, 30 percent of major government procurement contracts are set-aside for local contractors. Foreign contractors obtain imported goods and services exclusively through Saudi agents. Furthermore, an economic offset requirement has been invoked which

mandates reinvestment of a portion of the government contract value in indigenous industries for certain high value government procurement contracts.

## Trade Barriers

Import licenses are not required for virtually all goods. Foreign exchange for imports is readily available and no restrictions on financial transfers or exchange controls exist.

## Labor Law

Most of the provisions dealing with labor law and employee's rights are included in the Labor and Workmen's Regulations of 1969. The establishment of labor unions is prohibited and basically there is no collective labor law in the Kingdom.

The regulations provide for enforcement of employee's rights, record-keeping and reporting, protection of women and children, inspection of places of work provision of medical and other facilities, etc. Labor benefits are mandatory and may not be waived.

According to the regulations, every employee is entitled to a written employment contract, although an employment contract does not necessarily have to be in writing in order to be valid.

With minor exceptions, the maximum work week is eight hours per day for a six day week. During the month of Ramadan, the maximum work week decreases to thirty-six hours.

The Saudi Labor Regulations distinguish between specified and unspecified term contracts. If the employment relationship is for a specified period, the employee may only be terminated "for cause" as defined in the Regulations, which usually means a fundamental breach of the employment contract by the employee. If the employment contract states no specific term then the worker may be terminated for a valid reason only, which does not reach to the level of "cause". In all cases, the employee must be given a requisite statutory termination notice.

Saudi labor laws ensure preferential treatment for Saudis in hiring over equally qualified foreign nationals, mandating that three-quarters of every employer's work force must consist of Saudis and that no less than 51 percent of the employers' total payroll be paid to Saudis.

## Environmental Law

Saudi Arabia is a signatory to several international treaties concerning the environment. These treaties include:

- The 1967 Outer Space Treaty;
- The Kuwait Regional Convention for the Protection of the Marine Environment from Pollution;
- The 1992 Regional Convention for the Conservation of the Red Sea and the Gulf of Aden Environment;
- The 1989 Basel Convention on the Control of Transboundary Movements of Hazardous Wastes and their Disposal.

# SYRIA

## Recent Political Developments

In 1999, President Hafiz al-Asad was re-elected to his 5th term as President of Syria capturing 99.4 percent of the vote. He has served in that position since taking power in a 1970 coup. But the most important development may be the grooming of his son Bashar, to eventually succeed him.

President Asad's health for years has been bad, but it recently has been reportedly deteriorating. After seemingly putting peace with Israel on the back-burner in late 1999 to ensure his son's position as heir, Assad surprisingly announced that he would send his foreign minister to meet with Israeli Prime Minister Ehud Barak in Washington. The December summit was the highest-level talks between the two countries. The meeting was held although Israel refused to agree to withdraw to June 4, 1967 borders, a Syrian demand for resuming talks.

While the meeting brought great euphoria, the negotiations are expected to be tough. Many believe an agreement

| | |
|---|---|
| Population | 16 million (1999) |
| Population Growth Rate | 3.3% |
| Religion | 70% Sunni Muslim, 12% Alawi, 14% Christian (various sects), 3% Druze and small number of Jews, Yazidis and other Muslim Sects |
| Government | Presidential Republic |
| | Arabic (English and French are widely spoken; Kurdish is spoken among the Kurd minority) |
| Work Week | Commercial: Saturday–Thursday 9:00–14:00; 16:00–19:00 & 17:00–20:00 Public Sector: Saturday–Thursday 8:00–14:00 Banking: Saturday–Thursday 8:00–14:00 |
| Monetary Unit | Syrian Pounds (SP) |
| Exchange Rate | SP 42.75 = US$1 |

can be reached within a year. If a treaty is struck, it will likely lead to a treaty with Lebanon and a withdraw of Israeli troops from southern Lebanon.

## Recent Economic Developments

Syria remains one of the Middle East's most isolated economies, resisting the economic trends sweeping the rest of the region, such as privatization. The government still keeps intact many policies that protect home-grown industries at the expense of attracting foreign investment. Such policies include high tariffs and numerous import restrictions and limited access to capital for those in the private sector.

The country's economy depends primarily on oil, remittances from Syrians working abroad (primarily in Lebanon) and agriculture. Its economy is also affected by external matters such as foreign aid, the peace process and relationship with neighboring states. The country's economy is damaged by its inclusion on the US list of countries that sponsor terrorism.

Nevertheless, Syria has great growth potential from its geographic location, a population with a long history of entrepreneurship, sufficient natural resources, high tourism potential, relatively fertile land and inexpensive raw materials.

Investing in these areas and further opening the economy can have a large impact on the country's inhabitants.

Syria's population is sixteen million with a 3.5 percent annual growth rate. This factor and Syria's relative domestic stability have made it an increasingly attractive destination for foreign investment, especially Arab, during 1991 to 1995. During this period, the average GDP growth stood at 7 percent at constant prices, and per capita GDP grew by more than 3.7 percent per year. From 1994 to 1995, Syrian GDP grew by 19.2 percent, and industrial production increased by about 16 percent.

Since the break-up of the Soviet union, Syria has become increasingly oriented towards Western Europe, and, in particular, the EU. Exports to Europe hit over 60 percent of total exports versus about 25 percent to Arab countries. Imported goods from Europe account for nearly 50 percent of total imports.

Petroleum and related products account for about 60 percent of exports. Other ranking items include clothes, fruit, vegetables and cotton. Roughly one-third of imports are machinery and transport equipment, and road vehicles make up more than 11 percent of the total. Iron and steel account for about 15 percent of all imports, while chemical and related products capture 10 percent.

The economic gains in the first half of the 1990s have not been widely distributed. Additionally, unemployment is a growing concern as roughly 60 percent of the population is estimated to be under the age of twenty. Water is another problem as Syria may face a serious water shortage by the end of the decade given current water policies.

During the early 1990s, the Syrian economy experienced several years of brisk growth. Between 1990 and 1995 average GDP growth stood at 7 percent at constant prices, and per capita GDP grew by more than 3.7 percent per year. From 1994 to 1995, Syrian GDP grew by 19.2 percent, and industrial production increased by about 16 percent. And in 1996, GDP grew by 7.2 percent and industrial production by 5.1 percent.

But the economy began to experience a downturn because of a worldwide recession, declining oil prices and agriculture commodities as well as a reduction in foreign aid. More troubling for the country's long-tern economic outlook is the amount of oil remaining. It is believed that without any new discoveries—and current exploration have not yielded positive results—the country may turn into an oil importer within the next 5–6 years. There are, however, other alternatives to lure foreign investors in its gas development, exploration, production and export.

There are many areas that must be reformed before the country can hope to invigorate its economy by means other than oil. The government still maintains many policies that inhibit large growth. The country has restricted imports, imposed high tariffs, and banned imports of products that compete with local industries. The country is also burdened with a large external debt, which hampers Syria's access to international capital markets and promised loans from the European Investment Bank.

A government study estimates that it will cost the country $6 billion to revamp the country's feeble industry and implement the reforms necessary to gain acceptance into the Euro-Mediterranean Partnership. The report concluded that besides infrastructure development, vocational skills need to be developed, industrial facilities rehabilitated and Syrian industries made more competitive.

The country's inclusion on US's list of states that sponsor terrorism is a political hurdle that negatively impacts the country's economy. This causes US firms interested in business or investment opportunities to consider US export controls, the lack of guaranteed trade financing and additional tax implications.

Although the country has a long path of reform ahead, it has begun to take initial steps in this direction. As the government slowly opens its economy to foreigners, it has told the public sector to increase efficiency and prepare for competition. Furthermore, the government in the last seven years has been opening to private participation some sectors that have formerly been solely in the public domain, such as food processing, textiles and pharmaceuticals. But the main benefactors of the opening to the private sector are those businessmen with close or family contacts to the top political echelons.

The country has also taken important strides during the 1990s in developing its rickety communication infrastructure. The country has awarded hundreds of millions of dollars in contract that is expected to increase the country's fixed lines by 1 million by 2004. This would bring Syria's fixed lines to 1.65 million.

The government has also announced tenders for GSM service and Internet, which is now available only on a limited scale to government entities. Cellular service is not available.

Syria is also upgrading its power-generation capacity. This capacity is now 6,500 megawatts, although there are still regular short power outages in large cities, especially in the summer. A total of 97 percent of the population have electricity. Furthermore, several studies have been commissioned such as investigating the possibility of launching investment and foreign trade banks, and opening a stock market, something which would require increased transparency and expose the economy's true condition. Thus far, neither program has advanced past the preliminary declaration stage.

The country's 1998 exports were roughly $2.2 billion, a 30 percent drop from the year before, which the government attributed to the drop in oil and cotton prices. Those two commodities comprise about 81 percent of the country's total exports.

## Economic Policy

From the 1960s until recently, the Syrian government pursued policies aimed at expanding the public sector, with tight controls imposed on private sector activity. During the 1980s, the country suffered from a severe foreign exchange shortage, aggravated by a fall in remittances and aid flows from the Gulf and a severe drought in 1989-1990 that forced the government to sharply boost food imports.

As the government imposed draconian foreign exchange and trade controls, a parallel economy emerged, based on large-scale smuggling to and from neighboring Lebanon. The Syrian government cracked down on smuggling in May 1993, and most of the pre-smuggled commodities can now be imported via official channels. Smuggling has not, however, been eradicated.

Syria's economy in the 1990s is undergoing a slow and controlled transition toward a market system. Since 1990, foreign exchange controls have eased due to a renewal of external foreign exchange flows, both official and private. Additionally, the government has taken gradual liberalization measures to open up the economy. Until recently, the government pursued policies aimed at expanding the public sector, with tight controls imposed on private sector activity. All large industry, including the banking and insurance sectors, was nationalized in the 1960s and continued to grow with the help of Arab aid in the 1970s. With a liberalization of trade and foreign exchange controls, a greater proportion of economic activity is now within legal channels, but the parallel economy remains a key element of the economy.

Since 1991, private sector investment has picked up noticeably, as businessmen have taken advantage of incentives offered under a new investment law, Law No. 10. Liberalization measures implemented in recent years now permit private enterprise to retain foreign exchange from exports, 75 percent for industrial products and 100 percent for agricultural commodities, and to finance permitted imports for inputs and a number of basic commodities using foreign exchange gained from exports.

Although it has retained a monopoly on wheat and flour imports, the government widened the list of imports permitted to the private sector, including items formerly reserved for public sector trading companies, such as rice, sugar and tea.

In 1990, the government established an official parallel rate, known as the neighboring countries' rate, to provide further incentives for remittances and for trade through official channels. This rate and others more closely reflect the real value of the Syrian pound. Use of such rates continues to expand, a trend that should eventually lead to unification of the multiple rates presently used for different purposes.

**Economic Indicators**

|  | 1999* | 1998 | 1997 |
|---|---|---|---|
| Real GDP (US$ billions) | 12.10 | 12.10 | 12.65 |
| Per Capita GDP (US$) | 790 | 800 | 837 |
| Real GDP Growth (percent) | 0 | −4.4 | 0 |
| Inflation (%; official) | 2 | 2 | 2.2 |
| Unemployment (%; official) | 7 | 7 | 7 |
| Exports (fob, US$ billion) | — | 3.09 | 4.06 |
| Imports (fob, US$ billion) | — | 3.26 | 3.6 |
| Trade Balance (US$ billion) | — | −0.17 | 0.46 |
| Government Revenues (US$ billions) | — | 4.11 | 4.05 |
| Government Expenditures (US$ billions) | — | 4.73 | 4.42 |
| Overall Deficit (US$ billion) | — | 0.62 | 0.37 |
| Gas Production (millions of cubic meters) | — | 2,487 | 2,270 |

## Foreign Aid

Between 1977–1994, Syria received cash transfers from Arab Gulf states of almost US$ 17 billion in total, helping the government to sustain a defense establishment budgetary burden that amounted to some 50 percent of its annual budget expenditure. The emphasis of the aid shifted after 1991 to supporting specific projects, allowing Syria to buy power stations, a one million line telephone network and a new sewerage system.

In early February 1995, the European Union (EU) approved a new aid package of about US$ 50 million to finance development projects in Syria, despite concern about Syria's debt problems at the time (Syria owed some US$ 750 million to European creditors prior to receiving French assistance). The aid package included financing to set up a Syrian export promotion center, responding to one of the EU's concerns that Syria's export revenues are too dependent on oil. Other projects in the package included the upgrading of water and electricity systems, technical assistance to the banking sector and a tourism venture.

## Foreign Debt

As of the end of 1999, Syria's external debts stand at about US$ 20 billion, which is owed to Russia and to a number of European countries. France's decision to settle its debt problem with Syria was highly appreciated by Damascus, although not stated publicly, and could open the way to an EU-Syrian trade agreement. Syria hopes that it will be in line for substantial debt relief once a peace agreement is reached with Israel.

## Exchange Rates

The Syrian exchange rate is a complicated system that has been an inhibiting factor in attracting foreign investment. Beginning in 1998, the government reduced the number of exchange rates from eight to three. The official rate is SP 11.2 to $1, while the currency's real value is worth SP 50 to $1.

Academics, businessmen and economists have urged the government for years to implement a simplified system. Thus far there has only been little change. For example, beginning January 1, 1995, the government attempted a rate unification, calculating government accounts at the neighboring countries' official rate of SP 43=US$ 1, rather than the previous SP 23=US$ 1. The official rate of SP 11.2=US$ 1, which had been in existence since 1988, was still used to calculate some transactions, including hotel bills paid by foreigners and various government transactions. The SP 23=US$ 1 rate remained in effect for some customs tariffs. In contrast, the black-market rate in Damascus hovered between SP 48 to 54=US$ 1 since the early 1990s, while the rate in Beirut is around SP 54=US$ 1.

## Major Economic Domains

### Industry
Presently, Syria's industrial sector is weak, concentrating on basic products such as foods, chemicals and soaps. Industries suffer from obsolete equipment and technologies and a lack of available capital. Under these condi-

tions, the industry sector will be unable to offset lost oil revenues in the event that the petroleum industry begins to dry up.

Textiles constitute the largest manufacturing industry in Syria. Other industries include petrochemicals, fertilizers, cement, soap, glass, food processing, sugar processing, tobacco, iron and steel, tanning and vegetable oil.

Syrian manufacturing industries began to grow in the 1960s. The government encouraged industrialization by raising tariffs on imported consumer goods and by providing tax exemptions and credit for domestic industries.

Heavy industry, banking, insurance and utilities remain in the public sector. Food processing, textiles, pharmaceuticals and transportation have slowly been opened to the private sector during the last seven years.

## Agriculture

Syria's total crop production may decline by roughly 30 percent in 1999 because of a serious drought during the first six months. Further exacerbating the problem has been the country's wide use of irrigating pumps, which have caused the water table to drop significantly.

The country's principal found crop is wheat. In 1998, the country harvested 4.1 million tons of wheat, while it is expected to yield only 2.3 million tons in 1999.

Syria is comprised of 20 percent arable land. Syria produces a wide variety of crops, some in sufficient quantity for export. The major crops are cereals, primarily wheat and barley, cotton, tobacco, grapes, olives, citrus fruits and vegetables. Agricultural land is privately owned for the most part.

## Tourism

The tourism sector in Syria has developed slowly, partly because of ambivalence on the part of the government, which is hesitant about permitting a massive influx of foreign visitors, and partly because Syria's image abroad has deterred would-be tourists from visiting. In recent years, the average number of tourists visiting Syria was about two million, most of them from Arab countries. The Syrian government had anticipated an increase in the number of tourists to six million by 2000, but without a peace agreement, this will be a difficult target to meet. In 1999, the number of tourists amounted to about 1.3 million.

## Business Environment

### *Franchising*

Syrian regulations have made foreign franchising virtually impossible. There is one American fast-food franchise in the country.

The concept of franchising, especially the prospects for opening the first major American fast food restaurant, has captured the imagination of many Syrians. Many capable and well-capitalized Syrian businessmen have applied for major American fast food franchises, but have been refused.

### Best Business Prospects

| Rank | Sector |
|------|--------|
| 1 | Oil & Gas Exploration Equipment, Piping & Supplies |
| 2 | Telecommunications |
| 3 | Electricity |
| 4 | Cotton Yarn Spinning |
| 5 | Fertilizer & Chemical Processing Plants |
| 6 | Silo Storage for Grains |
| 7 | Irrigation Equipment |
| 8 | Pharmaceuticals |
| 9 | Medical Equipment & Supplies |
| 10 | Computers |
| 11 | Tourism |
| 12 | Port Facilities |
| 13 | Fast Foods & Franchising |

The best prospects for agricultural products are corn, soybeans and soy products, rice, cigarettes, vegetable seeds and almonds.

## Legal Review

### Judiciary

According to the Constitution of 1973, the Syrian Arab Republic is a democratic, popular, socialist and sovereign state with a republican system of government. The Constitution establishes Islamic jurisprudence as a main source of legislation.

Two judicial systems operate in Syria: the Courts of General Jurisdiction and the Administrative Courts. Transcendent authority over all courts of law rests with the Supreme Constitutional Court, which deals almost exclusively in matters of constitutional law and other internal affairs of state.

## Courts of General Jurisdiction

The Courts of General Jurisdiction are separated into six branches, all of which are further categorized by Civil and Penal Chambers (with the exception of the Personal Status Courts). These branches are: (1) The Court of Cassation; (2) Courts of Appeal; (3) Tribunals of First Instance; (4) Tribunals of Peace; (5) Personal Status Courts; and (6) Courts for Minor Offendors.

The Court of Cassation, the highest court, hears appeals from the lower courts and can overturn judgments rendered by Courts of Appeal in criminal and civil cases.

The Courts of Appeal preside over a separate governorate (*Mouhafazat*) each and are divided into Civil and Penal Chambers. Each Court of Appeal hears appeals of decisions in cases previously tried before the Tribunals of First Instance and the Tribunals of Peace.

There are several Tribunals of First Instance located in each governorate. Each Tribunal is divided into several divisions according to nature of the cases presented.

The Tribunals of Peace preside over minor civil and criminal matters and are abundant in each governorate. The Personal Status Courts deal mostly in personal status and family matters and vary according to the religion and ethnic origin of the litigants. The jurisdiction of the Courts for Minor Offendors applies accordingly to matters relating to minors. The Administrative Courts adjudicate matters involving the state and its agencies.

## Recognition of Foreign Judgments

Foreign judgments can only be executed in Syria if they relate to civil or to commercial disputes upon the approval of the Court of First Instance in the governorate where the judgment is to be executed. If there is no bilateral treaty on mutual recognition with the country concerned, the Syrian court will re-examine the case and scrutinize the foreign court's opinion. If a bilateral treaty exists, the Court will limit its scrutiny to violations of Syrian public policy.

## Dispute Resolution

Generally, both domestic and international disputes are arbitrable, unless otherwise specified in statutory provisions. Public or government institutions cannot agree to submit to arbitration unless provided for by statute. The state can only agree to arbitrate if it is bound by treaty. International arbitration held in Syria is subject to Syrian law and is generally covered by the same rules governing domestic arbitration. The enforcement of international arbitration awards generally follows the same rules as the enforcement of foreign court decisions.

Furthermore, Syria is a contracting party to the New York Convention on the Recognition and Enforcement of Foreign Arbitral Awards. Few investment disputes have actually occurred during the past few several years. Such disputes are usually settled (often after long delays) through negotiations or by enforcement of a contractual arbitration clause.

### Business Forms and Structures

## Companies Law

According to Syrian commercial law contained in Legislative Decree No. 149 of 1949, there are several forms in which entities may be registered in Syria and through which business may be conducted. These are: (1) capital company (either a shareholding or a limited liability company); (2) general partnership; (3) limited partnership; (4) joint venture; and (5) branch of a foreign company. All of these forms enjoy an independent legal personality except for the joint venture.

Foreign enterprises wishing to establish a branch or to carry out work in Syria must register with the Foreign Companies Department of the Ministry of Foreign Trade. The participation of foreign entities may not exceed 49 percent of invested capital. As a limiting measure, foreign companies and individuals of non-Arab origin may not own real property, but may only rent facilities in order to meet their commercial and residential needs, unless the government issues a decree permitting a particular foreign company to own real property.

## Shareholding Companies

A non-Syrian company may establish a shareholding company in Syria provided that: (1) the majority of shareholders are Syrian nationals; (2) the Ministry of Economy and Foreign Trade authorizes the venture; and (3) there is a minimum capital investment of SP 50,000.

Shareholding companies must set aside 10 percent of their net profits annually, as a legal reserve that can be discontinued when its total reserves equal at least 50 percent of the share capital of the company. The legal reserves set aside may not exceed 25 percent of the company's net profits per year. Foreign nationals who are members of the board may not exceed the proportion of their relative shareholding participation in the company's capital. In addition, a majority of the members of the board must be Syrian nationals.

In public shareholding companies, at least two members of the board of directors are required to be representatives of the employees. Members of the board of directors are individually liable for any violation of laws, regulations or the terms of the company's articles of association. The board must convene once a month, in Syria, and at least one member more than half of the total number of board members must be present. Voting by proxy or by writing is not permitted. The board of directors must have full authority to deal with all matters pertaining to the company's normal conduct. A general assembly of shareholders is required to convene at least once a year.

## Limited Liability Company

In order to form a limited liability company, a copy of the company's constitution must be deposited at the Primary Civil Court within a month of establishment. Capital investment of not less than SP 25,000 is required. An application to register a limited liability company should also be submitted to the Ministry of Supply and Interior Trade (along with a copy of the Constitution) which, if it shall approve the application, shall issue a certificate of registration.

## Partnerships

Foreign individuals or corporate bodies are permitted to enter into a general or limited partnership provided a written agreement is signed by all partners, an application is submitted to the Ministry of Supply and Interior Trade and provided that the foreign entity is not a bank, insurance company, law or accounting firm.

## General Partnership

In a general partnership all partners are jointly liable to the full extent of their personal fortunes. A minimum of two partners is necessary to found a general partnership. At least one of the general partners' names must be included in the title of the company along with a description signifying it is a partnership.

## Limited Partnership

A limited partnership includes limited partners, who are liable only to the extent of their capital investment, in addition to a general partner or partners, who have unlimited liability. A foreign company or individual can be a partner in either type of partnership.

## Joint Ventures

There are few joint ventures between Syria and foreign firms. The largest are in the oil sector.

Due to special privileges and exemptions, which include tax and customs duty exemptions, relaxation of foreign currency controls and the easing of some bureaucratic restraints, joint ventures are considered to be very practical. In order to establish a joint venture, a law or legislative decree must be issued to approve the proposal. In order for a foreign business to set up a joint venture, it must first establish its presence in Syria in some other manner.

## Branch Offices

Companies wishing to establish a branch in Syria are required to submit a request to the Foreign Companies Department of the Ministry of Economy and Foreign Trade. Following authorization, registration of the company must be published in the Official Gazette. The general manager of a branch must be a Syrian national.

There are no special requirements for the financing of the branch, but the transfer of capital from the branch is restricted. Any amounts transferred must receive prior authorization from the Ministry of Economy.

## Commercial Agency

Generally, Syrian law does not require a foreign firm that wishes to do business in Syria to have an agent or a local distributor. Syrian businesses may order directly from abroad without seeking to establish an agent/distributor relationship.

Legislative Decree 151 of 1952 governs the licensing and registration of agents acting for foreign companies. The agent must apply for a license to the Ministry of Economy and Foreign Trade. In addition to providing the agents particulars as required in the application, a notarized, Arabic translation of the agency agreement between the agent and the foreign company must accompany the application. Agents may only be Syrian nationals or a company registered in Syria whose partners or shareholders are Syrian nationals.

## Currency and Banking

## Foreign Currency Control

Exchange control is carried out on behalf of the government by the Central Bank, which may authorize certain banks and agencies to deal in foreign exchange.

While the import of foreign currency by non-residents into Syria is not restricted, the exportation of Syrian currency abroad is, in most circumstances, prohibited. On leaving Syria, non-residents are only permitted to take out of Syria the amount of foreign currency that they declared as carrying upon entering Syria.

Non-residents employed in Syria are allowed to remit abroad in foreign currency 50 percent of their salary (including benefits) and 100 percent of their severance pay after paying Syrian income tax.

Non-resident companies registered and operating in Syria may open bank accounts in both foreign and Syrian currency. The source of such bank accounts must be currency transferred from abroad or Syrian earned currency, respectively. Only 50 percent of the net profits of foreign investment may be remitted abroad. Foreign funds of a capital nature require the approval of the Central Bank in order to be sent abroad. Furthermore, real property may not be owned by non-residents without prior approval from government authorities.

## Banking

The Syrians banking system is controlled entirely by the government, and no private or foreign bank may operate in Syria. There are five banks: the Commercial Bank of Syria, the Agricultural Cooperative Bank, the Industrial Bank, the Real Estate Bank, and the People's Credit Bank. Banking operations and the money supply is regulated by the Central Bank.

The Central Bank of Syria, Commercial Bank of Syria, Industrial Bank, Agricultural Cooperative Bank, Loan and Savings Bank, Real Estate Bank, the General Syrian Insurance Agency and the General Postal Savings Establishment, however, provide the usual services provided by banks elsewhere with the notable exception that the specialized sector banks listed are designed to provide services specifically for businesses dealing in a particular sector.

The services offered to non-resident companies by Syrian banks are generally limited to providing bank accounts in foreign and Syrian currency and bank guarantees; non-resident companies that obtain a bank guarantee based on their existing funds on account may, however, receive loans from Syrian banks in Syrian currency.

Interest rates in Syria are low (between 2 and 10 percent); in real terms, given the average yearly inflation rate, they are negative. The private sector can borrow at rates of 7 to 10 percent, but the government's priority is to lend to the public and mixed sector at favorable rates. Credit, therefore, is limited.

As the Syrian economy becomes more privatized and continues to grow, the high costs for finance available through the banks in Syria may become a burden on development. Nevertheless, presently there are no measures that will allow private banks.

Syria also does not have an organized capital, foreign exchange and financial market. The government is currently studying a number of proposals for the formation of a stock exchange for the benefit of firms operating under the new Investment Law but no decision has been taken.

Other projected reforms include scrapping Law No. 24, which prohibits Syrians from holding foreign currency but which is also contradicted by Law No. 10 which permits investors to deal in foreign currency.

## Intellectual Property

Patents and trademarks can be registered with the Patent and Trademark Office. Syria is a signatory to the Paris Convention for the Protection of Industrial Property and to the Madrid Agreement concerning the suppression of false statements of origin.

### *Patents*

Law No. 47 of 1946, amended by Legislative Decree No. 28 of 1980, provides that a patent is valid for a period of fifteen years from the date of application, but an extension of its validity is possible. Renewal fees must be paid every year for the first five years and then consecutively for each five year period thereafter. Working of a patent within two years of its grant is compulsory, and working of a patent within three years of filing the application is compulsory in order to claim priority.

### *Trademarks*

Protection for trademarks is provided under Legislative Decree No. 28 of 1980. It grants protection for ten years from the date of registration and is renewable for ten year periods thereafter. The international classification of goods and services is followed in Syria for trademark registrations. The use of trademarks in Syria is not compulsory for filing applications for registrations or for maintaining trademark registrations in force.

Trademark applications are examined initially to determine that the mark is not identical to or closely resembles previously registered trademarks covering the same goods or services. Thereafter, the applicant may be requested by the Boycott of Israel Office to provide a declaration regarding the Arab boycott of Israel. Failure to provide the boycott declaration will result in delay in registration. Once the file is complete and cleared, the Trademark Office registers the trademark immediately.

## Copyright

There is no official system of copyright protection in Syria. In the book industry, however, major political infringements do not appear to be a problem as most books are in Arabic and by Arab authors. There are some individual entrepreneurs who copy records, cassettes and videos for resale. These operations are not sanctioned by the Syrian government.

## Taxation

Syria's system of income tax is apportioned into three main income categories: (1) profits from an industrial, commercial, or non-commercial activity; (2) wages; and (3) income derived from movable capital assets.

Legislative Decree No. 85 of 1949 regulates income tax. It is subject to wide interpretation by tax officials and tax committees. The Tax Department administers Syria's tax laws and is supervised by the Ministry of Finance.

### Taxation of Companies

A business profits tax is charged on net profits derived from professional and industrial, commercial and non-commercial activities, as well as on net profits from all other activities not specifically subject to the wage tax, to the tax on income from personal property or to the real property tax. The business profits tax is levied on the profits of individuals as well as on the profits of corporate entities. Non residents are subject to the business profits tax on all profits arising from sources or activities in Syria.

The business profit tax is applied in progressive rates between 10 percent to 45 percent, depending on the amount of taxable income. Shareholding companies and industrial limited liability companies are taxed at a flat rate of 32 percent and 42 percent respectively.

Dividends are not subject to a withholding tax provided such dividends are paid from company profits. The company profits from which dividends are paid are taxed under the business profits tax unless specifically exempted.

## Taxation of Individuals

An individual is liable to the same taxes as a company on his business income, income from movable capital and real property. In addition to these taxes, individuals are also subject to a wage and salary tax. Income, taxable under the wage and salary tax, includes the basic salary, bonuses, overtime, allowances and foreign benefits. This income is taxed at progressive rates of 5 percent to 12.5 percent. Foreign employees working in Syria are subject to the same rules and rates as those applied to Syrian employees.

## Other Taxes

### Tax on Income from Movable Capital

Tax on income from movable capital applies to interest, royalties and foreign source dividends. Royalty payments are subject to this tax and payable by the recipient, unless the royalty payments would be subject to the tax on business profits for the recipient.

The tax is levied at a flat rate of 7.5 percent on such income received by a Syrian resident and at a rate of 15 percent on such income received by a non-resident, unless reduced by an applicable tax treaty.

### Real Property Tax

Real property gains are taxed at rates ranging from 17 percent to 60 percent. A property registration fee is due upon the registration of real estate, its sale, assignment or inheritance. The fee amounts to 10 percent of the value of the property, as estimated by the Ministry of Finance.

### Stamp Duty

A stamp duty is imposed on the documents relating to the formation of companies, contracts, deeds and a variety of other instruments and transactions in Syria. The stamp duty is charged at a fixed or proportional rates depending on the type of transaction and is levied at a rate of 0.624 percent on contracts signed in Syria.

### Treaties for the Prevention of Double Taxation

Syria has entered into tax treaties for the prevention of double taxation with Cyprus, Czechoslovakia, India and Romania. Under these treaties, business profits of a foreign company that is a resident of a signatory country, arising from its business conducted in Syria, are taxable in Syria, provided that such business is carried out by a permanent establishment of such company in Syria. Furthermore, Syria is also a party to the Agreement for the Avoidance of Double Taxation and Prevention of Tax Evasion between the States of the Arab Economic Union Council.

## Investment and Trade

### Investment Incentives
### Encouragement of Investment Law (Law No. 10)

The Encouragement of Investment Law, No. 10 of May 1991, was enacted to encourage investments in economic and social development projects, approved by the Supreme Council of Investment, which is composed of various government ministers. Applications for approval of projects must be filed with the relevant ministry that will forward them to the Council for approval.

Approved projects may then import all equipment and supplies needed, without limitation, in order to establish, develop or enlarge the project. Such importation is exempt from taxes, customs and any other duties. Nonetheless, taxes and duties are levied on all imported equipment that is used to operate the project on a continuing basis.

Depending on the type of project, certain tax exemptions are granted for periods ranging from five to seven years. Furthermore, all projects covered under Law No. 10 are exempt from Syrian foreign exchange control. After five years, the portion of foreign investment equal to the amount of shares held in such a project may be repatriated to the foreign investor, based on the actual value of the project. The amount transferred may not exceed the initial currency investment. Should circumstances that are beyond the control of the investors arise, repatriation may begin within the first six months of the project. Annual profits and interest earned, through the use of foreign capital, may be transferred abroad.

The Investment Law's main provisions are as follows:

- The project must correspond to the government's aim for the relevant sector;

- Import of production inputs such as machinery, equipment and vehicles is free of customs duty;
- Mixed-sector companies in which the Syrian government's stake is at least 25 percent or companies that export 50 percent of their products receive a seven year tax holiday;
- Private-sector companies receive tax incentives five years;
- Foreign exchange capital can be repatriated after five years, and, if the project fails through circumstances out of the investor's control, such capital can be repatriated after six months;
- Profits can be transferred freely;
- 50 percent of expatriate salaries and 100 percent of expatriate severance pay can be repatriated.

A 1996 decision by Syria's Supreme Council for Investment states that the expansion, modernization and development of projects under the 1991 Investment Law No. 10 will not receive any new tax benefits. Seven years after the law's implementation, it has not achieved its goal of attracting foreign investment. Businessmen complain that the law is irrelevant under current business conditions. Most foreign investment in Syria has come from expatriates or businessmen from Arab countries. Furthermore, many projects approved under this law were never executed because of marketing and other bureaucratic problems.

## Incentives for the Tourism Industry

Several laws provide incentives for the tourism industry and certain other industries. These incentives, under Decision 186, include a seven year exemption from all taxes on the operation of tourist establishments, an exemption from paying income tax on up to 50 percent of the profits, certain import and customs exemptions, and some exemptions allowing bank accounts to be maintained in foreign currency.

According to Decrees 46 and 162 and Law No. 36, investments in hotels, restaurants and approved tourism projects enjoy certain benefits which may include an exemption from tax for between five to seven years, for example, hotels, restaurants and entertainment areas having a deluxe or first class rating.

Imported building materials, furniture and installations for these tourism businesses are also exempt from customs duties if such imports are used in order to enable a hotel or restaurant to maintain its deluxe or first rate rating.

## Trade Regulations

Before 1990, Syrian policy was geared to substituting imports with domestically produced goods. The government, however, has eased regulations to the point that advance deposits for imports of food and industrial inputs have been abolished. The most significant change has been in financial transactions. According to statistics by the Syrian government, 95 percent of exported and imported goods are priced at the neighboring countries' rate, which has gradually replaced the alternative rates for different goods. Furthermore, exporters do not have to exchange their foreign exchange earnings with the Commercial Bank of Syria if they then want to finance imports. The 25 to 30 percent share in foreign export proceeds that must be exchanged at the commercial banks are now also subject to the neighboring exchange rate.

All documentary transactions for imports must be by a letter of credit opened at the Commercial Bank of Syria. Typically, the bank requires the importer to cover 100 percent of the transaction from his own resources offshore or from funds generated by exports. Syrian importers often use free-of-payment or 180-day-credit facilities clauses. In this case, the importer pays through his offshore bank either cash in advance or via L/C, and the bill of lading is then sent to the Commercial Bank of Syria. Alternatively, an importer may use foreign exchange earned from exports and deposited in the Central Bank of Syria.

## Free Trade Zones

Free trade zones have been established in Damascus, Aleppo, Tartus, Latakia, the Damascus international airport and in Adra. Article 6 of Decree 84 of 1972 encourages certain kinds of investments in free trade zones, authorizes the importation of foreign goods to these zones, and permits re-exportation that is not subject to the laws on foreign trade, customs duties or taxes. The Ministry of Economy and Foreign Trade may authorize the establishment of warehouses in a free trade zone.

Up to 20 percent of imports to such warehouses may be granted an exemption from the usual limitations imposed on imports into the Syrian market, provided they do not compete with local industries or with a state-run monopoly. Priority in establishing an operation in a free trade zone is given to industries that use components or raw materials produced in Syria, complement existing industries in Syria, satisfy a local demand or employ a large number of Syrian workers.

## Trade Agreements

A cooperation agreement has existed between Syria and the EU since 1977 that sets preferential tariffs for a wide range of agricultural produce as well as import ceilings for crude oil, petroleum products and cotton fabrics. These ceilings are above normal customs duties applicable to third countries. Syria is also included in the EU plan that allows industrial products to enter the EU market duty free. There are special regulations to the agreement, regarding technical and financial cooperation, which were renewed in 1991 and are now focused on supporting Syrian economic reform measures, especially in private sector development in agriculture, manufacturing, science and technology, as well as external trade.

Syria entered an agreement for Economic and Social Cooperation and Coordination with Lebanon in September 1993, which regulates the general framework of bilateral relations between the two countries in such areas as trade, movement of people and capital, residence, employment and transport. The sale of agricultural products in both countries is conducted by a joint Syrian-Lebanese marketing company. Other later concluded bilateral accords regulate water sharing in the Orontes river, labor relations (addressing the legalization of an estimated 500,000 or more Syrian workers in Lebanon), tourism and cultural relations.

Trade agreements with other countries, especially Arab countries specify products that can be traded in both directions under preferential terms. Such trade is often limited to specific transactions, such as the importation of equipment under a particular contract or tender. No formal trade relations exist with Israel, although illegal trade has become more prominent since the peace process began.

While the political sector is characteristically hesitant and reserved, the existing illegal trade indicates that the private sector seems interested in entering into trade and general business relations with Israel as soon as the political barriers will be removed.

## Customs

Customs duties can range from 1 percent to over 100 percent on certain items. Law No. 1 of 1980 created a Unified Tax on Imports which ranges from 6 percent for goods exempt from customs, and from 35 percent for goods subject to customs tariff, to more than 100 percent. Machinery and materials imported for new industrial investment, under certain circumstances, may, upon application to and approval from the government, be exempt from import duties.

The customs procedures require that goods imported be accompanied by invoices that list the producer of the goods and their country of origin in Arabic. The invoice must also include an Israeli boycott clause and, in some cases, a health declaration.

## Private Sector Investment

Until the 1990s, private sector involvement in industry was limited by a number of regulations. In the past decade, the relaxation of certain restrictions allowed the private sector to import parts, equipment and other industrial inputs. Currently, private sector involvement is significant in the textile, food, leather, paper, and chemicals sectors, while heavy industry remains state-dominated. The Syrian government, however, has started to open up these industries to private-sector investment as the public sector cannot meet rising demand. There are plans to open the country's first privately-run sugar factory, and a private Saudi-Syrian joint venture has plans to open a cement factory.

In agriculture, the private sector dominates approximately two-thirds of cultivable land, with state-farms and cooperatives accounting for the remainder.

## Public Sector Procurement

Public sector procurement in Syria is regulated by Decrees No. 195 of 1974 and No. 349 of 1980, which set forth regulations governing contracts and tenders for public establishments, companies and enterprises. The decrees impose a number of regulations requiring the buying entity to solicit bids by announcing requirements through the Daily Bulletin of Official Tenders. The announcement of tenders with deadlines of less than forty-five days is not uncommon, however, suggesting that in certain cases, the contest may have already been decided beforehand.

Foreign companies may bid directly or through the use of a duly-registered Syrian agent. Offers, accompanied by a bid bond of 5 percent of the offer value may be submitted. Before an L/C is obtained, the supplier must submit a 10 percent performance bond. The Commercial Bank of Syria requires that all bonds be issued according to the Syrian Official Text.


## Environmental Law

In 1979, Syria appointed a Minister of State for Environmental Affairs and has since continued to make much headway in developing the country's environmental institutional capabilities by creating a General Commission for Environmental Affairs (GCEA) under the direction of the Minister. This basic framework for environmental protection is constrained, however, by acute shortages in human, physical and financial resources.

In 1994, a World Bank project was instituted in Syria (Program Syria 21) to formulate an Environmental Action Plan with the participation of the GCEA in order to address the country's pressing environmental issues by the promotion and integration of environmental considerations in all development activities. Program 21 began its activities in mid-1995 and has since instituted certain changes to the decision-making process and a reform policy for seven river-basin projects.

Syria is a party to several international agreements for the protection of the environment, including the International Convention for Civil Liability for Oil Pollution Damage (and its amendments); the Convention on the Establishment of an International Fund for Compensation for Oil Pollution Damage; the International Convention Relating to Intervention on the High Seas in Cases of Oil Pollution Casualties; the Convention for the Protection of the Mediterranean Sea against Pollution; the Agreement for the Establishment of a General Fisheries Council for the Mediterranean (as amended); the Convention concerning the Protection of Workers against Ionizing Radiation; the Treaty banning Nuclear Weapon Tests in the Atmo-

sphere, in Outer Space and Underwater; the Agreement for the Establishment of a Commission for Controlling the Desert Locust in the Near East;
the Convention concerning Protection against Hazards of Poisoning arising
from Benzene and the Convention for the Protection of the World Cultural
and Natural Heritage.

# TUNISIA

## Recent Political Developments

On October 24, 1999, more than 90 percent of Tunisia's eligible voters voted for the incumbent president, Zine al-Abidine Ben Ali. This is the 62-year-old leader's third 5-year term. This was also the first time in Tunisia's 43-year history that opposition candidates were allowed to challenge the president.

Still, human rights groups said that despite the government's declared commitment to political pluralism and press freedom, the gap between rhetoric and substantive action remains wide. When Ben Ali recently promised greater political liberalization, many still questioned whether there will in fact be any modification in the tough measures used to restrain Islamists, trade unionists and human rights activists.

Following the election, Ben Ali backed up his election promises of economic reform and growth by reshuffling his cabinet and appointing the economist Mohamed Ghannouchi as the state's new prime minister.

In general, Tunisia is considered safe from an Islamic fundamentalist take-over. The thirty-one year rule of Tunisian President Habib Bourghiba (1956-87) left the country relatively free of bureaucratic corruption and steered it clear of the same command economy structure that decimated Algeria.

| Profile | |
|---|---|
| Population | 10.02 million (1992) |
| Religions | Over 99% Moslem with a very small indigenous Jewish community |
| Government | Republic with an elected parliament |
| Languages | Arabic, French |
| Work Week | Private Sector: Monday–Friday Banking: Monday–Saturday |
| Monetary Unit | Tunisian Dinar (TD) |
| Exchange Rate | TD 1.18=$US 1 |

## Recent Economic Developments

Tunisia, the Maghreb's smallest country, has one of the region's healthiest economies. Since 1997, the country's GDP has expanded by about 5.6 percent annually, an outstanding rate compared to its neighbors. Inflation has been held below 4.0 percent.

One of the main strengths of the economy is its diversity. The service sector (primarily tourism) comprises roughly 34 percent of GDP, manufacturing industries, 17.8 percent, agriculture, 11 percent, and non-manufacturing industries, primarily phosphate mining and hydrocarbons, which contribute about 4.5 percent of GDP.

Tourism and textile production are the two sectors earning the highest revenue. The latter totals about $800 million and comprises roughly 33 percent of the manufacturing sector.

The country has recently entered into a Free Trade Accord with the EU under which it will remove tariff and other trade barriers on most non-agricultural goods, services and capital by 2008.

The road to this country's economic success began in 1986 when the country turned from its socialist past and sought guidance from the IMF and World Bank.

Tunisia simplified its tax system and reduced tax rates, with a fixed maximum rate of 35 percent for businesses. Banking and financial sectors were partly liberalized and restructured. Some public companies were privatized and foreign trade and domestic prices de-controlled. As of 1997, 87 percent of prices were deregulated at the production level and 85 percent at the distribution level. Also, 97 percent of imports no longer require prior licensing. Maximum tariff rates on a broad range of imports, however, rose from 43 to 287 percent in July 1996.

All of these measures have made their impression felt on the population. According to Tunisian government statistics, more than 60 percent of the population is middle class. Only 6.7 percent falls below the poverty threshold. The national savings rate is 23 percent and 79 percent of Tunisians own their own homes. Over 85 percent of Tunisian homes are connected to the electrical grid, and 70 percent have potable water.

In July 1999, the IMF predicted that Tunisia's GDP would have real growth of 6.5 percent with inflation holding at 3 percent. Its economy was helped by good harvests and a large diversion of Mediterranean tourists to Tunisia because of the war in the Balkan and security concerns in Turkey.

Tourism is crucial to the country's economy. During the first 9 months of 1999, the number of arriving tourists rose 16.7 percent to 4.63 million and the level of European tourists increased by 16.1 percent. This is significant because tourism is the country's main source of foreign exchange revenues. Through November1999, the country's foreign exchange earnings from tourism totaled TD 1.82 billion, which is greater than all of 1998's figures of TD 1.71 billion.

The country's current account deficit is projected to reach 3.7 percent of GDP compared with 3.4 percent in 1998. Fiscal revenues increased by 0.5 percent of GDP despite a removal of trade tariffs. Debt service declined by 0.4 percent of GDP and privatization receipts rose to 1.8 percent of GDP in 1998.

Tunisia's trade volume with its African and Arab neighbors increased 6.5 percent in 1998 to TD 1.042 billion. Its trade deficit with these countries was TD 56.8 million down from 129.8 million in 1997. Exports to sub-Sahara Africa jumped by 27 percent and recorded an 11.5 percent increase with Gulf countries.

Investment intentions in Tunisia's industry sector in 1998 rose 15.9 percent to TD 1.166 billion ($988.1 million) from TD 1.006 billion. This leap was spurred primarily by increased investment in the building sector which rose 64.4 percent to TD 193 million from TD 117 million and in the mechanical and electrical sector which leaped 59.3 percent to TD 170 million.

Intentions of investment in the chemical sector declined 21.2 percent to TD 97 million from TD 123 million. Intentions of investment with the participation of foreigners totaled TD 383 million, down 13.7 percent from TD 444 million. Intentions of investment in services were down 50.3 percent to TD 291 million from TD 584 million.

The country, which is a World Trade Organization member, is most interested in foreign investment that boosts export earnings, attracts technology, creates rather than cuts jobs and minimally competes with domestic industry.

Unemployment is one of the country's most serious problems at more than 25 percent. President Ben Ali called job creation "the priority of priorities." By January 2000, the "National Employment Fund" may start its activities. This program was announced last October and is part of a multi-initiative to develop employment opportunities.

The government has also launched the "mise à niveau" program, which was designed to raise productivity of Tunisian business during the next 10 years to allow them to be able to better compete on the global level. This will take on added importance when the service sector is opened to foreign competition in 2001 under WTO and EU FTA agreements. The other goal of the "mise à niveau" program is to improve the country's infrastructure, communications and other trade-and-investment related capabilities.

The European Investment Bank (EIB) is helping in this endeavor, lending its North African neighbor 83.1 million Euros to finance public and private sector projects. Besides this, the government issued in August 1999 its first Eurobond, raising 225 million Euros.

## Government Role in the Economy

The government has been slowly stepping back from the economy and encouraging the private sector to assume a greater role. Still, the government's role in the economy is greater than that of other countries at comparable levels of development.

While the government has had a cautious privatization program, it does face some important obstacles such as fears of mass firing in massive layoffs in unprofitable and overstaffed public companies.

The government of Tunisia has been methodically reducing its role in the economy. Although the privatization program is supported by the National Labor Federation (UGTT), the government is moving carefully to avoid mass firings in unprofitable public companies.

The government is focusing on the stock market as the principal vehicle for the privatization program. Specific targets are companies operating in competitive sectors.

The most dramatic re-orientation has occurred in the financial and banking sectors. The Central Bank is gradually shifting to a supervisory and regulatory role. Interest rates were officially deregulated and commercial banks allowed to move into the long term credit market. The government made

## Economic Indicators

| | 2000 | 1999 | 1998 | 1997 |
|---|---|---|---|---|
| GDP Growth (percent) | 6.0(T) | 6.2 | 5.0 | 5.4 |
| Exports (TDbn) | | 6.370* | 6,532 | 6,148 |
| Imports (TDbn) | | 9.182* | 9,476 | 8,794 |
| Inflation | | 2.7 | 3.1 | 3.7 |
| Tourism Earnings (TD bn) | | 1.82* | 1.71 | 1.55 |
| Remittances (in cash and TD mn) | | 683* | 654 | 616 |
| Foreign Direct Investment (including energy) (TD mn) | | 277.5** | 760 | 406 |
| Current Account Balance (TD mn) | | −222.8 | −769 | −655 |
| Unemployment*** | | | 15.2 | 15.4 |
| Expenditure (budgeted TD bn) | 10.510 | 9.590 | 8.726 | |
| Revenues (budgeted TD bn) | 6.580 | 6.185 | 5.175 | |
| Government Net Deficit (excluding debt amortization) (budgeted TD bn) | −0.750 (T) | 0.910 (E) | | |
| Deficit as % GDP | 2.7 (T) | 3.6 (E) | | |

(T) = target
(E) = estimate
*Through November 1999
**Through September 1999
***Provisional

the Tunisian Dinar convertible for current account transactions, and currency trading was privatized.

In the financial markets, the former state-controlled stock exchange, the Bourse, was privatized. The new structure is composed of brokerage houses. Similarly, a privately held central stock clearing house company was established. The state will continue to exercise its supervisory and regulatory role through the Financial Market Council.

## Reforms Policy

Tunisia, under the influence of president Ben Ali, has implemented an International Monetary Fund-style economic stabilization program, highlighted by rigorous budget balancing, foreign trade liberalization and private sector incentives. Consequently, economic growth rates have surged.

Most of this capital came from European Union investors who were encouraged by Tunisia's proximity to southern Mediterranean markets, relatively low cost labor force and enhanced fiscal transparency.

If there are any gathering storm clouds on the Tunisian horizon, they are probably in the area of nascent privatization, where turf conscious Tunisian bureaucrats frequently erect obstacles for local businessmen. Barriers, however, are slowly falling (particularly in the area of agriculture), and all signs now point towards considerably higher levels of both local and foreign investment and sustainable overall economic growth.

## Business Environment

### Privatization

In 1999, the government increased to 152 the number of major privatization projects planned for the coming years. The sale of these enterprises are expected to yield revenues of more than TD 7.645 billion (roughly $6.37 billion). The government is also planning to publish lists of those firms to be sold as a way of attracting more foreign investors.

In 1998, money raised from the sale of two cement factories was enough for the government to cover its foreign exchange needs for the year. In total, the government sold 20 state-owned enterprises in 1998.

Germany's Siemens Ag and India's KEC International won two separate contracts to install a 225-kV grid link between Tunisia and Libya. The connection is planned to be completed by the first quarter of 2001, and it will complete a larger Mediterranean grid linking Egypt, Libya, Tunisia, Algeria, Morocco, Spain and Italy.

A Swedish consulting firm was hired by the government to propose a restructuring plan for the railway sector and the refocusing of the activities of the state-owned rail company SNCFT.

### Stock Exchange

The Tunis Stock exchange is a 34-share capitalization-weighted index. Trade on the exchange is fully electronic and conducted among authorized brokerage houses while remaining under the supervision of the staterun Financial Market Council.

The Tunis Stock Exchange was established in 1969. Tunisian companies on the stock exchange are required to publish semi-annual corporate reports audited by a certified public accountant. Due to a decree issued in 1995, it is easier today for foreigners to purchase shares in Tunisian companies. Foreigners can buy up to 10 percent of a company's shares on the Tunis Stock Exchange and up to 30 percent of a private company without central bank approval.

The Tunisian stock exchange is also playing a role in the country's search for development capital, though up until now foreign interest has been relatively low, largely because of small trading volumes and related fears of insider manipulation.

## Major Projects

In June 1998, the government negotiated a build-own-operate contract for a 470 MW combined cycle electrical power plant. The country's power demand is expected to grow at 7 percent a year. The state electricity and gas utility is planning to add 100–300 MW every two years beginning in 2001.

The country is also planning build-operate-transfer contracts to build a series of major highways. The first will be 60-kilometer Tunis-Bizerte link. The Tunis-Bousalem will be 140 kilometers and the M'saken-Gabes, 250 kilometers.

Finally, the country is planning to spend $2 billion to $3 billion during the next 5 to 10 years on environmental programs, such as landfill construction and wastewater treatment.

Bouygues has won construction projects for the Tunis City of Science, a science and technology institute, and various housing projects throughout Tunis. The company also won a contract to complete the proposed Tunis headquarters of the Arab League, unfinished since the league moved back to Cairo, which is now slated to become the Tunisian broadcasting center.

## Franchising

The first major fast food chain to open a store came to Tunis in 1994. But in 1996, the government opposed franchise agreements with foreign companies and blocked projects underway. There is growing interest in franchising and many Tunisian entrepreneurs are seeking contacts with foreign franchisers.

## Best Business Prospects

| Rank | Sector |
|------|--------|
| 1 | Electrical Power Systems |
| 2 | Telecommunications Equipment |
| 3 | Construction & Engineering Services |
| 4 | Pollution Control Equipment & Services |

# Legal Review

Tunisia is a Civil Law Republic, founded upon a constitution that embodies the principles of sovereignty of the people and separation of powers between the branches of government. The Republic is divided into twenty-three regions, each of which has its own local government and is competent to conduct and manage local affairs.

## Judiciary

Judicial powers are vested in the Court of Justice (Court de Cassation). The judicial branch of government has criminal, administrative and civil systems.

### Civil Court System

The civil court system is divided into four levels; the District Courts, Courts of First Instance, Appeal Courts, and the Supreme Court.

### District Courts

District Courts have jurisdiction to hear matters the value of which does not exceed TD 7,000 as well as matters relating to nationality and labor issues. A single judge hears cases in the District Courts. Appeal of a judgment from a District Court is made to the Courts of First Instance.

## Courts of First Instance

A Court of First Instance is located in each of Tunisia's twenty-three regions in Tunisia. The Courts of First Instance are vested with the power to hear all civil and commercial matters without regard to the monetary value of the claim, including divorces and applications for immediate relief in urgent matters. The Courts of First Instance also hear appeals of decisions from the District Courts. Each Court of First Instance is composed of a panel of three judges.

Cases which began in by the Courts of First Instance, may be appealed to the Appeal Courts. Appeals of District Court judgments decided by Courts of First Instance may not be appealed to the Appeal Courts, but, rather, relief may be sought from the Supreme Court.

## Appeals Courts

The Appeals Courts have jurisdiction to hear appeals of decisions rendered by the Courts of First Instance except where the decision was an appeal from a decision of a District Court. The Appeal Courts cover several regions, and, therefore, cases from several Courts of First Instance are heard by the same Appeals Court.

## Supreme Court

The Tunisian Supreme Court examines decisions appealed from either the Appeals Court or from the Courts of First Instance sitting in its appellate capacity to determine whether the law was correctly applied by the lower court. The Supreme Court does not examine the substantive aspects of the case on appeal, and only points of law may be appealed to it. Submitting a matter to the review of the Supreme Court does not automatically stay execution of the original judgment. A stay of execution may be granted by the First President of the Supreme Court; the applicant making the motion for such a stay must deposit a bond with the court to secure the judgment.

In the event that the Supreme Court voids a lower court judgment, the matter is resubmitted to another judge or panel of judges of the court which rendered the original judgment. For example, a voided judgment from the Appeals Court covering several regions would be resubmitted to an Appeals Court covering a different area. In the event that the court, on rehearing the matter, fails to comply with the ruling of the Supreme Court regarding the application of law, the matter is heard by the full panel of the Supreme Court whose decision on the case is binding.

## Criminal Court System

The criminal court system is very similar in structure to the civil court system. Misdemeanor offenses are handled by the District Courts, while all other criminal offenses, except felonies, are submitted to the Courts of First Instance for determination. Felony crimes are submitted to the criminal courts division of the Appeal Courts after an indictment has been issued by a judge based on the findings of the grand jury (*Chambre des Mises en Accusation*).

## Administrative Court System

The administrative court system is responsible for resolving disputes between individuals and the government and any governmental subdivision or agency.

**Business Forms**

## Companies Law

The commercial law of Tunisia recognizes two types of companies; share companies and companies of persons (partnerships). Foreigners are permitted to hold shares in Tunisian companies without restriction. In companies organized for the purpose of certain commercial and service activities, however, permission of the Higher Investment Board is required in order for foreign investment to exceed 49 percent. Transfers of shares representing in excess of 10 percent of the voting rights in such a company requires a separate approval.

## Share Companies

Share Companies may be established as either a joint stock company or a limited liability company.

## Joint Stock Companies

Joint stock companies may be established with a minimum of seven shareholders. The minimum nominal value per share in a joint stock company is TD 5. The board of directors of a joint stock company is comprised of between three to twelve directors. The directors appoint the chairman and general manager of the company.

While foreigners may serve as directors of joint stock companies without any limitation, officers of the company are subject to Tunisian labor law which gives preference to Tunisian nationals. Foreign ownership in businesses which engage in certain fields is restricted by decree to no more than 49 percent of the share capital unless special permission is obtained from the Higher Investment Board.

In existing companies, transfers of shares representing more than 10 percent of the voting rights require approval.

Joint stock companies are used primarily to conduct investment operations and activities. From the perspective of the availability of financing, banks prefer the financing arrangements available to joint stock companies.

## Limited Liability Companies

Limited liability companies may be established with a minimum of two shareholders. The shareholders appoint a manager who is endowed with all the powers of the company with regard to and toward third parties, even if the shareholders of the company have taken measures to limit the powers granted to the manager. For this reason, limited liability companies are used primarily for small projects and family businesses. All shares must be nominative and bearer shares are allowed only with the permission of the Ministry of Finance.

## Foreign Companies

A foreign company may establish and register a branch in Tunisia by obtaining a Merchant Card from the Ministry of Trade. The process for obtaining a Merchant Card and registering in Tunisia is significantly easier for foreign companies which have engaged in a contractual relationship with a Tunisian company.

A copy of the contract with the Tunisian company, the incorporation documents of the foreign company and all records and board decisions of the foreign company relating to the creation of the foreign branch must be submitted along with the application for registration to the Ministry of Trade.

In 1996, legislation authorizing the creation of International Trade Companies (ITC) was adopted. An ITC is a non-resident company in which the share capital is held by Tunisian or non-Tunisian residents where at least 66 percent of such share capital is paid through convertible foreign currency, An ITC may engage wholly in export, and 80 percent of its turnover must originate from exportation.

## Partnerships

Under Tunisian law, partnerships, or a company of persons, may be formed. The unlimited liability of the persons forming such a partnership or company of persons for its obligations is a deterrent to using this corporate form.

## Commercial Agency

Foreign companies wishing to effect business in Tunisia without establishing a corporate entity in Tunisia must appoint a Tunisian citizen to act as their agent. Agency and representation activities are reserved to Tunisian citizens under the applicable law. An agent wishing to act for a foreign company must conclude a contract with the foreign principal and then apply to the Ministry of Trade for authorization. While the terms of an agency contract are freely negotiable, the contract may not provide for exclusivity.

## Currency and Banking

### Foreign Currency Control

Foreign exchange controls in Tunisia are regulated by the Foreign Trade and Foreign Exchange Code of 1976. The government has undertaken a review of the Code and is in the process of instituting liberalization changes. The Tunisian Dinar is not fully convertible to foreign currencies, however, in recent years, Tunisia has relaxed foreign exchange control provisions regarding current account transactions. A currency account transaction law was enacted in 1993 which incorporates liberalizing provisions in this regard. Today the Tunisian Dinar is commercially convertible for all *bona fide* trade and investment operations. Foreign investors in Tunisian companies are entitled to repatriation capital and may receive dividends in foreign currency.

In the area of importation of goods, all import documents which involve payments must be handled through authorized banks. Foreign currency may be purchased from the Central Bank of Tunisia (CBT) or from banks which have been designated by the CBT for the payment of imports, subject to licensing restrictions and provided that the license has been obtained prior to importation. Payments for exports received in foreign currency ordinarily must be repatriated within ten days of payment.

Capital transfers are subject to the approval of the CBT. Non-residents are allowed to repatriate invested capital and net proceeds of such investment in foreign currency.

## Banking

The CBT monitors the commercial, development and investment banks operating in Tunisia. The commercial banks provide short and mid-term credit. Development banks grant only long-term credit for the financing of large scale projects in tourism, agriculture and industry. Investment banks, which were recently created, are responsible for promoting investment projects and managing capital risks.

New legislation enacted in 1994 is aimed at broadening the range of banking services and products available, easing restrictions regarding loan approvals, and increasing competition in the banking industry. These new laws also created a new type of banking category which specializes in providing financial management banking services for business enterprises.

## Intellectual Property

Tunisia is a signatory of the Paris Convention for the Protection of Industrial Property and the Paris Convention Regarding Trademarks, as revised in the Hague, London and Stockholm. Tunisia is a member of the World Intellectual Property Organization and is a signatory of the UNCTAD agreement on the protection of patent and trademarks. Tunisia has withdrawn from the Madrid Agreement regarding trademarks.

## Patents

Patent applications are examined by the Patent Office only with regard to form and, while novelty of an invention is examined, merit is not. A patent application, together with the grant of a patent are published in the Official Gazette. Opposition to a patent application must be filed within two months of the date when the application was filed. Applications for the issue of letters patent should be made before the invention has been published, used or otherwise received sufficient publicity to allow it to be put into practice.

The protection period of a patented invention is twenty years from the date on which the patent application was filed. Working of a patent is an official requirement, and must be done for two consecutive years, starting within three years of the date on which the patent application was filed or two years from the date on which the patent was granted. Nominal working of a patent, by way of direct offer or solicitation, is sufficient to meet the standards.

Rights in a patent may be transferred or assigned to third parties, including, by the laws of succession, to heirs.

## Designs and Industrial Models

Designs and industrial models may be protected through registration. There is no novelty examination conducted regarding the application for registration of a design or industrial model. Any interested party who has filed an application with regard to the same or similar design or model may file a request for cancellation of the infringing design or model before a competent tribunal.

A design or industrial model registration is granted for five, ten or fifteen years, beginning on the date the application for registration was filed. The registration of a design or industrial model, as well as its cancellation or assignment, are published in the Official Gazette and entered into the designs register. There are no provisions regarding the compulsory working or licensing of a design or industrial model.

## Copyright

The Tunisian Copyright Law of 1994 determined the Copyright as the right of the owner of the work to have the exclusive right to copy the work in a material form, whatever its type is, and to present his work to the public. The protected work may be it literary, scientific or artistic, whatever its value or the purpose for which it is prepared.

According to Article 18 of the Law, the copyright shall be valid during the author's lifetime and shall continue for fifty calendar years after the author's death. The copyright with respect to photographic works is valid, according to Article 19, for twenty-five calendar years as from the date of work completion. The copyrights assignable by sale, wholly or partially, according to Article 22.

The Law establishes the Tunisian Institution for the Protection of Copyright. The Institution has several functions, including the protection of copyright.

Any party which does not respect copyright as defined by the law, shall be obligated to pay damages to the owner of this right. The law also establishes monetary sanctions for violations or infringements. A person who violates the law may be obliged to pay fines ranging from TD 500 to 5,000.

## Trademarks

As a result of Tunisia's withdrawal from the Madrid Agreement with regard to trademarks, in 1988, trademark applications thereafter should be filed in Tunisia by anyone interested to protect a trademark right in order to secure his interests and to be availed of the protections under the laws of Tunisia.

Registration is a necessary element to gain protection and is ordinarily issued directly upon filing an application for registration. A trademark registration is valid for fifteen years from the date on which the application for registration was filed. It may be renewed indefinitely for similar periods of time. Tunisia does not require use of a trademark as a condition for maintaining registration.

Tunisia follows the International Classification of goods and services.

## Taxation

The Tunisian tax system was entirely revised in 1990 and is contained in the Income Tax Act of 1989. The new tax laws include two direct tax regimes: income tax and corporate tax. The value added tax is an important indirect tax revenue regime. It should be noted that the tax laws should be considered in conjunction with the tax incentives available to investors and businesses (see, the Investment Incentives section below), in order to understand the tax system and a taxpayer's tax liability in Tunisia.

### *Income Tax*

Income tax is imposed on individuals based on income, including a partner's share of profits in partnerships and profits derived by members of a joint venture. The marginal tax rates are:

| Income in TD | Tax Rate |
|---|---|
| 0–1,500 | 0% |
| 1,501–5,000 | 15% |
| 5,001–10,000 | 20% |
| 10,001–20,000 | 25% |
| 20,001–50,000 | 30% |
| Over 50,000 | 35% |

Individuals, like companies, are subject to Tunisian income tax only on income arising in Tunisia. The tax law deems all income of a Tunisian, regardless of where his work was performed and where the income was paid, to have arisen in Tunisia. As a result, a Tunisian resident individual is subject to the Tunisian income tax on his worldwide employment income.

Dividends paid by companies to shareholders are not taxed, and investments made in certain companies may be tax-deductible.

A non-resident is subject to the Tunisian income tax at the normal graduated rates on income received in consequence of employment by a local employer (whether a resident employer or a Tunisian permanent establishment of a non-resident employer) as well as to the various flat rate withholding taxes.

## Corporate Tax

Companies are subject to a flat tax rate of 35 percent on net profits. Profits generated from exports are deductible from taxable profits. Foreigners are exempted from taxes on transfer of dividends, the proceeds from the sale of shares and capital gains. Thus, dividends distributed by a company are not subject to tax. Furthermore, investments made by a company in an entity which enjoys tax incentives are deductible from taxable income, up to 35 percent of the investing company's taxable income. Since 1994, remuneration paid by a company to its directors is taxed.

## Indirect Taxes

Value added tax was introduced in Tunisia in 1988 to replace the turnover tax levied on production, consumption and services. Ordinarily VAT is levied at 18 percent; certain priority goods are, however, subject to a lower rate of 10 percent, and certain luxury goods are subject to a rate of 29 percent.

Employers and their employees are subject to a social security tax. In addition, various employees must pay a flat rate professional training tax on salaries paid to employees at the rate of 1 percent in the manufacturing industry and 2 percent in all other industries.

Another indirect tax levied in Tunisia is a land registration tax. This tax is levied at a rate of 5 percent of the value of real property acquired.

## Treaties for the Prevention of Double Taxation

Relief from double taxation is available through tax treaties to which Tunisia is a signatory. Tunisia has entered into tax treaties with most Arab countries, European Union countries, the United States, Canada and some East European countries such as Romania, Bulgaria and Slovakia. Also, Tunisia has entered into a treaty with the United States, according to which Tunisian students who study in the United States, full-time or for specialized training, are exempt for not longer than five years from paying US income tax on some amounts such as payments from abroad made in respect of their studies, or as grants or allowances.

## Investment Incentives and Trade

### Investment Incentives

Tunisia has enacted several laws to encourage foreign investment in the industrial, agricultural and tourism sectors. Legislation promoting foreign investment in the service sector has been drafted and may be adopted by the Government.

Foreign investors wishing to invest in these sectors under the enabling legislation may do so through the form of a partnership (Association of Person) or as either a public or private company (Association of Capital).

In order to promote economic growth, narrow existing trade imbalances and increase exports, Tunisia offers extensive investment incentives. These incentives have been available since the 1970s. The Investment Incentives Code, which became effective in January 1994, promotes these goals. The Investment Incentives Code offers two types of incentives. The first kind of investment incentives is applied to all investment projects, except projects relating to mining, energy and finance. The second kind of investment incentives is reserved for projects engaged in specified fields or projects of a special nature.

All investment projects, except projects relating to mining, energy and finance are entitled to the following investment incentives:

- A deduction from taxable income, of up to 35 percent of net income or profits, for income or profits reinvested in share capital or invested in capital increase;
- A suspension of VAT and sales tax on locally produced equipment;
- A reduction of 10 percent from customs duties and the suspension of VAT and sales taxes on imported equipment for which there is no Tunisian manufactured substitute;
- An option to apply an installment method of depreciation for production plants and equipment, excluding office equipment, having a life expectancy of more than seven years.

The second kind of investment incentives is available to investment projects in the field of exporting (whether in whole or in part), regional development projects, or projects engaged in agriculture, environmental protection, research and development and new small enterprises. The investment incentives are substantial and vary depending on the field in which the enterprise engages and the industry concerned. A brief overview of some of the incentives available follows:

- A full deduction of income or profits from taxable income or corporate taxable income for a period of ten years, and a reduction of up to 50 percent beginning in the eleventh year;
- A full tax allowance in respect of profits reinvested in share capital or in the increase of the company's registered share capital;
- A full tax allowance in respect of profits reinvested in the company;
- Financial support for amounts paid for social security levies;
- Investment bonuses equal to 8 percent of the cost of the investment made;
- The option to elect a flat-tax rate of 20 percent of gross earnings.

In addition to the incentives available under the Investment Incentives Code, non-residents enjoy the tax-free transfer of capital invested in the investment project and the profits arising as a result thereof. Also, non-residents may freely repatriate their profits and capital upon the sale of their holdings in such investment projects.

The High Commission for Investments is authorized to grant further incentives to investment projects deemed to be of special or significant importance. Such benefits may take the form of exemptions from income tax or corporate tax for a period up to five years, state funded contributions to the costs of infrastructure development, an investment bonus of up to 5 percent of the total investment in the project or the suspension of tariffs and taxes levied on equipment.

## Trade Agreements

Tunisia prides itself on maintaining preferential trading-partner relations with African, Arab and Mediterranean nations. Tunisia has entered into trade agreements with forty-one developed and developing countries, which granted Tunisia most-favored-nation status. Tunisia has entered into bilateral and regional trade preference agreements with the European Union and the Arab Maghreb Union as well as certain agreements under the framework of the Inter-Arab Cooperation, the Inter-African Cooperation and the

Organization of the Islamic Conference. Furthermore, Tunisia is a member of the world trade organization (WTO) and is a signatory to the Global System on Trade Preferences.

In 1995, the Tunisian government and the European Union negotiated a major economic agreement on free trade. The pact establishes the framework for free trade between Tunisia and the European Union. The agreement, which came into effect in 1997, has a twelve year phase-in period.

## Free Trade Zones

Over 130 companies have submitted requests to invest in Tunisia's two free trade zones. Sixty companies, of which fifty are foreign, made requests to operate in the Bizerte Harbor Free Trade Zone, located sixty kilometers north of Tunis. Most of these companies are French, but requests have also come from American, German, British, Danish, Belgian, Japanese, Indonesian and Egyptian companies. These foreign companies are seeking to invest in the electronics, metals, pharmaceuticals and food industries.

The second free trade zone, in Zarzis Harbor, is 450 kilometers south of Tunis, near the Libyan border. Over seventy foreign companies have already submitted requests to invest in this zone, most of them French. The Zarzis zone spans over 380,000 square meters. Twenty million dollars have been invested to establish this zone, part of which will be utilized to expand the harbor facilities at Zarzis. The harbor is currently used to import oil from Libya, among other activities.

## Customs

Since March 1994 and the enactment of Law No. 94-41, which embodies the policy of the free trade principle adopted in other liberalization measures, Tunisia has allowed the free importation and exportation of goods, with the exception of restrictions relating to national security, public order, health and hygiene and the protection of flora, fauna and natural heritage.

Tunisia's basic tariff rate ranges from 10 percent to 43 percent. In addition, several years ago Tunisia imposed a temporary supplemental duty on certain imports that compete with locally produced goods. This duty was originally scheduled to be phased out at the end of 1994, but remains in effect.

## Labor Law

Employment relations in Tunisia are governed by the Labor Code of 1956. Labor contracts may be for a definite or an indefinite period of time. A definite period contract may specify that it is valid for either a limited period of time or for a specific task. If the parties continue such a contract after the agreed expiration date, then it becomes a contract for an indefinite period.

A labor contract may be terminated by agreement of the contracting parties or as a result of resignation or dismissal of the employee. In the latter case, the employee is entitled to severance pay. The Labor Code sets standards regarding other employment conditions, such as the maximum number of work hours per week, the minimum wage level, overtime work rate and annual leave. Regional labor inspectors are responsible for the enforcement of such regulations. Worker health and safety standards are regulated and enforced by the Social Affairs Ministry.

### Foreign Labor

The law providing incentives to foreign investors has granted wide employment facilities for expatriate personnel. For instance, foreign managers acting in their capacity as employers are not required to hold a work contract, and their company or enterprise may, with a simple declaration to the appropriate authorities, hire up to four expatriate technicians who may choose either a foreign social security system or the Tunisian system to which they must contribute a fixed amount set at 20 percent of their gross income.

Social security payments in respect of Tunisian employees are paid by the employer who contributes 20 percent of the employee's wage to the system and deducts 6.25 percent from the employee's wages for this purpose to be paid on the employee's behalf.

### Trade Unions

The right of workers to form unions is secured in the Tunisian Constitution and in the Labor Code. The right of unions to strike is conditional upon the fulfillment of certain conditions, such as giving ten days advance notice and receiving the approval of the Central Labor Federation.

Tunisian law protects the right to organize and to bargain collectively. Working conditions (such as wages) are fixed through the negotiation of approximately forty-five collective bargaining agreements, which determined standards applicable to entire economic sectors.

The government must confirm the collective bargaining agreements, though it cannot modify them. After government confirmation, the agreements are published in the official journal, a mandatory condition for the legal validity of the agreements.

## Environmental Law

Although Tunisia has enacted several laws pertaining to environmental protection, enforcement of environmental legislation has not been consistent until recently, due both to the lack of staff and resources. In addition, the legal instruments available in the past were not highly effective.

The creation of the National Environmental Protection Agency (ANPE) in 1988, however, led to the development of a National Action Plan for the Environment (NAPE), which attempts to draw together existing environmental legislation and programs and to provide a strategy for natural resource conservation, pollution control and land-use management. To that end, article 8 of Air Pollution and Noise Emissions Law No. 88-91 dictates that any industrial, agricultural or commercial establishment as well as any individual or corporate entity carrying out activity that may cause pollution to the environment, is obliged to eliminate or to reduce discharges and, eventually, to recycle rejected matter. The ANPE may initiate legal proceedings against violators or reach a compromise with the polluting entity.

Legislation pertaining to environmental protection includes the Wildlife Protection Law No. 88-20; the Water Pollution Law No. 75-16; and the Marine Pollution Law No. 75-16.

In addition, Tunisia is a member of ISO. In June, 1997, the Technical Committee for the Elaboration of Standards adopted the ISO 14,000 Series relating to industrial atmospheric emission standards.

Tunisia has entered into several international conventions and agreements dealing with environmental problems and aspects, including:

- Convention of the Prohibition of the Development, Production and Stockpiling of Bacteriological (Biological) and Toxin Weapons, and on Their Destruction;
- Convention on International Trade in Endangered Species of Wild Fauna and Flora;
- Convention for the Protection of the Mediterranean Sea Against Pollution;
- Treaty Banning Nuclear Weapon Tests in the Atmosphere, in Outer Space and Under Water; and
- International Convention Relating to Intervention on the High Seas in Cases of Oil Pollution Casualties.

# UNITED ARAB EMIRATES

## Recent Political Developments

The United Arab Emirates (UAE) is a member of the Gulf Cooperation Council, which includes Saudi Arabia, Oman, Qatar, Bahrain and Kuwait.

The main external political situation confronting the UAE is its ongoing dispute with Iran over three islands: Abu Musa and the Lesser and Greater Tumbs. The UAE claims that the Islands, now controlled by Iran, belong to them. They were occupied by the Shah in 1971. The Iranians insist the islands are under its sovereignty.

In 1999, the situation caused tension between the UAE and Saudi Arabia after the latter hosted a visit by Iranian President Mohammad Khatami. The UAE denounced the visit and accused Saudi Arabia of sacrificing regional allies to improve relations with the Islamic Republic.

| | |
|---|---|
| Population | 2.85 million (1999), including 80% expatriates |
| Religion | 90% Muslim |
| Government | Federation of Emirates |
| Languages | Arabic (English is widely spoken) |
| Work Week | Private Sector: Saturday–Thursday 8:30–13:00; 16:30–20:00 Public Sector: Saturday–Thursday 8:30–13:00 Oil Sector (Dubai): Sunday–Thursday 8:00–17:00 |
| Monetary Unit | UAE Dirham (DH) |
| Exchange Rate | DH 3.67=US$ 1 |

On the domestic front and in an effort to curb the problem of illegal laborers, the government passed a law expelling all foreign laborers in violation of their visas. In reality though, the government needs the foreign workers because nationals refuse to accept labor jobs.

## Recent Economic Developments

Both the United Arab Emirates political and economic systems make the country an anomaly in the Gulf. Politically, the United Arab Emirates is structured as a federation of seven Emirates located on the Arabian Peninsula. The seven Emirates are Abu Dhabi, Dubai, Sharjah, Ajman, Umm Al Qaiwain, Fujairah, and Ras Al Khaimah. Each emirate is ruled by a Sheikh, who maintains a high degree of autonomy as well as control over natural resources, including oil, and commercial activity. This means that there is unequal distribution of wealth, with Abu Dhabi and Dubai, the emirates's with the greatest hydrocarbon reserves, taking the lion's share.

The UAE economically differentiates itself from its neighbors through diversified economic base. While oil has been the main factor driving the country to having the region's second largest economy – an estimated $46 billion GDP in 1998 – it has taken much greater steps to wean itself from oil dependency. The country's economic health compared with its neighbors became evident during the 1998 oil-price crisis, when the country's oil revenue dropped 31 percent. The private sector, however, compensated with non-oil sector GDP growing 4.7 percent. This allowed the government to even increase expenditures by 7.1 percent, unlike all of its Gulf neighbors that are implementing austere spending measures to soften the blow of their lost oil revenue.

There are other positive signs indicating a healthy and growing economy. The country is close to launching a stock market; it has kept unemployment in check; and it has passed progressive privatization legislation that has received praise from outside the country.

The country has kept in place its extensive cradle-to-the grave welfare system for UAE nationals. The system includes subsidies, grants, loans and free services. Many subsidized services are also provided for foreigners, who comprise roughly 80 percent of the 2.6 million population. Unemployment among nationals may in the future become a problem and Emiratization of the country's economy.

Before the exploitation of petroleum deposits in the 1960s, the UAE had a subsistence economy, consisting mostly of fishing, date farming, camel husbandry, trading, and pearling. Today, the UAE is a prosperous country of global economic significance.

The UAE's GDP, which is dependent on oil prices, has followed a roller coaster pattern, soaring during the 1970s and declining precipitously throughout the 1980s. These swings in income have caused the authorities to look for ways to diversify the economy, particularly in Dubai, where oil production is declining. The search for diversification has been only partially successful. Oil revenues remain as the engine that powers the economy.

Continued low oil prices during 1998 decreased UAE's GDP by nearly 6 percent. Still, a closer look at the data reveals the government's success in protecting its economy from such fluctuations through economic diversification. In 1997, it was officially reported that the oil sector of the economy accounted for 30 percent of GDP, the lowest in the GCC.

In 1998, oil revenues declined by 31 percent, from $14.6 billion to $10.1 billion. The depressed oil-price caused oil's portion of GDP to drop to 21.7 percent in 1998.

Most of the country's budget is provided by Abu Dhabi, the wealthiest emirate. The proposed 1999-2000 budget reflects the positive impact the UAE's diversified economy has compared to its Gulf neighbors. Rather than announcing spending cutbacks, the UAE government announced it is increasing spending to $6.24 billion from the $5.829 billion predicted in 1998. The budget deficit is predicted at $676.294 million compared to $479 million in 1998. Revenues are expected to reach $5.566 billion in the coming year compared with $5.35 billion in the 1998-1999 fiscal year. The increased government spending is earmarked for housing projects for UAE nationals and for higher education and social welfare programs.

The government sector includes the accounts for the federal government as well as the accounts of the seven individual emirate governments. Only the federal budget, a small percentage, is published.

GDP growth estimates for 1998-1999 range between 6 and 8 percent and greatly depend on oil prices. But even if the amount reaches the lower end, it would still offset the 5.8 GDP decrease from the previous year.

Besides the diversification, the economic strength is attributed to various characteristics such as an open and free economy, substantial oil and gas reserves, stronger cooperation among emirates and considerable net overseas assets. The Abu Dhabi Investment Authority, for example, may have more than $150 billion invested abroad which can generate returns of up to $10 billion annually, roughly equal to oil export revenues.

Another important step in economic diversification is expected to occur this year with the opening of a stock exchange, which will be the second largest GCC bourse after Saudi Arabia's. This development will also help the country by promoting market regulation and transparency.

The country is also pushing forward its privatization program, preparing the way for the private sector to assume control of power and water facilities. The country recently introduced legislation for this move that has been hailed for its transparency and goals.

While the country's economic health continues to improve, there remain aspects that need to be addressed such as poor transparency in national accounts, over-dependency of the federal budget on oil, chronic fiscal imbalances, heavy reliance on an expatriate workforce and delayed restructuring in the public sector.

## Economic Indicators

|  | 1999 | 1998 | 1997 | 1996 |
|---|---|---|---|---|
| GDP (current prices, DH bn) | 185.1 | 170.1 | 180.6 | 175.8 |
| GDP Growth (percent) | 5.2 | −5.85 | 2.76 | 12.03 |
| GDP Per Capita (DH 1,000) | 63.0 | 62.5 | 59.2 | 62.3 |
| Balance of Payments (DH bn) |  | 2.76 | 1.20 | 2.28 |
| Trade Balance (DH bn) | 25.0 | 10.01 | 27.16 | 26.99 |
| Exports & Re-exports (DH bn) |  | 112.85 | 124.86 | 121.82 |
| Oil Exports (DH bn) | 35.31 | 35.70 | 49.10 | 52.00 |
| Imports (DH bn) | 100.0 | 102.84 | 97.7 | 94.83 |
| Average Inflation rate (estimates, %) |  | 1.5–2 | 2-3 | 3–4 |
| Unemployment |  | 2.7 | 2.6 |  |
| Current Account (US$ bn) |  | 1.78 | 6.31 |  |

## Oil Sector

The UAE has nearly 98 billion barrels of proven oil reserves, equaling about 9.8 percent of total proven world oil reserves. It also holds 5.8 trillion cubic meters of proven natural gas reserves, approximately 4.6 percent of the total world proven reserves. This places the UAE as the fourth largest holder of gas reserves. A majority of these resources are located in Abu Dhabi, which has 94 percent of the oil and 92 percent of the gas.

In 1998, oil price deflation caused the country's value of oil exports to decline 27.3 percent, gas exports, 23.5 percent, and petroleum derivatives by 14 percent. This price drop caused the OPEC countries to cut production. The UAE's production at the end of 1999 is near its quota of 2 million barrels per day, still significantly below capacity.

Dubai produces at maximum capacity. Abu Dhabi is completing a $5 billion program that will extend its capacity to 2.6 million barrels per day, and the emirate is considering further expansion.

The country is now preparing for two major downstream projects, petrochemicals and refinery expansion believing that Abu Dhabi needs to add value to its basic product to increase income from it. Abu Dhabi is also working to generate more revenues from its gas reserves.

## Non-Oil Sector

Several factors have contributed to the growth of the non-oil sector in recent years including government investments in electricity, water, and other infrastructure, development of financial services, and strong demand for re-exports. An open economic system, free movement of capital and financial stability have also contributed. The government has played an important and supportive role by providing incentives and subsidies, along with a high level of government expenditure in housing.

The largest contributors, as a percentage of GNP, after oil (21.7 percent in 1998) are, in descending order, wholesale and retail services (12 percent), government services (11.6 percent), business (10.7 percent) and construction (9.6 percent).

The Dubai Port Authority's container traffic increased by over 10 percent recent years. Trans-shipment business also expanded significantly. Local and re-export business now accounts for 50 percent of the total container volume handled by the DPA.

Most of the incoming traffic is destined for re-export, although Dubai's growing population, expanding consumer market and construction booms are taking an increasing share of imports.

The attractive Jebel Ali Free Zone has significantly reduced the UAE's dependence on trans-shipment. Over 1,200 companies from over seventy countries and major corporations such as Sony, Aiwa, Black & Decker, Nissan, Honda and Coleman are present in the zone. Recent investor includes the US-based Mars.

To attract even more investment, major upgrades are underway. By the year 2003, the DPA expects its two ports, Jebel Ali and Mina Rashid, will have thirty ship-to-shore cranes.

## Agriculture

The main growth sectors in agriculture are vegetable oils, beverages bases, breakfast cereals, poultry parts, fresh apples and pears, honey, frozen vegetables and snack foods.

The local food processing industry continues to expand offering export opportunities for semi-processed agricultural products. Major growth sectors are beverages (juices and soft drinks), dairy products (ice cream and yogurt), snack foods and biscuits.

## Public Finance

The UAE has a mixed economy, with the most productive assets owned by the government of the individual Emirates, but considerable scope is given to private enterprise. Its legal regime favors UAE nationals over foreigners. In both Abu Dhabi and Dubai, international oil companies maintain equity interests in their operations.

Some banks are privately owned. They represent one of the principal types of commercial establishment in which stock is sold to the public.

Foreign contractors or service businesses require UAE nationals sponsors, one for each Emirate in which they do business. Foreigners are not allowed to own land in Abu Dhabi or Dubai.

The government sector includes the accounts of the federal government as well as accounts of the seven individual Emirate governments. Only the federal budget, a small part of the total, is published.

As noted above, the UAE enjoys a booming re-export trade. Traditional re-export markets are the Gulf Cooperation Council (GCC) states and Iran, but UAE traders have aggressively sought out new markets in such areas as Russia, the newly independent states of central Asia and in South Africa.

## Business Environment

### *Privatization*

Abu Dhabi recently announced an ambitious initiative to privatize its power and water sectors. To this end, the emirate implemented a new regulatory framework for these industries contained in "Law no. 2 of 1998 Concerning the Regulation of the Water and Electricity Sector," which is user-friendly and creates transparency. The government published an English copy of the law.

The main features of the plan include the creation of a new public body that is responsible for government policy in the sector. It also calls for creating a new regulatory agency designed to encourage local and foreign investment while protecting the interests of the country and its nationals. Furthermore, the law calls for dismantling the assets of the former government Water and Electricity Department into various separate bodies.

Abu Dhabi's goals are to improve efficiency and service, promote local and foreign private sector investment and maximize revenues from an asset sales processes. At the same time, the legislation ensures continued security of water and electricity and promotes opportunities for UAE nationals.

The plan, which is to be the model for the other emirates, is expected to reduce the government's capital expenditures and subsidies. In Abu Dhabi, it costs 7 cents to generate one kilowatt an hour while the selling price is 4 cents to non-emirate nationals and commercial offices and two cents to nationals. It is estimated that government subsidies for this sector total $271.7 million a year.

## Stock Exchange

The UAE government is expected to approve the opening of a stock exchange within the next year. In December 1999, the government presented a bill that regulates the establishment of the Securities Commission and the Stock Market.

The bill states that the commission will be managed by a Board of Directors chaired by the Secretary for Trade and Industry. The board will consist of two members form the Trade and Industry Department, two from the Treasury, one from the Central Bank and four monetary experts. Board membership terms will be three years with the option of a one year second term. People who serve on the board of directors of publicly listed company's are barred from serving on the commission's board. The bill also states that the exchanges will be electronically linked to allow trading in all parts of the country.

Shares are currently traded informally. When it is launched, the exchange will be the region's second biggest. One major source of dispute has been on the issue of allowing foreigners to invest in the market. A few mutual funds now permit limited foreign ownership of shares.

Public stock companies may be registered in the UAE, despite the absence of an official stock exchange. Shares of public companies are bought and sold through private investment agencies, and share price information is based on the latest transactions.

The UAE stock market is believed to currently have a market capitalization of more than DH 67 billion, and the primary market is also expected to become very active in the future. The Emirates Bank group has established the Emirates Equity Index (Emnex), a composite of thirty-one actively traded UAE stocks. There are also sub-indices for the three main market segments—banking, services and insurance.

## Major Projects

The government's continued investment in infrastructure has been an important driver of growth. The main focus of this investment is electricity and water. Government officials predict that the population of nationals will be reach 1.31 million by 2005 and 2.194 million by 2012. This means that in 13 years, 9.3 million telephone lines will be needed and demand for power and water by 2012 will be 3,630mW and 1,150 million gallons per day.

In 1996 the total installed electrical capacity was 7,466 mw. Abu Dhabi had 45 percent of capacity and Dubai, 26 percent. The former is expected to double power output and population by 2010. Per capita electricity consumption in Abu Dhabi in 1996 was 13,433 kW, while per capita water consumption was 82,861 gallons, much used in desert agriculture, one of the world's highest rates. The UAE has the highest per capita consumption of desalinated water in the world. Planned water and power projects are estimated to cost $8.425 billion.

The government has also made telecommunications a priority. Under the Thuraya project, awarded for nearly $2 billion to Hughes Space and Communications, two satellites will be launched to provide enhanced GSM telecommunication and television services. There is also a planned cable television network that will deliver services to 10,000 a piece in Abu Dhabi and Dubai.

There are several new free zones in the planning or early construction stages. The most significant is the Abu Dhabi's Saadiyat Island Free Zone, an estimated $3 billion project that is expected to concentrate on bulk commodity trading rather than manufacturing.

In Abu Dhabi other planned or current projects include a $330 million expansion of the Abu Dhabi and Al Ain Airports and a $543 million development of an industrial city in Mussafah area that includes a 1,380-hectare industrial area with utility buildings, offices, a police station and a clinic.

Dubai also has projects in the works, including the $300 million Dubai "Emirates Hills" residential gated community project with two 18-hole golf courses. A new Dubai Airport in Jebel Ali for Dubai Municipality is being constructed as well as the $408 million Business park in Jebel Ali for Dubai Investment Park and Development Company. And in the emirate of Ajman, there is the $135 million Ajman Free Zone Expansion for the Ajman Free Zone Authority.

Other projects include the US$ 530 million expansion of Dubai Airport, a US$ 500 million expansion of Abu Dhabi and Al-Ain airports, the building of a number of new hotels, including a new 280-room Hyatt between Umm al-Nar and Shahama and a 416-room Park Plaza hotel near the Dubai World Trade Center, as well as two office towers in Dubai of 305 and 350 meters respectively and a new Sharjah world trade center, which will include a 320-meter tower and a 20,000 square-meter exhibition hall.

## Build Operate Transfer

One of the first BOT projects in the water treatment sector is the Ajman wastewater project. Concessionaires are Black & Veatch US International and the Abu Dhabi-based KEO International Consultants. One hundred million dollars will be invested in the first phase of development and the overall project is expected to require an investment of US$ 600 million. The concession will extend for twenty-five years, and the operators are expected to recover their outlay through house connection charges as well as through the treatment of waste water.

## Franchising

Currently, franchises are operating in the fast foods industry; dine-in restaurants and clubs; auto leasing; apparel; soft drink bottling; beauty products; hotels; toys; photography; jewelry; vending machines; dry cleaning; furniture; hardware; natural health products; publications; and sporting goods. The largest segment is the fast food franchise group which is highly sought after by local companies. Most of the major US fast food companies are already established in the market. The industry, however, is currently going through a major restructuring with several major franchises being sold to new owners. These changes are seen as a positive change from weaker to stronger management, and not as a reflection of weakness in the market. There remains considerable potential for franchises of all kinds.

There is no special legislation for franchises in the UAE. General contract and commercial law apply to franchise agreements. UAE law mandates that only UAE citizens or corporations wholly owned by UAE citizens are allowed to conduct retail operations, the most common type of franchise. Foreign businesses must work through a local partner as licensee or enter into a joint venture. Franchisees usually prefer to own 100 percent of the franchise themselves. In other cases, the franchisee enters into a joint venture with the franchiser to operate all outlets as company-owned stores employing local managers.

As with other types of business operations in the UAE, the selection of the local partner is critical. One common practice used by franchisers in the past that has, in many cases, caused considerable problems and significant lost sales is the selection of a master distributor to cover the entire Gulf through the use of sub-distributors in each country. Each market is different and requires qualified local partners to exploit its opportunities.

**Leading Business Opportunities**

| Rank | Sector |
|------|--------|
| 1 | Defense Industry Equipment |
| 2 | Oil and Gas Field Machinery |
| 3 | Architecture/Construction/Engineering Services |
| 4 | Telecommunications Equipment |
| 5 | Air Conditioning & Refrigeration |
| 6 | Computers & Peripherals |
| 7 | Automotive Parts and Service Equipment |
| 8 | Electrical Generation Equipment |
| 9 | Water Resources Equipment |

# Legal Review

The legal system of the UAE is based on its constitution that was approved by the Federal National Council in 1996. This replaced the provisional documents which had been renewed every five years since the country's creation in 1971. The Constitution establishes the principal instruments of Federal authority as follows:

- The Supreme Council of the Federation – composed of the seven sheikhs of the seven Emirates – has the power to enact legislation, establish policy, appoint persons to office and to assume supreme supervision of the Federation's affairs. Decisions should be approved by a majority of five, which must include the votes of the sheikhs of Abu-Dhabi and Dubai.

- The President and Vice President of the Federation are elected by the Supreme Council from among its members and have overall responsibility for the administration of federal laws and affairs.
- The Council of Ministers performs the function of a cabinet.
- The Federal National Council has advisory authority.
- The Federal judiciary.

The constitution provides a rather detailed list of citizen rights and liberties and lays down the rules of priority between federal and Emirate legislation. Under Article 151 of the constitution, federal law has precedence over legislation of the Emirates.

## Judiciary

The Federal judicial system in the UAE consists of Federal Courts of First Instance, two Federal Courts of Appeal in Sharjah and Abu Dhabi and a Federal Supreme Court in Abu Dhabi, the latter composed of five judges including a President of the Court. The Supreme Court has both appellate and original jurisdiction. The individual Emirates retained their own Islamic *Shari'a* courts which exist parallel to the Federal Courts. Dubai, however, has not merged its courts with the federal judiciary and the rules for admission to the Dubai bar are different than those for admission to the federal bar.

Most advocates in the UAE were, and primarily still are, expatriates. But the government has begun to enforce Law No. 21 of 1991 under which only UAE nationals can represent clients in local courts. Expatriate lawyers may only serve as legal consultants.

## *Alternative Dispute Resolution and Arbitration*

UAE courts usually enforce the intention of the parties to arbitrate disputes as expressed in a contractual arbitration clause. The courts, however, sometimes substitute clauses providing for arbitration outside of the UAE for local venue. UAE courts will often not enforce foreign judgments or honor contractual choice of law provisions.

Arbitration proceedings are usually carried out by the individual Emirates though their respective Chambers of Commerce and Industry which are quasi-state organizations. The Dubai Chamber of Commerce has published

Rules of Commercial Conciliation and Arbitration which are used by its Commercial Conciliation and Arbitration Center.

In this context, it should also be noted that according to Dubai Law No.4 of 1997 (amending and clarifying a 1996 law), the government of Dubai must consent to being sued. According to a July 1992 Directive, however, no such consent is required if an arbitration clause in any contract to which the government is a party is invoked.

## Business Forms and Structures

### Companies Law

Under Federal Law No. 8, business organizations may take one of seven forms: 1) Public Shareholding Companies; 2) Private Shareholding Companies; 3) Limited Liability Companies; 4) General Partnerships; 5) Limited Partnerships; 6) Partnerships Limited by Shares; and 7) Shareholding Companies. Companies not taking one of these forms are not legally recognized, and persons contracting in their name will be jointly and severally liable for the obligations arising from such contracts. Exceptions apply only for companies located in a Free Trade Zone. There are also requirements determining minimal capital contributions, the number of directors and shareholders, and incorporation procedures. Provisions concerning mergers and dissolution or conversion of companies are also included in the same law. Each entity must be registered and licensed with the UAE Federal Ministry of Economy and Commerce and with the appropriate authority in the Emirate in which its office will be located.

Furthermore, the law states the general rule that participation of UAE nationals should never be less than 51 percent in any commercial enterprise. Some business forms and structures are generally not available to foreign investors, as will be elaborated below.

### Public Shareholding Companies

A minimum of 55 percent of the shares of a public shareholding company must be offered to the general public. The minimum amount of capital for a public shareholding company is DH 10 million, of which a minimum of 25 percent must be settled on subscription. A shareholder's liability is limited to the nominal value of his shares in the company's capital. A PSC must have at least 10 founders, unless a government entity is involved, in which case the number may be lower. Shares are registered in a share register and cannot be issued at a price lower than nominal value; all shares have equal rights. This type of company must a minimum of 3 and maximum of 12 board of directors. The chairman, as well as a majority of the board, must be UAE nationals.

If a public shareholding company loses half its capital, its board of directors is required to call a general meeting of shareholders to consider the continuation or dissolution of the company. If the board fails to call such meeting or if the meeting fails to reach a decision on the subject, any interested party may file a lawsuit seeking the dissolution of the company.

## Private Shareholding Company

A private shareholding company must have a minimum of three shareholders. The minimum capital of a private shareholding company is DH 2 million. Shares may not be offered to the public. The private shareholding company's incorporating documents must preclude public offering of shares.

## Limited Liability Company

A limited liability company can be formed by a minimum of two and a maximum of 50 people. Shareholder liability is limited to the value of shares held in the company's capital. The minimum capital required to establish a limited liability company is DH 150,000 in Abu Dhabi and DH 300,000 in Dubai. Management is handled by no more than five designated managers, who are not necessarily members of the company. Non-UAE nationals may own up to 49 percent of an LLC.

The Companies Law provides that an LLC may engage in any lawful activity except insurance, banking and investment of money for others.

## Partnerships

### General Partnership
General partnerships are formed by two or more UAE nationals who are jointly and severally liable for its debts. This form is generally not available to non-nationals. Only the names of actual partners can be included in the company name, but the company may have a special trade name.

Interests of a partner can be transferred as stipulated in the partnership agreement or with the approval of all partners. The management may include one or more managers who are UAE nationals and who may or may not be partners in the company. The dissolution of a partnership may occur on the death, insanity, bankruptcy or withdrawal of one of the partners. The remaining partners, however, may unanimously decide to continue the partnership, provided that such decision is registered in the commercial register.

## Limited Partnership

A limited partnership is composed of one or more general partners who are jointly and severally liable for all of its debts, and one or more limited partners who are liable for the limited partnerships debts only to the extent of his capital contribution. A limited partner may not participate in the management or have his name appear in the name of the partnership. All general partners must be UAE nationals.

## Partnership Limited by Shares

A partnership limited by shares has both general partners with unlimited liability and partners whose liability is limited by their shares in the capital. General partners must be UAE nationals while participating partners may be non-nationals. The capital must be at least DH 500,000 and has to be divided into negotiable shares of equal value. Some formalities regarding the incorporation of a joint stock company are also applicable to a partnership limited by shares.

## Joint Ventures

A joint venture is formed by agreement between two or more natural persons or legal entities, and its objectives and terms are governed by the joint venture contract. This agreement is not subject to registration in the Commercial Register.

A joint venture may be carried out only in the private name of one of the UAE national partners.

## Structures Available to Foreign Investors

### General

A foreign investor may chose to participate with up to 49 percent in a company formed in one of the structures open to foreign investors. Despite the requirement that the majority of shares must be held by UAE nationals, it is still believed by some to be the easiest solution to carry out business in the UAE. Other available methods are the establishment of a branch or the use of commercial agency agreements. Special attention should also be paid to the possibilities offered by the Free Trade Zones where businesses are exempt from most requirements applicable in the regular UAE territory.

## Branches

A foreign company may establish a branch in the UAE but a local sponsor or agent is required who must be either a citizen of the UAE or a company wholly-owned by citizens of the UAE. A branch must be registered with the local chamber of commerce and the municipality. Since February 1990, branches of foreign companies (including those already in existence) are also required to register with the Ministry of Economy and Commerce. Exceptions are made pursuant to government approval.

Under Commercial Law No. 8 of 1984 and Ministerial Decision No. 69 of 1989, a branch office of a foreign company does not have a separate legal entity. It merely represents the mother company and carries out business under its name. A branch office is usually permitted to promote and to market the products of its parent and enter into transactions and offer service to customers in its name. The UAE agent will render the necessary services for obtaining of licenses, visas and other permits and run the business of the office without assuming any financial obligation.

## Commercial Agency

In order to make use of and conduct commercial agency activities, a foreign business is required to appoint an agent (an UAE national or a company owned by UAE nationals) for doing business in the UAE. Commercial agencies are governed by the Federal Commercial Agencies Law, Federal Law No. 18 of 1981, as amended by Law No. 14 of 1988. According this law, all commercial agency agreements have to be registered with the Federal Ministry of Economy and Commerce.

The Federal Commercial Agencies Law grants a commercial agent certain statutory rights which cannot be waived by contract. The most important are (1) any agent is entitled to territorial exclusivity in at least one Emirate and, accordingly, will receive infringement commissions on transactions concluded by the principle himself or by others within his territory; (2) the agent is entitled to prevent products subject to their agency from being imported into the UAE, if the agent is not the consignee; and (3) it is not permissible for a principle to terminate an agency agreement without the agent's approval except for reasons accepted by the Commercial Agencies Committee of the Ministry of Economy and Commerce, even if the term of the agreement has been initially limited by agreement. In absence of a justifiable reason, the failure to renew an agreement may entitle the agent to compensation.

It is possible to appoint an agent with rights to the entire UAE or for each or more than one of the single Emirates. The agents may themselves appoint distributors or sub-agents.

According to the Court de Cassation (Federal Court of Appeal) in Abu Dhabi, any dispute arising out of commercial agencies must be submitted first to the Commercial Agencies Committee and any judgment of the courts given without such first submission will be null and void.

## Business Licenses

All of the Emirates regulate both foreign and domestic business activity by requiring that any office for the conduct of business located in an Emirate must be properly licensed by the municipal authorities where located. The following kinds of business activities involve different kinds of licenses which allow the licensed business to conduct business as provided below: Representative Office License Activity of a representative office is limited to business or sales promotion activities and may be used as regional headquarters or a liaison facility. It may not import goods, effectuate sales or make contractual commitments.

Trade licenses allow the holder to import, sell, export and conduct general business with regard to certain identified goods or product lines. General trade licenses, which allow the import and export of all types of products and unrestricted engagement in a general trading business are rarely issued.

An industry license is required for the establishment and conduct of industrial activity with regard to the specific kind of manufacturing, processing or other industrial activity to be undertaken.

Service License authorizes various specified forms of service activity to be conducted.

Architects, engineers, business consultants, doctors, legal and accounting firms and other professionals and consultants are required to obtain professional licenses.

## Construction License

There are several kinds of construction licenses relating to different fields of construction activity. A general construction license, which authorizes the licensee to carry out all types of construction, including civil, mechanical, electrical, petroleum and other related activity, is also available.

## Currency and Banking

The UAE has no restrictions or regulations on foreign exchange. Capital, profits, interest, and royalty payments may be repatriated freely. The local currency has been tied traditionally to the US dollar at the rate of US$ 1 to DH 3.67.

## Banking

The current domestic financial market is best described as "over-banked." It consists of forty-eight local and foreign commercial banks, two restricted license (specialized) banks, and thirteen foreign bank representative offices.

Central bank regulations announced on April 5, 1993, set the minimum capital to risk-weighted asset ratio at 10 percent, which is 2 percent higher than the minimum level recommended by the Basel Concordat committee on banking supervision. The reduction of higher risk assets may cause concomitant declines in UAE bank profits, but it is anticipated that this will strengthen the banking industry.

Most banks provide trade, project and consumer financing. They re-export financing accounts for a large portion of trade finance, and this is viewed as having substantial prospects for growth. Loan decisions are based on project viability and the credit worthiness of the parties involved. Short-term loans (3-6 months) by commercial banks are offered at current interest rates. Project loans are given for five years. Consumer financing is also growing rapidly. Furthermore, the local banking system has well established correspondent relationships with international banks.

In the UAE, the marketing of financial products and services is regulated by the UAE Central Bank under Federal Law No. 10 of 1980 (the Central Bank Law and related banking resolutions). Enforcement of Central Bank policy, however, is often undertaken by the local licensing authorities in the various Emirates.

The Central Bank Law establishes five principal categories of institutions in the UAE—commercial banks, investment banks, financial establishments, financial intermediaries, and monetary intermediaries – all of which must be licensed by both the Central Bank and the local licensing authorities. In addition to these five categories, current practice in the individual Emirates permits the licensing of financial or investment consultants. These consultants are not required to obtain a Central Bank license.

## Commercial Banks

The Central Bank Law defines a commercial bank as any establishment which customarily receives funds from the public, grants credit and banking facilities, and conducts other banking operations prescribed for commercial banks either by law or by customary banking practice. In the UAE, customary banking practice includes the marketing and sale of investment products and services, including the sale of securities and various funds.

## Investment Banks

Central Bank Resolution No. 21 of 1988 regulates the activities of investment banks. Investment banks are defined as merchant or development banks or banks which provide medium or long term financing. The Central Bank Resolution authorizes investment banks in the UAE to offer financial products and services, including the issuance of financial instruments and the management of investment portfolios.

On June 1, 1997, the Emirates Bank Group, which is controlled by the Dubai government, launched UAE's first mutual investment fund with an initial capital of about US$ 8.2 million. The fund offers non-UAE nationals their first opportunity to invest in the UAE's tightly restricted equity market up to a limit of DH 500,000. The huge response by foreign investors prompted the UAE Central bank to raise its original ceiling of 20 percent of foreign investment to 49 percent. When the fund closed for public subscription on June 15, 1997 the investment totaled to US$ 74.5 million.

## Financial Establishments

The Central Bank Law permits financial establishments to lend money and to undertake other financial transactions but does not allow them to accept deposits. The Central Bank has adopted a policy that prohibits financial establishments from offering financial products and services. In comparison to commercial banks, the only activity that financial establishments may undertake which commercial banks may not is the lease of equipment and machinery.

## Financial Intermediaries

Financial intermediaries are brokers. Regulations issued under the UAE Central Bank Law allow licensed brokers to market and to sell foreign and local shares and financial instruments in consideration for a commission. Local and foreign companies may obtain a brokerage license from the UAE Central Bank.

## Monetary Intermediaries

Monetary intermediaries are money changers. They are not authorized to market or to sell investment products and services.

## Investment Consultants

The UAE Central Bank has not published regulations on investment consultancy. Under the existing policies of the individual Emirates, a company licensed as an investment consultant may advise and assist clients in pursuing various investment strategies but may not directly sell investment products. Sales of products introduced by consultants are, therefore, typically booked outside the UAE. Consultants are also not expected to receive investment funds from clients, although they may assist in the transfer of those funds. Consultants may not provide credit facilities or open accounts for clients but may assist them in opening accounts with brokers and banks. If properly authorized by the client, the consultant could also manage such accounts.

The UAE Central Bank has issued instructions to local municipalities that they may issue investment consultancy licenses but only after first consulting the Central Bank.

The UAE Central Bank has recently moved towards a tighter policy regarding investment companies and financial consultants. In the future, such companies will have to obtain a license from the Central Bank and to report under the rules it has established. Investment Companies for the purpose of these regulations have been defined as undertakings which are involved in investment in securities or in the management of trust funds or investment portfolios on behalf of others. The minimum paid up capital for investment companies (including branches of foreign companies) is DH 25 million, increasing to a larger amount depending on the activities of the company. Financial consultants, on the other hand, are deemed to be individual professionals or groups of professionals providing advice to individuals or companies about the value of securities and other financial instruments or giving recommendation about investing. For these, licenses can be issued with a minimum paid in capital of DH 1 million.

## Accountants and Auditors Regulations

Thus far, no local professional body of accountants has been established in the UAE, but many of the large, international accounting firms maintain offices in the UAE. According to the new Federal law Concerning the Organization of the Auditing Profession No. 22 of 1995 and the supplementing Ministerial Resolutions No. 49 of 1996 and No. 7 of 1997, foreign accounting firms can now only be listed in the register of active accountants if they have operated in the UAE prior to the effective date of the 1995 law. Further, the new law requires that all foreign firms will have to take on UAE nationals as partners. A five year transition period is granted to the existing firms to comply with the new standards.

## Intellectual Property

New federal laws were enacted in 1992 granting protection for patents, trademarks and copyrights. However, since UAE became a member of GATT, the established rules are being revised to comply with WTO (TRIPS) standards.

The revised laws are expected to be implemented by January 2000. UAE has already signed the Paris Convention.

## Patents

Once an application for the grant of a patent is filed, it is examined with respect to compliance with formalities and patentability under the Patent Law including its novelty, inventiveness and industrial applicability. In the case of refusal, the applicant has the right to appeal to the Committee in the Patent Office. Accepted applications are published in the Official Gazette, and any interested party has the right to appeal to the Committee within sixty days as of the date of publication in the Official Gazette. In the absence of opposition, the letters-patent or the utility certificate is issued.

A patent is valid for fifteen years and renewable for a period of no more than five years. Patents granted for process inventions relating to drugs and pharmaceuticals are granted for a non-renewable period of ten years.

The right to a patent may be assigned or licensed. An assignment shall have no effect against third parties unless it has been recorded at the Patent Office and published in the Official Gazette.

Working of patents in the UAE is an official requirement. If the owner of a patented invention does not satisfy the stipulated working requirements within four years from the filing date or three years from the grant date of the patent, if the working has ceased for two consecutive years, the use does not cover the demands of the UAE, or the owner refuses to license it under contract on fair terms, then the patent will be subject to compulsory licensing under the provisions of the law. The corresponding periods for a utility model is three years as of the filing date and two years as of the grant. Importation of products made under the patent does not satisfy the use requirement.

## Designs and Industrial Models

The examination procedure for designs and industrial models is same as that for patents. A design or industrial model registration is valid for five years and renewable for two additional consecutive five year periods. Annuities have to be paid within the final three months of the protection period, but late payment with a surcharge is possible within thirty days as of the elapse of the due date.

## Trademarks

The international classification of goods and services is followed in the UAE.

Once a trademark application is filed, the application is examined as to its registrability. Trademark applications accepted by the Registrar are published in the Official Gazette. Also, publication upon acceptance is effected in two local, daily Arabic newspapers and the cuttings of the notices, as published in the newspapers, are to be submitted to the Trademark Office. Any interested party may file a notice of opposition to the registration of the trademark within thirty days from the date of last publication. The decision of the Registrar regarding the opposition may be appealed to the Committee in the Trademark Office, and the Committee's decision may be appealed to the competent court. In the absence of opposition, a trademark is registered and the relevant certificate of registration is issued.

A trademark registration is valid for ten years from the date of filing the application and renewable for similar periods.

The ownership of a registered trademark can be assigned with or without the commercial enterprise using the trademark. Unless an assignment has been recorded in the register and published in the Official Gazette, the assignment shall have no effect *vis-à-vis* third parties.

Any interested party may request the court to cancel a trademark registration if the owners fail to use such a trademark in the UAE for five consecutive years from the date of registration.

## Copyrights

Copyright interests can be protected under the Copyright and Authorship Protection Law No. 40 for the year 1992.

Registration with the competent authority is optional, but a registration shall be regarded as the authoritative reference to the copyrighted information. Non-registration shall not entail infringing upon the author's right. A copyright registration is valid for the lifetime of the author plus twenty-five years after his death. The validity period for cinematographic films, works of applied art, works made by corporate bodies, works of art published under pen names, and works published for the first time after the author's death are protected for twenty-five years only. The validity period of photographic works is ten years only.

## Taxation

### *Income Tax*

The UAE does not have any enforced federal income tax legislation for general business. An income tax decree has been enacted by each Emirate, but in practice, the enforcement of these decrees is restricted to foreign banks and to oil companies. This practice is not likely to change in the near future as the relevant mechanisms with which to implement the tax decrees have not yet been established. The decrees indicate, however, that if taxation were enforced, taxes could be imposed retroactively.

Foreign banks are taxed at 20 percent of their taxable income in the Emirates of Abu-Dhabi, Dubai and Sharjah. The tax is restricted to the taxable income which is earned or deemed to be earned in that particular Emirate. Oil Companies (which include any chargeable person that deals in oil or right to oil both off-shore and on-shore) pay a flat rate of 55 percent on their taxable income in Dubai and 50 percent in the other Emirates. In addition, they pay royalties on production.

Personal incomes, including all forms of salary and capital gains wherever arising, are not subject to taxation in any of the Emirates.

### *Customs Duty*
Under the terms of an agreement on customs tariffs with countries of the GCC, all Emirates are bound to levy a minimum customs duty of 10 percent on luxury goods and 4 percent on the C.I.F. value of all other goods imported, excluding certain items such as alcohol and cigarettes. Recently, the federal government has approved a tobacco tax rate of 50 percent.

In practice, however, exemptions are made for a wide range of goods. In cases where customs duties are charged, it is generally restricted to 1 percent.

### *Other Local Taxes*
Municipal taxes are levied in most Emirates on annual rental paid at 5 percent for residential premises and 10 percent for commercial premises.

Other local taxes include a 5 percent tax on hotel services and entertainment.

## Investment and Trade

General Foreign investment in capital, technology or expertise is more than welcome in the UAE. Generally, any locally incorporated company must be at least 51 percent owned by UAE nationals, but the apportionment and distribution of profits is not similarly constrained.

### *Free Trade Zones*

Dubai, which has far less oil wealth than Abu-Dhabi, has undertaken a major promotion campaign to attract more foreign investment and tourism. Its vast Jebel Ali Free Trade Zone now houses more than 950 international operations, most of which engage in the distribution or light to medium manufacturing of products for domestic consumption and export. The Zone is built around the Dubai Port Authority's Jebel Ali Terminal and enables customers to take full advantage of the port's ISO-certified container and general cargo operations. A Free Zone Authority is assisting in administrative proceedings.

The principal advantage of free trade zones in the UAE, and especially Jebel Ali, is that companies locating in a free zone may be 100 percent foreign owned. Registration procedures tend to be relatively simple. Furthermore, since the nominal customs duty is only 4 percent and as much as 3 percent of it is often rebated, the entire country is a virtual Free Trade Zone.

Dubai Law No. 2 of April 3, 1993, is designed to treat equally goods manufactured by firms which are at least 51 percent owned by UAE or GCC nationals and which are licensed by the Ministry of Finance as UAE products, regardless of whether manufactured inside or outside free trade zones. The net effect of the law will be to exempt products produced in free trade zones from UAE customs duty. Over the long term, it is hoped that all GCC countries will cease to levy import duties on free zone products.

Under Dubai Law No. 9 of 1992, a company may set up a separate legal entity, referred to as a free zone establishment (FZE). The entity needs only one shareholder, whose liability may be limited to the amount of share capital paid in to the FZE (minimum share capital DH 1 million). No memorandum or articles of incorporation will be necessary. The Jebel Ali Free Zone Authority will provide to every applicant upon request the implementation regulations for foreign investors in the zone. The Zone Authority also maintains a FZE register.

The Jebel Ali Free Zone provides an opportunity to businesses to base their manufacturing, warehousing and trading operations in the Free Zone without the normal requirements attendant to the conduct of business in the Arab Gulf States. Businesses in Jebel Ali are exempted from the requirement of local ownership, payment of taxes and duties and are guarantied the freedom to transfer capital, profits and salaries. The Jebel Ali Free Zone Authority allows foreign companies to establish branch operations in Jebel Ali without any requirements of local sponsorship or agency. It is now also possible to incorporate wholly-owned subsidiaries in the Jebel Ali Free Zone. Gulf nationals may also establish operations which are not incorporated.

Recently, new Free Trade Zones similar in structure to the Jebel Ali Zone were opened at Dubai International Airport and in Sharjah International Airport.

## Trade Agreements

The UAE is a member of the GCC, and as such, is subject to the GCC agreements regarding trade. These agreements are described in the section on Trade Agreements in the chapter on Bahrain.

The UAE is a signatory to the General Agreement on Tariffs and Trade (GATT).

## Customs

Tariffs reflect the cost of the imported goods as indicated on the supplier's or manufacturer's invoice. In accordance with GCC initiatives, new customs duties were announced August 1, 1994, which provide a consistent duty of 4 percent on the CIF value of imports throughout the UAE.

It is expected that many items imported by the government, including personal effects, goods in transit, foodstuffs and medicines will be duty-free.

## Real Estate Investment

Until recently, in foreign ownership of land was not restricted in practice throughout the UAE with the exception of Abu-Dhabi and Dubai, where even transfers between Abu-Dhabi citizens are subject to government approval. A proposed federal real estate law, however, would prohibit foreigners and foreign companies (except those from other GCC states) to hold property, granting a transitional period to those who already own property. Enforcement, however, will likely take into consideration individual cases. Since land is available at nominal rents under the Organization of Industrial Affairs Act, the proposed law is generally believed to have hardly any adverse effect on foreign investment.

Building permits are granted only to construction engineers, and any construction without the appropriate permit from the local municipality will be illegal.

One of the most obvious ways to exploit land is to grant leases, particularly in the UAE, where the majority of the residents are expatriates, and, therefore, are obliged to rent. Until 1994, Sharjah was the only Emirate to have enacted a landlord and tenant law of general applicability. Sharjah's Landlord and Tenant Law of 1977, as amended in 1986, applies to almost all kind of leases. It requires leases to be registered with the municipal authorities.

Legislation regarding renting of real property in Abu-Dhabi, which was enacted in 1994, is more comprehensive than the Sharjah law, and covers all lease contracts. It requires that leases be registered with the relevant municipality. It further requires that lease agreements be in writing. Nonetheless the law also provides that the terms of a lease, though in writing may be established by all means of proof including oral or other extrinsic evidence not incorporated in the written lease.

## Collaterization of Loans

Governed by the Federal Commercial Transactions Law No.18 of 1993, various types of securities are available to secure loans and facilities granted by banks and financial institutions. These include a mortgage on land, a pledge on movable assets, a pledge on shares in a joint stock or limited liability company as well as a pledge on the commercial business on the whole (comprising material and intangible assets for the practice of commercial business). The latter two, which are particularly attractive to foreign investors not owning land, do not bar those pledging from managing their pledged business in the ordinary course of business.

## Public Sector Procurement

In the UAE, government projects are generally put out to tender. The required qualifications, specializations and other terms and conditions for participation vary according to the project and the authority concerned. Certain tenders are offered internationally, but where local tenders are concerned, only those companies licensed and registered with the department concerned are eligible to bid. In order to qualify to participate, one or more of the following may apply:

- The tenderer shall be a firm registered in the UAE;
- A foreign party may only participate if it has a UAE agent with the necessary documents;
- The tenderer should hold a valid license from the Economic Department;
- The tenderer must be a member of the Dubai Chamber of Commerce.

Abu-Dhabi has its own detailed rules and requirements for contractors who wish to be permitted for tender, imposing special registration requirements and placing limits on the commission the local agent involved is permitted to receive.

Environmental Law Over the past few years, various municipalities in the UAE have developed a relatively large body of environmental regulations based on local orders, many of which contain strong enforcement provisions. Among the Emirates, Dubai has the most developed system of environmental regulations, requiring permits from the local municipality for activities relating to water usage (sewage/drainage, liquid waste) and to air pollution. The environmental standards imposed are closely monitored by the local municipality, which has the power to clean up at the polluter's expense, to enforce discontinuance of drainage or to cancel existing permits. Furthermore, the operator of a facility is required to perform monthly tests and to send the results to the municipality.

On a federal level, the UAE created in 1993 the Federal Environmental Authority (FEA), which has since prepared a draft of environmental protection legislation for a comprehensive federal law that is supposed to bring new cohesiveness to the current fragmented system of environmental protection. In addition to provisions regarding the general protection of the environment, the proposed law contains specific chapters on water, soil and air pollution, noise pollution, the protection and preservation of wildlife, protected areas, environmental disasters and the handling of hazardous materials and waste. It also calls for eliminating pollution from sources outside the UAE and for full compliance with UAE treaty obligations. Companies will be required to comply with its provisions within two years from the date of publication. The executive regulations are to be published six month after enactment of the draft law. Entities formed after the enactment will have to comply with its provisions in order to obtain a license; the licensing authorities will require environmental impact studies from applicants. Furthermore, environmental protection will generally have to be considered in all government decisions.

General enforcement of the law will be undertaken by the Ministry of Justice. Violators of the proposed provisions will have to compensate individual victims of environmental damage. It is not clear, however, whether the law allows a private cause of action for the victims or whether the Ministry will administer such claims. On the other hand, the law does state expressly that environment protection societies may institute civil litigation against an offender.

The UAE recently joined the United Nations Framework Convention on Climate Control and is a party to various international treaties regarding environmental protection, including the 1969 Brussels Convention Relating to Intervention on the High Seas in Case of Oil Pollution Casualties and its 1973 Protocol; as well as the same convention relating to Civil Liability for Oil Pollution Damage; the 1971 Convention on the Establishment of an International Fund for Compensation in Oil Pollution Damage; the 1972 London Convention on the Prevention of Marine Pollution by Dumping from Ships and Aircraft (as amended); the Convention on International Trade in Endangered Species of Wild Fauna and Flora; Annex 16 on Environmental Protection of the 1944 Chicago Convention on International

Civil Aviation, the Kuwait Regional Convention for Cooperation on the Protection of the Marine Environment from Pollution; the 1985 Vienna Convention for Protection of the Ozone Layer with its 1987 Montreal Protocol on Substances that Deplete the Ozone Layer; the 1986 IAEA Conventions on Early Notification of a Nuclear Accident and on Assistance in the Case of a Nuclear Accident or Radiological Emergency.

# YEMEN

## Recent Political Developments

In 1967, following Britain's withdrawal from Yemen, the country split into two, with the National Liberation Front in the North and the communist People's Democratic Republic of Yemen (PDRY) established in the south. Relations between the two sides were hostile and characterized by border disputes, armed clashes and unification talks, which lasted for a decade. And following the reunification, the two sides again battled in a civil war.

Throughout this time, President Ali Abdallah Saleh was the ruler in the north and since reunification, over the entire country. He was reelected on September 26, 1999, garnering 96.3 percent of the vote. The opposition party called the vote a "mockery," because their candidate was among those barred from running. International observers said the polling process was generally fair, but many believed the millions of dollars spent on the elections could have been put to better use.

Yemen has become active in regional politics. It is eager to gain membership in the Gulf Cooperation Council (Saudi Arabia, the UAE, Kuwait, Bahrain, Oman and Qatar). Its application has been rejected for various reasons, including the country's tense relations with some member countries, especially Saudi Arabia. The two countries are engaged in a border dispute, that frequently includes cross-border gunfire. Comments from both sides in late 1999 suggest that a settlement may be approaching.

| Profile | |
|---|---|
| Population | 18.1 million (1999 estimate) |
| Population Growth Rate | 3.7 percent |
| Religions | 99% Muslim with some Jews, Christians, Hindus. |
| Government | Republic |
| Languages | Arabic (Many businessmen and government officials speak English.) |
| Work Week | Public Sector: Saturday–Thursday |
| Monetary Unit | Yemeni Rial (YR) |
| Exchange Rate | YR160=$1 |

## Political Violence

Tribal groups have traditionally used kidnapping of foreigners as a way to pressure the foreign community to obtain projects, services or focusing government attention on the redress of grievances. These "traditional" kidnappings changed on December 28, 1998, when 16 tourists were kidnapped and killed. These kidnappers, however, belonged to no particular tribe and, although they stole money and jewelry from their captives, they professed themselves to be devout Muslims, prepared to die for their cause.

Still, in most kidnappings, the victims generally are treated well and released unharmed after two to three weeks. Over the past six years, Yemeni tribesmen have kidnapped more than 100 Westerners, demanding improvements to their villages and personal handouts in exchange for the victim's safe release.

The tribesmen are particularly sensitive where oil and mineral extraction are concerned. There is a sense among those living in the mineralrich areas that they are not getting a fair share of the wealth. To help build community relations and preserve the peace, investors in such ventures should consider hiring more local tribesmen than they might first judge economically necessary. Financing communitybased buildings and services, such as in health care and basic education, can help ensure troublefree investment in nonurban areas.

Yemen possesses a rich culture, a long history and beautiful terrain. Yet it has one of the region's smallest tourism industries. The reasons are numerous, but perhaps the biggest is the tribal kidnappings of foreigners. President Abdullah Salih is seeking to end all kidnappings, recognizing the impact this has on the country's tourism industry. He praised local security forces for securing the release of two French tourists kidnapped January 17, 2000, saying, "[W]henever security forces act in a speedy, effective and firm manner, the state's prestige is enhanced and the criminals and all those who dare to sabotage the society's security and stability are deterred" (Republic of Yemen Radio).

To help end these kidnappings, the president created a special anti-terrorism unit, headed by his eldest son. Moreover, the government created special courts in which to try kidnappers. Convicted offenders may receive the death penalty.

## Political System

There are two functioning parallel political systems: an emerging modern democracy and an ancient tribal system dependent on patronage and consensus. The government is divided into three branches: the executive with the President appointing a cabinet headed by a Prime Minister; the legislative with a 301 member unicameral parliament; and the judicially consisting of three levels of courts.

## Recent Economic Developments

Yemen is the poorest country in the Middle East, with an average national per-capita of less than $1 a day. In the years after its 1990 unification, the economy suffered as government spending, inflation and unemployment rose sharply. However, in the last half decade, under the guidance of the IMF and World Bank, the country has begun to turn around its oil-fueled economy. Since 1995 when reforms began, the local currency was floated and stabilized, triple-digit inflation curbed to single-digit and many government-subsidies have been abolished.

The country is building a free trade zone in Aden that it hopes will transform Yemen's economic and commercial capital into a major tans-shipment hub. It is also pinning future hopes on its large Liquefied Natural Gas resources. Its location, history and culture also suggest a potentially lucrative tourism sector.

But many obstacles must be overcome before the country can attract tourists and the needed large-scale foreign investment. Such obstacles include widespread smuggling, corruption, kidnapping of foreigners and an inadequate infrastructure. Other challenges include high population growth, water scarcity, inadequate infrastructure, non-utilized natural resources and economic, monetary and administrative reforms.

The changes and reforms, however, are not just economic, but are political and cultural. Existing side-by-side with the young modern state is a complex and ancient tribal system that has rules and alliances that often clash with the government's. Gaining acceptance of modern economic and political principles will be perhaps a crucial key in continuing the economic turnaround.

Unification was declared May 22, 1990. Various factors contributed to the unified country's poor economic performance in the first few years after the unification. First, there were enormous costs associated with the unification, including the need for increasing expenditures particular for wages and defense. Second, just months after the unification, Iraq invaded Kuwait, an act that had negative economic consequences for Yemen. For example, Yemen never received $50 million in promised aid from Iraq. Furthermore, Yemen's reaction to the crisis angered the Gulf States. So angered was Saudi Arabia, that it, and eventually the other Gulf States, expelled all Yemeni workers. This resulted in 1.2 million Yemenis returning to Yemen, the loss of a $1 billion injection into the economy from remittances home and swelling unemployment. Furthermore, the country fell into a nearly 4-year long civil war.

Between 1990 and 1994, real GDP contracted and unemployment rose significantly. Budget deficits rose from 13 percent to 17 percent of GDP along with inflation to more than 70 percent. But beginning in 1995, the country began an impressive turnaround as it overhauled its macro structure under the guidance of the IMF. Real growth reached 7 percent in 1995 and 3 percent the following year. Inflation dropped to 12 percent by 1996 and the budget deficit comprised only 2.3 percent of GDP that year.

The picture has remained bright into the late 1990s. Government officials expect GNP to grow by about 4 percent in 1999, that is compared with 2.7 in 1998 and 5.2 in 1997.

Oil is the country's main revenue source, comprising 98.6 percent of total exports in 1997. And despite the sharp drop in oil prices in 1998 and the beginning of 1999 – which slashed the country's export earnings by the equivalent of 10 percent of GDP – the government has injected stability into the macro-economic system, improved the state budget, stabilized the exchange rate and reduced the inflation rate to 1 percent. The government was able to reduce the money growth rate from 34.7 percent in 1994 to 10.7 percent in 1997, and the budget deficit from 17.4 percent of GDP to 4 percent in the same time period.

Both the IMF and World Bank have praised these developments and have pledged further funds as long as reforms proceed. The World Bank said it would commit as much as $700 million during the next three years compared with $420 million during the previous three. These funds would be earmarked for improving the civil service, stimulating the private sector, and promoting the sustainable use of water and to developing education and health services.

This year, the World Bank did commit $50 million to help reform the public sector management. Yemen wants to borrow $876 million from international donors and the World Bank between 1999–2002.

While the country's first round of macro-structural improvements has been successful, the country has many areas to improve. The monthly per capita is $32.44 in urban areas and $23.81 in rural. (Those figures, however, could double with the inclusion of smuggling and the *qat* trade.) As of 1998, its maximum electricity capacity is 609 megawatts, but actual output is between 35-400 and that only reaches 30 percent of the population. Water and sewage services are even less adequate. Residents in the country's third largest city, Taiz, receive public water once ever 30–40 days. In some parts of Sana'a, raw sewage runs onto major thoroughfares. Unemployment exceeds 30 percent and illiteracy hovers at around 58 percent.

The 3.7 percent population growth rate, one of the region's highest, must be curbed while consumption of scarce renewable water supplies, which is occurring at 140–150 percent of recharge rate, needs to be reduced. According to experts, subsidies must be eliminated, and the government must also develop a transparent legal environment that can objectively and independently resolve disputes. Consequently, the government bureaucracy should be streamlined. Currently, the state employs 400,000 people, with wages consuming 60 percent of the state budget.

The government must eliminate the massive smuggling network, something that may create a confrontation with the tribal aspect of society. Smuggling is estimated to be a YR 70 billion (nearly $0.5 billion) a year business, roughly 30 percent of Yemen's total imports. Furthermore, smuggling cost the treasury YR 1.4 billion in income tax each year. Approximately 65 percent of incoming food supplies and 35 percent of pharmaceutical enter the country illegally.

According to local industrial sources, smugglers have saturated the market with all types of merchandise, causing thousands of workers to lose their jobs in the past couple of years.

## Economic Indicators

|  | 1998 | 1997 | 1996 |
|---|---|---|---|
| Nominal GDP (US$ billions) | 6.68 | 5.79 | 5.23 |
| GDP Growth (percent) | 6.1 | 5.19 | 4.4 |
| GNP Growth (percent) | 2.7 | 5.2 | 5.6 |
| Nominal GNP Per Capita (US$) | 327 | 306 | 280 |
| Total Government Expenditure as % of GDP | 43 | 44 | 43 |
| Inflation (%) | 27.3 | 6.3 | 5 |

## *Oil and Gas Sector*

An exportable amount of oil was first discovered in Yemen in 1984 in the Marib Governorate. Since then, petroleum has been the driver of Yemen's economic growth. By the end of 1997, oil production from three fields pushed the country's output to 385,000 bpd. Currently, the country is producing 380,000 bpd.

More important than oil to the Yemen's petroleum industry's future is Liquefied Natural Gas (LNG). The country plans to process and export the 17 trillion cubic feet of proved and associated and natural gas reserves. In 1995, Yemen concluded a gas development agreement with Total and in January 1997 agreed to include Hunt Oil, Exxon and Yukong of South Korea in the project. It is believed that during 25 years $3.5 billion will be invested in the project, which is expected to yield roughly 5.2 million tons of LNG a year.

## *Non-Oil Sector*

### *Aden Free Trade Zone and Aden Container Terminal*
In 1999, the first phase of the Aden Container Terminal (ACT) was launched. This $188 million facility will have the capacity to handle 500,000 twenty-foot equivalent units. It is part of a $580 million planned free trade zone at its southern port of Aden, which is anticipated to transform Yemen's economic and commercial capital into a major transshipment hub.

The zone will have six quays and a 16 meter-deep navigational channel, increased from 12, with all service and facilities to accommodate the world's largest container vessels.

The country plans to offer facilities and fast turnaround for the largest carriers now plying routes from Europe through the Suez Canal and the Red Sea to Southeast Asia, Australia and the Far East[7].

Free Zone incentives include exemption from taxation on industrial and commercial profits for 15 years with a possible extension for an additional 10 years; 100 percent foreign ownership permitted and encouraged; free transfer of capital and profits outside of the Aden Free Zone, not subject to exchange controls; and exemption from income tax on salaries, and bonuses of non-Yemeni employees working on Aden Free Zone projects.

## Agriculture

Agriculture has been and remains a key industry in Yemen, employing more than half of the workforce. While its role in the economy has diminished somewhat over the years, it is still crucial. In 1970, for example, agriculture absorbed 75 percent of the labor force and comprised 45 percent of GDP. In 1996, those figures dropped to 58 percent and 15 percent, respectively.

During the 1970s and 1980s, the agriculture sector underwent a significant transformation, evolving from traditional farming into a more modern industry. This transformation was fueled by investment, market expansion and protectionist policy.

Today Yemeni agriculture is market-oriented. It relies on irrigation and has enormous qat farming, which covers 10 percent of prime farmland. Many crops have strong economic potential such as cotton, grapes, papaya and coffee.

A main agricultural problem facing the country is sustainability. Many of the crops they produce, such as qat and cotton, are water intensive. There is already ground water overuse, a deterioration of upper watersheds and an increased risk of floods. It will be necessary to implement water conservation methods and to improve productivity to fuel growth. This will be crucial to help satisfy the country's growing population, which is expected to nearly double to 30 million within the next 20 years.

---

[7]  Reuters News Service Sept. 11, 1999

The World Bank reports that cultivation, retailing and distribution of Qat, a naturally-grown narcotic, account for up to 25 percent of Yemen's Gross Domestic Product. But experts agree that this plant offers little economic benefit, since very little of it is exported. In fact, qat-chewing is virtually a national pastime. During the afternoon, the country comes to a virtual standstill while people indulge in social chewing sessions. The problem has become such a national issue, that the president publicly announced his commitment to dropping the habit and urged others to follow his example. Furthermore, the government passed laws that would limit the places and times that people could chew Qat.

The government's main concerns with this endemic are as follows:

- There are adverse affects on human health and productivity, which have economic implications. Studies show that people consume more Qat than any other fruit or vegetable;
- "Qat sessions" result in a loss of 1 million human-hours a day;
- Qat cultivation uses more land than does wheat, fruit or vegetable farming. Qat farming currently consumes 70 percent of all agricultural land and 55 percent of ground water, further exacerbating an existing water scarcity problem.

## Tourism

Yemen has a unique culture, history and geography, which can be important lures for tourists. This potential cannot be fully met, however, until the infrastructure is improved and violent attacks and kidnappings are stopped.

But kidnappings are not the only issue putting the country in the region's unenviable 18th place in terms the number of tourists visitors. Other realities include the following:

- Tourist attractions and accommodations are generally insufficient and of low quality and are virtually non-existent beyond major cities. One-star hotels constitute 55 percent of all hotels in Yemen;
- Insufficient tourism laws;
- Polluted streets and tourist areas.

# Investment Opportunities

While many industries remain undeveloped in Yemen, many also offer good investment opportunities, excluding hydrocarbon exploration and production. They include, tourism, health services, power generation, fisheries, ship repair and maintenance and consumer products.

## Leading Business Opportunities

| Non-Agriculture Sector |
| --- |
| Automotive Parts & Services |
| Medical Instruments, Supplies & Pharmaceuticals |
| Agricultural Machinery & Equipment |
| Electrical Power Systems |
| Food/Processing/Packaging Equipment |
| Oil/Gas Field Machinery |
| **Agriculture Sector** |
| Corn |
| Soybean Meal |
| Canned Fruits & Vegetables |
| Honey |
| Rice |

# Legal Review

In general, Yemen has many adequate business laws on the book. The problem has been enforcement. It is not uncommon for the outcome of cases to depend on someone's relationship with government officials rather than the facts of a case.

The country, for example, has solid investment, labor and tax laws. The problem is the little transparency in implementation. Yemen must clarify procedures, create implementation regulations and install enforcement mechanisms.

## Trade Regulations and Standards

### Trade Barriers

The government eliminated import licensing in 1996 and cut tariff rates into four bands between 5 percent and 25 percent ad valorum. The government instituted an excise tax on industrial inputs and a production tax on local manufacturers to create a level playing field between imports and local industrial products. The country no longer enforces the secondary and tertiary aspects of the Arab boycott of Israel.

### Customs Valuation

Since July 1, 1996, imports have been valued by customs at the exchange rate determined by the market. Law 37/1997 regulates the new tariff on imported goods. Customs procedures, while improved, remain the biggest trade barrier.

### Import Licenses

The government eliminated licensing in 1996.

### Export Controls

Exports, which are taxed by the government, must be licensed only for statistical reasons. The Ministry of Fisheries limits the export of certain categories of seafood products. Exports of antiques and archeological items exceeding $100 in value are prohibited. Customs officials at the airport often arbitrarily confiscate souvenirs without compensation.

### Import/Export Documentation

These documents can be obtained from the Ministry of Supply and Trade and/or the ministry governing a company's activities. Health certificates are required to export animal and fisheries products.

### Temporary Entry

Equipment may be brought temporarily into Yemen to work on specific project, but it must be removed after the project's completion. In general, foreign companies use local agents to import the equipment so it can remain in the country for longer periods. If the equipment is sold or remains in Yemen, it will be taxed.

## Labeling, Marking Requirements

Foodstuff and/or pharmaceuticals imported into Yemen must contain the production and expiration date printed clearly on the package. GCC and International standards are followed.

## Prohibited Imports

The government prohibits importation of seven items: pork and pork products, coffee, alcohol, narcotics, some types of fresh fruits and vegetables, weapons and explosives, and rhinoceros horn.

## Standards

Various government organizations are responsible for standards and product quality control, including the Standardization, Meteorology, and Quality Control Organization of the Ministry of Industry, the Customs Authority, and the Environmental Department of the Ministry of Urban Planning.

Yemen belongs to the International Standards Organization (ISO 9000), the Organization of Meteorology International League (OMIL), and the Arab Standards Organization. The Standardization, Meteorology, and Quality Control Organization is responsible for testing imports and can remove them from the market if they do not meet standards.

## Free Trade Zones/Warehouses

The Yemeni government passed its Free Trade Zone Law (number 4) in 1993, and designated 170 sq. km. in Adeas for the first such zone. In March 1996, the government contracted a Saudi company to develop the Aden Free Zone. The Port of Singapore Authority, a minority shareholder, is constructing a modern container terminal and other seaport facilities, a power station, hotel/conference center, new airport, and developing industrial estates. No other free trade zones have been designated.

## Franchising

Yemen's Investment Code (Law 29 of 1997, amended) encourages franchising. Pizza Hut opened its first restaurant in 1995.

## Investment Issues

The General Investment Authority (GIA), established in March 1992, is responsible for implementing Yemen's Investment Law 22 of 1991. The authority is to promote investment opportunities, license investment projects and assist investors in overcoming impediments.

The GIA is particularly interested in investment projects in the following sectors: agriculture and livestock resources, including fishing; tourism, health, education, technical and vocational training at all levels; transportation; telecommunications; construction and housing; and industry.

### Banking

As of 1998, there were seven commercial banks operating in Yemen: five private and two public. There are also three public-sector banks specializing in industry, agriculture and housing that operate under the Central Bank of Yemen (CBY). Three Islamic banks opened between 1996-1997.

In February 1998, the CBY allowed the market to set loan and deposit rates above a bottom rate for savings accounts of 10 percent. The year before, the government established a special commercial bank described in the Standby Agreement with the IMF.

### Stock Exchange

Under the guidance of the World Bank, the Central Bank of Yemen (CBY) is considering establishing a stock market in the next few years. Most experts inside and outside the government, however, feel that the country lacks the expertise to do so in the near future. It is also doubtful that enough citizens have money to invest in the market.

### Efficient Capital Markets and Portfolio Investment

In late 1995, the CBY offered treasury bills to the public and received an overwhelmingly positive response. However, commercial banks make up a disproportionately large percentage of T-Bill holders, keeping approximately 30 percent of their assets in the bills. Because there are only a few wealthy and dependable traders with whom the commercial banks can lend, their main alternative source of revenue is T-bill interest. Thus, there is a large and underused pool of cash sitting in CBY coffers that could and should be put to better use.

## Expropriation and Compensation

Article 13 of Law 22 stipulates that "projects may not be nationalized or seized. Moreover, their funds may not be blocked, confiscated, frozen, withheld, or sequestered by other than the courts of law." Real estate can only be expropriated in the national interest, according to the law and court judgement. If it does occur, the owner must be compensated at the market value.

There is no evidence that the Yemen Arab Republic (former North Yemen) ever expropriated property. The Socialist Peoples' Democratic Republic of Yemen, however, (former South Yemen) did expropriate until the 1990 unification. The government of the unified Republic of Yemen has not expropriated property.

## Dispute Settlement

As of 1998, Yemen had not yet signed any international conventions on arbitration. Business disputes in the meantime may be handled by informal arbitration or within the court system.

The court system, however, is widely regarded as inefficient and subjective in its judgments. A special court that was established for resolving commercial disputes is presided over by the same judges in the old system. Thus, they still have no power to enforce their rulings. This situation is due to change as a judicial reform process was to begin in September 1998.

The best method is for foreign investors to establish a partnership with a Yemeni familiar with the system, and by including international arbitration clauses in their contracts. In cases involving interest, most judges base their decisions on the *Shari'a* (Islamic), which prohibits interest payments.

## Performance Requirements/Incentives

No performance requirements are specified. Incentives include the following: exemption from customs fees and taxes levied on a project's fixed assets; tax holiday on profits for a 7-year period, renewable up to a maximum of 18 years (subject to restrictions specified in the GIA Investment Guide); the right to purchase or rent land and buildings; and the right to import production inputs and export products without restrictions and registration in the import/export register.

## *Right to Private Ownership*

Foreigners may freely own property in Yemen. Foreign companies and establishments, however, generally must trade in Yemen through a Yemeni agent. Law 23 of 1997, "Regulating Agencies and Branches of Foreign Companies and Firms," outlines the requirements for establishing a Yemeni agent.

Chapter 3 of Law 23 permits foreign companies and firms to conduct business in Yemen by establishing foreignowned and managed branches in the following fields: banking; industrial activities (no limitations are specified); oil and minerals; agriculture and livestock, including fisheries; technical and consultancy services; tourism and hotels; and contracting/construction of infrastructure projects such as roads, airports, public utilities and residential settlements.

Foreign establishments wishing to open branches in their own names in Yemen must obtain a permit by decree from the Minister of Supply and Trade, subject to Law 23 and other laws in force at the time of application. However, as a practical matter, establishments should plan to engage a Yemeni partner.

## Intellectual Property Rights

Adequate IPR laws have been enacted (law 19 of 1994). The problem is the weak legal system. Influence with the judge and government is often more important than the facts. The country is not a member of WIPO or other International IPR conventions. The country has a record of inadequate protection for IPR, including trademarks and patents.

# SELECTED BIBLIOGRAPHY

*General Note*

The major information sources used for composing this book are as follows:

- Info-Prod Databases (these databases are updated daily and cover business, economic and legal issues on the entire region. Part of their information appears in leading international on-line vendors such as Reuters, Lexis-Nexis, Gale, FT, the Dialog Corporation).
- Middle East Business Watch published by Info-Prod Research (Middle East). This is a comprehensive package of real time intelligence products. It consists of the following elements:
  1. *Middle East Hotline* concentrates on highlighting the immediate commercial implications of crucial political developments. It is issued several times a week to offer the quickest analysis possible.
  2. *Middle East Briefing* provides in-depth coverage of major political, security, and macro-economic developments in the region. The frequency is fortnightly, and each issue is designed to make clear the connection between individual country trends and real business opportunities.
  3. *Middle East Risk Ratings* contain information on current commercial and political risk in 19 Middle Eastern nations. Updated quarterly, each set of ratings includes a detailed breakdown of the relevant factors which impact on an individual country's stability, as well as a cogent analysis of its relative political strengths and weaknesses.
- The US department of commerce databases which provided valuable information on the region's countries.

- Regional governmental publications including statistical books, foreign trade periodicals and the official gazettes.
- World Bank and IMF reports.
- Local press & media reports, including business and economic magazines and national news agencies.
- International news agencies (Reuters, BBC, AFP, AP).

Additionally, the book was based on the following sources:

## Algeria

- Abd Al-Hamid Ahdab, "Arbitration With the Arab Countries", Kluwer Law International, January 1999.

## Bahrain

- Coopers & Lybrand, Jawad Habib & Co., Bahrain, A Guide for Businessmen and Investors, 1992.
- The Economic Intelligence Unit, United Kingdom, Country Report—Bahrain, various editions.
- Gulf States Newsletter.
- International Bureau of Fiscal Documentation, Bahrain.
- Kiss A. C. (ed.), United Nations Environment Progamme, Selected Multilateral Treaties in the Field of the Environment, 1983.
- Middle East Executive Reports, various issues.
- Price Waterhouse, Doing Business in Bahrain, 1984.
- Swain, F., The Commercial Laws of Bahrain, Ocean Publications, Inc., 1986.
- An Exporter's Guide To Trading In The Gulf—Legal Aspects, Nabarro Nathanson, January 1999.

## Egypt

- Allied Accountants, Flash Report: The Egyptian Unified Tax Law No. 187 of 1993, 1994.
- Campbell, D., Legal Aspects of Doing Business In the Middle East, Kluwer Law International, Vol. 5, July 1996.
- Deloitte, Touche, Tohmatsu International, Egypt—International Tax and Business Guide, 1994.

- Egypt—USA: Presidents' Council, A Report Prepared for the Middle East/North Africa Economic Conference III, 1996.
- German—Arab Chamber of Commerce.
- Helmy, T. & Hamza, S.M. (Baker & McKenzie), Breaking New Grounds in Egypt, 1992.
- Middle East Executive Reports, various issues.
- Middle East Library for Economic Services.
- Price Waterhouse, Doing Business in Egypt.
- The Economist Intelligence Unit.
- Zeazaa, S. & Ghannam, M.A., The Commercial Law of Egypt, Oceana Publications, 1995.

## Israel

### Sources in English:

- "Agreement Between the Government of the State of Israel and the Government of the Hashemite Kingdom of Jordan on Irbid Qualifying Industrial Zone", 1997.
- Bavly Millner & Co., Israel Means Business 1995, Federation of Israeli Chambers of Commerce, 1995.
- Horvath, Bavly, Millner & Co., Foreigners in Israel, 1993.
- Kaplan, A., Israeli Business Law: An Essential Guide, Kluwer Law International, 1996.
- Luboshitz, Kasierer & Co., Israel: Business & Taxation 1977/8, 1997.
- Somekh, Chaikin, Doing Business in Israel, 1995.
- Yehuda Rave & Co., and Kesselman & Kesselman, Free Trade with the USA and the EC & EFTA via Israel, 1993.
- Standard & Poor's, Directory of Public Companies and Financial Institutions, Israel 1999.
- "Israel's Shohat has to Fix Budget First", Reuters News Service, July 6, 1999.

### Sources in Hebrew:

- Belinski, E., Capital Investment Laws: Theory & Practice, 1988.
- Felmann, A., Company Law in Israel: Principles & Practice, Carta, 1994.
- Hadari, Y., Capital Gains Tax of Real Estate, Yonatan, 1994.
- Narkis, P., Trademarks and Patents Law, Tamar, 1991.
- Rafael, A. & Mehulal, Y., Income Tax, 3rd Edition, Shoken, 1955.

- Shafat, Y.H. & Hendler, Z., Foreign Currency Control, Admiot, 1994.
- Sussmann, Y., The Law of Civil Procedure, 7th Edition, Aminon, 1995.

## Jordan

- "Agreement Between the Government of the State of Israel and the Government of the Hashemite Kingdom of Jordan on Irbid Qualifying Industrial Zone", 1997.
- Chamber of Commerce of Rotterdam, Seminar on the Trade Opportunities with Israel and Jordan Seen in the Perspective of a Changing Middle East, October 1995.
- Dallal, I.M., Jordan, in Campbell, C. (Ed.), Legal Aspects of Doing Business in the Middle East, Kluwer Law and Taxation Publishers, 1992.
- The Economist Intelligence Unit, various issues.
- Ernst & Young International Business Series, Doing Business in Jordan.
- International Bureau of Fiscal Documentation, The Hashemite Kingdom of Jordan, Supp. No. 60, January 1993.
- Investment Promotion Co., Investment Promotion Law (No. 16 for 1995, Jordan).
- Middle East Executive Reports, various issues.

## Kuwait

- Gulf States Newsletter, various issues.
- Middle East Executive Reports, various issues.
- TMP Agents, Abu Ghazaleh Intellectual Property, Registration Requirements Worldwide, 1995.

## Lebanon

- Doing Business in the Middle East, Kluwer Law and Taxation Publishers, 1992.
- Middle East Executive Reports, various issues.
- Sand, P.H. (ed.), The Effectiveness of International Environmental Agreements, 1992.
- TMP Agents Abu Ghazaleh Intellectual Property, Registration Requirements Worldwide, 1995.

## *Morocco*

- Bakkali, A. Esq., The Commercial Laws of Morocco, Oceana Publications, 1995.
- GPBM, Investing in Morocco, 1994.
- Middle East Executive Reports, various reports.
- Nelson, L. (ed.), Digest of Commercial Laws of the World, Oceana Publications, 1995.
- Price Waterhouse, Doing Business in Morocco, 1991, Supp. 1994.
- SASB Bulletin, Morocco to Place a New Law on IP Protection, October 1995.

## *Oman*

- Amison, M., Oman, *in* Campbell C. (Ed.), Legal Aspects of Doing Business in the Middle East, Vol. 5, Kluwer Law and Taxation Publishers, USA, 1992.
- Featherstone, Y., The Commercial Laws of the Sultanate of Oman, Oceana Publications, USA, 1983.
- Hill, Thomas W., Jr., The Commercial Legal System of the Sultanate of Oman, The International Lawyer, Summer 1983, Vol. 17, No. 3.
- Law of Commercial Agencies and its Regulations (translation to English), Oman Chamber of Commerce and Industry, Third Edition, 1993.
- McHugo, J., The Legal Structure for Investment in Oman in the 1990's: A Case Study of an Arabian Gulf Oil Exporting Economy, The International Lawyer, Vol. 24, No. 4, 1990.
- Middle East Executive Reports, various issues.
- Peat, Marwick, Mitchell & Co., Investment in Oman, 1992
- The Economist Intelligence Unit.
- TMP Bulletin, various issues.

## Palestinian Authority

- Abukhater, M., Agricultural Economist Urges Palestinian Membership in GATT, Palestine Business Report, Vol. 2, No. 6, June 1997.
- Abukhater, M., Palestine Stock Exchange Changing Investment Approaches, Palestine Business Report, Vol. 2, No. 6, June 1997.

- Abukhater, M., The Paris Economic Protocol: Three Years Later, Palestine Business Report, Vol. 2, No. 5, May 1997.
- Al Zaeem, S. & Associates, Overseas Private Investment Corporation Checklist, April 1996.
- Bahu, R., Melloul, E., and Walsh, W., Banking Reform in the Palestinian Territories, 1995.
- Draft: Basic Law for the National Authority in the Transitional Period, Occasional Document Series, No. 5, February 1996.
- Hoda Abdel Hadi & Partners, Intellectual Property Around the World, HAH Bulletin, Vol. 8, Winter 1997.
- Intellectual Property Protection in the Limited Palestinian Autonomy, TMP Agents, Abu Ghazaleh Intellectual Property, 1995.
- Intellectual Property Protection in the Palestinian Region, 7 Journal of Proprietary Rights, 1995.
- Mazen E. Qupty & Associates, Legal Aspects of Doing Business in Palestine, 1995.
- Middle East Executive Reports, various issues.
- Quigly, J., Legal Aspects of Doing Business in Palestine Judicial Anatomy in Palestine: Problems and Prospects, Dyton Law Review, Vol. 21, No. 3, Spring 1996.
- The Small Business Support Project, How to Conduct Business in the Palestinian Territories, January 1996.
- Taba Trade Leaders and Coordinating Committee, Market Access Study, August 1995.

*Sources in Hebrew:*
- Kaplan, Y., Cohen, A. & Sherman, Y., Tax Arrangements Between Israel and the Palestinian Authority, Globes, 25.1.96.

## Qatar

- Gulf States Newsletter, various issues.
- The Foreign and Commonwealth Office and the Department of Trade and Industry, General Report: Qatar Agency Regulation, UK, 1994.
- Guidelines in Course of Execution of Law No. 4/1986 Organizing Commercial Agents Affairs, Qatar.
- Majdalany, G., The Commercial Laws of Qatar, Oceana Publishers Inc., New York, 1986.

- Middle East Executive Reports, various issues.
- Salih, B., Qatar, in Campbell, D. (Ed.), Legal Aspects of Doing Business in the Middle East, Kluwer Law and Taxation Publishers, USA, 1992.
- TMP Bulletin.

## Saudi Arabia

- Campbell, C. (ed.), Legal Aspects of Doing Business in the Middle East, Vol. 5, 1996.
- Ernst & Young, Doing Business in Saudi Arabia, 1993.
- Khan, S.M., The Commercial Laws of the Kingdom of Saudi Arabia, Oceana Publications, 1989.
- Moores Rowland International, Saudi Arabia Investment and Taxation Guide, 1993.
- Nader, M.M.J. & Alameldin, M.I., A Legal Practical Guide for the Businessman in Saudi Arabia, Nader Law Offices, 1994.
- Price Waterhouse, Doing Business in Saudi Arabia, 1993.
- Sand, P.H. (ed.), The Effectiveness of International Environmental Agreements, 1992.
- Energy Compass, May 28, 1999.
- Economist Intelligence Unit.

## Syria

- Campbell, D., Legal Aspects of Doing Business in the Middle East, London 1995.
- Deloitte, Touche, Tohmatsu International, Syria: International Tax and Business Guide, 1992.
- Halbach, A.J., Brand, H.A.D., Helmschrott, C.G.H. & Strace, D., New Potentials for Cooperation and Trade in the Middle East, Weltforum Verlag Gmbh, 1995.
- International Bureau of Fiscal Documentation, Arab Republic of Syria, Supp. No. 61, April 1993.
- The International Lawyer, Vol. 14, No. 2, Spring 1980.
- Middle East Business Intelligence.
- Nelson, L., The Commercial Laws of Syria, Oceana Publications, 1992.

- Sinan, N., Syria, *in* Campbell C. (Ed.), Legal Aspects of Doing Business in the Middle East, Kluwer Law and Taxation Publishers, 1992.

*Sources in Hebrew:*
- Feiler, G., The Syrian Market and Prospects for Cooperation with Israel, Tel Aviv University Press, 1996.

# Tunisia

- Agency for the Promotion of Industry, Incentives for Investment in Manufacturing Industries and Industry-Related Services in Tunisia, 1994.
- Bellagha, A., Tunisia, in Campbell C. (Ed.), Legal Aspects of Doing Business in the Middle East, Kluwer Law and Taxation Publishers, 1992.
- Campbell, D., Legal Aspects of Doing Business in the Middle East, London, 1996.
- General Agreement on Tariffs and Trade, Trade Policy Review Mechanism—Tunisia, Reports by the Government and by the Secretariat, May 1994.
- Journal of International Arbitration, various issues.
- Middle East Commercial Law Review.
- Middle East Executive Reports.
- Registration Requirements Worldwide, TMP Agents, 1995.
- TMP Bulletin.

# United Arab Emirates

- Al Tamimi & Company, Jurisdiction of the Ubu Dhabi Court is a Matter of Public Policy and the Parties may not Agree Otherwise, Law Update News, October 1995.
- Al Tamimi, E., United Arab Emirates Trademark Law, The International Business Lawyer, February, 1995.
- Angell NBA, Islamic and Western Banking: A Comparison with Selected Legal Issues, June 1994.
- Campbell, C. (Ed.) Legal Aspects of Doing Business in the Middle East, Supp. 2, Vol. 5, 1996.
- Deloitte & Touche, International Tax and Business Guide, UAE.
- Dubai Ports Authority: 1997 Handbook, 1997.

- Ernst & Young, Doing Business in the United Arab Emirates, 1990.
- Essex PND, Khartoum OAET, Wellington ATK & Birmingham JRB, The Commercial Laws of the United Arab Emirates, Oceana Publications, 1986.
- Gulf States Newsletter.
- Jebel Ali Free Zone Authority Dubai, Your Global Business Base: Investors Guide.
- MECLR, Vol. 1, Issue 3, 1995.
- Middle East Executive Reports.
- Peat Marwick, Banking in the UAE, 1992.
- TMP Bulletin.
- United Arab Emirates: Land Law in the UAE, (1995) 20 International Legal Practitioner 6.
- UN Conference on the Environment and Development, A Survey of Existing Legal Instruments, Cambridge, 1992.
- US-Arab Chamber of Commerce, Doing Business in the Gulf—A Guide to Available Legal Structures, 1994.